DATE DUE

DEMCO 38-296

Published by Centric Media, Inc.

International Standard Book Number: 0-9667679-1-8
International Standard Serial Number: 1521-9364

Printed and bound in the United States of America.

TABLE OF CONTENTS

Introduction 2

How to Use This Book 2

History of the Bicycle 3

Choosing Cycling Equipment 6
   Bicycles
   Saddles
   Helmets
   Gloves
   Shoes and Pedals
   Other Accessories

Fitting 13
   Fitting Parameters
   Bicycle Sizes and Conversion Table

Buying a Used Bicycle 16
   New vs. Used
   Centric Media's Pricing Disclosures
   Condition of the Bicycle
   Buyer and Seller
   Retail Price
   Delivery
   Inspection and Warranty
   Used Bicycles at Stores
   Bicycle Store Pricing Policies
   Individual Sellers
   Pawnshops
   Police Auctions
   Inspection Checklist
   Buying Skills
   Selling Tips

Classic and Antique Bicycles 25

Bicycle Theft Prevention 26
   Centric™ BicycleLINK Registration System

Pricing Data 30

INTRODUCTION

Congratulations on buying the premiere edition of the world's only guide to used bicycle prices. *Centric™ BicycleLINK Blue Book* helps buyers and sellers locate each other, examines the quality or the *reasonable roadworthiness* of bicycles, and determines fair prices for used bicycles.

The publisher of the *Centric™ BicycleLINK Blue Book* takes very seriously its role in standardizing the prices of used bicycles. The bike values contained herein are the result of careful evaluations conducted by Centric Media, Inc., based on marketplace information that it deems reliable. The values are intended only as a guide. **Centric Media, Inc., assumes no liability for any errors or omissions.**

HOW TO USE THIS BOOK

The book is divided into two parts: Part I presents a general discussion of the issues involved in buying and selling a bicycle, while Part II contains new and used **retail** bicycle prices from 1994 to 1999.

Industry professionals and serious riders will find Part I to be an excellent refresher course. It is the *first in-depth* look at the used bicycle industry. The professional and serious hobbyist should also consider buying the **Centric™ BicycleLINK CD-ROM** and obtaining a subscription to its **Web site (http://www.bicyclelink.com)** for an excellent review of issues in the general industry concerning both used and new bicycles. In any event, professional and serious riders should avail themselves of the free portion of the Web site that includes the **Centric™ BicycleLINK Yellow Pages and classified listings** for links to manufacturers, stores, suppliers, and customers industry-wide, as well as used bicycle listings.

An individual buying a bicycle should pay particular attention to the sections in Part I entitled **Choosing Cycling Equipment, Fitting, Inspection Checklist,** and **Buying Skills**. Obviously, Centric Media, Inc., urges buyers to read the section on bicycle registration and to use the **Centric™ BicycleLink** world-wide registration system.

An individual bicycle seller should focus on the sections in Part I entitled **Centric Media Pricing Disclosures, Condition of the Bicycle, Buyer and Seller, Bicycle Store Pricing Policies, Individual Sellers,** and **Selling Tips**.

To use the pricing guidelines requires reading the section entitled **Condition of the Bicycle** and understanding the standard "*reasonably roadworthy*". If a bicycle meets that standard, its retail price should fall in the middle of the pricing range provided.

HISTORY OF THE BICYCLE

Today, the bicycle is the primary transportation of the human race. About 1.6 billion bicycles are in use throughout the world – in cosmopolitan cities, along remote country lanes, and in the smallest villages – and hundreds of millions of bikes are manufactured every year to meet the continuing demand for cheap wheeled transport.

Yet the bicycle is hardly a new vision of how humans can move. Historians speculate about Leonardo da Vinci's 1490s drawings and a 1580s stained glass window in England that appear to depict a two-wheeler. The first widely recognized two-wheeler in actual use, however, was the pedal-less *Celerifere*, a toy of the French nobility in the 1790s.

The more famous *Draisienne* followed that toy in 1816, still without pedals. The front wheel could be steered, and this two-wheeler was eventually mass-produced in Europe, particularly in England.

Ernest Michaux added cranks to the two-wheeler in 1855. At the age of 14, Michaux copied the crank from a hand-grinding wheel in his father's locksmithy and started a revolution in human transportation – the Velocipede.

By 1870, sophisticated metal Velocipedes were in production in Europe and the United States. Over time, they gave way to the Ordinary or high-wheeler.

The Ordinary was the beginning of the heyday of bicycling. It was speedy and capable of long trips on poor roads, so its use spread fast and far. In a day when a skilled person might earn 25 cents per hour in wages, a good Ordinary sold for $75 to $125, making it more expensive than building a house. Nevertheless, they sold at a furious pace.

Ordinaries had a big problem, however. When the front wheel came up against any obstacle that it could not roll over, the bike simply pitched the rider headfirst onto the ground. Called a "header," this characteristic problem spawned the "safety bicycle" in the 1890s.

With two wheels of equal size, plus a roller chain geared transmission, the safety bicycle was the direct ancestor of today's machines. Not only were these practical machines, but also, with a slight adaptation, they attracted thousands of women to cycling.

Now having transportation that did not need assistance from anyone, women gained a larger measure of freedom than they had enjoyed. The bicycle revolutionized female attire, making it a subject of controversy. Schools sprang up to teach women to ride. Many historians point to the safety bicycle as the beginnings of suffrage, women's rights, and feminism.

Brakes, lights, innovative tires, and inventions of every sort were created to accompany the safety bicycle. In fact, patents filed in the 1890s laid the groundwork for a startling number of "state of the art" inventions a century later, in the 1990s.

In England, in 1909, the Raleigh bicycle, equipped with a Sturmey Archer Three-Speed hub, started production. The classic three-speed bicycles based on the Sturmey Archer Three-Speed hub design spread worldwide along with the British Empire. Furthermore, these designs are still in production in British-built plants in India, Africa, and China.

In the 1930s, British-built "lightweight" bicycles, suitable for the packed earth of country roads, were being imported into the United States. Used on the gravel roads of the day, lightweights were unfortunately not as sturdy as the riders in the U.S. required.

The American balloon-tired cruiser bicycle, equipped with a coaster brake, emerged out of a need for unbreakable rough-road bicycles. Evolving rapidly into the "gas tank" cruisers of the 1950s, these bicycles are still in production. Now some even are made with titanium frames and sophisticated internal hub transmissions – yet they would blend into any street scene of the 1950s.

In the 1960s, the high-rise bicycle – a 20-inch wheel bicycle for children – was the success story of the decade. The Schwinn Sting-Ray was the most desired bicycle of the day, selling in tremendous volume.

By the late 1960s, European lightweight derailleur-equipped bicycles began to appear in the United States. Common in Europe since the 1940s, with the Italians and the French dominating both racing and the production of high-performance bicycles, the 10-speed changed the look of American cycling. The new look featured the dropped handlebar position, which also reduced drag and increased speed.

The 10-speed bicycle fueled the astonishing "Bike Boom" of the 1970s, during which Baby Boomers just reaching their physical peak pedaled throughout the United States and Canada, as well as many countries in Europe.

The Japanese introduced their first 10-speeds into the United States in the early 1970s. The quality and value of their exports quickly gained them a dominant position in the marketplace – even as it drove most European makers and virtually all domestic manufacturers out of the adult bicycle market in the United States.

At the same time in the United States, BMX racing was being born in and started to hit its stride late in the decade. BMX bicycles were descendants of the high-rise bicycles of the 1960s. This exciting sport involved youthful riders racing on a short, closed dirt track.

In the early 1980s, a few California riders started putting derailleur gears on old balloon-tire cruisers and riding them down steep mountain roads. The bicycles they created were the first mountain bikes. Those California riders, such as Gary Fisher, Tom Ritchey, and Mike Sinyard (Specialized), are now as famous as the labels on a number of popular brands of mountain bikes.

During the same period, a few American bicycle manufacturers started domestic production of aluminum and carbon fiber bicycles. Superior products resulted in rapid growth and helped unseat Japanese bicycle companies, who till then had held a dominant position. This new U.S. production, combined with the emergence of Taiwan and China as quality lower price bicycle builders, emphasized the worldwide nature of the bicycle business in the 1980s and 90s.

The early 1980s saw the creation of the "Freestyle" or trick bicycle. Originally a street sport, riding it grew into a jaw-dropping spectacle of flying, leaping bicycles and dancing riders. ESPN, ESPN2, and other television networks often feature this "X-treme" new sport.

Now in the late 1990s, the hybrid bicycle, the road bike, and the mountain bike have proved to be the dominant machines of the decade.

In the near future, electrically assisted bicycles, recumbent bicycles, and aerodynamic chassis for bicycles promise new levels of comfort, speed, and efficiency for bike-lovers.

From their beginning, bicycles have been high technology. The steel two-wheelers of the 1860s were the most sophisticated machines of their day. The ball bearing, the tensioned spoked wheel, seamed and seamless tubing, pneumatic tires, roller chains, planetary gears, and many more key mechanical inventions were first created for the bicycle, and some even percolated out to improve other devices that people find useful.

Today, the bicycle continues to be the most energy- and cost-efficient transportation device in the world. Bikes are still high technology. They are made from the most advanced materials, with bicycle builders using the same materials and techniques that the most advanced military aircraft use.

After all, the first airplane was built in a bicycle shop.

CHOOSING CYCLING EQUIPMENT

BICYCLES

The questions below are starting points for choosing a bicycle and appropriate accessories:

1. What bicycles has the buyer had in the past that he or she liked?
2. Where will the buyer ride? Is it asphalt or dirt? Is it hilly or flat?
3. How often will the buyer ride?
4. Why is the buyer riding: for transportation, exercise, or fun?
5. How long will typical rides last?
6. With whom will the buyer ride? What type of bike does he or she ride?
7. Will the buyer commute on this bike? In what weather?
8. Does the buyer need to carry camping gear or groceries on this bike?
9. What is the buyer's budget?

Here are some types of bicycles, together with guidelines on their usage and pricing.

General Rule. Most quality adult bicycles will start at $300. The buyer will get quantum increases in quality for small increases in price up to about $700. Above $700, the increases in performance become more expensive, until at about $1,200 it starts taking a lot of money to get a bicycle that has small (but, for experts, significant) increases in quality and performance. Above $2,000, a buyer is purchasing some of the best machines mankind can build, often identical to the state-of-the-art machines used by the world's finest racers.

Prices given here are approximate entry points for the product category described.

Kids' Bikes

Toys (less than $100):

These bicycles have heavy, mild steel frames and cheap components. They often come with training wheels. They break easily, the seat stem is short, and they have virtually no resale value. They are good for one thing: teaching kids to ride a two-wheeler. As soon as the children learn, they are going to need a new bike. Stores such as Toys Я Us or Sears carry the widest selection. This item is a great flea market or garage sale $5 purchase.

Real Kids' Bikes ($100 – $300):

These good-quality bikes for children range from the simplest one-speed coaster brake cruisers, through BMX bikes, to 15-speed mountain bikes. They are equipped with high-tensile steel frames and inexpensive components. Stores such as Sportsmart and Sears carry a wide variety of this quality bike.

Beginner trick bicycles are also found in this price range.

Road Bikes

This type of bike generally features 10 – 24 gears, thin road tires and rims, and dropped handlebars.

Inexpensive Road Bikes ($200 – $350):

Most major brands start their adult line in this price category. This bike typically features a high-tensile/chrome molybdenum frame with relatively inexpensive components. A lower riding position for the upper body, together with more efficient rims and tires, makes these bicycles faster and easier to pedal on pavement than cruisers or mountain bikes. A buyer taking short rides on paved bike paths and roads for fun will find this quality and price satisfactory.

Mid-Range Road Bikes ($350 – $550):

This range consists of good bikes for daily riding on roads and bike paths. They are usable for long tours, amateur triathlons, beginning racing, club rides, and daily training.

The majority of bicycle shop sales ring up a $350 – $550 sale. Bicycles at this price are sturdy and have durable components.

The upper range ($550 – $1,200) features aluminum frames, titanium steel, or chrome molybdenum steel frames and excellent components. The performance in this category is very hard to differentiate from that of the most expensive bikes in the world. This range combines light frames and strong components with a wide selection of products.

The price range suits the discriminating rider who enjoys touring, rides centuries (100 miles) for exercise on a regular basis, is a regular weekend rider, or commutes, especially if longer distances are involved (and if there's a very safe place to store the bike at work or school).

Road Racing Bikes (more than $600):

These bicycles feature lightweight frames and components, dropped handlebars, and narrow tires and are designed to go fast on pavement. They are long-lasting, state-of-the-art bicycles for the daily fast rider. They are used by top triathletes, serious club riders, cross-country racers, and riders requiring daily training.

Bicycles in this category are equipped with aluminum, carbon, titanium, or chrome molybdenum frames with the best components in the world. They are virtually indestructible if not abused.

The top echelon of road bicycle ($2,000 – $5,000) is frequently custom made and purchased directly from the finest bicycle makers around the globe. They are the bicycle world's equivalent of building a racing sailboat, promoting a racecar, or piloting a high-performance aircraft (though, of course, biking is far less costly than any of those other hobbies).

Mountain Bikes

City Bikes (more than $250):

The term "city bikes" describes lower-end bikes with mountain bike frame styling, narrower tires, and usually a more upright riding position. In essence, these bikes have a mountain frame but road wheels and tires and therefore ride better on pavement than does a mountain bike. They do not do well off the road, but can go on well-maintained dirt trails.

These bicycles are good bikes for neighborhood cruising, commuting, and errand running.

Mountain Bikes ($200 – $400):

These models offer heavier, stronger frames and lower-end components and are, therefore, not ideal for heavy trail-riding. These models tend to break components when ridden heavily, wear rapidly, and are not as agile or fun as the more expensive mountain bikes.

They are good for all-purpose use on- or off-road, as well as for commuting, and can be used on beach, gravel, dirt, or pavement.

Mountain Bikes ($400 – $1,000):

These excellent-quality off-road bikes are good all-purpose bikes for daily riding and club participation. They are also excellent commuters (if they can be stored safely) and can be used for beginning mountain bike racing.

Mountain Bikes (more than $1,000):

These excellent all-purpose bikes offer lightweight, strong frames of aluminum, carbon, or chrome molybdenum and the finest and most durable of components. They can be used for racing and heavy off-road riding and are extremely tempting to thieves.

Down-Hill Bikes (more than $1,000):

These single-purpose mountain bikes have long travel dual suspension and extra braking capacity. They are heavier and more expensive than comparable mountain bikes and are designed to maintain control at high speed when descending a mountain.

Hybrids (more than $350):

The term "hybrid" refers to a bicycle that is between a road bike and a mountain bike. The frame reinforcement is intermediate, the handlebar is placed in the upright position, and the rims and tires are road versions. More precisely, these bikes have road bike frame geometry (as opposed to the mountain bike frame geometry on the city bike) with medium-width tires and mountain bike gearing, saddle, and handlebars. Excellent commuters, these bikes are almost as easy to pedal on the road as a road bike and are nearly as versatile as a mountain bike. The down side is that they are neither fish nor fowl. They are slower on pavement than a road bike and cannot withstand much off-road use.

Other Bikes

Cruisers (more than $100):

Cruising bikes are good old-fashioned fun. They offer heavy frames, fat tires, and gearing from single-speed to seven-speed rear hubs. They are great for casual riding around the neighborhood, short trips, and errands. They work well on pavement as well as hard-packed sand and gravel and campground trails and are, in that sense, hybrid. Of course, they are relatively slow but with comfortable riding position and seats.

Freestyle Bikes (more than $200):

These trick bicycles are designed for doing stunts and tricks and, more frequently, good for looking very cool. They have extremely strong frames, wheels, and components that add to the price but make them very durable. Essentially, a freestyle bike is a BMX. The distinguishing characteristics are the thinner tires, pegs to stand on over the front and rear axles, and its light weight (to allow for trick or stunt riding).

Mountain Racing Bikes (more than $1,000):

Designed for long, hard training and race-day speed and handling, mountain racing bicycles are versatile and quite comfortable. The model for the lower-priced mountain bikes must be durable, agile, and fast.

Criterium Bikes (more than $1,200):

These machines are designed for short, fast racing courses. Criterium bikes are fun to ride but require constant rider attention. The gearing, as well as virtually all the other features of this type, renders them useful only for racing.

Time Trial Bikes (more than $1,000):

Designed for time trial competition, these bikes are built for aerodynamic efficiency. Most riders do not regard them as comfortable. Strictly speaking, they are useful only for racing and triathlons.

Adult Tricycles (more than $200):

Designed to carry as much as several sacks of groceries in a large basket, these bikes are popular with folks who have a diminished sense of balance or simply do not need to go far or fast (or perhaps live in a neighborhood with uneven pavement and sidewalks). They are very comfortable, fun, and popular as neighborhood cruisers and errand runners.

Tandems (more than $600):

A bicycle built for two allows two riders of unequal skill or strength to ride together (for example, a parent and a child or young teen), and to go farther and faster than they could go on single bicycles. Popular with families and couples, these bicycles today are a fast-growing segment of cycling.

Recumbents (more than $500):

By putting the rider in a reclining position, the recumbent bicycle becomes more aerodynamic than a conventional bicycle. Many riders consider it also to be a more comfortable position. Finally, the use of more of one's musculature makes them fast, easy to pedal, and increasingly popular. Recumbents may represent the bicycle trend of the future.

Motored Bicycles (more than $500):

Bicycles equipped with internal combustion engines have been popular in France, and in Europe in general, for many years. In the United States, electrically powered bicycles are growing rapidly in popularity and are being manufactured in Europe, China, and domestically.

HPV, or Human Powered Vehicles:

A community of researchers and scientists is involved in developing more efficient human-powered vehicles. While these vehicles are occasionally seen on the roads, they may be difficult to locate in bicycle retail stores.

Information about special need or experimental vehicles can be found at **http://www.bicyclelink.com**.

SADDLES

Comfortable seats are of paramount importance to cyclists. Fortunately, today's saddles come in many sizes and shapes so that almost anyone can find a comfortable seat.

Gel-padded saddles are almost always more comfortable for beginning to intermediate riders. High-mileage riders will usually gravitate toward non-gel seats that gradually are fit to the rider's rear end through breaking in while riding. Gel seats and pads do deteriorate with usage, and an older or worn gel seat is not comfortable. Seats that incorporate gel into their original design work much better than add-on gel padding.

There is a trade-off on saddle size. A large saddle provides lots of square inches to support the rider's weight, but at the same time the rider is sitting on the muscles he or she uses to ride. The pressure can cause those muscles to ache painfully.

A small saddle keeps the rider from sitting on those muscles, but the rider has only a few square inches to support his or her weight. This concentration of weight can cause chafing, soreness, and bruising.

Perhaps, as people get older and heavier, they need more square inches. As riders become stronger and fitter, they need fewer square inches of seat. But each person's posterior can be uniquely made comfortable.

Generally, women are more comfortable on a saddle that is short and wide. A variety of saddles have wider bases, shorter noses, and often "cut-outs" in the nose to make them even more comfortable and, for some people, a "must-have." Some saddles, made for men, have the cut-out feature on a longer nose and a narrower base.

Bicycle shorts are a great help because they are basically seamless and provide a smooth fabric between seat and skin. Most shorts also have a bit of extra padding in the seat.

HELMETS

Serious accidents do occur, and so, a helmet is a necessity. Cool helmets make great gifts.

How Do You Know if Bicycle Helmets Really Protect?

It is no accident that people – young and old – who wear bicycle helmets when they ride are practicing an important safety precaution. No one plans to crash on a bicycle, but it can happen at any time. Injury statistics based on hospital reports on accidents involving bicycles are staggering. *Wearing a bicycle helmet can help save a life.*

It is not enough, however, to buy and wear any old helmet. Not all helmets are alike. Those certified by an independent third party, such as, the Safety Equipment Institute (SEI), are tested to meet the most current bicycle helmet safety standards. SEI certifies helmets to the ASTM F-1447 bicycle helmet standard and has just started certifying to the new Consumer Product Safety Commission (CPSC) bicycle helmet standard.

When the SEI label appears on bicycle helmets you know not only that the product conforms to the bicycle helmet standard but also that the manufacturer consistently turns out quality products. Only when the product models annually pass the stringent laboratory tests and the manufacturer passes SEI's quality assurance audit does the SEI label go on the helmet.

Once a certified bicycle helmet is on your head, the fit of the helmet is critical to providing protection. You must follow the fit instructions supplied by the helmet manufacturer. The helmet should sit level on the rider's head and should not be able to be moved much in any direction.

Manufacturers also are required to provide instructions on replacement of a helmet. All helmets must be replaced when they have been involved in a crash or have been damaged by solvents. For more information on certified helmets, contact SEI at 1307 Dolly Madison Blvd., Suite 3A, McLean, VA 22101. E-mail: *info@SEInet.org* or Web site: *http://www.SEInet.org.*

GLOVES

Cycling gloves are important and generally overlooked safety accessories. Hands bear the brunt of spills and falls. Good gloves, especially those padded with gel, prevent road rash and gouging.

SHOES AND PEDALS

Rubber-treaded pedals are generally standard equipment on bicycles but are not completely safe. Accidents can occur when the rider's foot slips off the pedal while pedaling hard. Toe clips and straps, also called rat-trap pedals, are metal or plastic retainers that keep the rider's feet in place on the pedal. The tightness of the strap can be adjusted to suit the rider. These pedals allow the rider to be confident that this or her feet will stay on the pedals, and are fairly easy to get into and out of after a little practice. To a minor extent, they also allow the rider to pull up on the pedal as well as push down, increasing riding efficiency somewhat.

At one time, cleats were used to help secure the shoe even more reliably on the pedal but are seldom used nowadays. They have been replaced by clip-less pedal systems, which consist of special pedals that connect to special cleats attached to a cycling shoe. They work rather like ski bindings – step down to fasten, turn the heel to the outside to release. These pedals are often used by both road and mountain riders.

Pedaling is easiest when the rider wears a shoe designed for cycling. To support the foot on the pedal, cycling shoes are made lightweight and almost too stiff to walk in, and they have solid attachments for cleats. Especially with clip-less pedals, cycling shoes are as necessary as correct shoes for any other sport, perhaps even more so, because cyclists can push much harder against their pedals than other athletes will push against the ground.

OTHER ACCESSORIES

Serious riders should also budget for flat-tire repair kits, hydration systems (in other words, water bottles), sunglasses, pumps, and car bicycle racks. A rider is far better off with a good bike, shorts, helmet, shoes, gloves, water bottle, flat-repair kit, and bicycle rack than with a great bike and no accessories.

FITTING

The human body connects with a bicycle at five points: two hands, two feet, and one pair of buttocks. All of these points need to be properly fitted to the bike for size and comfort.

To emphasize, we are all different. Each human body is uniquely stretched (cramped) over a bicycle. A torso leans forward toward the handlebars, arms reach out to the grips, and legs reach down to power the pedals. All these bodily dimensions need to be appropriate in relation to the bicycle parts for the individual rider, otherwise pain will result and riding will become less efficient and even physically harmful.

On all bicycles, it is preferable to carry 60 to 70 percent of the rider's weight on the rear wheel. But a good riding position allows a rider to shift weight back and forth between the wheels and between his or her arms, rear, and legs as needed for riding conditions. The rider should be able to sit up high enough to relax the back muscles, as well as to lean far enough forward to apply maximum force on the pedals.

FITTING PARAMETERS

(Please note that the frame size of the American-invented mountain bike tends to be given in inches, while the frame size of the European-originated road bike tends to be expressed in centimeters. There are 2.54 centimeters in an inch, but the conversion is not quite exact. A chart is provided at the end of this section).

There are three basic measurements used to fit someone on a bicycle frame:

1. The frame size – not adjustable; therefore, one must buy the proper frame size

2. Stem length and handlebar width (minimally adjustable)

3. Seat height (adjustable)

The height measurement from the center of the crank axle to the top of the seat tube is the "frame size." Frame size helps determine two primary parameters: the height of the bicycle and its length. These measurements contribute to how far the rider's legs can extend, whether he or she can comfortably straddle the top tube when stopped, and how far forward the rider leans when seated on the bicycle.

Height of the frame is important and, as noted, is the dimension used to describe a frame size. Ironically, however, the length of the top tube of the frame is actually more important than the height.

The post of the saddle allows adjustment of several inches. Changing the stem allows an adjustment of only about one-half inch (maximally). Therefore, it is better practice to get the top tube length right first and *then* adjust for height using the saddle.

On all bicycles, the rider leans forward a bit. The length of the top tube of the frame, combined with the forward reach of the stem, controls how far forward a rider leans. The farther forward the rider leans, the more he or she can use the powerful muscles in the lower back, buttocks, and legs to push hard, making peddling easier. Conversely, the farther forward the rider leans, the more fatigue he or she will feel in the back, neck, shoulders, arms, and hands.

Bicycle sizing has changed over time, and many of today's adults grew up at a time when bicycles were described by their wheel size. Today, however, wheel diameter is not a contributor to frame size or bicycle fit other than straddle height. A 26-inch wheel is usually used on off-road bikes, a 70-cm or 28-inch (or 27-inch) wheel is used on road bicycles. The size of the wheel is a function of the purpose the bicycle will serve.

The actual height of the top tube is called the "straddle height." Straddle is easy to understand – if the straddle height is taller than the inseam, getting off the bike in a hurry may be painful. Generally speaking, the straddle height should be 2 inches below the crotch for road bikes and 4 inches below the crotch for mountain bikes.

Unfortunately, a buyer's frame measurements are not consistent between types of bikes. A rider who rides a 19-inch mountain bike may require a 24-inch (60-cm) road bike. Also unfortunately, different manufacturers have different ideas about what a frame length should be (just as do clothing manufacturers in different countries). There is wide variation in the length of frames that are the "same size."

After the basic frame size has been established through trial and error and experience and a bicycle has been selected, the second fitting tailors the bicycle to suit. It is exactly like having pants or a skirt hemmed – except an ill-fitting bicycle is a lot more painful than short pants or a dress-hem one trips over!

Installing a stem that fine-tunes the length of the frame to the buyer's body, selecting a seat (see below) that is comfortable, adjusting the post, and choosing grips or handlebars that fit the buyer's shoulders and hands – all these choices are worthwhile investments of time and money.

Fatigue or stress in the back or shoulders is a bad sign. Often revealed on longer rides, neck and shoulder pain may require changes in the handlebars or stem to make the bike comfortable.

Finally, the rider's hands should rest comfortably and at shoulder width apart on the grips or bar tape. Elbows should be bent. Brake levers should be placed and of a size to be easily reached and operated.

BICYCLE SIZES AND CONVERSION TABLE

1 inch = 2.54 centimeters

Below are common frame sizes with metric equivalents shown for sizes used on road bikes. Note that the inch and metric equivalent are not exact but reflect actual industry usage.

14 inch[1]

14.5 inch

15 inch

16 inch

16.5 inch

17 inch

17.5 inch

18 inch

19 inch = 49 cm

20 inch = 51 cm

21 inch = 54 cm

22 inch = 56 cm

23 inch = 58 cm

24 inch = 60 cm

25 inch = 63 cm

26 inch = 66 cm

Sizes outside these ranges will usually be available only in a custom bicycle.

Most bicycle makers will build their bikes in either odd or even sizes — with many exceptions. Some manufacturers will build half sizes, while many will exclude the largest and smallest sizes.

---

[1] The reason that the table does not convert all the sizes is that mountain bikes are described in inches and road bikes in inches or centimeters. Frame sizes that are not shown with metric equivalent are mountain bike sizes only.

BUYING A USED BICYCLE

Approximately 100 million used bicycles are in use in the United States, and about 10 percent of the market is replenished each year. It is a market that is growing every year. (Source: World Market Report, Interbike Directory.)

Until this book, the **Centric™ BicycleLINK Blue Book**, very little has been known about the used bicycle market. Also, until the development of these pages, there was no reliable place to get market information on the value of used bicycles.

There appear to be no legal national or regional distributors of used bicycles.

Retail stores do sell used bicycles in college towns across the country. It is unknown, however, what percentage of used bicycle sales is made through these stores. Such stores frequently offer inspection, repair, and/or warranties with used bicycles.

A direct market between buyer and seller also exists. These sales take place between friends, on the Internet, at flea markets and garage sales, and through classified advertising.

Tens of thousands of bicycles are stolen in this country every month. Most bicycles do not reappear anywhere in the U.S. bicycle market. Many "hot" bicycles stock the backyards of the thieves; reportedly, however, the great bulk of these bicycles is channeled through fencing operations and finally exported through Miami and other ports to the Caribbean and elsewhere.

NEW VS. USED

Buying a new bike assures the purchaser of the opportunity to buy a bicycle that fits correctly, that is mechanically new and perfect, and that gives the buyer the widest choices in style, type, price, and appearance.

When purchased from a bicycle shop, the bicycle will have been professionally assembled, and a service department will back up the manufacturer's warranty and fit.

The chief disadvantage of new bicycles is that, while they are a great value, they are much more expensive than used bicycles. Also, there are many interesting or unique older cycles that have no new equivalents.

Buying a used bike is a way to get a lot of bicycle for the money. After less than four years, quality bikes of all sorts can be purchased for approximately half or less of what they fetch new. In fact, a used bike may often be purchased for what it can be sold for later. In effect, the used bike may hold its entire value, just like a classic sports car.

Many used bikes come with accessories and upgrades installed that cost nothing extra and represent considerable value.

Finally, when buying a used bicycle, a proper inspection should reveal virtually all defects. Each piece of the equipment is in view and can be tried out. The mechanical issues of a used bicycle should be relatively easy for careful buyers to detect and resolve.

CENTRIC MEDIA'S PRICING DISCLOSURES

The current practices of pricing used bicycles have been rather haphazard. Centric Media, Inc., commissioned a continuing study by Cambridge Systematics, Inc. Hundreds of transactions were tracked by model, price category, age, and condition. At the request of Centric Media, industry analysts reviewed new and used bicycle market trends for geographic and seasonal factors.

Many specific lessons have come out of the data. They clearly show that cheap bicycles and expensive bicycles do not hold value over the first years as well as intermediately priced bicycles (between $400 and $700). In certain geographic areas (for example, the Northeast) where seasons fluctuate, prices are higher in season and lower out of season, though they maintain the same averages as the rest of the country. Other specific lessons are reviewed below.

The economist conducting the study, however, found a great inconsistency in the data. The inconsistency makes sense in a market where no standard has been set and little communication occurs.

Therefore, Centric Media is continuing the study for an additional two years in order to help provide a framework for the market as well as to track market transactions through its Web page. Certain disclaimers are in order:

> THE RELIABILITY OF THE CURRENT AVERAGE PRICES MAY VARY IN A RANGE OF 15 PERCENT FROM THE PRICE STATED IN THE TABLES.

> LIKE ALL COMMODITIES, THE PRICES OF USED BICYCLES CAN GO UP AND DOWN WITH GENERAL MARKET CONDITIONS AND SPECIFIC INDUSTRY TRENDS.

The **Centric™ Bicycle Blue Book** has relied on prior market structuring models, as well as new and used bicycle prices, to set the prices in its Bicycle Blue Book. As noted, the Cambridge Systematics study is scheduled to continue for two years. Centric Media's CD-ROM customers can gain access to the most-up-to-date pricing for specific models from the Web site by following the directions there.

CONDITION OF THE BICYCLE

The pricing of any bike, including that by Centric Media, Inc., requires that the bicycle be reasonably roadworthy, which means fully functioning with all components, brake pads, and tires in reasonable condition. Thus, for example, all other things being roadworthy, a bicycle with brand new tires is worth more than the same bicycle described in the standard pricing. As with a car, if a bicycle is beat up, obviously it is worth less. If it is pristine, it's worth more.

Whenever a used bicycle has serious appearance, mechanical, or structural deficiencies, the value plummets. However, a used bike in pristine condition will usually bring only a little more than a used bike in average condition. The reason is that the difference between the prices of new bicycles and used bicycles is small enough that the new bicycle price caps how high the used bicycle price can go up.

BUYER AND SELLER

In bike buying, buyer and seller are equally motivated. Both buyer and seller have an opportunity to check out market information (including Centric Media, Inc.).

RETAIL PRICE

The price quoted is the retail price. If the buyer is a reseller, a discount equal to the standard retailer's margin is appropriate. (Such discounts may range from 40 percent to 60 percent.)

DELIVERY

The price is free on board (FOB) from a point within reasonable driving distance for the buyer. Therefore, if the bicycle needs to be shipped to the buyer's city, that cost is considered to be a seller's expense.

INSPECTION AND WARRANTY

A store inspection is worth $25 to $30, while a one-year warranty is worth approximately $100 to $150, depending on whether the buyer is in a high-cost or low-cost portion of the United States. Those amounts are not included in the Bicycle Blue Book price.

USED BICYCLES AT STORES

Many, but not all, bicycle shops sell used bikes. Some stores actively discourage used bicycle sales.

Most bicycle shops acquire used bikes through two major sources: trade-ins, and unclaimed repairs. Some stores specialize in used bikes and will buy them for cash.

In some cases, a mechanic will have inspected the bike; in other cases, the store will have inspected and repaired the bike; and in still other shops the bicycle is sold "as-is." Some bicycle shops will provide a warranty with a used bike.

BICYCLE STORE PRICING POLICIES

In bicycle stores, the widely used rule of thumb is: "Used bicycles tend to sell for about half of what they sold for new — if they are completely functional, look good, and have no mechanical problems."

Since prices have gone up slowly over the decades, this rule of thumb even applies to older model years. For example, a Schwinn Varsity that sold for $99 in 1974, and that is still sound and looks good, will often sell for $50. And a 1995 Trek 820 that sold new for $399 will likely sell for about $200.

The following formulas summarize current practices for many stores in valuing trade-ins and used bicycles for purchase and resale:

Original retail price	$_____	(1)
Divided by 2	$_____	(2)
Value of services/repairs	$_____	(3)

The store then makes this calculation:

Original price	$_____	(2)
Minus repairs	$_____	(3)
Subtotal	$_____	(4)

The subtotal (item 4) is the amount that many stores will pay for the trade-in. If, however, the bicycle is one that may not be readily in demand and will likely take additional time to sell, the bicycle may require a further discount to account for the inventory cost.

For the sales price, a store adds its mark-up to the subtotal (item 4) above.

INDIVIDUAL SELLERS

Most used bikes are sold to friends, at flea markets or garage sales, or through advertising, including bicycle and other bulletin boards, in classifieds, or on the Internet. Obviously, a buyer must be more self-reliant when dealing with an individual rather than a reputable bicycle shop. There is much more price flexibility as well, especially when considering what price the seller would get from a bicycle store.

When responding to an advertisement, a buyer should determine the make, model, year, and size of the bike. The **Bicycle Blue Book** determines its current retail market value.

PAWNSHOPS

No surprise here that pawnshops are in the money business. They make their profits by lending money at high interest rates to individuals who need small loans. The goods taken in as security are returned to the borrower when the loan is repaid. When the loan is not repaid, the pawnbroker sells the goods to recover his money. That sale is also usually made on high interest terms. Pawnbrokers are interested in the loan, not the bike.

POLICE AUCTIONS

One of the great myths of the used-bike world is that bargains can be found at police auctions.

Law enforcement agencies pick up thousands of bicycles in the course of a year. Only a few will be identified and returned to their owner. (*Most are not registered!*) At regular intervals, the agency will hold an auction and sell the remaining bicycles to the highest bidder.

Most agencies store bikes out-of-doors in piles, in exposed conditions. The bikes rust, especially the chains and cables. The frames and forks get bent.

Police auction bikes often must be completely reconditioned. The sales are best for finding bike parts. For individuals who want a good bike, the police auctions are a poor bet.

INSPECTION CHECKLIST

Items that may be needed for a proper inspection include: 14 and 15 mm wrenches; 4,5, and 6 mm allen wrenches; pump; chain or gear gauge; spoke wrench; patch kit; tire irons; a rag; helmet; shorts; and riding shoes.

Initially, the buyer should ask the seller for any paperwork (such as manual and sales receipt) on the bicycle and its history, including reason for selling, any upgrades, major repairs, storage location, and accidents. The buyer should ask the seller at this point what is the asking price and what accessories are included. Inspecting the bicycle involves checking the following:

1. *Type*: Mountain, hybrid, road, or specialty (racing, time-trial, and so on).

2. *Make, model, and price*: The make, model, and original price should be confirmed

in the store or the manufacturer's Web page.

3. *Frame size (measured from center crank to top of seat tube)*: Individual buyers are sometimes tempted to buy the wrong size because the seller is offering a great deal. The temptation should be resisted. The discomfort on the back, neck, knees, hands, shoulders, arms, and parts south is not worth it.

4. *Signs of accidents*: Scrapes on the outside of the brake levers, edges of the saddle, bent handlebars, cranks, or derailleur mounting bolt are sure signs of a crash. Scrapes, dents, ripped seats, rust, lack of lubrication, broken spokes, and gouges are all signs of possible abuse or accidents. Or, the fork blades may be bent backward, which can be difficult to spot.

5. *Frame alignment*: Examine the front and back for straightness.

6. *Frame and fork dents or surface damage*: Dented frame tubes cannot be repaired and may indicate a badly abused bike. The bicycle should be turned upside down to check the lower tubes and also see if water runs out of the seat post strut. Running fingers over the frame welds will check for cracks and other damage.

7. *Chain and derailleur rust and wear*: On expensive bicycles, a chain gauge should be used to determine wear and tear. Rusty chains, cables, and components are usually expensive to replace. Most bicycle shops will not accept a bike with a rusty chain, knowing that it will also need a new freewheel and other parts.

8. *Corrosion in general*: Paint blisters indicate rust, which is difficult to stop on a steel frame. Difficulty turning the lug nuts, quick release levers, adjusting barrels, or spoke nipples is an indication of corrosion. A sun-faded saddle is an indication that a bicycle has been left out in the elements. A "salty" surface on aluminum is another indication of corrosion.

9. *Derailleur gearing and controls*: The gears in the derailleur can be checked for wear and tear, using a gauge. The number of gears in both front and back should be verified. Gear levers or handle controls should move easily and be conveniently located.

10. *Rim alignment*: Brakes are compressed until barely touching the rim. If spinning the tire and rim results in rubbing and releasing, the rim is out of alignment. Rims more that 1 inch out of alignment probably cannot be repaired. Dented rims will require replacement.

11. *Tire quality*: Tires must be pumped to recommended pressure to check for ballooning. Depending on quality, tires cost between $6 and $30 for just the tire and $3 and $10 for installation.

12. *Brake pads and cables*: For safety purposes, it is very important to compress the brake levers hard to determine that they are in perfect working order. Worn

brake pads will require replacement. The pads cost from $4 to $30 each, and installation is generally an additional $8 to $15 each. Brake pads on specialty or very expensive bikes can be surprisingly costly.

13. *Saddle*: A bicycle's saddle is relatively expensive to replace, costing between $8 and $100.

14. *Cranks*: Firmly grasp the frame and shake the crank back and forth. Any movement indicates crank or bearing problems, which can cost from $10 to $60 to repair.

15. *Hubs*: Both wheels must spin without noise from the hub. Fixing or replacing hubs can cost between $10 and $200.

16. *Quick releases*: Quality bicycles offer quick release on the hubs and seat posts.

17. *Overall cleanliness and condition*: The handlebar tape or foam should be in good condition. The frame paint can have some flecks or scratches, but it should be in fairly good condition.

18. *Test ride*: The buyer should take the bicycle on as extensive a test ride as possible. Prior to leaving, the buyer should adjust the seat post to its proper height. The brakes must be checked carefully and tried on flat terrain! A "face plant" is not an approved inspection technique. To reiterate, the frame straddle height should allow 2 inches of clearance for road bikes and 4 inches for mountain bikes. The ride should include both flat and hilly terrain.

Most bicycle stores will safety inspect a bicycle for free and will offer a detailed estimate for any needed repairs.

BUYING SKILLS

Negotiation comes down to some basic, universal rules:

- Get the seller to quote a price first.
- Who needs whom? A student may need a bicycle in September more. A seller leaving town may have to lower the price to move a bicycle quickly.
- Instincts are important. If something seems wrong, if the deal seems too good to be true, it probably is.
- Love is for people and pets, not deals.
- There is nothing wrong with asking for a lower price.
- Time is valuable.
- Buyers and sellers shouldn't "burn bridges."

- Niceness counts.

- Bicycles with unusually small or large frames usually command lower prices.

- The relationship with a bicycle store can help. If a mechanic in the store helps out, a tip is in order.

SELLING TIPS

Selling a bicycle directly to a buyer will usually, but not always, result in a higher price. The suggestions below are in the order from the most to the least important, and the latter suggestions are for sellers who have more time than money. The seller should do the following:

1. At a minimum, clean the bike and pump up the tires.

2. Find the original receipt, the owner's manual, and any other paperwork that goes with the bike.

3. Make sure the bike is safe for a test ride.

4. Remove all the accessories. They will not help get a higher price, and they may be sold separately or used on another bike.

5. Most buyers do not value upgrades. Original equipment should be reinstalled only if the seller can make use of the upgraded components.

6. Clean the bike thoroughly. Get the dirt and grease out of every nook and cranny.

7. Oil the chain.

8. Touch up the paint.

9. Wax the bike.

10. Replace damaged seats, handlebar tape, or grips.

11. Replace badly worn tires.

The seller should set the price *after* getting the bicycle ready for sale.

Sellers can advertise the bike in a number of locations:

1. *Metropolitan newspapers:* Most large papers are expensive places in which to place even a small classified ad. However, they reach so many people that a sale may be assured.

2. *College newspapers, flea market magazines, neighborhood advertisers:* These publications offer low-cost advertising and are usually the most effective place to advertise. Posting ads on bulletin boards in student centers, laundries, community

bulletin boards, grocery stores, and bicycle shops (those that allow it) is also worthwhile.

3. *Club newsletters*: Many bicycle clubs produce newsletters that offer classified advertising. Sellers can also take the bike to cycling events.

4. *The Web*: Posting a bike for sale on the Internet has the advantage of being free. Both local and national listings are available. (See the classified section at ***http://www.bicyclelink.com***)

CLASSIC AND ANTIQUE BICYCLES

Antique bicycles are interesting and fun. More than one person has discovered a dusty old bike in the barn that was worth $3,000 or more to a collector.

This market is complicated and subtle. Here are some basic rules:

1. Very old bikes, such as Ordinaries (high wheelers), are something few people know much about. Real ones are extremely rare and can be valuable. Many excellent reproductions exist, though, with some old enough to be collectibles in themselves.

2. Balloon tire bikes with gas tanks are the most active category of antique bikes. Some models are valuable, depending on year, make, and condition. Boys' bikes are worth a lot more than girls' bikes.

3. Bikes from the 1960s are common, often resemble the bikes from the '50s, and do not bring high prices – yet. . .

4. Classic road racing bikes from the 1960s and 70s are not particularly valuable – yet. They will be.

The **Centric™ BicycleLINK Yellow Pages** at *http://www.bicyclelink.com* includes contacts for persons interested in classic and collector bicycles.

BICYCLE THEFT PREVENTION

Approximately 450,000 stolen bicycles are reported each year. It is estimated that those reports represent less than half of the actual number of bicycles stolen each year.

Bicycles virtually all come with a "Bicycle Theft Guarantee" that goes something like this: "If you don't lock your bike up, it's guaranteed that someone will steal it."

There are two physical methods to prevent bicycle theft: personal vigilance and quality locks. Vigilance means keeping the bike in sight at the office, while in an ATM line at the bank, or in a store.

Locking the bike (by an unremovable part like the frame) to an immovable object is the proper technique. Keeping the bike locked even when it is at home is necessary. An extraordinary number of bicycles are reported stolen from open garage doors and apartment patios. Kryptonite®-brand U-shaped locks are considered the most reliable in the industry.

Bicycle thieves are brazen. Centric Media customers have lost bikes that they leaned up against a storefront for "just a moment." Bicycle racers tell of bold thieves who drove up in a truck and stole bicycles only 20 feet from them. The thieves tossed the bikes into the back of a pickup and roared off before the startled racers could react.

A bicycle shop owner tells a story of a thief who came into the store, calmly got on a bike, and rode it out the open door of the store and sprinted away.

Where do stolen bikes end up? Evidence is strong that most of the bikes are exported. In Miami, reliable sources report that there is an area on the waterfront where small freighters and ferries depart regularly with decks completely covered with used bicycles. These bicycles are destined for Haiti, the Dominican Republic, and other islands. Sources speculate that these bicycles are stolen. Similar exports to Mexico are believed to occur.

The police often suspect bicycles are stolen but cannot do anything about it. They do not have probable cause to make a stop, nor has there been an effective national registration system to check ownership. Several new registration systems are now being implemented.

The Centric Media anti-theft registration system is detailed below. The system provides effective, transferable registration for the owner, as well as probable cause for police to investigate if the label is removed.

Most bicycle locks do not work particularly well and only serve to keep an honest person honest. If the thief has any tools or any expertise, most locks cannot even slow him down. Lightweight cable and most chains, as well as most locks, are susceptible to either "Swiss wire cutters" or bolt cutters. Very heavy chains work well, if they are combined with a similar sized padlock.

U-shaped locks come in several grades. The "imported" U-shaped locks are the least expensive and provide security for most situations. However, on a college campus, in a city, or in any place where a bicycle is left in a rack, the better grades of locks are necessary.

U-locks are attacked by thieves who carry car jacks (the Volvo jack is a favorite due to its compact size) and simply force the shackle open. Other methods of attack include freezing and shattering the lock, or cutting or removing the object the bicycle is locked to.

Kryptonite® is a widely recommended brand of bike lock. In New York City and other major metropolitan areas, many observers believe that Kryptonite's top-of-the-line locks are the only ones that have a chance of working.

Along with locking a bicycle up, registering it from Day One is an essential precaution.

CENTRIC™ BICYCLELINK REGISTRATION SYSTEM

The innovative Centric™ BicycleLINK Registration System relies on the modern miracle of the Internet and some old-fashioned technology to offer the only effective worldwide national bicycle registration system.

The need for a central system is clear. Most states delegate bicycle registration to cities. Local governments have no nationwide standards. In virtually all states, that bicycle information is not collated.

Unless the bicycle is recovered by the same city that originally licensed it, there is no way to contact the owner. The only places where stolen bicycles are reported are in a database, which covers all stolen items.

Stolen bicycles are often not reported in that system, and if reported, locators do not check the system.

The BicycleLINK registry works worldwide and effectively combats bicycle theft.

REGISTRATION

The owner links to **http://www.bicyclelink.com/registration/** and clicks on the registration button. The registrant fills out two sections which describe the personal information of the owner (including a private password) and general information about the bicycle, including the serial number.

The serial number can be found on the purchase receipt or information package that originally comes with the bicycle. Additionally, the serial number is usually stamped in the metal on the bottom of the crank set, lower frame tube, head tube, bottom bracket, seat tube, rear stay, or rear dropout. It is easy to detect when the bicycle is turned over onto its seat.

Some expensive custom bicycles, tandems, and recumbents do not have a serial number and may be registered by manufacturer alone. To recover a bicycle without a serial number after it is stolen, however, the registrant must report the theft. See below.

If the registrant has e-mail, Centric Media will send an e-mail confirmation in a few days. The registrant also receives a hard copy of the registration in the mail and an adhesive label. The registrant attaches the label (which is the best one on the market today) on the bicycle frame in accordance with the instructions. The label cannot be easily removed without leaving a mark on the substrate. The label holds a warning, a URL for Centric Media's Web site **http://www.bicyclelink.com,** and the telephone number

1-877-FOR-BIKERS (1-877-367-2453)

In order to perfect notification of registration, the owner may wish to use an electric pencil to etch the letters "BL" on the frame underneath the label.

NOTIFICATION OF STOLEN BICYCLES

In the unhappy event the bicycle is stolen, the owner should link immediately to **http://www.bicyclelink.com/registration/** and report the theft, following the instructions at the web site. To repeat, if the registered bicycle does not have a serial number, it is imperative that the registrant reports the theft to effectuate recovery.

RECOVERY

BicycleLINK is conducting educational outreach to police and other government departments, pawnshops, and bicyclists.

When the authorities recover a bicycle, or ownership comes into question during a transaction, the interested party contacts BicyleLINK on its toll free line (**1-877-FOR -BIKERS**) or logs on to the Internet to check the registration. The computer runs a check based on the bicycle description and serial number and notifies the owner by e-mail or postcard of the location of the bicycle.

Transfer

To transfer the bike, the owner logs on to **http://www.bicyclelink.com** and follows the instructions there. To transfer, you must have the personal password that was used in the original registration.

The registration lasts ten years. As of November 1, 1998, the cost is ten dollars ($10.00, or $1.00 per year.) Price is subject to change without notice.

Register now!

DISCLAIMER FOR CENTRIC BICYCLELINK BLUE BOOK

The bike values contained herein are the result of careful analysis conducted by Centric Media, Inc., based on marketplace information, which it deems reliable. The analysis compares the original sales prices of specific brands and models sold throughout the United States to used sales prices for the same brand and model. The values are intended only as a guide. Centric Media, Inc. assumes no liability for any errors or omissions.

INTRODUCTION TO PART II: PRICING SECTION

This section contains used price information for over 9,700 bikes manufactured between 1994 and 1998 and the suggested retail price for almost 2,000 models manufactured in 1999.

Follow these simple steps to find the **used price** range for a bicycle that you are interested in buying or selling:

1. Go to the section for the **Year** that the bike was manufactured.

2. Find the **Brand** of bike that you are looking for. These are listed alphabetically.

3. Under the **Brand** heading locate the **Model**.* These are listed alphabetically.

4. The price range for that bike is shown to the right of the **Model** name. The range is valid for bicycles that are in fair to good condition and that are still equipped with the original components.

To find the 1999 **suggested retail** price for a new model:

1. Go to the section for **1999**.

2. Find the **Brand** of bike that you are looking for. These are listed alphabetically.

3. Under the **Brand** heading locate the **Model***. These are listed alphabetically.

4. The suggested retail price for each bike is listed to the right of the **Model** name.

---

*Some manufacturers build different bikes with same model name but different components, forks, or different types of paint or finish. The price range will differ for different configurations of the same model name. If there is more than one listing for the model that you are looking up, information on components, fork, or finish is provided so that you will find a unique price or price range for your specific bike. In a few cases the models are not distinguished by name, components, fork, or finish. For those we have specified simply "other features" to explain the different prices.

MODEL

PRICE RANGE

Aegis 🚲

Carbon Mountain	$ 809 –	$ 1,095
Carbon Road	$ 688 –	$ 931

Alex Moulton 🚲

5	$ 831 –	$ 1,124
AM 14	$ 885 –	$ 1,197
APB 14	$ 667 –	$ 902

Alpinestars 🚲

AL-D560	$ 444 –	$ 601
AL-D735	$ 639 –	$ 865
AL-D900	$ 739 –	$ 1,000
CR-D50	$ 191 –	$ 258
CR-D100	$ 236 –	$ 319
CR-D300	$ 267 –	$ 361
CR-D560	$ 355 –	$ 481
CR-D735	$ 561 –	$ 759
CR-T100	$ 245 –	$ 331
CR-T560	$ 359 –	$ 486

Barracuda 🚲

A2B	$ 219 –	$ 296
A2E	$ 444 –	$ 601
A2M	$ 326 –	$ 442
A2R	$ 297 –	$ 402

Basso 🚲

Astra C: Record	$ 888 –	$ 1,201
Coral Track	$ 565 –	$ 764
Evolution C: Record	$ 896 –	$ 1,212
GAP C: Athena	$ 728 –	$ 985

C: – Components   F: – Fork

MODEL	PRICE RANGE

Basso (*continued*)

GAP TI	$ 790 – $ 1,069
Loto Chorus	$ 813 – $ 1,100
TI Hardtail C: LX	$ 798 – $ 1,079
TI Hardtail C: Record	$ 891 – $ 1,206

Bianchi

Advantage	$ 213 – $ 288
Alfana	$ 440 – $ 596
Avenue	$ 166 – $ 225
Boardwalk	$ 248 – $ 335
Campione d'Italia	$ 428 – $ 579
Carbon Virata	$ 644 – $ 871
Cobra	$ 859 – $ 1,162
Denali	$ 536 – $ 725
EL C: Chours	$ 944 – $ 1,277
EL C: Record	$ 1,078 – $ 1,458
EL C: Veloce	$ 796 – $ 1,078
Eros	$ 373 – $ 504
Genius C: Chorus	$ 969 – $ 1,311
Genius C: Record	$ 1,112 – $ 1,505
Genius C: Veloce	$ 828 – $ 1,121
Giro	$ 536 – $ 725
Grizzly	$ 593 – $ 802
Grizzly RC	$ 828 – $ 1,120
Ibex	$ 366 – $ 496
Kodiak	$ 203 – $ 274
Lynx	$ 263 – $ 356
Nyala	$ 203 – $ 274
Ocelot	$ 166 – $ 225
Osprey	$ 282 – $ 382
Peregrine	$ 405 – $ 548

C: – Components   F: – Fork

MODEL	PRICE RANGE

Bianchi *(continued)*

Model	Price Range
Premio	$ 228 – $ 309
Project-3	$ 312 – $ 422
Project-5	$ 446 – $ 603
SBX C: Chorus	$ 859 – $ 1,162
SBX C: Record	$ 1,028 – $ 1,390
SBX C: Veloce	$ 693 – $ 937
Super Grizzly RC	$ 1,078 – $ 1,458
Timber Wolf	$ 146 – $ 197
Veloce	$ 656 – $ 887

Bike Friday

Model	Price Range
Companion	$ 341 – $ 462
New World Tourist	$ 514 – $ 695
Pocket Llama	$ 665 – $ 900
Pocket Rocket	$ 609 – $ 824
Sport	$ 555 – $ 751

Breezer

Model	Price Range
Beamer	$ 815 – $ 1,102
Jet Stream	$ 691 – $ 935
Lightning	$ 815 – $ 1,102
Storm	$ 479 – $ 648
Thunder	$ 532 – $ 720
Venturi	$ 844 – $ 1,142

Bridgestone

Model	Price Range
BUB	$ 154 – $ 208
CB-1	$ 161 – $ 218
MB-1	$ 565 – $ 764
MB-2	$ 516 – $ 697
MB-3	$ 347 – $ 470

C: – Components   F: – Fork

MODEL	PRICE RANGE

Bridgestone *(continued)*

Model	Price Range
MB-3 SUS	$ 426 – $ 576
MB-4	$ 285 – $ 385
MB-4 SUS	$ 347 – $ 470
MB-5	$ 263 – $ 356
MB-5 SUS	$ 306 – $ 414
MB-6	$ 196 – $ 265
RB-1	$ 516 – $ 697
RB-2	$ 319 – $ 431
RB-T	$ 302 – $ 408
XO-3	$ 343 – $ 465
XO-4	$ 241 – $ 326
XO-5	$ 177 – $ 240

Brompton

Model	Price Range
Unspecified	$ 343 – $ 465

Burley

Model	Price Range
Bossa Nova	$ 807 – $ 1,092
Duet	$ 653 – $ 884
Rock 'n Roll	$ 653 – $ 884
Rock 'n Roll Allsop	$ 717 – $ 970
Samba	$ 516 – $ 697
Zydeco	$ 445 – $ 601

Cannondale

Model	Price Range
C-600	$ 437 – $ 591
C-2000	$ 764 – $ 1,034
Delta V-400	$ 357 – $ 483
Delta V-500	$ 410 – $ 554
Delta V-600	$ 402 – $ 543
Delta V-700	$ 550 – $ 744

C: – Components   F: – Fork

MODEL   PRICE RANGE

Cannondale (continued)

Model	Price Range	
Delta V-1000	$ 638 – $	863
H-300	$ 213 – $	288
H-400	$ 263 – $	355
H-600	$ 380 – $	514
H-800	$ 459 – $	621
Killer V-900	$ 487 – $	658
Killer V-2000	$ 638 – $	863
Killer V-3000	$ 887 – $	1,200
M-300	$ 213 – $	288
M-400	$ 263 – $	355
M-500	$ 357 – $	483
M-600	$ 402 – $	543
M-700	$ 445 – $	602
M-800	$ 459 – $	621
MCX-24	$ 213 – $	288
MT-2000	$ 867 – $	1,172
MT-3000	$ 983 – $	1,330
R-300	$ 291 – $	394
R-400	$ 334 – $	452
R-500	$ 357 – $	483
R-600	$ 460 – $	623
R-700	$ 581 – $	786
R-800	$ 596 – $	806
R-900	$ 664 – $	899
R-1000	$ 871 – $	1,179
R-2000	$ 989 – $	1,338
RT-3000	$ 957 – $	1,295
Super V-1000	$ 792 – $	1,071
Super V-2000	$ 925 – $	1,251

C: – Components   F: – Fork

MODEL	PRICE RANGE

Cannondale *(continued)*

Model	Price Range
T-700	$ 433 – $ 586
T-1000	$ 735 – $ 994
Track 1000	$ 567 – $ 768

Casati

Model	Price Range
Ellisse EL O/S	$ 868 – $ 1,174
Gold Line SLX	$ 831 – $ 1,124
Record SL	$ 738 – $ 999

Cignal

Model	Price Range
Bimini	$ 142 – $ 192
Cherokee	$ 98 – $ 133
Dorado C: LX	$ 283 – $ 382
Kokomo	$ 123 – $ 166
Melbourne Express	$ 316 – $ 428
Montego	$ 118 – $ 160
Montero	$ 123 – $ 166
Nevada	$ 252 – $ 341
Ozark	$ 147 – $ 198
Rialto	$ 98 – $ 133
Scirocco	$ 98 – $ 133
Shenango	$ 189 – $ 256
Silverado	$ 261 – $ 353
Ventura	$ 175 – $ 237
Zanzibar	$ 225 – $ 305

Ciocc

Model	Price Range
SL Racing (Excel)	$ 443 – $ 599

C: – Components   F: – Fork

MODEL   PRICE RANGE

Co-Motion

Model	Price Range
Bofus Off-Road	$ 862 – $ 1,167
Bofus Road	$ 862 – $ 1,167
Cutthroat XTR	$ 840 – $ 1,137
Double Espresso	$ 899 – $ 1,216
Espresso Dura-Ace C: STI	$ 850 – $ 1,150
Espresso C: Record Ergo	$ 841 – $ 1,138
Espresso C: Ultegra	$ 716 – $ 968
Java	$ 856 – $ 1,159
Speedster	$ 807 – $ 1,092

Counterpoint

Model	Price Range
Opus IV CL	$ 885 – $ 1,197
Presto C: CL	$ 625 – $ 846
Presto C: SE	$ 680 – $ 920
Presto C: SE63	$ 739 – $ 1,000
SE Triad	$ 831 – $ 1,124

Cycle Pro

Model	Price Range
Capri	$ 61 – $ 83
Comp	$ 71 – $ 96
Explorer	$ 56 – $ 76
Ladybug	$ 56 – $ 76
Raider	$ 61 – $ 83

Dean

Model	Price Range
New XT Aluminum	$ 877 – $ 1,187
New XT Aluminum, Shock	$ 885 – $ 1,197
New XT Titanium	$ 899 – $ 1,217
Shimano C: Ultegra Steel	$ 872 – $ 1,180
Shimano C: Ultegra Titanium	$ 901 – $ 1,219
XTR Aluminum	$ 899 – $ 1,217

C: – Components   F: – Fork

MODEL	PRICE RANGE

Dean *(continued)*

| XTR Aluminum, Shock | $ 901 – $ 1,219 |
| Zap Steel | $ 900 – $ 1,218 |

DeRosa

Heritage Edition 1957	$ 816 – $ 1,103
Nuovo Classico TSX	$ 857 – $ 1,159
Primato EL/OS	$ 899 – $ 1,216

Diamondback

Apex	$ 351 – $ 474
Approach	$ 166 – $ 225
Ascent	$ 260 – $ 351
Axis TR	$ 583 – $ 789
Axis TT C: LX	$ 757 – $ 1,024
Axis TT C: XT	$ 892 – $ 1,207
Cross Country	$ 141 – $ 190
Dual Response	$ 797 – $ 1,078
Dual Response CM	$ 628 – $ 850
Expert	$ 248 – $ 335
Interval	$ 176 – $ 239
Lake Side	$ 201 – $ 272
Master	$ 394 – $ 533
Outlook	$ 109 – $ 148
Parkway	$ 115 – $ 155
Prevail TT	$ 868 – $ 1,175
Response Elite	$ 455 – $ 616
Response Sport	$ 329 – $ 445
Sorrento	$ 166 – $ 225
Sorrento Sport	$ 196 – $ 266
Topanga	$ 211 – $ 285
Traverse	$ 141 – $ 190

C: – Components   F: – Fork

MODEL	PRICE RANGE

Easy Racer

Gold Rush Replica	$ 831 – $ 1,124
Tour Easy	$ 638 – $ 863

Eddy Merckx

Century TSX	$ 857 – $ 1,159
Corsa SL	$ 761 – $ 1,029
MX Leader	$ 901 – $ 1,219
Titanal	$ 816 – $ 1,103

Fuji

Absolute	$ 177 – $ 240
Ace	$ 191 – $ 259
Blaster	$ 106 – $ 143
Blaster 6	$ 101 – $ 136
Blvd C: XC	$ 120 – $ 163
Club	$ 327 – $ 442
Crosstown	$ 101 – $ 136
Discovery	$ 196 – $ 265
Discovery SX	$ 250 – $ 338
Dynamic	$ 196 – $ 265
Mt. Fuji SX	$ 580 – $ 785
Odessa	$ 106 – $ 143
Outland	$ 245 – $ 332
Outland SX	$ 298 – $ 403
Regis	$ 120 – $ 163
Roubaix	$ 407 – $ 550
Royale	$ 241 – $ 326
Sagres	$ 149 – $ 202
Sandblaster	$ 149 – $ 202
Suncrest	$ 298 – $ 403
Suncrest SX	$ 399 – $ 540

C: – Components   F: – Fork

MODEL	PRICE RANGE

Fuji *(continued)*

Model	Price Range
Sunfire	$ 135 – $ 182
Sunfire SX	$ 177 – $ 240
Supreme	$ 135 – $ 182
Team	$ 516 – $ 697
Thrill	$ 177 – $ 240
Thrill SX	$ 219 – $ 296
Tiara	$ 140 – $ 189
Touring Series	$ 327 – $ 442

Gary Fisher

Model	Price Range
Advance	$ 168 – $ 227
Aquila	$ 272 – $ 368
Hoo Koo E Koo	$ 327 – $ 442
Montare	$ 364 – $ 492
Mt. Tam	$ 611 – $ 826
Nevada City	$ 692 – $ 937
Paragon	$ 445 – $ 601
Procaliber	$ 799 – $ 1,081
Procaliber Ltd.	$ 901 – $ 1,219
Rangitoto	$ 272 – $ 368
Supercaliber	$ 639 – $ 865
Tassajara	$ 210 – $ 283
Tyro	$ 168 – $ 227
Ziggurat	$ 739 – $ 1,000

Giant

Model	Price Range
Allegre	$ 299 – $ 404
ATX-760	$ 280 – $ 378
ATX-870	$ 260 – $ 352
ATX-875	$ 260 – $ 352
ATX-890	$ 299 – $ 404

C: – Components   F: – Fork

MODEL   PRICE RANGE

Giant (continued)

Model	Price Range
Cadex ALM-1	$ 373 – $ 504
Cadex CFM-1	$ 616 – $ 834
Cadex CFM-2	$ 535 – $ 723
Cadex CFM-3	$ 458 – $ 619
Cadex CFR-1	$ 577 – $ 781
Cadex CFR-3	$ 408 – $ 552
Cadex TCM	$ 745 – $ 1,008
Iguana	$ 199 – $ 270
Innova	$ 183 – $ 247
Kronos	$ 220 – $ 298
Nutra	$ 157 – $ 213
Perigee	$ 166 – $ 224
Prodigy	$ 230 – $ 311
Rincon	$ 136 – $ 184
Sedona ATX	$ 220 – $ 298
Yukon	$ 162 – $ 219
Yukon SE	$ 183 – $ 247

Giordana

Model	Price Range
AL Titanium	$ 738 – $ 999
XL Cronometro	$ 665 – $ 900
XL Eco	$ 780 – $ 1,056
XL Strada	$ 653 – $ 884
XL Superleggero	$ 831 – $ 1,124
XL Ultra	$ 896 – $ 1,212

Green Cycles

Model	Price Range
Hornet	$ 899 – $ 1,216

C: – Components   F: – Fork

MODEL	PRICE RANGE
GT	🚲
Aggressor	$ 145 – $ 196
Avalanche AL	$ 341 – $ 462
Avalanche AL F: Rock Shox	$ 415 – $ 561
Backwoods	$ 221 – $ 299
Bravado LE	$ 459 – $ 622
Bravado LE F: Rock Shox	$ 553 – $ 748
Cirque	$ 191 – $ 258
Corrado	$ 363 – $ 492
Corrado F: Rock Shox	$ 429 – $ 580
Discovery	$ 117 – $ 158
Edge Aluminum	$ 696 – $ 942
Edge Chromoly	$ 720 – $ 974
Edge Zap Aluminum	$ 723 – $ 979
Edge Zap Chromoly	$ 737 – $ 997
Force	$ 274 – $ 371
Fury	$ 546 – $ 739
Karakoram	$ 274 – $ 371
Karakoram F: Rock Shox	$ 341 – $ 462
Outpost	$ 121 – $ 164
Outpost Trail	$ 105 – $ 142
Pantera AL	$ 267 – $ 362
Pantera AL F: Rock Shox	$ 331 – $ 448
Rage	$ 473 – $ 640
Ricochet	$ 295 – $ 399
RTS-1	$ 702 – $ 949
RTS-2	$ 557 – $ 754
RTS-3	$ 432 – $ 584
Strike	$ 363 – $ 492
Talera	$ 137 – $ 185
Team RTS	$ 740 – $ 1,001
Tequesta	$ 206 – $ 279

C: – Components   F: – Fork

MODEL		PRICE RANGE

GT *(continued)* 🚲

Timberline	$ 168 – $ 227
Timberline FS	$ 221 – $ 299
Vantara	$ 141 – $ 191
Zaskar	$ 511 – $ 691
Zaskar F: Rock Shox	$ 592 – $ 802
Zaskar LE	$ 679 – $ 918

Haro 🚲

Escape	$ 347 – $ 470
Escape Comp	$ 389 – $ 527
Extreme	$ 507 – $ 686
Impulse	$ 660 – $ 893
Impulse Comp	$ 877 – $ 1,186
Intense	$ 125 – $ 169
Missile	$ 116 – $ 156
Vector V1e	$ 125 – $ 169
Vector V2c	$ 156 – $ 211
Vector V3a	$ 175 – $ 237
Vector V4s	$ 230 – $ 311
F-26a	$ 738 – $ 999

HH 🚲

America	$ 884 – $ 1,197
Dirty Harry	$ 580 – $ 785
Fudendo	$ 498 – $ 674
Pista	$ 608 – $ 822
The Menace	$ 532 – $ 720

Ibis 🚲

Cousin It Mountain	$ 860 – $ 1,163
Cousin It Road	$ 860 – $ 1,163

C: – Components   F: – Fork

MODEL	PRICE RANGE

Ibis (continued) 🚲

Mojo	$ 893 – $ 1,209
Scorcher	$ 435 – $ 589
Touche	$ 860 – $ 1,163

Iron Horse 🚲

Amigo	$ 271 – $ 367
AT100	$ 177 – $ 239
AT150	$ 204 – $ 277
AT200	$ 223 – $ 301
AT50	$ 125 – $ 169
AT70	$ 144 – $ 195
Bronco	$ 120 – $ 162
Eliminator 24	$ 153 – $ 207
Elite	$ 100 – $ 136
MT400	$ 241 – $ 325
MT500R	$ 271 – $ 367
MT600	$ 326 – $ 442
MT650R	$ 406 – $ 550
MT700R	$ 625 – $ 846
MT1000R	$ 896 – $ 1,212
Tango	$ 498 – $ 674
XT1500	$ 125 – $ 169
XT1800	$ 144 – $ 195
XT2100	$ 172 – $ 233
XT5000	$ 271 – $ 367

Jamis 🚲

Aragon	$ 175 – $ 237
Aurora	$ 424 – $ 574
Citizen	$ 147 – $ 198

C: – Components   F: – Fork

MODEL	PRICE RANGE

Jamis (continued)

Model	Price Range
Coda	$ 291 – $ 394
Cross Country	$ 147 – $ 198
Dakar	$ 851 – $ 1,151
Dakota	$ 547 – $ 740
Diablo	$ 345 – $ 467
Dragon	$ 638 – $ 863
Durango	$ 203 – $ 274
Eclipse	$ 532 – $ 720
Eureka	$ 316 – $ 428
Exile	$ 248 – $ 335
Explorer XR	$ 291 – $ 394
Quest	$ 405 – $ 548
Tangier	$ 207 – $ 280
Ukiah	$ 166 – $ 224

Jazz

Model	Price Range
Bold Moves	$ 112 – $ 152
Inferno	$ 155 – $ 210
Latitude	$ 112 – $ 152
Rocket	$ 123 – $ 167

Kestrel

Model	Price Range
200ESL C: Dura-Ace STI	$ 896 – $ 1,212
200SCi/105 C: STI	$ 653 – $ 883
200SCi C: Athena	$ 797 – $ 1,078
200SCi C: Ultegra STI	$ 778 – $ 1,053
500SCi C: Ultegra STI	$ 856 – $ 1,158
CS-X C: Deore LX	$ 714 – $ 966
CS-X C: Deore XT	$ 843 – $ 1,141

C: – Components   F: – Fork

MODEL	PRICE RANGE

KHS

Model	Price Range
Aero Comp C: Ultegra	$ 595 – $ 806
Aero Sport	$ 214 – $ 289
Aero Turbo C: STI	$ 414 – $ 560
Comp	$ 351 – $ 475
Comp FZ	$ 437 – $ 591
Cross Sport	$ 161 – $ 218
Descent	$ 306 – $ 413
Montana	$ 110 – $ 149
Montana Crest	$ 195 – $ 264
Montana Junior	$ 125 – $ 169
Montana Sport	$ 172 – $ 233
Montana Super	$ 115 – $ 156
Montana Trail	$ 139 – $ 188
Pro	$ 515 – $ 697
Pro FZ	$ 595 – $ 806
Summit	$ 245 – $ 331
Tandemania	$ 326 – $ 442
Tandemania Comp	$ 548 – $ 742
Team	$ 680 – $ 919
Ti Issue	$ 851 – $ 1,151
Ti Team	$ 894 – $ 1,210

Kingcycle

Model	Price Range
Unspecified	$ 799 – $ 1,080

Klein

Model	Price Range
Adept	$ 699 – $ 945
Adroit C: XT	$ 900 – $ 1,218
Aeolus C: Dura-Ace	$ 896 – $ 1,212
Aeolus C: Ultegra	$ 774 – $ 1,047
Attitude C: XT	$ 834 – $ 1,129

C: – Components   F: – Fork

MODEL	PRICE RANGE

Klein (continued) 🚲

Attitude C: XT/S	$ 882 – $ 1,193
Attitude C: XT2	$ 860 – $ 1,164
Attitude C: XTR	$ 900 – $ 1,217
Attitude C: XTR/S	$ 900 – $ 1,217
Attitude C: XTR2	$ 891 – $ 1,206
Fervor C: LX	$ 555 – $ 751
Fervor C: LX/S	$ 588 – $ 796
Fervor C: STX	$ 479 – $ 648
Fervor C: STX/S	$ 516 – $ 697
Panache	$ 531 – $ 718
Performance	$ 531 – $ 718
Pinnacle C: LX	$ 617 – $ 834
Pinnacle C: STX	$ 547 – $ 740
Pulse C: LX	$ 865 – $ 1,170
Pulse C: XT	$ 840 – $ 1,136
Quantum II	$ 732 – $ 990
Quantum Pro	$ 899 – $ 1,216
Quantum Pro C: Ultegra	$ 832 – $ 1,126
Quantum C: Ultegra	$ 671 – $ 907
Quantum C: Veloce	$ 595 – $ 806
Quantum Z C: RX-100	$ 443 – $ 599
Quantum Z C: Veloce	$ 548 – $ 742

Kona 🚲

AA	$ 426 – $ 576
Cinder Cone	$ 310 – $ 419
Cinder Cone, Shock	$ 387 – $ 524
Explosif	$ 515 – $ 697
Fire Mountain	$ 218 – $ 295
Hahanna	$ 186 – $ 252
Haole	$ 901 – $ 1,219

C: – Components   F: – Fork

MODEL	PRICE RANGE

Kona *(continued)*

Hot	$ 738 – $ 999
Kilauea	$ 462 – $ 626
Kula	$ 580 – $ 785
Lava Dome	$ 267 – $ 361
Lava Dome, Shock	$ 351 – $ 475

LeMond

GAN Team	$ 826 – $ 1,118
V2 Boomerang	$ 890 – $ 1,204
V2 High Modulus	$ 824 – $ 1,115
V2 Standard Modulus	$ 803 – $ 1,087

Lightning

P-38	$ 705 – $ 954
P-38S	$ 799 – $ 1,081

Linear

Unspecified	$ 516 – $ 697

Litespeed

Catalyst	$ 738 – $ 999
Obed	$ 738 – $ 999
Obed F/S	$ 815 – $ 1,102
Ocoee	$ 875 – $ 1,183

Macalu

Pro OX3	$ 479 – $ 648
Professional	$ 565 – $ 764
Titanium 21	$ 780 – $ 1,055
Titanium Racing (Excel)	$ 680 – $ 920
Titanium SL	$ 901 – $ 1,219

C: – Components   F: – Fork

MODEL   PRICE RANGE

Mandaric

Model	Price Range
2 Jump	$ 881 – $ 1,192
Cromor	$ 439 – $ 594
Victoria	$ 868 – $ 1,174

Marin

Model	Price Range
Bear Valley	$ 289 – $ 391
Bear Valley SE	$ 339 – $ 459
Bobcat Trail	$ 219 – $ 296
Eldridge Grade	$ 415 – $ 561
Hawk Hill	$ 196 – $ 265
Hidden Canyon	$ 181 – $ 246
Highway One	$ 877 – $ 1,186
Indian Fire Trail	$ 580 – $ 785
Muirwoods	$ 241 – $ 326
Nail Trail	$ 411 – $ 556
Palisades Trail	$ 274 – $ 371
Pine F.R.S.	$ 790 – $ 1,069
Pine Mountain	$ 516 – $ 697
Point Reyes	$ 481 – $ 650
Redwood	$ 387 – $ 524
Rocky Ridge	$ 515 – $ 697
Sausalito	$ 326 – $ 442
Stinson	$ 200 – $ 271
Team FRS	$ 885 – $ 1,197
Team Issue	$ 815 – $ 1,103
Team Marin	$ 692 – $ 937
Zig Zag Trail	$ 596 – $ 806

Marinoni

Model	Price Range
Corsa C: Ultegra STI	$ 610 – $ 826
Corsa Veloce C: Ergo	$ 515 – $ 697

C: – Components   F: – Fork

MODEL	PRICE RANGE

Marinoni (continued)

Giro Chorus C: Ergo	$ 761 – $ 1,029
Record C: Ergo, Leggero	$ 868 – $ 1,174
Record C: Ergo, Panache	$ 885 – $ 1,197
Sprint Stratos C: Ergo	$ 406 – $ 550
Squadra C: Athena Ergo	$ 639 – $ 865
Ultimo C: Dura-Ace STI	$ 857 – $ 1,159

Masi

Gran Corsa	$ 579 – $ 783
Team 3V	$ 705 – $ 954
Titanium	$ 901 – $ 1,219
Tre Volumetrica	$ 885 – $ 1,197

Medici

Pro-Strada Osso	$ 799 – $ 1,081

Miele

Alfa	$ 223 – $ 301
Beta	$ 437 – $ 591
Equipe	$ 739 – $ 1,000
Gara T.T.	$ 414 – $ 560
Invictus C: STI	$ 575 – $ 778
Kawartha	$ 276 – $ 373
Lupa	$ 306 – $ 413
Mercury	$ 207 – $ 280
Muskoka	$ 195 – $ 264
Pegasus	$ 297 – $ 402
Saturn	$ 223 – $ 301
Titan	$ 367 – $ 497
Turista	$ 318 – $ 430
Zeus	$ 625 – $ 846

C: – Components   F: – Fork

MODEL	PRICE RANGE
Mondonico	🚲
Adventure SL	$ 666 – $ 902
Diamond C: SLX	$ 769 – $ 1,040
EL-OS	$ 894 – $ 1,210
Futura	$ 565 – $ 764
Mongoose	🚲
Alta	$ 241 – $ 326
Crossway 425	$ 186 – $ 252
Crossway 625	$ 214 – $ 289
Hilltopper	$ 214 – $ 289
Hilltopper C: SX	$ 267 – $ 362
IBOC Champion	$ 1,025 – $ 1,387
IBOC Comp	$ 384 – $ 520
IBOC Comp C: SX	$ 506 – $ 684
IBOC Crit	$ 482 – $ 652
IBOC Pro C: SX	$ 620 – $ 838
IBOC Road	$ 575 – $ 778
IBOC Team C: SX	$ 823 – $ 1,114
IBOC World	$ 705 – $ 954
Maneuver	$ 130 – $ 176
Mount Grizzly	$ 102 – $ 138
Rockadile	$ 267 – $ 362
Rockadile C: SX	$ 333 – $ 451
Switchback	$ 158 – $ 214
Sycamore	$ 186 – $ 252
Threshold	$ 133 – $ 180
Ultra Storm	$ 139 – $ 188

C: – Components   F: – Fork

MODEL	PRICE RANGE
Montague	🚲
909	$ 223 – $ 302
949	$ 327 – $ 442
MX-7	$ 223 – $ 302
Triframe Tandem	$ 738 – $ 999
Motiv	🚲
Backcountry	$ 248 – $ 335
Cross	$ 177 – $ 240
Highridge	$ 106 – $ 143
Rockmonster	$ 385 – $ 521
Rockpoint	$ 173 – $ 234
Rockridge	$ 140 – $ 189
Stonehill	$ 86 – $ 117
Vortex	$ 495 – $ 670
Mountain Goat	🚲
Mudslinger	$ 884 – $ 1,197
Road Goat	$ 896 – $ 1,212
Route 66	$ 844 – $ 1,142
Whiskeytown Racer	$ 831 – $ 1,124
Mountain TEK	🚲
1001 SIS	$ 130 – $ 176
2002 SIS	$ 177 – $ 240
Carbon C: XT	$ 692 – $ 937
Comp C: LX	$ 356 – $ 481
Comp C: XT	$ 541 – $ 731
Extreme	$ 182 – $ 246
Peak	$ 306 – $ 414
Vertical	$ 232 – $ 314

C: – Components   F: – Fork

MODEL	PRICE RANGE

Mt. Shasta

Model	Low	High
Arrowhead	$ 144	$ 195
Kilimanjaro	$ 214	$ 289
Legacy	$ 134	$ 182
Palomar	$ 249	$ 337
Saddleback	$ 125	$ 169
Serengeti	$ 163	$ 220
Sonora	$ 111	$ 150
Sport	$ 115	$ 156

Nashbar

Model	Low	High
1000MT	$ 498	$ 674
1000RT	$ 403	$ 545
1000X	$ 547	$ 740
3000X	$ 149	$ 201
5000X	$ 263	$ 356
6000T	$ 214	$ 289
7000R	$ 379	$ 513

Nishiki

Model	Low	High
Arroyo	$ 161	$ 218
Backroads	$ 205	$ 277
Beta	$ 444	$ 601
Blazer	$ 125	$ 169
Bravo A	$ 106	$ 143
Century	$ 130	$ 176
Colorado	$ 250	$ 338
Cornice	$ 376	$ 508
FS-4	$ 746	$ 1,009
Manitoba	$ 180	$ 243
Optima	$ 272	$ 368

C: – Components   F: – Fork

MODEL	PRICE RANGE

Nishiki *(continued)*

Pinnacle	$ 461 – $ 624
Pueblo	$ 142 – $ 192
Rally	$ 105 – $ 142
Sport	$ 180 – $ 243

Norco

Arctic	$ 177 – $ 239
Avanti	$ 284 – $ 385
Axia	$ 406 – $ 550
Bandit	$ 347 – $ 470
Bigfoot	$ 254 – $ 343
Blitz	$ 318 – $ 430
Bush Pilot	$ 172 – $ 233
Katmandu	$ 149 – $ 201
Kokanee	$ 200 – $ 270
Monterey Cross	$ 204 – $ 277
Nitro	$ 501 – $ 678
Quest	$ 139 – $ 188
Radius	$ 186 – $ 252
Rampage	$ 666 – $ 902
Rampage Titanium	$ 901 – $ 1,219
Sasquatch	$ 399 – $ 539
Sonic	$ 739 – $ 1,000
T.N.T.	$ 791 – $ 1,071
Torque	$ 548 – $ 742
Turbine	$ 326 – $ 442
Turbine C: STI	$ 391 – $ 529
Vector	$ 326 – $ 442
Voltage	$ 258 – $ 349

C: – Components   F: – Fork

MODEL   PRICE RANGE

Nordic

Model	Price Range
Bike Standard	$ 182 – $ 246
Track 4-Wheeler	$ 284 – $ 385
Track Good Life Bike	$ 144 – $ 195
Track Good Life III Trike	$ 232 – $ 313

Novara

Model	Price Range
Arriba-S	$ 295 – $ 400
Aspen	$ 193 – $ 262
Aspen-S	$ 239 – $ 323
Corsa	$ 147 – $ 198
Dirt Rider	$ 98 – $ 133
PonDeRosa-S	$ 358 – $ 484
Randonee	$ 283 – $ 382
Strada	$ 272 – $ 368
Team	$ 609 – $ 824
Trionfo	$ 514 – $ 695

Parkpre

Model	Price Range
Alumax	$ 414 – $ 560
Comp Limited	$ 301 – $ 408
Grand Sport	$ 149 – $ 201
Leisure Sport	$ 137 – $ 186
Pro 825	$ 666 – $ 902
Pro Elite	$ 877 – $ 1,186
Scepter Comp	$ 367 – $ 497
Solitude	$ 223 – $ 301
Sport Limited	$ 191 – $ 258
Team 925	$ 511 – $ 691
Team 925R	$ 524 – $ 709
X Comp SE	$ 245 – $ 331

C: – Components   F: – Fork

MODEL	PRICE RANGE

PB Derailleur 🚲

| Pacific/Aspen | $ 327 – $ 442 |

Performance 🚲

M-104	$ 445 – $ 601
M-204	$ 339 – $ 459
M-304	$ 298 – $ 403
M-404	$ 232 – $ 314
M-504	$ 205 – $ 277
M-604	$ 175 – $ 237
M-704	$ 147 – $ 199
R-104	$ 399 – $ 540
R-204	$ 302 – $ 408
TM-1000 C: LX	$ 564 – $ 764
TM-1000 C: XT	$ 639 – $ 865
TR-1000 C: Dura-Ace	$ 780 – $ 1,056
TR-1000 C: Ultegra	$ 680 – $ 919
X-204	$ 168 – $ 227
X-304	$ 135 – $ 182

Peugeot 🚲

Alpin Pro	$ 418 – $ 565
Appalaches	$ 241 – $ 325
Azur	$ 218 – $ 295
Biarritz	$ 444 – $ 601
Carbone 900	$ 739 – $ 1,000
Carbone 1000	$ 780 – $ 1,056
Churchill	$ 115 – $ 156
Dune	$ 167 – $ 227
Energy	$ 318 – $ 430
Evasion	$ 130 – $ 175
Horizon	$ 218 – $ 295

C: – Components   F: – Fork

1994

MODEL / PRICE RANGE

Peugeot *(continued)*

Model	Price Range	
Legende	$ 267 – $	361
Liberty	$ 195 – $	264
Nature	$ 241 – $	325
Panorama	$ 149 – $	201
Prestige	$ 297 – $	402
Success	$ 306 – $	413
Urbano	$ 172 – $	233
Village	$ 115 – $	156
X-Country	$ 314 – $	425

Pinarello

Model	Price Range	
Krono T/T	$ 738 – $	999
Maxim	$ 901 – $	1,219
Monviso	$ 857 – $	1,159
Stelvio	$ 692 – $	937
Team Banesto Cromovan	$ 899 – $	1,216

Pogliaghi

Model	Price Range	
Track	$ 692 – $	937

ProFlex

Model	Price Range	
254	$ 347 – $	470
454	$ 366 – $	495
554	$ 444 – $	601
754	$ 548 – $	742
854	$ 610 – $	826
954	$ 844 – $	1,142
Arcadia	$ 316 – $	428
Newport	$ 218 – $	295

C: – Components   F: – Fork

MODEL

PRICE RANGE

Raleigh

Model	Price Range	
C30	$ 112 – $	151
C40	$ 120 – $	162
C50	$ 159 – $	214
CT200	$ 175 – $	237
CT300	$ 196 – $	265
CT400	$ 239 – $	324
DXR	$ 69 – $	93
DXR 6	$ 87 – $	117
ER1	$ 73 – $	99
ER3	$ 104 – $	140
ER6	$ 99 – $	134
ER7	$ 129 – $	175
Florosaurus	$ 59 – $	80
Honeysaurus	$ 53 – $	71
M15	$ 90 – $	121
M20	$ 91 – $	123
M30	$ 110 – $	148
M40	$ 124 – $	167
M50	$ 142 – $	193
M60	$ 179 – $	242
Microsaurus	$ 53 – $	71
MT200	$ 223 – $	301
MT300	$ 265 – $	359
MT400	$ 335 – $	453
MT500	$ 396 – $	535
MT700	$ 513 – $	693
MTi 1000	$ 622 – $	841
MXR	$ 59 – $	80
R40	$ 133 – $	180
RT300	$ 215 – $	291

C: – Components   F: – Fork

MODEL		PRICE RANGE

Raleigh *(continued)*

Model	Price Range	
RT500	$ 254 – $	344
RT505LE	$ 395 – $	535
RT600	$ 458 – $	620

Rans

Nimbus	$ 547 – $	740
Nimbus C: XT II	$ 665 – $	900
Response	$ 405 – $	548
Stratus	$ 547 – $	740
Stratus C: XT II	$ 665 – $	900
Tailwind	$ 316 – $	428

ReBike

707	$ 209 – $	283
818	$ 241 – $	325
ReTrike 707	$ 263 – $	355
ReTrike 707ss	$ 263 – $	355
ReTrike 707vp	$ 276 – $	373

Research Dynamics

Coyote 2	$ 207 – $	280
Coyote 4	$ 252 – $	341
Coyote Alu 5	$ 541 – $	731
Coyote Carbon 5	$ 692 – $	937
Coyote Pro 4	$ 378 – $	511
Coyote STX	$ 252 – $	341
Coyote Team 6	$ 831 – $	1,124
Coyote Titanium 5	$ 780 – $	1,056

Richard Sachs

Signature 531	$ 901 – $	1,219

C: – Components   F: – Fork

MODEL	PRICE RANGE

Ritchey

Model	Price Range
Comp-23	$ 692 – $ 937
Comp Shocker I	$ 807 – $ 1,092
Comp Shocker II	$ 780 – $ 1,056
Everest	$ 816 – $ 1,103
Lite Beam	$ 816 – $ 1,103
P-21 Team W.C.S.	$ 823 – $ 1,114
P-21 W.C.S.	$ 790 – $ 1,069
P-22	$ 728 – $ 985
P-22 Team	$ 790 – $ 1,069
Skyliner	$ 901 – $ 1,219
Ultra	$ 596 – $ 806

Romic

Model	Price Range
Ace Race	$ 851 – $ 1,151
Athena Tourer	$ 676 – $ 915
Edco IGP Racer	$ 838 – $ 1,134
Edco Supertour	$ 791 – $ 1,071
Icarus Tourer	$ 807 – $ 1,091
Sport Ride	$ 625 – $ 846
Sportx	$ 706 – $ 956
Superbe Pro	$ 727 – $ 984
Track Record	$ 599 – $ 810
Tri Star Racer	$ 767 – $ 1,037
Veloce Sport	$ 611 – $ 826

Ross

Model	Price Range
Adventurer	$ 102 – $ 138
Aristocrat	$ 203 – $ 274
Centaur	$ 241 – $ 325
Chimera	$ 111 – $ 150
Griffon	$ 132 – $ 179

C: – Components   F: – Fork

MODEL		PRICE RANGE

Ross *(continued)* 🚲

Mt. Hood	$ 258 – $ 349
Mt. Jefferson	$ 91 – $ 123
Mt. Katahdin	$ 151 – $ 205
Mt. McKinley	$ 574 – $ 777
Mt. Olympus	$ 173 – $ 234
Mt. Pocono	$ 95 – $ 129
Mt. Rainier	$ 291 – $ 394
Mt. Rushmore	$ 123 – $ 166
Mt. Snow TS	$ 280 – $ 379
Mt. St. Helens	$ 237 – $ 321
Mt. Washington	$ 137 – $ 186
Mt. Whitney	$ 385 – $ 521
Pegasus	$ 159 – $ 214
Peryton	$ 96 – $ 130

Ryan 🚲

Vanguard	$ 611 – $ 826

Sampson 🚲

TSC	$ 815 – $ 1,103

Santana 🚲

Arriva	$ 884 – $ 1,197
Cilantro	$ 884 – $ 1,197
Fusion	$ 884 – $ 1,197
Rio	$ 815 – $ 1,102
Visa	$ 815 – $ 1,102
Vision	$ 815 – $ 1,102

C: – Components   F: – Fork

MODEL	PRICE RANGE

Schwinn

Model	Price Range
CrissCross	$ 199 – $ 270
CrossCut	$ 259 – $ 350
CrossFit	$ 150 – $ 202
CrossTrail	$ 227 – $ 306
Frontier	$ 116 – $ 157
High Plains	$ 199 – $ 270
High Sierra SS	$ 358 – $ 484
High Timber SS	$ 408 – $ 552
Hurricane	$ 150 – $ 202
Impact	$ 172 – $ 232
Moab	$ 227 – $ 306
Moab SS	$ 280 – $ 379
Paramount RS-30	$ 481 – $ 650
Paramount RS-60	$ 661 – $ 894
Paramount RS-80	$ 857 – $ 1,160
Passage	$ 280 – $ 379
R 5.0	$ 618 – $ 836
Sidewinder	$ 133 – $ 180
Sierra	$ 306 – $ 414

Scorpio

Model	Price Range
AL 550	$ 316 – $ 428
AT 200	$ 132 – $ 179
AT 400	$ 189 – $ 256

Scott

Model	Price Range
Boulder	$ 347 – $ 470
Chenango	$ 271 – $ 367
Cheyenne	$ 297 – $ 402
Comp Racing CST	$ 444 – $ 601
Mohaka	$ 144 – $ 195

C: – Components   F: – Fork

MODEL	PRICE RANGE

Scott *(continued)*

Model	Price Range
Montego	$ 160 – $ 217
San Diego	$ 218 – $ 295
San Francisco	$ 167 – $ 227
Sandoa	$ 241 – $ 325
Seattle	$ 144 – $ 195
Sonoma	$ 284 – $ 385
Tampico	$ 195 – $ 264
Ultimate	$ 830 – $ 1,123
Unitrack CC	$ 347 – $ 470
Unitrack FSR	$ 639 – $ 865
Unitrack ST	$ 284 – $ 385

Serotta

Model	Price Range
Colorado ATX	$ 858 – $ 1,161
Colorado CR	$ 887 – $ 1,201
Colorado TG	$ 774 – $ 1,047
Colorado TTR	$ 875 – $ 1,184
Max II	$ 722 – $ 976

Signature

Model	Price Range
Minotaur	$ 196 – $ 265
Super Gran Tour	$ 175 – $ 237
Triad	$ 354 – $ 478

Simoncini

Model	Price Range
Europa SLX Classic	$ 653 – $ 884
Strada Titanium C: Record	$ 838 – $ 1,134
Strada Titanium C: Stratos	$ 625 – $ 846
TSX Classic	$ 790 – $ 1,069

C: – Components   F: – Fork

MODEL	PRICE RANGE

Softride 🚲

Model	Price Range
Contour	$ 367 – $ 497
Cross 360	$ 284 – $ 385
Husky	$ 306 – $ 413
Solo	$ 692 – $ 937

Specialized 🚲

Model	Price Range
Allez	$ 390 – $ 527
Allez Comp	$ 474 – $ 641
Allez Pro	$ 628 – $ 849
Allez Sport	$ 323 – $ 437
Crossroads	$ 156 – $ 211
Crossroads Cruz	$ 131 – $ 177
Crossroads Sport	$ 195 – $ 264
Crossroads XP	$ 234 – $ 317
Epic	$ 474 – $ 641
Epic Comp	$ 553 – $ 749
Epic Pro	$ 697 – $ 943
Globe 3	$ 146 – $ 197
Hardrock	$ 141 – $ 190
Hardrock 6	$ 114 – $ 155
Hardrock FS	$ 205 – $ 277
Hardrock Sport	$ 156 – $ 211
Hardrock Ultra	$ 186 – $ 251
Hot Rock	$ 90 – $ 121
M2 Pro	$ 761 – $ 1,029
M2 Road (Limited Edition)	$ 944 – $ 1,277
Rockhopper	$ 220 – $ 297
Rockhopper 18	$ 126 – $ 170
Rockhopper Comp	$ 300 – $ 406
Rockhopper Comp FS	$ 345 – $ 467
Rockhopper FS	$ 281 – $ 381

C: – Components   F: – Fork

MODEL	PRICE RANGE

Specialized *(continued)*

Model		Price Range		
Rockhopper Sport	$	253	– $	343
S-Works Steel	$	697	– $	943
Shockrock 20	$	156	– $	211
Shockrock FS 24	$	161	– $	217
Stumpjumper	$	411	– $	556
Stumpjumper FS	$	534	– $	722
Stumpjumper FSR	$	761	– $	1,029
Stumpjumper M2	$	453	– $	614
Stumpjumper M2 FS	$	663	– $	897

Spectrum

Model		Price Range		
Custom Steel C: Ergo	$	898	– $	1,214
Custom Steel C: STI	$	872	– $	1,180
Custom Steel Track Suntour	$	739	– $	1,000
Stock Titanium C: Ultegra	$	898	– $	1,214

Sterling

Model		Price Range		
Deluxe Touring	$	898	– $	1,214
Eco Sport Tandem	$	877	– $	1,186
Access F/S	$	609	– $	824

Terry

Model		Price Range		
Athene	$	325	– $	439
Chrom	$	551	– $	745
Classic	$	597	– $	807
Jacaranda	$	444	– $	600
Jacaranda S	$	594	– $	804
Symmetry	$	410	– $	555

Thebis

Model		Price Range		
Trike 201	$	737	– $	997

C: – Components   F: – Fork

MODEL	PRICE RANGE

Timberlin

Model				
City Slicker	$	120	– $	163
Crossroads	$	135	– $	182
Destiny	$	120	– $	163
Escapade	$	205	– $	277
Fastrax	$	106	– $	143
Land Rover	$	108	– $	146
Millenium	$	327	– $	442
Rendezvous	$	232	– $	314
Rendezvous, Shock	$	323	– $	437
Ridge Runner	$	168	– $	227
Short Cut	$	113	– $	153
Stomper	$	101	– $	136
Trail Blazer	$	327	– $	442
Trail Blazer RS	$	407	– $	550
Urban Express	$	130	– $	176
Wildwoods	$	173	– $	234

Titan

Model				
Titanium Compe	$	692	– $	937

Torelli

Model				
Corsa Strada C: Ergo	$	429	– $	581
Countach	$	666	– $	902
EL-OS	$	891	– $	1,206
Express	$	739	– $	1,000
Super Strada	$	508	– $	688

Trek

Model				
370	$	207	– $	280
520	$	443	– $	600
700	$	148	– $	200

C: – Components   F: – Fork

MODEL	PRICE RANGE

Trek (continued)

Model	Price Range
720	$ 170 – $ 229
730	$ 213 – $ 288
750	$ 290 – $ 392
750 MetroTrack	$ 359 – $ 485
800	$ 148 – $ 200
820	$ 170 – $ 229
830	$ 197 – $ 266
830 SHX	$ 224 – $ 302
850	$ 224 – $ 302
850 SHX	$ 290 – $ 393
920	$ 238 – $ 322
930	$ 261 – $ 353
930 SHX	$ 337 – $ 457
950	$ 397 – $ 537
970	$ 509 – $ 689
1200	$ 349 – $ 473
1220	$ 364 – $ 492
1400	$ 478 – $ 647
2120	$ 509 – $ 689
2200	$ 540 – $ 731
2300	$ 647 – $ 875
5200	$ 798 – $ 1,079
5500	$ 973 – $ 1,316
7000	$ 337 – $ 457
7000 SHX	$ 509 – $ 689
7600	$ 419 – $ 567
8000	$ 465 – $ 630
7900	$ 510 – $ 691
8700	$ 502 – $ 680
9200	$ 741 – $ 1,003
9500	$ 1,004 – $ 1,358

C: – Components   F: – Fork

MODEL   PRICE RANGE

Trek (continued)

9800	$ 741 – $ 1,003
9900	$ 973 – $ 1,316
T50	$ 577 – $ 781
T100	$ 741 – $ 1,003
T200	$ 1,004 – $ 1,358

Ultimax

Crow	$ 95 – $ 129
Goshawk	$ 120 – $ 162
Snipe	$ 144 – $ 195

Univega

Activa Action	$ 148 – $ 201
Activa Country	$ 180 – $ 244
Alpina 5.1	$ 232 – $ 314
Alpina 5.3	$ 288 – $ 389
Alpina 5.5	$ 337 – $ 456
Alpina 5.7	$ 385 – $ 521
Alpina S7.3	$ 332 – $ 449
Alpina S7.5	$ 380 – $ 514
Alpina S7.7	$ 473 – $ 639
Boralyn R8.8	$ 910 – $ 1,231
Boralyn S8.7	$ 780 – $ 1,055
Boralyn S8.9	$ 967 – $ 1,308
Carbolite R7.2	$ 427 – $ 578
Carbolite R7.4	$ 525 – $ 711
Carbolite R7.6	$ 630 – $ 852
CB 6.3	$ 459 – $ 621
CB S8.3	$ 589 – $ 797
Ground Force	$ 146 – $ 197
Ground Force-S	$ 191 – $ 258

C: – Components   F: – Fork

MODEL | PRICE RANGE

Univega (continued)

Model	Price Range
Rover 3.3	$ 148 – $ 201
Rover 3.5	$ 175 – $ 236
Rover S4.3	$ 201 – $ 272
Shockblok 10.3 Ti	$ 1,065 – $ 1,441
Via Carisma	$ 217 – $ 293
Via De Oro	$ 317 – $ 429
Via Monega	$ 268 – $ 362

Ventana

Model	Price Range
El Martillo	$ 862 – $ 1,167
Marble Peak	$ 872 – $ 1,180

Yokota

Model	Price Range
Ahwahnee	$ 166 – $ 224
Ahwahnee Cross	$ 175 – $ 237
El Capitan	$ 486 – $ 658
Granite Peak	$ 213 – $ 288
Grizzly Peak	$ 480 – $ 650
Half Dome	$ 885 – $ 1,197
Quicksilver	$ 245 – $ 331
Silver Peak	$ 855 – $ 1,156
Tuolumne	$ 128 – $ 173
Tuolumne Cross	$ 130 – $ 176
Twin Peak	$ 639 – $ 865
Yosemite	$ 265 – $ 359
Yosemite Comp	$ 298 – $ 403
Yosemite Pro	$ 362 – $ 489

ZeroBike

Model	Price Range
Cannibal	$ 565 – $ 764
Red Zone	$ 811 – $ 1,098

C: – Components   F: – Fork

MODEL	PRICE RANGE

Aegis

Model	Price Range
Mountain C: XT Deluxe	$ 842 – $ 1,139
Mountain C: XT Standard	$ 800 – $ 1,082
Road C: 600 Ultegra STI	$ 811 – $ 1,097
Road Campy Chorus C: Ergo	$ 878 – $ 1,187

AMP Research

Model	Price Range
B-3 C: LX	$ 743 – $ 1,006
B-3 C: XT	$ 821 – $ 1,110
B-4 C: LX	$ 873 – $ 1,181
B-4 C: XT	$ 920 – $ 1,245

Angletech

Model	Price Range
Counterpoint – Presto SE	$ 740 – $ 1,001
Counterpoint – Presto SE63	$ 777 – $ 1,051
Counterpoint – Presto SS	$ 861 – $ 1,164
Counterpoint – Triad SE63	$ 956 – $ 1,293
Montaque – Road with Altitude	$ 842 – $ 1,139
Rans – V-Rex GL 63	$ 800 – $ 1,083
Rans – V-Rex SS	$ 945 – $ 1,279
Tri-King	$ 956 – $ 1,293

Auburn

Model	Price Range
CR-20R	$ 264 – $ 357
CR-20RX	$ 340 – $ 460
CR-20S	$ 199 – $ 269
JR-20RX	$ 273 – $ 370

Balance

Model	Price Range
AL-150	$ 210 – $ 285
AL-150 F: RST 170	$ 248 – $ 336
AL-250	$ 249 – $ 337

C: – Components   F: – Fork

MODEL   PRICE RANGE

Balance (continued)

Model		Price Range
AL-250	F: RST 170	$ 301 – $ 407
AL-350		$ 296 – $ 400
AL-350	F: Manitou Comp	$ 382 – $ 517
AL-350	F: ProForx	$ 370 – $ 500
AL-350	F: RST 170	$ 329 – $ 445
AL-450		$ 359 – $ 485
AL-450	F: Manitou Comp	$ 438 – $ 592
AL-450	F: Manitou Magnum	$ 453 – $ 613
AL-450	F: ProForx	$ 426 – $ 577
AL-550		$ 418 – $ 565
AL-550	F: Manitou 4	$ 535 – $ 724
AL-550	F: Manitou Comp	$ 492 – $ 666
AL-550	F: Manitou Magnum	$ 507 – $ 686
AL-750		$ 492 – $ 666
AL-750	F: Manitou 4	$ 601 – $ 813
AL-750	F: Manitou Comp	$ 562 – $ 761
AL-750	F: Manitou Magnum	$ 576 – $ 779
FS-450	F: Manitou 4	$ 600 – $ 811
FS-450	F: Manitou Comp	$ 560 – $ 758
FS-450	F: ProForx	$ 550 – $ 744
FS-550	F: Manitou 4	$ 671 – $ 908
FS-550	F: Manitou Comp	$ 636 – $ 861
FS-550	F: Manitou EFC	$ 700 – $ 948
FS-550	F: Manitou Magnum	$ 649 – $ 877
FS-550	F: ProForx	$ 627 – $ 848
FS-750	F: Manitou 4	$ 726 – $ 982
FS-750	F: Manitou Comp	$ 694 – $ 939
FS-750	F: Manitou EFC	$ 752 – $ 1,017
FS-750	F: Manitou Magnum	$ 705 – $ 954
FS-750	F: ProForx	$ 685 – $ 927
Killer-B		$ 194 – $ 262

C: – Components   F: – Fork

MODEL	PRICE RANGE

Balance (continued) 🚲

Killer-B 24	$ 208 – $ 282
TTPro-550	$ 795 – $ 1,076
TTPro-550 F: Manitou 4	$ 844 – $ 1,141
TTPro-550 F: Manitou Comp	$ 836 – $ 1,131
TTPro-550 F: Manitou Magnum	$ 839 – $ 1,135
TTPro-550 F: ProForx	$ 830 – $ 1,123
TTPro-750	$ 836 – $ 1,132
TTPro-750 F: Manitou 4	$ 890 – $ 1,204
TTPro-750 F: Manitou Magnum	$ 878 – $ 1,188

Barracuda 🚲

A2B	$ 245 – $ 332
A2E	$ 552 – $ 747
A2Fast	$ 573 – $ 775
A2M	$ 407 – $ 551
A2R	$ 322 – $ 436
A2RS	$ 365 – $ 494
A2T	$ 777 – $ 1,051
A2V	$ 606 – $ 820
A2Z	$ 203 – $ 274
Cuda Comp	$ 669 – $ 905
XX Team	$ 497 – $ 673

Battle 🚲

A.X.E. AL	$ 907 – $ 1,228
A.X.E. Carbon	$ 920 – $ 1,245
A.X.E. Elite	$ 777 – $ 1,051
Tomahawk Aluminum	$ 941 – $ 1,273

Bianchi 🚲

| Advantage | $ 217 – $ 294 |

C: – Components   F: – Fork

MODEL | PRICE RANGE

Bianchi (continued)

Model	Price Range	
Alfana	$ 464 – $	628
Avenue	$ 178 – $	241
Campione D'Italia	$ 464 – $	628
Carbon Virata	$ 585 – $	792
Denali RC	$ 729 – $	986
EL International	$ 1,061 – $	1,435
Eros	$ 468 – $	634
Genius	$ 1,153 – $	1,560
Grizzly RC	$ 984 – $	1,332
Ibex	$ 373 – $	505
Kodiak	$ 223 – $	302
Lynx	$ 272 – $	368
Nyala	$ 217 – $	294
Ocelot	$ 178 – $	241
Osprey	$ 272 – $	368
Peregrine	$ 439 – $	594
Premio	$ 288 – $	390
Premio Triple	$ 290 – $	392
Project-1	$ 262 – $	354
Project-3	$ 368 – $	498
Strada	$ 155 – $	210
Super Grizzly	$ 1,089 – $	1,474
Super Ibex	$ 585 – $	792
Timber Wolf	$ 161 – $	217
Trofeo	$ 352 – $	477
TSX Chorus	$ 963 – $	1,303
Veloce	$ 628 – $	850

Bike Friday

Model	Price Range	
Companion	$ 422 – $	571
New World Tourist	$ 461 – $	624

C: – Components   F: – Fork

MODEL	PRICE RANGE

Bike Friday *(continued)*

Pocket Llama	$ 536 – $ 726
Pocket Rocket	$ 556 – $ 752

BikeE

HZ	$ 422 – $ 571
MZ	$ 362 – $ 489

Bilenky

Clubsman	$ 810 – $ 1,096
Hedgehog Twin	$ 961 – $ 1,300
Midlands	$ 765 – $ 1,035
Sterling	$ 959 – $ 1,297
Trans-Am	$ 860 – $ 1,163
Travel Clubsman	$ 841 – $ 1,138

BMC

SU2	$ 752 – $ 1,018
SU2 Race	$ 822 – $ 1,112
XU2	$ 670 – $ 906

Bottecchia

Team 3 SL	$ 639 – $ 864
Team EL-OS	$ 841 – $ 1,138

Boulder Bikes

Paris-Roubaix	$ 893 – $ 1,209
Paris-Roubaix C: AL	$ 967 – $ 1,308
Starship	$ 860 – $ 1,164
Starship C: AL	$ 941 – $ 1,273
Tourstar	$ 907 – $ 1,228

C: – Components   F: – Fork

MODEL		PRICE RANGE
Breezer		🚲
Beamer	$ 893	– $ 1,208
Jet Stream	$ 725	– $ 981
Lightning	$ 841	– $ 1,138
Storm	$ 461	– $ 624
Thunder	$ 536	– $ 726
Venturi	$ 877	– $ 1,186
Burley		🚲
Duet	$ 771	– $ 1,043
Rock 'n Roll	$ 771	– $ 1,043
Rock 'n Roll Softride	$ 827	– $ 1,119
Samba	$ 607	– $ 821
Zydeco	$ 463	– $ 627
Zydeco Mixte X	$ 501	– $ 678
Caloi		🚲
Elite	$ 327	– $ 442
Elite -DH5	$ 639	– $ 864
Elite XC	$ 423	– $ 573
Expert	$ 250	– $ 338
Expert-DH7	$ 463	– $ 626
Expert XC	$ 340	– $ 459
Max	$ 154	– $ 209
Pro	$ 273	– $ 369
Pro-DH6	$ 573	– $ 775
Pro XC	$ 374	– $ 506
Sigma	$ 382	– $ 517
Sigma XC	$ 523	– $ 708
Sigma DH4	$ 669	– $ 905
Sport	$ 222	– $ 300
Sport XC	$ 273	– $ 369

C: – Components   F: – Fork

MODEL | PRICE RANGE

Caloi *(continued)*

Model		Price Range	
Supra	$	203 – $	274
Supra XC	$	222 – $	300
Team-DH1	$	941 – $	1,273
Team-DH2	$	815 – $	1,103
Team-DH3	$	752 – $	1,018
Team C: LX	$	463 – $	626
Team C: LX-XC	$	606 – $	820
Team C: XT	$	573 – $	775
Team C: XT-XC	$	669 – $	905
Team XTR C: XC	$	878 – $	1,187
Ultra-Six	$	154 – $	209

Cannondale

Model		Price Range	
C 1000	$	614 – $	831
C 2000	$	751 – $	1,016
F 200	$	268 – $	362
F 400	$	368 – $	498
F 500	$	414 – $	560
F 600	$	496 – $	671
F 700	$	622 – $	841
F 1000	$	694 – $	939
H 300	$	233 – $	316
H 400	$	290 – $	392
H 600	$	376 – $	509
H 800	$	614 – $	831
Killer V 500	$	393 – $	531
Killer V 900	$	515 – $	696
M 300 LE	$	235 – $	318
M 300 LE Mixte	$	235 – $	318
M 300 SE	$	235 – $	318
M 400	$	297 – $	401

C: – Components   F: – Fork

MODEL	PRICE RANGE
Cannondale (*continued*)	🚲
M 500	$ 383 – $ 518
M 800	$ 502 – $ 679
M 900	$ 502 – $ 679
MC 400	$ 198 – $ 268
MC 500	$ 244 – $ 331
MT 1000	$ 766 – $ 1,037
MT 2000	$ 897 – $ 1,214
MT 3000	$ 1,016 – $ 1,374
R 300	$ 340 – $ 460
R 400	$ 401 – $ 542
R 500	$ 409 – $ 553
R 600	$ 477 – $ 645
R 700	$ 648 – $ 876
R 800	$ 658 – $ 890
R 900	$ 745 – $ 1,008
R 1000	$ 907 – $ 1,228
SR 900	$ 836 – $ 1,132
Super V 700	$ 622 – $ 841
Super V 900	$ 694 – $ 939
Super V 1000	$ 869 – $ 1,176
Super V 2000	$ 936 – $ 1,267
T 400	$ 340 – $ 460
T 700	$ 409 – $ 553
T 1000	$ 748 – $ 1,012
Track	$ 694 – $ 939
Cignal	🚲
Bimini	$ 155 – $ 209
Cherokee	$ 105 – $ 142
Dorado C: SX	$ 309 – $ 419
Kokomo	$ 130 – $ 176

C: – Components   F: – Fork

MODEL	PRICE RANGE

Cignal *(continued)* 🚲

Melbourne Express	$ 331 – $ 448
Montauk	$ 203 – $ 275
Montero	$ 130 – $ 176
Ozark	$ 155 – $ 209
Ozark 20	$ 89 – $ 121
Ozark 24	$ 105 – $ 142
Ranger	$ 84 – $ 114
Rialto	$ 110 – $ 148
Shenango	$ 184 – $ 249
Silverado	$ 264 – $ 357
Ventura	$ 184 – $ 249
Zanzibar	$ 208 – $ 281

Ciocc 🚲

| Cross | $ 538 – $ 727 |

Clark-Kent 🚲

F-12	$ 727 – $ 984
F-12 F: Manitou IV	$ 727 – $ 984
F-14	$ 822 – $ 1,112
F-16	$ 966 – $ 1,307
Ti-300	$ 869 – $ 1,176
Ti-300 Time	$ 869 – $ 1,176

Co-Motion 🚲

Bofus Off-Road	$ 947 – $ 1,282
Bofus Road	$ 935 – $ 1,266
Cappucino	$ 912 – $ 1,233
Espresso	$ 806 – $ 1,090
Espresso SNS	$ 877 – $ 1,186
Java	$ 931 – $ 1,259

C: – Components   F: – Fork

MODEL	PRICE RANGE

Co-Motion *(continued)*

Mocha	$ 799 – $ 1,081
Road fillet	$ 949 – $ 1,284
Road TIG	$ 860 – $ 1,163
Speedster	$ 883 – $ 1,194

Conejo

AP/5 C: LX	$ 843 – $ 1,140
AP/5 C: LX F: Judy XC	$ 864 – $ 1,169
AP/5 C: XT	$ 947 – $ 1,281
AP/5 C: XT F: Judy DH	$ 958 – $ 1,296
AP/5 C: XT F: Judy SL	$ 957 – $ 1,295
ARS/5 C: LX	$ 738 – $ 999
ARS/5 C: LX F: Judy XC	$ 767 – $ 1,038
ARS/5 C: XT	$ 905 – $ 1,225
ARS/5 C: XT F: Judy DH	$ 926 – $ 1,253
ARS/5 C: XT F: Judy SL	$ 925 – $ 1,251
ARS/5 C: XTR	$ 958 – $ 1,296
ARS/5 C: XTR F: Judy DH	$ 965 – $ 1,305
ARS/5 C: XTR F: Judy SL	$ 964 – $ 1,305

Counterpoint

Presto	$ 769 – $ 1,040
Presto Triad	$ 942 – $ 1,274

Cresswell Engineering

Rapide	$ 800 – $ 1,083

Crestone Peak

BMX Pro Racing	$ 282 – $ 382
Conclusion	$ 669 – $ 905
Desert Trekking	$ 520 – $ 703

C: – Components   F: – Fork

MODEL	PRICE RANGE

Crestone Peak *(continued)*

SAS Comp	$ 423 – $ 573
SAS Expert	$ 340 – $ 459
SAS Extreme	$ 684 – $ 925
SAS Pro	$ 573 – $ 775
The Symbol	$ 800 – $ 1,083
Trial Power	$ 463 – $ 626
Triathlon 105	$ 573 – $ 775
Twin Shock Comp	$ 415 – $ 562
Twin Shock Expert	$ 296 – $ 400
Twin Shock Extreme	$ 669 – $ 905
Twin Shock Pro	$ 555 – $ 751
VO2 Max Comp	$ 482 – $ 652
VO2 Max Expert	$ 361 – $ 489
VO2 Max Extreme	$ 746 – $ 1,009
VO2 Max Pro	$ 600 – $ 812

Crosstrac

Sonoma	$ 949 – $ 1,283
Sonoma Ultra	$ 967 – $ 1,308

De Rosa

Giro	$ 920 – $ 1,245
Giro w/pedal	$ 914 – $ 1,237

Dean

6061 Aluminum	$ 740 – $ 1,001
Aermet 100 Mountain	$ 941 – $ 1,273
Caffeinated Full Suspension	$ 953 – $ 1,289
Carbore Rigid	$ 936 – $ 1,267
Race BMX	$ 191 – $ 259
Steel Road	$ 861 – $ 1,164

C: – Components   F: – Fork

MODEL   PRICE RANGE

Dean (continued)   🚲

| Titanium Mountain | $ 959 – $ 1,297 |
| Titanium Road | $ 956 – $ 1,293 |

Diamondback   🚲

Apex	$ 335 – $ 453
Approach	$ 147 – $ 199
Ascent	$ 224 – $ 303
Ascent EX	$ 254 – $ 343
Assault	$ 108 – $ 146
Axis TT	$ 692 – $ 936
Axis TT Pro	$ 782 – $ 1,059
Cross Country	$ 126 – $ 170
Dual Response	$ 599 – $ 811
Dual Response Pro	$ 743 – $ 1,005
Expert	$ 265 – $ 358
Impression	$ 66 – $ 89
Interval	$ 165 – $ 224
Lakeside	$ 182 – $ 247
Master	$ 394 – $ 533
Mini Photon	$ 53 – $ 72
Mini Viper	$ 57 – $ 77
Outlook	$ 94 – $ 127
Outlook 24	$ 91 – $ 124
Parkway	$ 103 – $ 140
Photon	$ 70 – $ 95
Prevail TT	$ 767 – $ 1,038
Reactor	$ 129 – $ 174
Recoil	$ 100 – $ 135
Response Sport	$ 283 – $ 382
Sorrento	$ 139 – $ 188
Sorrento Sport	$ 169 – $ 229

C: – Components   F: – Fork

MODEL   PRICE RANGE

Diamondback *(continued)*

Model	Price Range
Topanga	$ 182 – $ 247
Venom	$ 108 – $ 146
Vertex	$ 385 – $ 520
Vertex TA	$ 529 – $ 715
Vertex TR	$ 502 – $ 680
Viper CB	$ 74 – $ 101
Viper FW	$ 83 – $ 112
WCF Vertex	$ 446 – $ 603
Wildwood	$ 128 – $ 173
Wildwood 24	$ 121 – $ 163

Dirt Research

Model	Price Range
Badlands	$ 227 – $ 307
Bandelier	$ 318 – $ 431
Bandelier Suspension	$ 401 – $ 543
Echo Canyon	$ 501 – $ 678
Hot Springs AL	$ 277 – $ 375
Hot Springs AL Suspension	$ 347 – $ 469
Hot Springs ST	$ 225 – $ 305
Hot Springs ST Suspension	$ 296 – $ 400
Kenai-Rigid	$ 520 – $ 703
Kenai F: Rock Shox	$ 595 – $ 805
Kings Canyon	$ 670 – $ 906
Kobuk	$ 264 – $ 357
Kobuk Suspension	$ 334 – $ 451
Pecos	$ 387 – $ 523
Pecos F: Rock Shox	$ 473 – $ 640
Voyageurs AL	$ 875 – $ 1,184
Wildcat Canyon	$ 941 – $ 1,273

C: – Components   F: – Fork

1995

MODEL	PRICE RANGE

Dyno 🚲

| Air | $ 145 – $ 196 |
| Slammer | $ 234 – $ 317 |

Easy Racers 🚲

EZ-1	$ 381 – $ 515
Gold Rush Replica	$ 878 – $ 1,188
Tour Easy	$ 697 – $ 943

Eddy Merckx 🚲

| Arcobaleno | $ 847 – $ 1,146 |
| Titanium A.X. | $ 931 – $ 1,260 |

Free Agent 🚲

Ambush	$ 124 – $ 168
Eluder	$ 94 – $ 127
Enforcer	$ 250 – $ 338

Fuji 🚲

Ace	$ 199 – $ 269
Anniversary Edition	$ 227 – $ 307
Blvd XC	$ 125 – $ 169
Crosstown	$ 105 – $ 142
Discovery	$ 296 – $ 400
Discovery C: SX	$ 403 – $ 546
Dynamic	$ 184 – $ 249
Finest	$ 296 – $ 400
Mt. Fuji C: SX	$ 538 – $ 728
Odessa	$ 105 – $ 142
Professional	$ 538 – $ 728
Regis	$ 125 – $ 169
Roubaix	$ 424 – $ 573

C: – Components   F: – Fork

MODEL	PRICE RANGE

Fuji (continued)

Model	Price Range
Sagres	$ 155 – $ 209
Sandblaster	$ 155 – $ 209
Suncrest	$ 383 – $ 518
Suncrest C: SX	$ 463 – $ 627
Sundance C: SX	$ 501 – $ 678
Sunfire	$ 135 – $ 182
Sunfire C: SX	$ 184 – $ 249
Supreme	$ 140 – $ 189
Tahoe	$ 227 – $ 307
Tahoe C: SX	$ 318 – $ 430
Team	$ 501 – $ 678
Thrill	$ 184 – $ 249
Thrill C: SX	$ 227 – $ 307
Tiara	$ 140 – $ 189
Touring Series	$ 318 – $ 430

Gary Fisher

Model	Price Range
Alfresco	$ 282 – $ 382
Aquila	$ 291 – $ 394
Cronus	$ 538 – $ 728
Hoo Koo E Koo	$ 374 – $ 506
Hoo Koo E Koo Greatful Dead	$ 463 – $ 627
Kai Tai	$ 331 – $ 448
Maniac	$ 213 – $ 288
Marlin	$ 189 – $ 256
Montare	$ 383 – $ 518
Mt. Tam	$ 607 – $ 821
Paragon	$ 501 – $ 678
Procaliber	$ 822 – $ 1,112
Rangitoto	$ 278 – $ 376
Supercaliber	$ 726 – $ 983

C: – Components   F: – Fork

MODEL	PRICE RANGE

Gary Fisher (continued)

Model	Price Range
Tassajara	$ 227 – $ 307
Tyro	$ 140 – $ 189
Zebranoh	$ 199 – $ 269

Giant

Model	Price Range
Acapulco	$ 127 – $ 172
Allegre	$ 343 – $ 464
Attraction	$ 87 – $ 117
ATX 760	$ 293 – $ 397
ATX 780	$ 343 – $ 464
ATX 860	$ 238 – $ 322
ATX 870	$ 281 – $ 380
ATX 875	$ 281 – $ 380
ATX 880	$ 322 – $ 436
ATX 890	$ 402 – $ 544
Awesome	$ 109 – $ 148
Boulder 24	$ 94 – $ 127
Boulder 26	$ 100 – $ 136
CFM-2	$ 475 – $ 643
CFM-3	$ 363 – $ 491
CFM-4	$ 299 – $ 404
CFR-1	$ 575 – $ 777
CFR-2	$ 439 – $ 594
Chaos	$ 84 – $ 114
Commotion	$ 89 – $ 120
Farrago	$ 123 – $ 166
Frantic	$ 75 – $ 102
Iguana	$ 193 – $ 261
Iguana SE	$ 238 – $ 322
Innova	$ 193 – $ 261
Kronos	$ 239 – $ 323

C: – Components   F: – Fork

MODEL	PRICE RANGE

Giant (continued)

Nutra	$ 147 – $ 199
Option	$ 105 – $ 142
Perigee	$ 171 – $ 232
Prodigy	$ 259 – $ 351
Rincon	$ 147 – $ 199
Sedona	$ 238 – $ 322
Sedona SE	$ 281 – $ 380
Taffy	$ 65 – $ 88
TCM	$ 685 – $ 927
Totally Awesome	$ 138 – $ 187
Yukon	$ 173 – $ 234
Yukon SE	$ 193 – $ 261

Giordana

Titanium AL	$ 878 – $ 1,188
XL ECO	$ 851 – $ 1,152
XL Strada	$ 699 – $ 945
XL Superleggero	$ 949 – $ 1,284

GT

Aggressor	$ 148 – $ 200
Arette	$ 116 – $ 157
Avalanche	$ 359 – $ 486
Avalanche Suspension	$ 433 – $ 586
Backwoods	$ 233 – $ 315
Cirque	$ 152 – $ 206
Edge	$ 751 – $ 1,017
Force	$ 281 – $ 380
Fury	$ 560 – $ 758
Karakoram	$ 298 – $ 403
Karakoram Suspension	$ 375 – $ 507

C: – Components   F: – Fork

MODEL	PRICE RANGE

GT *(continued)*

Model	Price Range
Outpost	$ 132 – $ 179
Outpost Trail	$ 112 – $ 151
Pantera	$ 273 – $ 370
Pantera Suspension	$ 352 – $ 477
Rage	$ 457 – $ 618
Rebound	$ 188 – $ 254
Ricochet	$ 281 – $ 380
RTS-1	$ 692 – $ 936
RTS-2	$ 524 – $ 709
RTS-3	$ 381 – $ 516
Strike	$ 365 – $ 494
Talera	$ 156 – $ 211
Team RTS	$ 771 – $ 1,044
Tempest	$ 195 – $ 264
Tequesta	$ 218 – $ 295
Timberline	$ 180 – $ 243
Timberline FS	$ 233 – $ 316
Vantara	$ 136 – $ 184
Zaskar	$ 544 – $ 736
Zaskar LE	$ 743 – $ 1,006
Zaskar Suspension	$ 621 – $ 840

GT BMX

Model	Price Range
Bullet 6-Speed	$ 125 – $ 169
Bullet 18-Speed	$ 165 – $ 223
Flame	$ 125 – $ 169
Fueler	$ 218 – $ 294
Interceptor	$ 135 – $ 182
Jr. Pro Series mini	$ 257 – $ 348
Little Timber	$ 105 – $ 142
Mach One	$ 169 – $ 229

C: – Components   F: – Fork

MODEL	PRICE RANGE

GT BMX (continued)

Model	Price Range
Mini Mach One	$ 169 – $ 229
Outbound 6-speed	$ 105 – $ 142
Performer	$ 165 – $ 223
Pro Freestyle Tour	$ 234 – $ 317
Pro Freestyle Tour Team	$ 318 – $ 430
Pro Series	$ 227 – $ 307
Pro Series Cruiser	$ 234 – $ 317
Pro Series Team Pro XL	$ 318 – $ 430
Vertigo	$ 142 – $ 193

Guerber

Model	Price Range
Pro Fred	$ 956 – $ 1,293

Haro

Model	Price Range
Blaster	$ 84 – $ 114
Escape	$ 361 – $ 489
Escape Comp	$ 838 – $ 1,134
Escape Sport	$ 412 – $ 557
Extreme	$ 440 – $ 595
Extreme Comp	$ 838 – $ 1,134
Group 1 ALi	$ 255 – $ 345
Group 1 Ci	$ 130 – $ 176
Group 1 Si	$ 167 – $ 226
Group 1 Ti	$ 110 – $ 148
Group 1 Zi	$ 100 – $ 135
Impulse Comp	$ 859 – $ 1,162
Master	$ 340 – $ 460
Megatube DV8 FW1	$ 125 – $ 169
Megatube DV8 Mag	$ 140 – $ 189
Megatube DV8 XC6	$ 130 – $ 176
Shredder Deluxe	$ 157 – $ 213

C: – Components   F: – Fork

1995

MODEL	PRICE RANGE

Haro *(continued)*

Model	Price Range
Shredder Standard	$ 135 – $ 182
Sport	$ 218 – $ 294
Vector V0i	$ 125 – $ 169
Vector V1e	$ 145 – $ 196
Vector V2	$ 169 – $ 229
Vector V24S	$ 125 – $ 169
Vector V24S Suspension	$ 169 – $ 229
Vector V3	$ 194 – $ 262
Vector V4	$ 255 – $ 345
Vector V5	$ 300 – $ 406

HH

Model	Price Range
America	$ 956 – $ 1,293
Dirty Harry	$ 697 – $ 943
Fudendo	$ 556 – $ 752
Furiosa Ti	$ 777 – $ 1,051
Furiosa 2 Ti	$ 698 – $ 945
Pista	$ 606 – $ 820
Professional	$ 907 – $ 1,227
Vitesse	$ 860 – $ 1,164

Ibis

Model	Price Range
Cousin-it	$ 967 – $ 1,308
EZ-Street	$ 907 – $ 1,228
Forte	$ 967 – $ 1,308
Touche	$ 967 – $ 1,308

Iron Horse

Model	Price Range
Amigo	$ 282 – $ 382
ARS 600	$ 273 – $ 370
ARS 700	$ 463 – $ 627

C: – Components   F: – Fork

MODEL
PRICE RANGE

Iron Horse (continued)

Model	Price Range
ARS 800	$ 639 – $ 864
ARS 900	$ 777 – $ 1,051
ARS Comp	$ 282 – $ 382
AT20	$ 115 – $ 155
AT50	$ 135 – $ 182
AT70	$ 165 – $ 223
Bronco	$ 120 – $ 162
Eliminator	$ 165 – $ 223
MT 100	$ 194 – $ 262
MT 200	$ 236 – $ 320
MT 400R	$ 250 – $ 339
MT 400R Suspension	$ 296 – $ 400
MT 500	$ 340 – $ 460
MT 500 Suspension	$ 424 – $ 573
Typhoon	$ 150 – $ 203
XT1500	$ 122 – $ 165
XT1800	$ 147 – $ 199
XT2100	$ 191 – $ 259

Jamis

Model	Price Range
Aragon	$ 184 – $ 249
Aurora	$ 374 – $ 506
Citizen	$ 155 – $ 209
Coda	$ 314 – $ 424
Cross Country	$ 155 – $ 209
Dakar	$ 663 – $ 898
Dakar Team	$ 842 – $ 1,139
Dakota	$ 463 – $ 627
Diablo	$ 374 – $ 506
Dragon	$ 663 – $ 898
Durango	$ 222 – $ 301

C: – Components   F: – Fork

MODEL	PRICE RANGE

Jamis *(continued)*

Model	Price Range
Eclipse	$ 556 – $ 752
Eureka	$ 309 – $ 419
Exile	$ 269 – $ 364
Explorer XR	$ 314 – $ 424
Quest	$ 444 – $ 600
Tangier	$ 222 – $ 301
Ukiah	$ 184 – $ 249

Kestrel

Model	Price Range
200EMS C: Dura-Ace	$ 961 – $ 1,300
200SCI C: 105	$ 739 – $ 1,000
200SCI C: Athena	$ 840 – $ 1,136
200SCI C: Ultegra	$ 842 – $ 1,139
500SCI C: Dura-Ace	$ 965 – $ 1,305
500SCI C: Ultegra	$ 920 – $ 1,245
CSX C: Deore LX	$ 698 – $ 945
CSX C: Deore XT	$ 800 – $ 1,082

KHS

Model	Price Range
Aero Comp	$ 698 – $ 945
Aero Special	$ 241 – $ 326
Aero Sport	$ 203 – $ 274
Aero Track	$ 318 – $ 430
Aero Turbo	$ 439 – $ 594
Alite 1000	$ 309 – $ 418
Alite 1000 F: Rock Shox Quadra 5	$ 402 – $ 544
Alite 3000	$ 482 – $ 652
Alite 3000-X	$ 606 – $ 820
Cross Sport	$ 139 – $ 189
Handi Cycle	$ 79 – $ 106
Montana	$ 104 – $ 141

C: – Components   F: – Fork

MODEL	PRICE RANGE

KHS *(continued)* 🚲

Montana Comp	$ 331 – $ 448
Montana Comp F: Rock Shox Mag 21	$ 447 – $ 604
Montana Comp FZ	$ 443 – $ 600
Montana Comp FZ F: Rock Shox Judy X	$ 559 – $ 756
Montana Crest	$ 188 – $ 255
Montana Descent	$ 296 – $ 400
Montana Descent F: Rock Shox Quadra	$ 368 – $ 498
Montana FXT-Comp	$ 463 – $ 626
Montana FXT-Team	$ 878 – $ 1,187
Montana Pro	$ 520 – $ 703
Montana Pro-X	$ 632 – $ 855
Montana Raptor	$ 109 – $ 148
Montana Raptor-X	$ 154 – $ 209
Montana Sport	$ 154 – $ 209
Montana Summit	$ 250 – $ 338
Montana T-Rex	$ 119 – $ 161
Montana T-Rex-X	$ 159 – $ 215
Montana Team	$ 772 – $ 1,044
Montana Trail	$ 134 – $ 182
Montana Trail-X	$ 179 – $ 242
Sundancer	$ 99 – $ 134
Tandemania AL	$ 623 – $ 842
Tandemania Comp	$ 573 – $ 775
Tandemania Sport	$ 340 – $ 459

Klein 🚲

Adroit	$ 965 – $ 1,306
Attitude	$ 920 – $ 1,244
Attitude Suspension	$ 941 – $ 1,273
Fervor C: LX	$ 637 – $ 862
Fervor C: STX-RC	$ 566 – $ 766

C: – Components   F: – Fork

MODEL	PRICE RANGE

Klein (continued)

Model	Price Range
Pulse C: LX F: Judy	$ 834 – $ 1,128
Pulse C: LX F: Ocelot	$ 790 – $ 1,069
Pulse C: XT F: Judy	$ 907 – $ 1,228
Pulse C: XT F: Ocelot	$ 877 – $ 1,186
Quantum	$ 603 – $ 816
Quantum II	$ 799 – $ 1,081
Quantum Pro C: Ultegra	$ 941 – $ 1,273

Kona

Model	Price Range
AA	$ 482 – $ 652
A'ha	$ 241 – $ 326
Cinder Cone	$ 361 – $ 489
Explosif	$ 606 – $ 820
Fire Mountain	$ 250 – $ 338
Hahanna	$ 215 – $ 291
Hei Hei	$ 966 – $ 1,307
Hot	$ 789 – $ 1,067
Humu Humu	$ 169 – $ 229
Kapu	$ 573 – $ 775
Keiki	$ 188 – $ 255
Kilauea	$ 520 – $ 703
Koa	$ 340 – $ 459
Ku	$ 789 – $ 1,067
Kula	$ 684 – $ 925
Lava Dome	$ 296 – $ 400
Muni-Mula	$ 423 – $ 573
Sex One	$ 555 – $ 751
Sex Too	$ 698 – $ 945

LBIC

Model	Price Range
EX 200	$ 145 – $ 196

C: – Components   F: – Fork

MODEL	PRICE RANGE

LeMond

GLX	$ 709 – $ 960
Titanium	$ 829 – $ 1,122
V2	$ 920 – $ 1,245

Lightning

M-5	$ 776 – $ 1,050
P-38	$ 777 – $ 1,051
P-38X	$ 869 – $ 1,176
Stealth	$ 538 – $ 727

Litespeed

Catalyst	$ 814 – $ 1,102
Hiwasse	$ 668 – $ 904
Obed	$ 830 – $ 1,123
Obed F/S	$ 859 – $ 1,162
Tachyon	$ 835 – $ 1,130

Macalu

Pro OX-II C: LX	$ 500 – $ 676
Pro OX-II C: XT	$ 573 – $ 775
Road Ti C: Chorus	$ 776 – $ 1,050
Road Ti C: Dura-Ace	$ 860 – $ 1,163
Road Ti C: Record	$ 893 – $ 1,208
Road Ti C: Ultegra	$ 739 – $ 1,000
Ti MTN C: XT F: Judy SL	$ 799 – $ 1,081
Ti MTN C: XTR F: Judy SL**	$ 841 – $ 1,138
Ti MTN F: MAG21	$ 726 – $ 982

Marin

Bear Valley	$ 287 – $ 388

C: – Components   F: – Fork

MODEL	PRICE RANGE

Marin *(continued)*

Model	Price Range
Bear Valley F: Manitou 4	$ 416 – $ 563
Bear Valley F: Manitou Comp	$ 360 – $ 487
Bear Valley F: Manitou Magnum	$ 381 – $ 515
Bear Valley F: Rock Shox Judy XC	$ 426 – $ 577
Bear Valley F: Rock Shox Mag 21	$ 387 – $ 524
Bear Valley F: Rock Shox Quadra 5	$ 350 – $ 473
Bear Valley S.E.	$ 322 – $ 436
Bear Valley S.E F: Manitou 4	$ 452 – $ 612
Bear Valley S.E. F: Manitou Comp	$ 398 – $ 539
Bear Valley S.E. F: Manitou Magnum	$ 418 – $ 566
Bear Valley S.E F: Rock Shox Judy XC	$ 462 – $ 625
Bear Valley S.E. F: Rock Shox Mag 2	$ 424 – $ 574
Bear Valley S.E. F: Rock Shox Quadra 5	$ 388 – $ 525
Bobcat Trail	$ 203 – $ 274
Eldridge Grade	$ 386 – $ 523
Eldridge Grade F: Manitou 4	$ 509 – $ 689
Eldridge Grade F: Manitou Comp	$ 458 – $ 620
Eldridge Grade F: Manitou EFC	$ 520 – $ 704
Eldridge Grade F: Manitou Magnum	$ 477 – $ 646
Eldridge Grade F: Rock Shox Judy XC	$ 519 – $ 702
Eldridge Grade F: Rock Shox Mag 21	$ 483 – $ 653
Eldridge Grade F: Rock Shox Quadra 5	$ 449 – $ 607
Hawk Hill	$ 179 – $ 242
Hidden Canyon	$ 154 – $ 209
Indian Fire Trail	$ 548 – $ 742
Indian Fire Trail F: Manitou 4	$ 645 – $ 873
Indian Fire Trail F: Manitou Comp	$ 602 – $ 815
Indian Fire Trail F: Manitou EFC	$ 655 – $ 886
Indian Fire Trail F: Manitou Magnum	$ 618 – $ 837
Indian Fire Trail F: Rock Shox Judy XC	$ 653 – $ 884
Indian Fire Trail F: Rock Shox Mag	$ 623 – $ 843

C: – Components   F: – Fork

MODEL	PRICE RANGE

Marin (continued)

Model	Price Range
Indian Fire Trail F: Rock Shox Quadra 5	$ 594 – $ 804
Muir Woods	$ 231 – $ 313
Nail Trail	$ 351 – $ 475
Nail Trail F: Manitou 4	$ 471 – $ 638
Nail Trail F: Manitou Comp	$ 418 – $ 566
Nail Trail F: Manitou EFC	$ 483 – $ 653
Nail Trail F: Manitou Magnum	$ 438 – $ 593
Nail Trail F: Rock Shox Judy XC	$ 481 – $ 651
Nail Trail F: Rock Shox Mag 21	$ 444 – $ 601
Nail Trail F: Rock Shox Quadra 5	$ 409 – $ 553
Nail Trail F.R.S.	$ 573 – $ 775
Palisades Trail	$ 255 – $ 344
Palisades Trail F: Manitou 4	$ 391 – $ 529
Palisades Trail F: Manitou Comp	$ 334 – $ 452
Palisades Trail F: Manitou Magnum	$ 355 – $ 481
Palisades Trail F: Rock Shox Mag 21	$ 362 – $ 490
Palisades Trail F: Rock Shox Quadra	$ 324 – $ 438
Pine Mountain	$ 435 – $ 589
Pine Mountain F: Manitou 4	$ 546 – $ 738
Pine Mountain F: Manitou Comp	$ 496 – $ 672
Pine Mountain F: Manitou EFC	$ 556 – $ 752
Pine Mountain F: Manitou Magnum	$ 515 – $ 696
Pine Mountain F: Rock Shox Judy XC	$ 554 – $ 750
Pine Mountain F: Rock Shox Mag 21	$ 520 – $ 704
Pine Mountain F: Rock Shox Quadra 5	$ 487 – $ 659
Point Reyes	$ 423 – $ 573
Redwood	$ 340 – $ 459
Rocky Ridge	$ 455 – $ 616
Rocky Ridge F: Manitou 4	$ 566 – $ 766
Rocky Ridge F: Manitou Comp	$ 519 – $ 702
Rocky Ridge F: Manitou EFC	$ 577 – $ 780

C: – Components   F: – Fork

MODEL	PRICE RANGE

Marin (continued) 🚲

Model	Price Range
Rocky Ridge F: Manitou Magnum	$ 536 – $ 726
Rocky Ridge F: Rock Shox Judy XC	$ 575 – $ 778
Rocky Ridge F: Rock Shox Mag 21	$ 542 – $ 733
Rocky Ridge F: Rock Shox Quadra 5	$ 510 – $ 690
San Rafael	$ 222 – $ 300
Sausalito	$ 287 – $ 388
Stinson	$ 179 – $ 242
Team F.R.S.	$ 800 – $ 1,082
Team Marin	$ 520 – $ 703
Team Marin F: Manitou 4	$ 614 – $ 830
Team Marin F: Manitou Comp	$ 569 – $ 769
Team Marin F: Manitou EFC	$ 623 – $ 843
Team Marin F: Manitou Magnum	$ 585 – $ 792
Team Marin F: Rock Shox Judy XC	$ 622 – $ 841
Team Marin F: Rock Shox Mag 21	$ 590 – $ 799
Team Marin F: Rock Shox Quadra 5	$ 560 – $ 758
Team Titanium	$ 811 – $ 1,097
Team Titanium F: Manitou 4	$ 864 – $ 1,169
Team Titanium F: Manitou Comp	$ 839 – $ 1,136
Team Titanium F: Manitou EFC	$ 870 – $ 1,176
Team Titanium F: Manitou Magnum	$ 849 – $ 1,148
Team Titanium F: Rock Shox Judy XC	$ 869 – $ 1,175
Team Titanium F: Rock Shox Mag 21	$ 852 – $ 1,152
Team Titanium F: Rock Shox Quadra 5	$ 835 – $ 1,129

Marinoni 🚲

Model	Price Range
Corsa C: Athena	$ 777 – $ 1,051
Leggero C: Chorus	$ 920 – $ 1,245
Panache C: Record	$ 967 – $ 1,308
Pista C: Superbe	$ 606 – $ 820
Sprint C: Mirage	$ 555 – $ 751

C: – Components   F: – Fork

MODEL	PRICE RANGE

Marinoni (continued)

Squadra C: Ultegra	$ 777 – $ 1,051
Turista	$ 752 – $ 1,018
Ultimo C: Dura-Ace	$ 967 – $ 1,308

Masi

Gran Corsa	$ 721 – $ 975
Team 3V	$ 799 – $ 1,081
Tre Volumetrica	$ 842 – $ 1,139

Maxam

Reveille	$ 212 – $ 287
Reveille DL	$ 296 – $ 400
Reveille LX	$ 250 – $ 338

Maxcycles

Cross Blast	$ 361 – $ 489
Extra-Comp	$ 361 – $ 489
Extra Blast	$ 266 – $ 359
Pro-Comp	$ 418 – $ 565
Ultra Comp	$ 512 – $ 693

MCS

Hurricane Jr.	$ 184 – $ 249
Magnum 24	$ 198 – $ 269
Magnum Mini	$ 179 – $ 242
Magnum Pro	$ 179 – $ 242
Magnum Team	$ 273 – $ 369
Magnum XLX	$ 179 – $ 242
XLX Team	$ 262 – $ 354

C: – Components   F: – Fork

1995

MODEL	PRICE RANGE

Mondonico 🚲

Diamond	$ 789 –	$ 1,067
EL-OS	$ 869 –	$ 1,176
Futura	$ 713 –	$ 964

Mongoose 🚲

Alta	$ 272 –	$ 367
Amplifier II	$ 758 –	$ 1,026
Confetti	$ 77 –	$ 104
Crossway 250	$ 161 –	$ 217
Crossway 450	$ 189 –	$ 256
Crossway 625	$ 231 –	$ 312
Crossway 850	$ 312 –	$ 422
DMC	$ 403 –	$ 545
Expert	$ 127 –	$ 171
Expert Pro	$ 169 –	$ 228
Hill Topper	$ 231 –	$ 312
Hill Topper SX	$ 285 –	$ 386
Hooligan	$ 236 –	$ 319
IBOC Comp	$ 415 –	$ 562
IBOC Comp SX	$ 514 –	$ 695
IBOC Crit	$ 415 –	$ 562
IBOC Pro	$ 538 –	$ 728
IBOC Pro SX	$ 717 –	$ 970
IBOC Road	$ 585 –	$ 791
IBOC Team SX	$ 875 –	$ 1,184
IBOC World	$ 758 –	$ 1,026
IBOC Zero G	$ 364 –	$ 493
IBOC Zero G SX	$ 441 –	$ 596
Menace	$ 112 –	$ 151
Motivator	$ 89 –	$ 120
Motivator Mini	$ 89 –	$ 120

C: – Components   F: – Fork

MODEL	PRICE RANGE

Mongoose *(continued)*

Mt. Grizzly	$ 103 – $ 140
Rockadile	$ 338 – $ 458
Rockadile SX	$ 390 – $ 528
Solution	$ 263 – $ 356
Solution Pro	$ 415 – $ 562
Stormer	$ 118 – $ 159
Switchback	$ 175 – $ 237
Sycamore	$ 189 – $ 256
Threshold	$ 152 – $ 206
Villain	$ 135 – $ 183
Villain Mags	$ 152 – $ 205
909	$ 232 – $ 313
MX-7	$ 232 – $ 313
Triframe Tandem	$ 822 – $ 1,112

Motiv

Back Country	$ 119 – $ 161
Duet Tandem	$ 318 – $ 430
Ground Pounder	$ 250 – $ 338
Highridge	$ 236 – $ 319
Sonora	$ 296 – $ 400
Stonegrinder	$ 169 – $ 229
Titanium	$ 822 – $ 1,112

Moulton

APB14	$ 599 – $ 810
APB14 Plus	$ 678 – $ 918
APB3	$ 511 – $ 691

Mountain Goat

| Joule | $ 851 – $ 1,152 |

C: – Components   F: – Fork

MODEL	PRICE RANGE

Mountain Goat (continued)   🚲

Mudslinger	$ 896 – $ 1,213
Route 66	$ 715 – $ 968
Whiskeytown Racer	$ 792 – $ 1,071

Mountain TEK   🚲

Boulder	$ 129 – $ 175
Carbon C: XT	$ 670 – $ 906
Comp C: STX	$ 362 – $ 489
Comp C: XT	$ 423 – $ 573
Extreme	$ 174 – $ 235
Peak	$ 250 – $ 338
Summit	$ 318 – $ 430
Team Issue	$ 878 – $ 1,187
Teton	$ 154 – $ 209
Traverse	$ 222 – $ 300
Vertical	$ 203 – $ 274

Nashbar   🚲

4000X	$ 222 – $ 300
4000XS	$ 248 – $ 335
5000R	$ 273 – $ 369
6000T	$ 245 – $ 332
Sport Tandem	$ 606 – $ 820

Nishiki   🚲

Backroads	$ 189 – $ 256
Blazer	$ 125 – $ 169
Bravo	$ 105 – $ 142
Cascade	$ 296 – $ 400
Century	$ 135 – $ 182
Colorado	$ 250 – $ 339

C: – Components   F: – Fork

MODEL

PRICE RANGE

Nishiki (continued)

Model	Price Range
Manitoba	$ 169 – $ 229
Pueblo	$ 145 – $ 196
Sport	$ 165 – $ 223

Norco

Model	Price Range
Arctic	$ 169 – $ 229
Avanti	$ 169 – $ 229
Axia	$ 327 – $ 442
Bigfoot	$ 250 – $ 338
Bush Pilot	$ 169 – $ 229
Cherokee	$ 114 – $ 155
Forza C: Dura-Ace	$ 878 – $ 1,187
Forza RX/100 C: Ultegra	$ 538 – $ 727
FTS-1	$ 726 – $ 982
Jammer SP	$ 159 – $ 215
Java	$ 463 – $ 626
Katmandu	$ 144 – $ 195
Kokanee	$ 203 – $ 274
Magnum	$ 241 – $ 326
Micro Mountaineer	$ 109 – $ 148
Milano	$ 193 – $ 261
Mini Mountaineer	$ 109 – $ 148
Monterey	$ 217 – $ 294
Mountaineer SL	$ 129 – $ 175
Nitro	$ 403 – $ 545
Nitro (suspension)	$ 435 – $ 589
Picante	$ 331 – $ 448
Quest	$ 139 – $ 189
Rampage	$ 538 – $ 727
Sasquatch	$ 331 – $ 448
Sasquatch (suspension)	$ 361 – $ 489

C: – Components   F: – Fork

MODEL	PRICE RANGE

Norco (continued) 🚲

Tango	$ 309	– $	418
Team Issue	$ 907	– $	1,228
TNT	$ 726	– $	982
Turbine	$ 423	– $	573

Novara 🚲

Alight	$ 215	– $	291
Arriba	$ 294	– $	397
Arriba-LT	$ 248	– $	336
Arroyo	$ 152	– $	206
Aspen	$ 191	– $	259
Corsa	$ 167	– $	226
Dirt Rider 20	$ 110	– $	148
Dirt Rider 24	$ 112	– $	152
Ponderosa	$ 403	– $	546
Pro-Ultimate	$ 500	– $	676
Randonnee	$ 294	– $	397
Team FS	$ 751	– $	1,016
Team SL	$ 668	– $	904
Trionfo	$ 571	– $	773
X-R	$ 227	– $	307

Nytro 🚲

TT650	$ 538	– $	727
TT650 600 C: Ultegra	$ 726	– $	982

Oryx 🚲

2000	$ 305	– $	412
2000S	$ 387	– $	523
3000	$ 353	– $	478
3000S	$ 428	– $	579

C: – Components   F: – Fork

MODEL

PRICE RANGE

Parkpre

Model	Price Range
Al-U-Max F: Manitou Comp	$ 461 – $ 623
Al-U-Max F: Manitou Magnum	$ 475 – $ 642
Al-U-Max F: PRF	$ 396 – $ 536
Al-U-Max F: Rock Shox Mag 21	$ 468 – $ 634
Comp 20	$ 112 – $ 152
Comp Limited F: Manitou Comp	$ 365 – $ 494
Comp Limited F: PRF	$ 296 – $ 400
Comp Limited F: Rock Shox Mag 21	$ 374 – $ 506
Comp Limited F: RST 381	$ 335 – $ 454
Grand Sport	$ 154 – $ 209
Mountain Comp F: PRF	$ 250 – $ 338
Mountain Comp F: RST 171	$ 282 – $ 382
Pro 825 F: Manitou 4	$ 710 – $ 960
Pro 825 F: Manitou EFC	$ 750 – $ 1,014
Pro 825 F: PRF	$ 628 – $ 849
Pro 825 F: Rock Shox Judy SL	$ 761 – $ 1,029
Pro 825 F: Rock Shox Judy XC	$ 718 – $ 971
Pro 825 F: Rock Shox Mag 21	$ 683 – $ 923
Pro Elite F: Manitou 4	$ 917 – $ 1,241
Pro Elite F: Manitou EFC	$ 934 – $ 1,263
Pro Elite F: PRF	$ 878 – $ 1,188
Pro Elite F: Rock Shox Judy SL	$ 938 – $ 1,269
Pro Elite F: Rock Shox Judy XC	$ 921 – $ 1,246
Pro Elite F: Rock Shox Mag 21	$ 905 – $ 1,225
Pro Image F: Manitou 4	$ 710 – $ 960
Pro Image F: Manitou EFC	$ 750 – $ 1,014
Pro Image F: PRF	$ 628 – $ 849
Pro Image F: Rock Shox Judy SL	$ 761 – $ 1,029
Pro Image F: Rock Shox Judy XC	$ 718 – $ 971
Pro Image F: Rock Shox Mag 21	$ 683 – $ 923
Scepter Comp F: Manitou Comp	$ 419 – $ 567

C: – Components   F: – Fork

MODEL	PRICE RANGE

Parkpre *(continued)*

Model	Price Range
Scepter Comp F: PRF	$ 353 – $ 477
Scepter Comp F: Rock Shox Mag 21	$ 428 – $ 579
Scepter Comp F: RST 381	$ 390 – $ 528
Solitude F: PRF	$ 203 – $ 274
Solitude F: RST 170	$ 239 – $ 323
Sport Limited F: PRF	$ 179 – $ 242
Sport Limited F: RST 156	$ 203 – $ 274
Team 925 F: Manitou 4	$ 565 – $ 764
Team 925 F: Manitou Magnum	$ 536 – $ 726
Team 925 F: PRF	$ 463 – $ 626
Team 925 F: Rock Shox Mag 21	$ 530 – $ 718
X-Comp	$ 250 – $ 338

Pashley

Model	Price Range
DP23 Frontload Trike	$ 529 – $ 716
MW3 Worktrike	$ 620 – $ 839
NO. 33 food vending trike	$ 566 – $ 766
Picabac Sprint	$ 538 – $ 728
Picador Sprint	$ 538 – $ 728
Premier	$ 668 – $ 904
Prestige	$ 636 – $ 860
Princess Original	$ 340 – $ 460
Princess Sovereign	$ 416 – $ 562
Prospero Original	$ 336 – $ 454
Prospero Sovereign	$ 399 – $ 540
RH3 Carrier Bicycle	$ 438 – $ 592
Roadster	$ 285 – $ 385
SW8 Delibike	$ 459 – $ 622
TB2 Police Cruiser	$ 438 – $ 592

C: – Components   F: – Fork

MODEL	PRICE RANGE

Pedalcraft 🚲

QuadraPed	$ 857 – $ 1,159
TriSpeeder	$ 772 – $ 1,045

Performance 🚲

Jungle	$ 193 – $ 261
M-105	$ 455 – $ 616
M-105-Suspension	$ 538 – $ 727
M-205	$ 423 – $ 573
M-205-Suspension	$ 482 – $ 652
M-305	$ 340 – $ 459
M-305-Suspension	$ 403 – $ 545
M-405	$ 296 – $ 400
M-405-Suspension	$ 340 – $ 459
M-505	$ 236 – $ 319
M-505-Suspension	$ 282 – $ 382
M-605	$ 184 – $ 248
M-705	$ 154 – $ 209
R-105	$ 423 – $ 573
R-205	$ 296 – $ 400
Salmagundi C: Dura-ace	$ 842 – $ 1,139
Salmagundi C: Ultegra	$ 726 – $ 982
TM-1000 C: LX	$ 590 – $ 798
TM-1000 C: LX-Suspension	$ 639 – $ 864
TM-1000 C: XT	$ 639 – $ 864
TM-1000 C: XT-Suspension	$ 712 – $ 964
TM-1000 C: XTR	$ 752 – $ 1,018
TM-1000 C: XTR-Suspension	$ 811 – $ 1,097
TR-1000 C: 105	$ 635 – $ 860
TR-1000 C: Ultegra	$ 693 – $ 937
X-205	$ 174 – $ 235
X-305	$ 139 – $ 189

C: – Components   F: – Fork

MODEL	PRICE RANGE

Peugeot

Model	Price Range
Alpin Pro	$ 459 – $ 622
Appalades	$ 249 – $ 336
Biarritz	$ 403 – $ 546
Dune Racing	$ 174 – $ 236
Dune Racing Suspension	$ 203 – $ 275
Horizon	$ 232 – $ 313
Legende	$ 296 – $ 400
Liberty	$ 198 – $ 269
Nature 500	$ 203 – $ 275
Nature 600	$ 227 – $ 307
Prestige	$ 327 – $ 442
Sprint	$ 208 – $ 281
Success	$ 338 – $ 458
X-Country	$ 336 – $ 454

Pinarello

Model	Price Range
Concept	$ 943 – $ 1,276
Stelvio	$ 789 – $ 1,067

Powerlite

Model	Price Range
P-11	$ 89 – $ 121
P-16	$ 105 – $ 142
P-19	$ 94 – $ 128
P-28	$ 137 – $ 186
P-38	$ 169 – $ 229
P-47	$ 218 – $ 294
P-51	$ 246 – $ 332
P-61	$ 340 – $ 460
P-Shooter	$ 74 – $ 100

C: – Components   F: – Fork

1 9 9 5

MODEL	PRICE RANGE

ProFlex

455	$ 383 – $ 518
555	$ 463 – $ 627
755	$ 590 – $ 798
855	$ 699 – $ 945
Animal	$ 822 – $ 1,112
Arcadia	$ 340 – $ 460
Attack	$ 538 – $ 728
Newport	$ 250 – $ 339

Python

Anaconda	$ 120 – $ 162
Apollo	$ 94 – $ 128
Boa	$ 340 – $ 460
Bonecrusher	$ 189 – $ 256
Mamba	$ 135 – $ 182
Medusa	$ 236 – $ 320
Serpent	$ 109 – $ 147
Strangler	$ 160 – $ 216

Raleigh

Boardwalk	$ 76 – $ 102
C30	$ 114 – $ 154
C40	$ 127 – $ 171
C50	$ 143 – $ 194
Coranado	$ 97 – $ 131
F-500 Police	$ 250 – $ 338
Florasaurus	$ 56 – $ 76
Honeysaurus	$ 52 – $ 70
M-20	$ 88 – $ 120
M-30	$ 106 – $ 143
M-40	$ 127 – $ 171

C: – Components   F: – Fork

MODEL	PRICE RANGE

Raleigh (continued)

Model	Price Range
M-400	$ 269 – $ 364
M-40GS	$ 122 – $ 166
M-50	$ 147 – $ 199
M-60	$ 172 – $ 232
M-80	$ 212 – $ 286
M-800	$ 358 – $ 484
M-9000	$ 423 – $ 572
Microsaurus Rex	$ 52 – $ 70
Mtn Scout	$ 91 – $ 123
MXR	$ 56 – $ 76
MXR Pro	$ 56 – $ 76
R500	$ 287 – $ 389
R600	$ 391 – $ 529

Rans

Model	Price Range
Nimbus	$ 668 – $ 904
Nimbus C: XT	$ 813 – $ 1,100
Response	$ 599 – $ 810
Rocket 20/20	$ 500 – $ 676
Stratus	$ 668 – $ 904
RansStratus C: XT	$ 813 – $ 1,100
Tailwind	$ 457 – $ 619
V-Rex	$ 631 – $ 854
V-Rex C: XT	$ 784 – $ 1,061

ReBike

Model	Price Range
2600 LE	$ 296 – $ 400
2600 SE	$ 282 – $ 382
ReBike 707	$ 227 – $ 307
ReBike 818	$ 264 – $ 357

C: – Components   F: – Fork

MODEL	PRICE RANGE

ReBike (continued)

ReTrike 707	$ 296 – $ 400
ReTrike 707VP	$ 305 – $ 412

Redline

MR-140	$ 135 – $ 182
PL-24 Cruiser	$ 189 – $ 256
Proline	$ 189 – $ 256
RL-240	$ 140 – $ 189
RL-340	$ 105 – $ 142
RL-340 Junior	$ 105 – $ 142
RL-440	$ 140 – $ 189

Research Dynamics

Coyote AFS Six	$ 752 – $ 1,018
Coyote Alu Five	$ 463 – $ 626
Coyote One	$ 147 – $ 199
Coyote Pro Four	$ 357 – $ 483
Coyote STX Single Track	$ 273 – $ 369
Coyote Team Extreme 20	$ 94 – $ 127
Coyote Team Extreme 24	$ 132 – $ 179
Coyote Team Six	$ 555 – $ 751
Coyote Titan	$ 842 – $ 1,139
Coyote Two	$ 215 – $ 291

Ritchey

Comp Shocker	$ 831 – $ 1,124
Crazy Pete	$ 692 – $ 936
Everest	$ 907 – $ 1,227
Lite Beam	$ 893 – $ 1,208
P-21	$ 880 – $ 1,191
P-21 WCS	$ 920 – $ 1,245

C: – Components   F: – Fork

MODEL	PRICE RANGE

Ritchey (continued)

Model	Price Range
P-22	$ 812 – $ 1,099
Project-20	$ 941 – $ 1,273

Robinson

Model	Price Range
24 Cruiser	$ 236 – $ 320
Junior	$ 241 – $ 326
MX	$ 174 – $ 236
Pro	$ 227 – $ 307
Rebel	$ 100 – $ 135
SST	$ 135 – $ 182
Team	$ 318 – $ 430

Romic

Model	Price Range
Athena Sport	$ 725 – $ 981
Chorus Sport	$ 811 – $ 1,097
Chorus Tourer	$ 832 – $ 1,126
Chorus Tourer Triple	$ 782 – $ 1,057
Eagle Track	$ 662 – $ 896
Eco Tour	$ 684 – $ 926
Lone Eagle	$ 684 – $ 926
RX-100 Tourer	$ 664 – $ 898
SportX	$ 752 – $ 1,018
Superace	$ 907 – $ 1,227

Ross

Model	Price Range
Adventurer	$ 110 – $ 148
Amazon	$ 82 – $ 110
Aristocrat	$ 203 – $ 275
Beach Commander	$ 100 – $ 135
Boomerang/Young Lady	$ 76 – $ 103
Chimera	$ 120 – $ 162

C: – Components   F: – Fork

MODEL	PRICE RANGE

Ross (continued)

Model	Price Range
Compact Clic	$ 100 – $ 135
Compact III	$ 110 – $ 148
Diamond Cruiser	$ 105 – $ 142
Diamond Trimatic	$ 125 – $ 169
Dune Commander	$ 100 – $ 135
Endo	$ 94 – $ 128
Eurotour	$ 110 – $ 148
Frenzy	$ 82 – $ 110
Gran Tour	$ 130 – $ 176
Griffon	$ 142 – $ 193
Mt. Cruiser	$ 130 – $ 176
Mt. Jefferson	$ 89 – $ 121
Mt. Katahdin	$ 174 – $ 236
Mt. Olympus	$ 203 – $ 275
Mt. Pocono	$ 100 – $ 135
Mt. Rushmore	$ 115 – $ 155
Mt. Snow 250	$ 120 – $ 162
Mt. Snow 252	$ 110 – $ 148
Mt. Snow 254	$ 140 – $ 189
Mt. Snow 256	$ 203 – $ 275
Mt. Washington	$ 127 – $ 172
Mt. Washington XOS	$ 127 – $ 172
Pegasus	$ 179 – $ 242
Peryton	$ 105 – $ 142
Piranha Pro 142	$ 100 – $ 135
Piranha Pro 144	$ 105 – $ 142
Piranha Pro 146	$ 122 – $ 165
Piranha Pro 148	$ 130 – $ 176
Pronto/Bitsy Lady	$ 48 – $ 65
Race BMX Comp Cro-Moly	$ 179 – $ 242
Race BMX Cro-Moly	$ 130 – $ 176

C: – Components   F: – Fork

MODEL	PRICE RANGE

Ross (continued) 🚲

Race BMX Mini Tri-Moly	$ 130 – $ 176
Race BMX Pro Aluminum	$ 250 – $ 339
Race BMX Tri-Moly	$ 115 – $ 155
Race FS Comp Cro-Moly	$ 203 – $ 275
Race FS Pro Aluminum	$ 285 – $ 385
Race Trail Power Aluminum	$ 463 – $ 627
Radical/Little Lady	$ 74 – $ 100
Shark 222/223	$ 125 – $ 169
Shark 226/227	$ 130 – $ 176
Slinger/Petite Lady	$ 69 – $ 93
Tailspin/Teeny Lady	$ 65 – $ 88
Unicorn	$ 100 – $ 135
Zwoom	$ 112 – $ 152
Zwoom XII	$ 150 – $ 203

Ryan Recumbent Cycles 🚲

DuPlex	$ 965 – $ 1,305
Vanguard C: LX	$ 684 – $ 926
Vanguard C: XT	$ 851 – $ 1,152

Santa Cruz 🚲

Tazmon C: XT	$ 901 – $ 1,219
Tazmon C: XT/LX	$ 821 – $ 1,110

Santana 🚲

Arriva	$ 941 – $ 1,273
Cilantro	$ 941 – $ 1,273
Fusion	$ 941 – $ 1,273
Rio	$ 860 – $ 1,163
Visa	$ 860 – $ 1,163
Vision	$ 860 – $ 1,163

C: – Components   F: – Fork

MODEL	PRICE RANGE
Schwinn	🚲
Clear Creek	$ 186 – $ 251
Frontier	$ 129 – $ 175
High Plains	$ 213 – $ 289
Homegrown USA Racing	$ 1,152 – $ 1,559
Homegrown USA Suspension	$ 1,281 – $ 1,732
Le Tour	$ 224 – $ 304
Moab Elite	$ 273 – $ 370
Moab Elite S	$ 300 – $ 406
Moab S	$ 246 – $ 333
Passage	$ 306 – $ 413
s[9 five] .1	$ 735 – $ 995
s[9 five] .2	$ 560 – $ 757
s[9 five] .3	$ 464 – $ 628
s[9 five] .4	$ 439 – $ 594
s[9 five] .5	$ 414 – $ 560
s[9 five] .6	$ 358 – $ 484
Searcher Express	$ 157 – $ 213
Searcher Range	$ 186 – $ 251
Searcher Ridge	$ 219 – $ 296
Searcher Transit	$ 129 – $ 175
Side Winder	$ 157 – $ 213
Side Winder 2.0	$ 129 – $ 175
Side Winder 2.4	$ 152 – $ 205
Super Sport	$ 464 – $ 628
Thrasher	$ 129 – $ 175
XS	$ 157 – $ 213
XS Pro	$ 213 – $ 289
Scorpio	🚲
AL-200	$ 227 – $ 307
AL-550	$ 323 – $ 436

C: – Components   F: – Fork

MODEL   PRICE RANGE

Scorpio (continued)

Model					
AT-50	$	105	– $	142
AT-100	$	97	– $	131
AT-200	$	140	– $	189
AT-400	$	213	– $	288
AT-J20 F: Pilot Jumbo	$	84	– $	114
AT-J20 F: Pilot Lite	$	63	– $	85
RA-200	$	318	– $	430

Scott

Model					
AFD 303	$	340	– $	459
AFD 903	$	832	– $	1,125
Arapahoe	$	159	– $	215
Boulder	$	296	– $	400
Comp Jr.	$	119	– $	161
Comp Racing CST	$	463	– $	626
Expression	$	331	– $	448
Instinct	$	188	– $	255
Magnum MK 1.0 CST	$	296	– $	400
Magnum MK 2.0 CST	$	361	– $	489
Mohaka	$	184	– $	248
Pro Racing CST	$	789	– $	1,067
Santa Cruz	$	222	– $	300
Seattle	$	169	– $	229
Summit	$	241	– $	326
Tampico	$	208	– $	281
Team Jr.	$	139	– $	189
Team Racing CST	$	657	– $	889
Vantage 1.0	$	327	– $	442
Vantage 2.0	$	463	– $	626
Vantage 3.0	$	654	– $	885

C: – Components   F: – Fork

MODEL	PRICE RANGE

SE Racing

Model	Price Range
Assassin Pro	$ 231 – $ 313
Assassin Pro XL	$ 231 – $ 313
Bronco	$ 99 – $ 134
Eagle	$ 144 – $ 195
PK Ripper	$ 241 – $ 326
PK Ripper XL	$ 241 – $ 326
Quadangle	$ 241 – $ 326

Serotta

Model	Price Range
ATX	$ 902 – $ 1,220
CSI	$ 944 – $ 1,277
TG	$ 834 – $ 1,129

Signature

Model	Price Range
Centaur	$ 250 – $ 339
Minotaur	$ 203 – $ 275
Mt. Hood	$ 383 – $ 518
Mt. Mckinely	$ 639 – $ 864
Mt. Rainier	$ 383 – $ 518
Mt. St. Helens	$ 262 – $ 354
Mt. Whitney	$ 463 – $ 627
Super Gran Tour	$ 179 – $ 242
Zemopi 484	$ 296 – $ 400
Zemopi 584	$ 424 – $ 573
Zemopi 684	$ 573 – $ 775
Zemopi 784	$ 822 – $ 1,112

Simoncini

Model	Price Range
SLX Europa C: Athena	$ 573 – $ 775
SLX Europa C: Chorus	$ 654 – $ 885

C: – Components   F: – Fork

MODEL	PRICE RANGE

Softride 🚲

Model	Price Range
360 Powercurve	$ 383 – $ 518
Contour Powercurve	$ 603 – $ 816
Husky Powercurve	$ 432 – $ 584
Qualifier 650C	$ 724 – $ 979
Solo 700C	$ 777 – $ 1,051
Sully Powercurve	$ 765 – $ 1,035
Traveler Powercurve	$ 639 – $ 864

Specialized 🚲

Model	Price Range
Allez Sport	$ 401 – $ 542
Crossroads	$ 163 – $ 221
Crossroads Cruz	$ 143 – $ 193
Crossroads Sport	$ 189 – $ 255
Crossroads XP	$ 305 – $ 413
Globe 3	$ 168 – $ 228
Globe 7	$ 233 – $ 315
Hardrock 20	$ 107 – $ 145
Hardrock FS	$ 213 – $ 289
Hardrock GS	$ 148 – $ 200
Hardrock GSX	$ 148 – $ 200
Hardrock Sport	$ 163 – $ 221
Hardrock Sport GX	$ 163 – $ 221
Hardrock Ultra	$ 189 – $ 255
Hot Rock	$ 86 – $ 116
M2 Road	$ 564 – $ 763
M2 Road Comp	$ 676 – $ 914
M2 Road Pro	$ 807 – $ 1,092
M2 Super Road Pro	$ 1,115 – $ 1,509
Rockhopper	$ 223 – $ 302
RockHopper 24	$ 133 – $ 180
RockHopper 26	$ 133 – $ 180

C: – Components   F: – Fork

MODEL	PRICE RANGE

Specialized (continued)

Rockhopper Comp A1	$ 342 – $ 463
Rockhopper Comp A1 FS	$ 396 – $ 536
Rockhopper FS	$ 310 – $ 419
Rockhopper Ultra	$ 262 – $ 355
Shockrock 20	$ 158 – $ 214
Shockrock 24	$ 163 – $ 221
Stumpjumper	$ 432 – $ 584
Stumpjumper FS	$ 556 – $ 752
Stumpjumper FSR	$ 776 – $ 1,050
Stumpjumper FSR Sport	$ 564 – $ 763
Stumpjumper M2	$ 483 – $ 653
Stumpjumper M2 FS	$ 602 – $ 815
Stumpjumper M2 FS Comp	$ 754 – $ 1,020

Spectrum

Steel C: Record	$ 965 – $ 1,305
Steel C: Chorus	$ 931 – $ 1,260
Steel C: Dura-Ace	$ 953 – $ 1,289
Steel Track C: Record	$ 878 – $ 1,188
Steel Track C: Suntour	$ 800 – $ 1,083

Supercross

Racer-X	$ 194 – $ 262
XLT Team	$ 305 – $ 412

Terry

Athene	$ 336 – $ 454
Chrom	$ 595 – $ 805
Classic	$ 667 – $ 902
Jacaranda S Static	$ 479 – $ 648
Jacaranda S Suspended	$ 620 – $ 839
Symmetry	$ 463 – $ 627

C: – Components   F: – Fork

MODEL	PRICE RANGE

Thebis 🚲

201	$ 840 – $ 1,136

Ti Cycles 🚲

Full-Suspension Chrome-moly	$ 832 – $ 1,126
Full-Suspension Titanium	$ 961 – $ 1,300
Mountain Chrome-moly	$ 777 – $ 1,051
Mountain Titanium	$ 967 – $ 1,308
Road Chrome-moly	$ 759 – $ 1,026
Road Titanium	$ 965 – $ 1,305
Semi-Unified Full-Suspension	$ 961 – $ 1,300
Tandem Chrome-moly	$ 949 – $ 1,284

Timberlin 🚲

City Slicker	$ 124 – $ 168
Crossroads	$ 144 – $ 195
Fastrax	$ 119 – $ 161
Landrover	$ 119 – $ 161
Millenium	$ 361 – $ 489
Ridge Runner	$ 169 – $ 229
Short Cut	$ 117 – $ 159
Stomper	$ 104 – $ 141
Urban Express	$ 139 – $ 189
Wildwoods	$ 174 – $ 235

Titus 🚲

Cyborg Fs AL	$ 966 – $ 1,307
Full Racing	$ 965 – $ 1,305
Hard Core Racer Mtn	$ 908 – $ 1,228
Hard Core Racer Road	$ 851 – $ 1,152
SFS Easton AL	$ 941 – $ 1,273
SFS Ti	$ 967 – $ 1,308

C: – Components   F: – Fork

MODEL	PRICE RANGE
Torelli	🚲
Corsa Strada	$ 463 – $ 626
Express	$ 789 – $ 1,067
Nitro Express	$ 835 – $ 1,130
Super Strada	$ 698 – $ 945
Trek	🚲
370	$ 216 – $ 293
470	$ 330 – $ 447
520	$ 472 – $ 638
700	$ 155 – $ 210
720	$ 172 – $ 233
730	$ 204 – $ 276
750	$ 280 – $ 379
800	$ 155 – $ 210
800 Sport	$ 128 – $ 173
820	$ 172 – $ 233
830	$ 204 – $ 276
830 SHX	$ 228 – $ 309
850	$ 233 – $ 315
930	$ 252 – $ 341
930 SHX	$ 344 – $ 465
950	$ 344 – $ 465
970	$ 431 – $ 582
970 SHX	$ 504 – $ 682
990	$ 660 – $ 892
1220	$ 379 – $ 513
2100	$ 472 – $ 638
2120	$ 562 – $ 761
2300	$ 625 – $ 845
5000	$ 726 – $ 982
5200	$ 842 – $ 1,140

C: – Components   F: – Fork

MODEL | PRICE RANGE

Trek (continued)

Model	Price Range
5500	$ 1,029 – $ 1,393
6500	$ 299 – $ 404
7000	$ 394 – $ 533
7000 SHX	$ 472 – $ 638
7600	$ 431 – $ 582
7900	$ 562 – $ 761
8000	$ 447 – $ 605
8000 SHX	$ 516 – $ 698
8700	$ 512 – $ 693
8700 SHX	$ 660 – $ 892
9200	$ 588 – $ 796
9800	$ 726 – $ 982
9800 SHX	$ 815 – $ 1,103
9900	$ 1,029 – $ 1,393
Cruiser Classic	$ 117 – $ 159
Mountain Lion 260SHX	$ 172 – $ 233
Mountain Lion 40	$ 100 – $ 135
Mountain Lion 90SHX	$ 163 – $ 220
Rocket	$ 82 – $ 110
T100	$ 472 – $ 638
T200	$ 938 – $ 1,269
Wizard	$ 76 – $ 103
Y22	$ 757 – $ 1,024
Y33	$ 1,069 – $ 1,446

Two "O" Delta Three

Model	Price Range
Versatile V	$ 670 – $ 906

Ultimax

Model	Price Range
Condor/Flamingo	$ 58 – $ 78
Eagle/Hummingbird	$ 58 – $ 78

C: – Components   F: – Fork

MODEL	PRICE RANGE

Ultimax (continued)

Model	Price Range
Goshawk 300	$ 122 – $ 166
Hawk & Kiwi	$ 94 – $ 127
Kingfisher 100	$ 104 – $ 141
Ptarmigan 200	$ 122 – $ 166
Sage Thrasher/Road Runner	$ 63 – $ 85
Snipe 500	$ 193 – $ 261
Swift 400	$ 139 – $ 189
Thrush	$ 122 – $ 166

Univega

Model	Price Range
Activa Action	$ 123 – $ 167
Activa Country	$ 151 – $ 204
Activa Trail	$ 194 – $ 263
Alpina 501	$ 220 – $ 298
Alpina 503	$ 356 – $ 481
Alpina 505	$ 356 – $ 481
Alpina 507	$ 406 – $ 549
Alpina 602-S	$ 288 – $ 389
Alpina 604-S	$ 356 – $ 481
Alpina 606-S	$ 430 – $ 582
Alpina 608-S	$ 593 – $ 802
Aluminum 701	$ 280 – $ 379
Aluminum 703	$ 330 – $ 447
Aluminum 706-X	$ 442 – $ 598
Aluminum 708-X	$ 513 – $ 693
Boralite B4C	$ 937 – $ 1,268
Boralite Road	$ 981 – $ 1,327
Boralyn	$ 819 – $ 1,108
Carousel	$ 57 – $ 77
Cave Man	$ 57 – $ 77
Cobra	$ 116 – $ 156

C: – Components   F: – Fork

MODEL | PRICE RANGE

Univega (continued)

Model	Price Range	
Dual Action	$ 536 –	$ 725
Dual Action Pro	$ 695 –	$ 940
Gran Rally	$ 612 –	$ 828
Hornet BMX	$ 80 –	$ 108
Hornet CX	$ 74 –	$ 101
Mad Dog	$ 66 –	$ 89
Merry Go Round	$ 66 –	$ 89
Mountain Force 101	$ 102 –	$ 138
Mountain Force 103	$ 102 –	$ 138
Mountain Force 105	$ 124 –	$ 168
Mountain Force 202-S	$ 140 –	$ 190
Mountain Force 204-S	$ 151 –	$ 204
Pro Comp	$ 776 –	$ 1,050
Rover 301	$ 116 –	$ 156
Rover 303	$ 146 –	$ 197
Rover 305	$ 178 –	$ 241
Rover 402-S	$ 157 –	$ 212
Sportour	$ 247 –	$ 334
Super G	$ 154 –	$ 208
Super G AL	$ 220 –	$ 298
Superstrada	$ 358 –	$ 484
Tandem Sport	$ 330 –	$ 447
Tandem Tour	$ 503 –	$ 681
Via Carisma	$ 220 –	$ 298
Via De Oro AL	$ 363 –	$ 491
Via Montega	$ 272 –	$ 369
Willow	$ 74 –	$ 101

Ventana

Model	Price Range	
Marble Peak	$ 893 –	$ 1,209
Marble Peak FS	$ 967 –	$ 1,308

C: – Components   F: – Fork

MODEL	PRICE RANGE

Vision

VR40AU	$ 461 – $ 624
VR40BU	$ 511 – $ 691
VR40EU	$ 461 – $ 624
VR40FU	$ 520 – $ 703
VR42AU	$ 603 – $ 816
VR42EU	$ 613 – $ 830
VR45AU	$ 832 – $ 1,126
VR45EU	$ 837 – $ 1,133

Vitus

992 C: Athena	$ 654 – $ 885
992 C: Chorus	$ 726 – $ 983
992 C: Record	$ 771 – $ 1,043

VooDoo

Bizango C: Deore LX F: Rock Shox Judy XC	$ 705 – $ 954
Bizango C: Deore LX F: Rock Shox Mag 21	$ 672 – $ 909
Bizango C: Deore LX F: Rock Shox Quadra 21R	$ 655 – $ 886
Bizango C: Deore LX F: Rock Shox Quadra 5	$ 637 – $ 862
Bizango C: Deore LX F: Tange	$ 600 – $ 811
Bizango C: Deore XT F: Rock Shox Judy XC	$ 818 – $ 1,107
Bizango C: Deore XT F: Rock Shox Mag 21	$ 793 – $ 1,073
Bizango C: Deore XT F: Rock Shox Quadra 21R	$ 780 – $ 1,055
Bizango C: Deore XT F: Rock Shox Quadra 5	$ 766 – $ 1,036
Bizango C: Deore XT F: Tange	$ 737 – $ 997
Bizango C: Deore XT/LX F: Rock Shox Judy XC	$ 751 – $ 1,017
Bizango C: Deore XT/LX F: Rock Shox Mag 21	$ 721 – $ 976
Bizango C: Deore XT/LX F: Rock Shox Quadra 21R	$ 705 – $ 954
Bizango C: Deore XT/LX F: Rock Shox Quadra 5	$ 689 – $ 932
Bizango C: Deore XT/LX F: Tange	$ 655 – $ 886
Bizango C: Deore XTR/XT F: Rock Shox Judy XC	$ 873 – $ 1,181

C: – Components   F: – Fork

MODEL	PRICE RANGE

VooDoo *(continued)*

Model	Price Range
Bizango C: Deore XTR/XT F: Rock Shox Mag 21	$ 853 – $ 1,154
Bizango C: Deore XTR/XT F: Rock Shox Quadra 21R	$ 842 – $ 1,139
Bizango C: Deore XTR/XT F: Rock Shox Quadra 5	$ 830 – $ 1,123
Bizango C: Deore XTR/XT F: Tange	$ 806 – $ 1,091
Bizango C: STX-RC F: Rock Shox Judy XC	$ 672 – $ 909
Bizango C: STX-RC F: Rock Shox Mag 21	$ 637 – $ 862
Bizango C: STX-RC F: Rock Shox Quadra 21R	$ 619 – $ 837
Bizango C: STX-RC F: Rock Shox Quadra 5	$ 600 – $ 811
Bizango C: STX-RC F: Tange	$ 561 – $ 759
Bokor C: Deore LX F: Rock Shox Judy XC	$ 655 – $ 886
Bokor C: Deore LX F: Rock Shox Mag 21	$ 619 – $ 837
Bokor C: Deore LX F: Rock Shox Quadra 21R	$ 600 – $ 811
Bokor C: Deore LX F: Rock Shox Quadra 5	$ 580 – $ 785
Bokor C: Deore LX F: Tange	$ 540 – $ 731
Bokor C: Deore XT F: Rock Shox Judy XC	$ 818 – $ 1,107
Bokor C: Deore XT F: Rock Shox Mag 21	$ 751 – $ 1,017
Bokor C: Deore XT F: Rock Shox Quadra 21R	$ 737 – $ 997
Bokor C: Deore XT F: Rock Shox Quadra 5	$ 721 – $ 976
Bokor C: Deore XT F: Tange	$ 689 – $ 932
Bokor C: Deore XT/LX F: Rock Shox Judy XC	$ 705 – $ 954
Bokor C: Deore XT/LX F: Rock Shox Mag 21	$ 672 – $ 909
Bokor C: Deore XT/LX F: Rock Shox Quadra 21R	$ 655 – $ 886
Bokor C: Deore XT/LX F: Rock Shox Quadra 5	$ 637 – $ 862
Bokor C: Deore XT/LX F: Tange	$ 600 – $ 811
Bokor C: Deore XTR/XT F: Rock Shox Judy XC	$ 842 – $ 1,139
Bokor C: Deore XTR/XT F: Rock Shox Mag 21	$ 818 – $ 1,107
Bokor C: Deore XTR/Xt F: Rock Shox Quadra 21R	$ 806 – $ 1,091
Bokor C: Deore XTR/XT F: Rock Shox Quadra 5	$ 793 – $ 1,073
Bokor C: Deore XTR/XT F: Tange	$ 766 – $ 1,036
Bokor C: STX-RC F: Rock Shox Judy XC	$ 619 – $ 837
Bokor C: STX-RC F: Rock Shox Mag 21	$ 580 – $ 785

C: – Components   F: – Fork

MODEL | PRICE RANGE

VooDoo (continued)

Model		Price Range	
Bokor C: STX-RC F: Rock Shox Quadra 21R	$	561 – $	759
Bokor C: STX-RC F: Rock Shox Quadra 5	$	540 – $	731
Bokor C: STX-RC F: Tange	$	498 – $	674
Canzo C: Deore LX F: Rock Shox Judy DH	$	882 – $	1,194
Canzo C: Deore LX F: Rock Shox Judy XC	$	853 – $	1,154
Canzo C: Deore LX F: Rock Shox Mag 21	$	830 – $	1,123
Canzo C: Deore LX F: Rock Shox Quadra 21R	$	818 – $	1,107
Canzo C: Deore LX F: Rock Shox Quadra 5	$	806 – $	1,091
Canzo C: Deore XT F: Rock Shox Judy DH	$	940 – $	1,272
Canzo C: Deore XT F: Rock Shox Judy XC	$	922 – $	1,248
Canzo C: Deore XT F: Rock Shox Mag 21	$	908 – $	1,228
Canzo C: Deore XT F: Rock Shox Quadra 21R	$	900 – $	1,217
Canzo C: Deore XT F: Rock Shox Quadra 5	$	891 – $	1,206
Canzo C: Deore XT/LX F: Rock Shox Judy DH	$	908 – $	1,228
Canzo C: Deore XT/LX F: Rock Shox Judy XC	$	882 – $	1,194
Canzo C: Deore XT/LX F: Rock Shox Mag 21	$	863 – $	1,168
Canzo C: Deore XT/LX F: Rock Shox Quadra 21R	$	853 – $	1,154
Canzo C: Deore XT/LX F: Rock Shox Quadra 5	$	842 – $	1,139
Canzo C: Deore XTR/XT F: Rock Shox Judy DH	$	960 – $	1,299
Canzo C: Deore XTR/XT F: Rock Shox Judy XC	$	950 – $	1,285
Canzo C: Deore XTR/Xt F: Rock Shox Mag 21	$	940 – $	1,272
Canzo C: Deore XTR/XT F: Rock Shox Quadra 21R	$	935 – $	1,264
Canzo C: Deore XTR/XT F: Rock Shox Quadra 5	$	929 – $	1,256
Canzo C: STX-RC F: Rock Shox Judy DH	$	863 – $	1,168
Canzo C: STX-RC F: Rock Shox Judy XC	$	830 – $	1,123
Canzo C: STX-RC F: Rock Shox Mag 21	$	806 – $	1,091
Canzo C: STX-RC F: Rock Shox Quadra 21R	$	793 – $	1,073
Canzo C: STX-RC F: Rock Shox Quadra 5	$	780 – $	1,055
D-Jab C: Deore LX F: Rock Shox Judy SL	$	859 – $	1,162
D-Jab C: Deore LX F: Rock Shox Judy XC	$	830 – $	1,123
D-Jab C: Deore LX F: Rock Shox Mag 21	$	806 – $	1,091

C: – Components   F: – Fork

MODEL   PRICE RANGE

VooDoo (continued)   🚲

Model		Price Range
D-Jab C: Deore LX F: Rock Shox Quadra 21R	$	793 – $ 1,073
D-Jab C: Deore LX F: Rock Shox Quadra 5	$	780 – $ 1,055
D-Jab C: Deore LX F: Tange	$	751 – $ 1,017
D-Jab C: Deore XT F: Rock Shox Judy SL	$	912 – $ 1,234
D-Jab C: Deore XT F: Rock Shox Judy XC	$	908 – $ 1,228
D-Jab C: Deore XT F: Rock Shox Mag 21	$	891 – $ 1,206
D-Jab C: Deore XT F: Rock Shox Quadra 21R	$	882 – $ 1,194
D-Jab C: Deore XT F: Rock Shox Quadra 5	$	873 – $ 1,181
D-Jab C: Deore XT F: Tange	$	853 – $ 1,154
D-Jab C: Deore XT/LX F: Rock Shox Judy SL	$	888 – $ 1,201
D-Jab C: Deore XT/LX F: Rock Shox Judy XC	$	863 – $ 1,168
D-Jab C: Deore XT/LX F: Rock Shox Mag 21	$	842 – $ 1,139
D-Jab C: Deore XT/LX F: Rock Shox Quadra 21R	$	830 – $ 1,123
D-Jab C: Deore XT/LX F: Rock Shox Quadra 5	$	818 – $ 1,107
D-Jab C: Deore XT/LX F: Tange	$	793 – $ 1,073
D-Jab C: Deore XTR/XT F: Rock Shox Judy SL	$	952 – $ 1,288
D-Jab C: Deore XTR/XT F: Rock Shox Judy XC	$	940 – $ 1,272
D-Jab C: Deore XTR/Xt F: Rock Shox Mag 21	$	929 – $ 1,256
D-Jab C: Deore XTR/XT F: Rock Shox Quadra 21R	$	922 – $ 1,248
D-Jab C: Deore XTR/XT F: Rock Shox Quadra 5	$	915 – $ 1,238
D-Jab C: Deore XTR/XT F: Tange	$	900 – $ 1,217
D-Jab C: STX-RC F: Rock Shox Judy SL	$	837 – $ 1,133
D-Jab C: STX-RC F: Rock Shox Judy XC	$	806 – $ 1,091
D-Jab C: STX-RC F: Rock Shox Mag 21	$	780 – $ 1,055
D-Jab C: STX-RC F: Rock Shox Quadra 21R	$	766 – $ 1,036
D-Jab C: STX-RC F: Rock Shox Quadra 5	$	751 – $ 1,017
D-Jab C: STX-RC F: Tange	$	721 – $ 976
HooDoo C: Deore LX F: Rock Shox Judy XC	$	561 – $ 759
HooDoo C: Deore LX F: Rock Shox Mag 21	$	520 – $ 703
HooDoo C: Deore LX F: Rock Shox Quadra 21R	$	498 – $ 674
HooDoo C: Deore LX F: Rock Shox Quadra 5	$	476 – $ 645

C: – Components   F: – Fork

MODEL	PRICE RANGE

VooDoo (continued)

Model		Price Range
HooDoo C: Deore LX F: Tange	$ 431 – $ 584
HooDoo C: Deore XT F: Rock Shox Judy XC	$ 705 – $ 954
HooDoo C: Deore XT F: Rock Shox Mag 21	$ 672 – $ 909
HooDoo C: Deore XT F: Rock Shox Quadra 21R	$ 655 – $ 886
HooDoo C: Deore XT F: Rock Shox Quadra 5	$ 637 – $ 862
HooDoo C: Deore XT F: Tange	$ 600 – $ 811
HooDoo C: Deore XT/LX F: Rock Shox Judy XC	$ 619 – $ 837
HooDoo C: Deore XT/LX F: Rock Shox Mag 21	$ 580 – $ 785
HooDoo C: Deore XT/LX F: Rock Shox Quadra 21R	$ 561 – $ 759
HooDoo C: Deore XT/LX F: Rock Shox Quadra 5	$ 540 – $ 731
HooDoo C: Deore XT/LX F: Tange	$ 498 – $ 674
HooDoo C: Deore XTR/XT F: Rock Shox JudyXC	$ 780 – $ 1,055
HooDoo C: Deore XTR/XT F: Rock Shox Mag 21	$ 751 – $ 1,017
HooDoo C: Deore XTR/Xt F: Rock Shox Quadra 21R	$ 737 – $ 997
HooDoo C: Deore XTR/XT F: Rock Shox Quadra 5	$ 721 – $ 976
HooDoo C: Deore XTR/XT F: Tange	$ 689 – $ 932
HooDoo C: STX-RC F: Rock Shox Judy XC	$ 520 – $ 703
HooDoo C: STX-RC F: Rock Shox Mag 21	$ 476 – $ 645
HooDoo C: STX-RC F: Rock Shox Quadra 21R	$ 454 – $ 614
HooDoo C: STX-RC F: Rock Shox Quadra 5	$ 431 – $ 584
HooDoo C: STX-RC F: Tange	$ 384 – $ 520
Wanga C: Deore LX F: Rock Shox Judy XC	$ 637 – $ 862
Wanga C: Deore LX F: Rock Shox Mag 21	$ 600 – $ 811
Wanga C: Deore LX F: Rock Shox Quadra 21R	$ 580 – $ 785
Wanga C: Deore LX F: Rock Shox Quadra 5	$ 561 – $ 759
Wanga C: Deore LX F: Tange	$ 520 – $ 703
Wanga C: Deore XT F: Rock Shox Judy XC	$ 766 – $ 1,036
Wanga C: Deore XT F: Rock Shox Mag 21	$ 737 – $ 997
Wanga C: Deore XT F: Rock Shox Quadra 21R	$ 721 – $ 976
Wanga C: Deore XT F: Rock Shox Quadra 5	$ 705 – $ 954
Wanga C: Deore XT F: Tange	$ 672 – $ 909

C: – Components   F: – Fork

MODEL	PRICE RANGE

VooDoo (continued) 🚲

Model	Price Range
Wanga C: Deore XT/LX F: Rock Shox Judy XC	$ 689 – $ 932
Wanga C: Deore XT/LX F: Rock Shox Mag 21	$ 655 – $ 886
Wanga C: Deore XT/LX F: Rock Shox Quadra 21R	$ 637 – $ 862
Wanga C: Deore XT/LX F: Rock Shox Quadra 5	$ 619 – $ 837
Wanga C: Deore XT/LX F: Tange	$ 580 – $ 785
Wanga C: Deore XTR/XT F: Rock Shox Judy XC	$ 830 – $ 1,123
Wanga C: Deore XTR/XT F: Rock Shox Mag 21	$ 806 – $ 1,091
Wanga C: Deore XTR/XT F: Rock Shox Quadra 21R	$ 793 – $ 1,073
Wanga C: Deore XTR/XT F: Rock Shox Quadra 5	$ 780 – $ 1,055
Wanga C: Deore XTR/XT F: Tange	$ 751 – $ 1,017
Wanga C: STX-RC F: Rock Shox Judy XC	$ 600 – $ 811
Wanga C: STX-RC F: Rock Shox Mag 21	$ 561 – $ 759
Wanga C: STX-RC F: Rock Shox Quadra 21R	$ 540 – $ 731
Wanga C: STX-RC F: Rock Shox Quadra 5	$ 520 – $ 703
Wanga C: STX-RC F: Tange	$ 476 – $ 645

Wynn 🚲

Model	Price Range
Cross America	$ 887 – $ 1,201
Cross Town	$ 862 – $ 1,167
Fire	$ 771 – $ 1,043
Orcas	$ 692 – $ 936
Passion	$ 882 – $ 1,193
Phase II	$ 890 – $ 1,204
Phase III	$ 965 – $ 1,306
Skookum	$ 947 – $ 1,281
Tahuya	$ 759 – $ 1,026
Wishbone - Track	$ 929 – $ 1,257

Zerobike 🚲

Model	Price Range
Cannibal	$ 599 – $ 810
Red Zone	$ 856 – $ 1,158
Red Zone DH	$ 965 – $ 1,305

C: – Components   F: – Fork

MODEL	PRICE RANGE

Aegis

Model	Price Range
Carbon ATB-1	$ 893 – $ 1,208
Carbon ATB-2	$ 823 – $ 1,114
Carbon ATB-3	$ 875 – $ 1,183
Carbon ATB-4	$ 813 – $ 1,099
Carbon Road-1	$ 983 – $ 1,331
Carbon Road-2	$ 943 – $ 1,276
Carbon Road-3	$ 849 – $ 1,149
Carbon Road-4	$ 798 – $ 1,080
Carbon Road-6	$ 987 – $ 1,335
Carbon Road-7	$ 916 – $ 1,240
Carbon Road-8	$ 867 – $ 1,174

Aero-Fast

Model	Price Range
#2448 Super Deluxe	$ 157 – $ 213
#2449 Heavy Duty	$ 139 – $ 188
#2456 Workhorse	$ 195 – $ 263
#2500 Deluxe Springer	$ 329 – $ 445
#2501 Deluxe Truss Rod	$ 283 – $ 383
#2502 Economy	$ 329 – $ 445
#2503 Beach Bomber	$ 207 – $ 280
#2504 Beach Bomber Economy	$ 157 – $ 213
#2505 St. Moritz	$ 195 – $ 263
#2506 Claybrook w/front carrier	$ 182 – $ 247
#2507 Gliderider	$ 217 – $ 293

Alpinestars

Model	Price Range
ASR-50	$ 187 – $ 253
ASR-100	$ 221 – $ 299
ASR-200	$ 245 – $ 332
ASR-300	$ 287 – $ 389
ASR-400	$ 346 – $ 468

C: – Components   F: – Fork

MODEL　　　　　　　　　　　　　　PRICE RANGE

Alpinestars *(continued)*

Model	Price Range
ASR-500	$ 390 – $ 527
ASR-600	$ 419 – $ 567
ASR-700	$ 492 – $ 665
ASR-900	$ 649 – $ 878
RSA-240	$ 390 – $ 527
RSA-340	$ 472 – $ 639
RSA-440	$ 619 – $ 838
RSA-740	$ 714 – $ 966
RSA-840	$ 795 – $ 1,076

American Flyer

Model	Price Range
Bobcat	$ 968 – $ 1,310
Terminator	$ 967 – $ 1,309
Z-1	$ 999 – $ 1,351

AMP Research

Model	Price Range
B3 LX F: AMP Research F3 XC	$ 820 – $ 1,109
B3 LX F: AMP Research F4 BLT	$ 858 – $ 1,161
B3 XT F: AMP Research F3 XC	$ 913 – $ 1,236
B3 XT F: AMP Research F4 BLT	$ 939 – $ 1,271
B3 XT w/disc brakes F: AMP Research F3 XC	$ 966 – $ 1,307
B3 XT w/disc brakes F: AMP Research F4 BLT	$ 982 – $ 1,328
B4 LX F: AMP Research F3 XC	$ 887 – $ 1,201
B4 LX F: AMP Research F4 BLT	$ 917 – $ 1,241
B4 XT F: AMP Research F3 XC	$ 958 – $ 1,296
B4 XT F: AMP Research F4 BLT	$ 976 – $ 1,320
B4 XT w/disc brakes F: AMP Research F3 XC	$ 992 – $ 1,342
B4 XT w/disc brakes F: AMP Research F4 BLT	$ 999 – $ 1,351

Angletech

Model	Price Range
Altitude SL	$ 901 – $ 1,219
Altitude T/C	$ 901 – $ 1,219

C: – Components　　　F: – Fork

MODEL	PRICE RANGE

Angletech/Pedal Craft

Tri Speeder	$ 932 – $ 1,261

Angletech/Rans

V-Rex GL63	$ 883 – $ 1,194

Balance

AL 150 F: Balance R.I.D.	$ 248 – $ 335
AL 150 F: RST 171B	$ 296 – $ 400
AL 250 F: Balance R.I.D.	$ 296 – $ 400
AL 250 F: RST 381	$ 353 – $ 477
AL 350 F: Answer Manitou Mach 5 Comp XC	$ 419 – $ 567
AL 350 F: Balance R.I.D.	$ 342 – $ 462
AL 450 F: Answer Manitou Mach 5 Pro XC	$ 491 – $ 664
AL 450 F: Balance	$ 408 – $ 552
AL 550 F: Answer Manitou Mach 5 Pro XC	$ 595 – $ 805
AL 550 F: Answer Manitou Mach 5 SX	$ 646 – $ 874
AL 550 F: Balance	$ 510 – $ 691
AL 750	$ 793 – $ 1,073
FS Pro 750 F: Answer Manitou EFC	$ 916 – $ 1,240
FS Pro 750 F: Answer Manitou Mach 5 SX	$ 884 – $ 1,195
Killer B	$ 228 – $ 309
Super B	$ 180 – $ 244

Barracuda

A2B	$ 290 – $ 392
A2E F: Answer Manitou Mach 5 SX	$ 585 – $ 792
A2E F: Rock Shox Mag 21	$ 585 – $ 792
A2M	$ 432 – $ 585
A2R	$ 335 – $ 454
A2RS	$ 452 – $ 612
A2T F: Answer Manitou Mach 5 SX	$ 842 – $ 1,139

C: – Components   F: – Fork

MODEL   PRICE RANGE

Barracuda *(continued)*   🚲

Model	Price Range
A2T F: Rock Shox Judy XC	$ 842 – $ 1,139
A2V F: Answer Manitou Mach 5 SX	$ 620 – $ 838
A2V F: Rock Shox Mag 21	$ 620 – $ 838
A2Z	$ 207 – $ 280
A2ZS	$ 255 – $ 345
Cuda Comp F: Answer Manitou Mach 5 SX	$ 714 – $ 966
Cuda Comp F: Rock Shox Judy XC	$ 714 – $ 966
XX Team	$ 512 – $ 692

Battle   🚲

Model	Price Range
Tomahawk LS F: Rock Shox Judy DH	$ 996 – $ 1,348
Tomahawk LS F: Rock Shox Judy XC	$ 946 – $ 1,280
VR	$ 992 – $ 1,341

Beyond Fabrications   🚲

Model	Price Range
G2-Al Integrated Suspension	$ 921 – $ 1,247

Bianchi   🚲

Model	Price Range
Advantange	$ 214 – $ 289
Avenue	$ 174 – $ 236
Bobcat	$ 123 – $ 167
Campione d'Italia	$ 474 – $ 641
Denali RC	$ 797 – $ 1,078
EL/OS Giro	$ 1,173 – $ 1,586
Eros	$ 489 – $ 661
Grizzly	$ 498 – $ 674
Grizzly RC	$ 978 – $ 1,323
Ibex	$ 454 – $ 615
Lynx	$ 252 – $ 341
Lynx SX	$ 322 – $ 435
Nyala	$ 214 – $ 289

C: – Components   F: – Fork

MODEL	PRICE RANGE

Bianchi *(continued)* 🚲

Model	Price Range
Ocelot	$ 180 – $ 244
Osprey	$ 306 – $ 414
Peregrine	$ 387 – $ 523
Premio	$ 284 – $ 384
Project 1	$ 268 – $ 363
Project 3	$ 353 – $ 478
San Remo	$ 532 – $ 719
Super G	$ 971 – $ 1,314
Super Grizzly	$ 1,201 – $ 1,625
Super Ibex	$ 702 – $ 950
Timber Wolf	$ 158 – $ 213
Trofeo	$ 348 – $ 471
TSX Chorus	$ 1,041 – $ 1,409
Veloce	$ 650 – $ 880
Volpe	$ 435 – $ 588

Bike Friday/Green Gear 🚲

Model	Price Range
Bike Two'sDay	$ 892 – $ 1,207
Metro	$ 299 – $ 405
New World Tourist	$ 471 – $ 637
Pocket Llama (MTB)	$ 547 – $ 740
Pocket Rocket (road)	$ 583 – $ 789

BikeE 🚲

Model	Price Range
7 speed	$ 368 – $ 499
21 speed	$ 430 – $ 582

Bilenky 🚲

Model	Price Range
Breakaway	$ 531 – $ 718
Breakaway Hedgehog	$ 558 – $ 755
Clubsman 853	$ 968 – $ 1,310

C: – Components   F: – Fork

MODEL	PRICE RANGE

Bilenky *(continued)*

Deluxe Tandem	$ 998 – $ 1,350
Hedgehog 853	$ 939 – $ 1,271
Hedgehog Twin	$ 998 – $ 1,350
Midlands	$ 853 – $ 1,154
Mud Puppy 853	$ 909 – $ 1,230
Planet 853	$ 985 – $ 1,333
Planet Track 853	$ 901 – $ 1,219
Pro-Am Deluxe	$ 794 – $ 1,075
Trans-Am deluxe	$ 741 – $ 1,003
Travel Clubsman S & S Coupler	$ 999 – $ 1,352

BLT

Basic Loaded Tour	$ 473 – $ 639

Bontrager

Privateer	$ 452 – $ 612
Privateer Comp	$ 652 – $ 883
Privateer S	$ 511 – $ 692
Race	$ 770 – $ 1,041
Race Lite	$ 842 – $ 1,139
Ti Lite	$ 985 – $ 1,333

Boulder Bikes

Defiant 100	$ 684 – $ 925
Defiant A/S 200	$ 756 – $ 1,023
Starship 100	$ 795 – $ 1,076
Starship AL 200	$ 892 – $ 1,207
Starship AL 300	$ 999 – $ 1,352

Bouncer

FAV Bouncing Scooter Bike	$ 132 – $ 179

C: – Components   F: – Fork

MODEL	PRICE RANGE

Breezer

Ignaz X	$ 342 – $ 463
Jet Stream	$ 842 – $ 1,139
Lightning	$ 863 – $ 1,168
Stream	$ 492 – $ 666
Thunder	$ 669 – $ 905

Brompton

L5	$ 366 – $ 495

Bruce Gordon

Rock 'n Road Tour	$ 842 – $ 1,139
Rock 'n Road Tour EX	$ 842 – $ 1,139

Bully

Big Block	$ 255 – $ 344

Burley

Rock 'n Roll	$ 789 – $ 1,068
Rumba	$ 684 – $ 926
Samba	$ 653 – $ 883
Samba Softride	$ 743 – $ 1,068
Zydeco	$ 512 – $ 692
Zydeco Mixte-X	$ 540 – $ 730

Caloi

Elite-XC	$ 390 – $ 527
Expert	$ 235 – $ 319
Expert-XC	$ 301 – $ 407
Pro	$ 255 – $ 344
Pro-XC	$ 346 – $ 468
Sigma	$ 346 – $ 468

C: – Components   F: – Fork

MODEL		PRICE RANGE		
Caloi (continued)				🚲
Sigma-XC	$	432	– $	584
Sport	$	207	– $	279
Supra	$	182	– $	246
Team-LX	$	390	– $	527
Team-LX-XC	$	512	– $	692
Team-XT-XC	$	731	– $	989
Cannondale				🚲
F1000	$	806	– $	1,090
F200	$	283	– $	383
F400	$	385	– $	521
F400 Polished	$	434	– $	587
F500	$	434	– $	587
F500 Polished	$	481	– $	651
F600	$	572	– $	773
F700	$	696	– $	941
F3000	$	1,010	– $	1,367
H200	$	229	– $	310
H300	$	262	– $	354
H400	$	335	– $	453
H600	$	480	– $	650
H700	$	541	– $	732
H800	$	593	– $	803
Killer V 500	$	434	– $	587
Killer V 500 Polished	$	481	– $	651
Killer V 900	$	593	– $	803
M200 LE	$	229	– $	310
M200 LE Mixte	$	229	– $	310
M200 SE	$	229	– $	310
M300	$	283	– $	383
M400	$	334	– $	452

C: – Components   F: – Fork

MODEL	PRICE RANGE
Cannondale (continued)	🚲
M500	$ 426 – $ 576
M800	$ 434 – $ 587
M900	$ 593 – $ 803
MT1000	$ 871 – $ 1,178
MT3000	$ 1,111 – $ 1,504
R300	$ 360 – $ 487
R400	$ 458 – $ 619
R500	$ 481 – $ 651
R500 Polished	$ 527 – $ 714
R500 Compact	$ 481 – $ 651
R600	$ 572 – $ 773
R700	$ 696 – $ 941
R800	$ 734 – $ 993
R800 Compact	$ 734 – $ 993
R900	$ 1,011 – $ 1,367
R900X	$ 797 – $ 1,078
R1000	$ 1,076 – $ 1,455
R2000	$ 1,127 – $ 1,525
RT2000	$ 960 – $ 1,299
SR500	$ 635 – $ 859
SR900	$ 903 – $ 1,221
Super V Active 1000	$ 932 – $ 1,261
Super V Active 2000	$ 973 – $ 1,316
Super V Active 3000	$ 1,094 – $ 1,481
Super V Carbon 700	$ 614 – $ 831
Super V Carbon 900	$ 771 – $ 1,043
T400	$ 360 – $ 487
T700	$ 483 – $ 654
T1000	$ 614 – $ 831

C: – Components   F: – Fork

MODEL	PRICE RANGE

Carbonframes

Tetra Pro Chorus	$ 993 – $ 1,343
Tetra Pro Ultegra	$ 982 – $ 1,328
Tetra Tri Dura-Ace	$ 999 – $ 1,352
Tetra Tri Ultegra	$ 990 – $ 1,340

Catamount Cycles

Catamount MFS LX	$ 873 – $ 1,181
Catamount MFS XT	$ 939 – $ 1,271
Catamount MFS XTR	$ 999 – $ 1,352

Cherry Bicycles

Cherry Bomb F: Buyer's choice C: Athena	$ 848 – $ 1,147
Cherry Bomb F: Buyer's choice C: Chorus	$ 895 – $ 1,210
Cherry Bomb F: Buyer's choice C: 105SC	$ 802 – $ 1,085
Cherry Bomb F: Buyer's choice C: 600 Ultegra	$ 856 – $ 1,158
Cherry Bomb F: Buyer's choice C: Dura-Ace	$ 965 – $ 1,306
Cherry Bomb MTB Components LX F: Rock Shox Quadra 21R	$ 761 – $ 1,029
Cherry Bomb MTB Components XT F: Rock Shox Quadra 21R	$ 840 – $ 1,136
Cherry Bomb MTB Components XTR F: Rock Shox Quadra 21R	$ 923 – $ 1,249
Cherry Bomb MTB C: LX F: Rock Shox Judy SL	$ 834 – $ 1,129
Cherry Bomb MTB C: LX F: Rock Shox Judy XC	$ 794 – $ 1,075
Cherry Bomb MTB C: LX F: Rock Shox Mag 21	$ 769 – $ 1,040
Cherry Bomb MTB C: XT F: Rock Shox Judy SL	$ 899 – $ 1,216
Cherry Bomb MTB C: XT F: Rock Shox Judy XC	$ 867 – $ 1,173
Cherry Bomb MTB C: XT F: Rock Shox Mag 21	$ 846 – $ 1,145

C: – Components   F: – Fork

MODEL	PRICE RANGE

Cherry Bicycles (continued)

Model	Price Range
Cherry Bomb MTB C: XTR F: Rock Shox Judy SL	$ 962 – $ 1,302
Cherry Bomb MTB C: XTR F: Rock Shox Judy XC	$ 942 – $ 1,274
Cherry Bomb MTB C: XTR F: Rock Shox Mag 21	$ 927 – $ 1,255
Cherry Cordial F: Buyer's choice C: Athena	$ 887 – $ 1,201
Cherry Cordial F: Buyer's choice C: Chorus	$ 927 – $ 1,255
Cherry Cordial F: Buyer's choice C: Record	$ 983 – $ 1,330
Cherry Cordial F: Buyer's choice C: 105SC	$ 848 – $ 1,147
Cherry Cordial F: Buyer's choice C: 600 Ultegra	$ 895 – $ 1,210
Dear John C: LX F: Rock Shox Judy XC	$ 755 – $ 1,022
Dear John C: LX F: Rock Shox Mag 21	$ 727 – $ 984
Dear John C: LX F: Rock Shox Quadra 21R	$ 719 – $ 972
Dear John C: LX F: Rock Shox Judy SL	$ 799 – $ 1,081
Dear John C: XT F: Rock Shox Judy SL	$ 871 – $ 1,179
Dear John C: XT F: Rock Shox Judy XC	$ 836 – $ 1,130
Dear John C: XT F: Rock Shox Mag 21	$ 813 – $ 1,099
Dear John C: XT F: Rock Shox Quadra 21R	$ 805 – $ 1,090
Dear John C: XTR F: Rock Shox Judy SL	$ 944 – $ 1,277
Dear John C: XTR F: Rock Shox Judy XC	$ 920 – $ 1,244
Dear John C: XTR F: Rock Shox Mag 21	$ 903 – $ 1,222
Dear John C: XTR F: Rock Shox Quadra 21R	$ 898 – $ 1,215
Fat Boy F: Buyer's choice C: Athena	$ 921 – $ 1,247
Fat Boy F: Buyer's choice C: Chorus	$ 954 – $ 1,291
Fat Boy F: Buyer's choice C: Record	$ 995 – $ 1,346
Fat Boy F: Buyer's choice C: 105SC	$ 887 – $ 1,201
Fat Boy F: Buyer's choice C: 600 Ultegra	$ 927 – $ 1,255
Titanium-DB	$ 997 – $ 1,349
Titanium F: Buyer's choice C: Athena	$ 980 – $ 1,326
Titanium F: Buyer's choice C: Chorus	$ 995 – $ 1,346

C: – Components   F: – Fork

1996

MODEL	PRICE RANGE

Cherry Bicycles (*continued*) 🚲

Model	Price Range
Titanium F: Buyer's choice C: 105SC	$ 961 – $ 1,300
Titanium F: Buyer's choice C: 600 Ultegra	$ 983 – $ 1,330
Titanium MTB-DB F: Rock Shox Judy XC	$ 999 – $ 1,352
Titanium MTB-DB F: Rock Shox Mag 21	$ 996 – $ 1,348
Titanium MTB-DB F: Rock Shox Quadra 21R	$ 995 – $ 1,346
Titanium MTB C: LX F: Rock Shox Judy SL	$ 983 – $ 1,330
Titanium MTB C: LX F: Rock Shox Judy XC	$ 968 – $ 1,310
Titanium MTB C: LX F: Rock Shox Mag 21	$ 958 – $ 1,296
Titanium MTB C: LX F: Rock Shox Quadra 21R	$ 954 – $ 1,291
Titanium MTB C: XT F: Rock Shox Judy SL	$ 999 – $ 1,352
Titanium MTB C: XT F: Rock Shox Judy XC	$ 993 – $ 1,343
Titanium MTB C: XT F: Rock Shox Mag 21	$ 987 – $ 1,335
Titanium MTB C: XT F: Rock Shox Quadra 21R	$ 985 – $ 1,332

Cignal 🚲

Model	Price Range
Bimini	$ 177 – $ 240
Cherokee	$ 117 – $ 158
Dorado SX	$ 264 – $ 358
Kokomo	$ 147 – $ 199
Lil Foxx	$ 65 – $ 87
Mantauk	$ 255 – $ 345
Melbourne Express	$ 338 – $ 457
Miss Daisy	$ 59 – $ 80
Montero	$ 142 – $ 193
Ozark C: Alivio	$ 167 – $ 227
Ozark C: Tourney TY-15	$ 91 – $ 144
Ranger	$ 96 – $ 130
Rialto	$ 122 – $ 165
Silverado	$ 320 – $ 432
Top Gun F: BMX tubular	$ 59 – $ 87
Village Velo 3 CB	$ 207 – $ 280

C: – Components   F: – Fork

140

MODEL		PRICE RANGE

Cignal *(continued)*

Village Velo CB	$	152 – $	206
Village Velo FW	$	137 – $	186
Zanzibar	$	207 – $	280

Ciocc

EL-OS Athena	$	873 – $	1,181
EL-OS Chorus	$	924 – $	1,250
EL-OS Record	$	989 – $	1,338
Gara Avanti	$	465 – $	629
Gara Mirage	$	502 – $	679
Gara Mirage Triple	$	517 – $	700
Gara Veloce	$	540 – $	730
Mini Max Athena	$	886 – $	1,198
Mini Max Chorus	$	933 – $	1,262
Mini Max Record	$	992 – $	1,343
SLX Athena	$	811 – $	1,098
SLX Chorus	$	873 – $	1,181
SLX Record	$	965 – $	1,306
SLX Veloce	$	708 – $	958
Thron Fillet Mirage	$	606 – $	820
Thron Fillet Mirage Triple	$	620 – $	838
Thron Fillet Veloce	$	640 – $	865
Thron Lugged Mirage	$	596 – $	806
Thron Lugged Mirage Triple	$	611 – $	827
Thron Lugged Veloce	$	630 – $	852

Co-Motion

Cappuccino	$	965 – $	1,306
Co-Pilot	$	794 – $	1,075
Co-Pilot Offroad	$	794 – $	1,075
Custom Fillet Offroad	$	933 – $	1,262

C: – Components   F: – Fork

MODEL	PRICE RANGE

Cignal (continued) 🚲

Custom Fillet Road	$ 93 – $ 1,262
Custom Softride	$ 925 – $ 1,252
Custom TIG Offroad	$ 883 – $ 1,194
Custom TIG Road	$ 883 – $ 1,194
Custom Titanium	$ 999 – $ 1,352
Custom Titanium Offroad	$ 999 – $ 1,352
Espresso	$ 831 – $ 1,124
Java	$ 989 – $ 1,338
Mocha	$ 929 – $ 1,257
Mocha Long	$ 929 – $ 1,257
Speedster	$ 945 – $ 1,279

Conejo 🚲

AP/5 Downhill	$ 991 – $ 1,340
AP/5 LX	$ 860 – $ 1,163
AP/5 XT	$ 969 – $ 1,310
ARS/5 LX	$ 777 – $ 1,051
ARS/5 XT	$ 888 – $ 1,201
ARS/5 XTR	$ 997 – $ 1,349
Puma Road	$ 999 – $ 1,352
Viper C: Shimano 105SC	$ 740 – $ 1,001
Viper C: Shimano 600 Ultegra	$ 793 – $ 1,073

Crankin Cycles 🚲

Dirt Rocket XT	$ 901 – $ 1,219
Dirt Rocket XTR	$ 969 – $ 1,311
Hot Rod 650	$ 925 – $ 1,252
Hot Rod 650 Ace	$ 955 – $ 1,292
Hot Rod 700 Ace	$ 964 – $ 1,304
Road Rocker 600	$ 883 – $ 1,194
Road Rocker 700	$ 932 – $ 1,261
Road Rocker Dura Ace	$ 946 – $ 1,280

C: – Components   F: – Fork

MODEL

PRICE RANGE

Croll

Model	Price Range
Mountain 853 C: Deore LX	$ 794 – $ 1,106
Mountain 853 C: Deore XT	$ 891 – $ 1,227
Mountain 853 C: Deore XTR	$ 969 – $ 1,333
Mountain Lugged C: Deore LX	$ 769 – $ 1,051
Mountain Lugged C: Deore XT	$ 863 – $ 1,168
Mountain Lugged C: XTR	$ 961 – $ 1,315
Mountain TIG F: Rock Shox Judy XC C: Deore LX	$ 699 – $ 958
Mountain TIG F: Rock Shox Judy XC C: Deore XT	$ 809 – $ 1,094
Mountain TIG F: Rock Shox Judy XC C: XTR	$ 929 – $ 1,278
Road C: Athena	$ 895 – $ 1,210
Road C: Chorus	$ 935 – $ 1,265
Road C: Record	$ 992 – $ 1,342
Road C: 105SC	$ 823 – $ 1,114
Road C: 600 Ultegra	$ 859 – $ 1,162
Road C: Dura-Ace	$ 945 – $ 1,278

Curve

Model	Price Range
Aermet 100 Mountain	$ 999 – $ 1,352
Aermet 100 Road	$ 999 – $ 1,352

Dan/Ed

Model	Price Range
MTB-1	$ 347 – $ 469
Super Cruiser	$ 347 – $ 469

De Bernardi

Model	Price Range
Aelle Avanti	$ 422 – $ 571
Aelle Mirage	$ 459 – $ 620
Aelle Mirage Triple	$ 477 – $ 645
Cromor Avanti	$ 459 – $ 620

C: – Components   F: – Fork

MODEL	PRICE RANGE

De Bernardi *(continued)*

Model	Price Range
Cromor Deluxe Mirage	$ 496 – $ 671
Cromor Deluxe Mirage Triple	$ 560 – $ 758
Cromor Deluxe Veloce	$ 582 – $ 787
Cromor Mirage	$ 496 – $ 671
Cromor Mirage Triple	$ 512 – $ 692
Cromor Veloce	$ 534 – $ 723
EL-OS Athena	$ 859 – $ 1,162
EL-OS Chorus	$ 912 – $ 1,234
EL-OS Record	$ 984 – $ 1,331
Max Athena	$ 881 – $ 1,192
Max Chorus	$ 929 – $ 1,257
Max Record	$ 991 – $ 1,341
SL Athena	$ 755 – $ 1,022
SL Chorus	$ 826 – $ 1,118
SL Veloce	$ 640 – $ 865
SLX Athena	$ 793 – $ 1,073
SLX Chorus	$ 858 – $ 1,161
SLX Record	$ 957 – $ 1,295
Thron Athena	$ 722 – $ 976
Thron Mirage	$ 564 – $ 763
Thron Mirage Triple	$ 578 – $ 782
Thron Touring Athena	$ 722 – $ 976
Thron Veloce	$ 599 – $ 811

De Rosa

Model	Price Range
Giro D'Italia	$ 946 – $ 1,280
San Remo Veloce	$ 757 – $ 1,024

Dean

Model	Price Range
Bam Bam	$ 994 – $ 1,345
Castanza	$ 917 – $ 1,241

C: – Components   F: – Fork

MODEL	PRICE RANGE

Dean *(continued)*

Colenel	$ 952 – $ 1,288
Jester	$ 917 – $ 1,241
Oscar	$ 914 – $ 1,237

Diamondback

Apex SE	$ 322 – $ 435
Approach	$ 161 – $ 217
Assault	$ 112 – $ 152
Assault EX	$ 130 – $ 176
Axis	$ 565 – $ 764
Crestview	$ 134 – $ 182
Expert	$ 306 – $ 414
Ignitor CB	$ 76 – $ 102
Ignitor FW	$ 80 – $ 109
Interval	$ 174 – $ 235
Lakeside	$ 204 – $ 276
Outlook	$ 103 – $ 139
Outlook 24	$ 101 – $ 136
Parkway	$ 107 – $ 145
Podium 1.0	$ 503 – $ 681
Podium 2.0	$ 608 – $ 822
Reactor	$ 130 – $ 176
Reactor Pro	$ 221 – $ 299
Response	$ 254 – $ 344
Response SE	$ 345 – $ 466
Sorrento	$ 139 – $ 188
Sorrento DX	$ 178 – $ 241
Sorrento SE	$ ·195 – $ 264
Topanga	$ 195 – $ 264
Topanga SE	$ 242 – $ 327
V-Link 1.0	$ 436 – $ 590

C: – Components   F: – Fork

MODEL

PRICE RANGE

Diamondback (continued)

Model	Price Range
V-Link 3.0	$ 565 – $ 764
V-Link Pro	$ 805 – $ 1,089
Venom	$ 117 – $ 158
Viper	$ 87 – $ 118
WCF 2.0	$ 418 – $ 566
WCF 4.0	$ 470 – $ 636
WCF 6.0	$ 608 – $ 822
WCF Pro	$ 847 – $ 1,146
Wildwood	$ 130 – $ 176
Wildwood 24	$ 108 – $ 146
Zetec	$ 470 – $ 636
Zetec Pro	$ 708 – $ 958

Dirt Research

Model	Price Range
Badlands	$ 269 – $ 364
Bandelier	$ 410 – $ 555
Echo Canyon	$ 512 – $ 692
Hot Springs	$ 309 – $ 418
Kenai F: Buyer's choice	$ 645 – $ 872
Kenai F: Rock Shox Judy XC	$ 650 – $ 879
Kenai C: Grip Shift/Deore XT	$ 580 – $ 785
Kenai C: Deore XT	$ 585 – $ 792
Kings Canyon	$ 684 – $ 926
Kobuk	$ 320 – $ 433
Pecos	$ 455 – $ 615
Voyageurs AL	$ 851 – $ 1,155
Wildcat Canyon	$ 999 – $ 1,352

Dyno

Model	Price Range
Air	$ 157 – $ 213
Blaze	$ 91 – $ 123

C: – Components   F: – Fork

MODEL	PRICE RANGE

Dyno (continued) 🚲

Compe	$ 140 – $ 189
Nitro	$ 132 – $ 179
Nitro 24	$ 147 – $ 199
Slammer	$ 264 – $ 358
Sonic	$ 190 – $ 287
VFR	$ 112 – $ 151
WSX	$ 96 – $ 130

Easy Racers 🚲

EZ-1	$ 388 – $ 525
Gold Rush Replica	$ 917 – $ 1,241
Tour Easy	$ 713 – $ 964

Eddy Merckx 🚲

Corsa 0.1	$ 863 – $ 1,168
OV Pro	$ 946 – $ 1,280
Strada	$ 743 – $ 1,005
Titanium AX	$ 958 – $ 1,296

Electra Bicycle Company 🚲

BMX 4	$ 245 – $ 332
Delivery 7	$ 301 – $ 407
Deluxe 1	$ 137 – $ 185
Deluxe 7	$ 255 – $ 344

Ellsworth 🚲

FS 2/XC	$ 999 – $ 1,352
Road	$ 968 – $ 1,310
Roots Cyclocross	$ 841 – $ 1,138
Sub 22	$ 841 – $ 1,138
Truth Aluminum FS	$ 882 – $ 1,193

C: – Components   F: – Fork

MODEL	PRICE RANGE

Fat Chance

Buck Shaver	$ 669 – $ 905
Chris Chance	$ 848 – $ 1,147
Yo Eddy! Team Fat Chance	$ 873 – $ 1,181

Free Agent

Air Raid	$ 157 – $ 212
Ambush	$ 137 – $ 185
Champ	$ 88 – $ 119
Cruiser Pro	$ 207 – $ 279
Eluder	$ 106 – $ 143
Enforcer	$ 255 – $ 344
Ground Zero	$ 192 – $ 259
Maverick	$ 101 – $ 136

Fuji

Ace	$ 207 – $ 280
Blaster	$ 122 – $ 165
Blaster SX	$ 157 – $ 213
Crosstown	$ 122 – $ 165
Del Rey	$ 187 – $ 253
Finest	$ 338 – $ 457
Folder	$ 172 – $ 233
Mt. Fuji SX	$ 620 – $ 838
Mt. Fuji LTD SX	$ 743 – $ 1,005
Nevada	$ 157 – $ 213
Odessa	$ 122 – $ 165
Professional	$ 901 – $ 1,219
Roubaix	$ 473 – $ 639
Sagres	$ 157 – $ 213
Sandblaster	$ 106 – $ 144
Sandblaster SX	$ 137 – $ 186

C: – Components   F: – Fork

MODEL	PRICE RANGE

Fuji (continued)

Model	Price Range
Suncrest	$ 329 – $ 445
Suncrest SX	$ 432 – $ 585
Sundance	$ 452 – $ 612
Sundance SX	$ 549 – $ 743
Sunfire	$ 132 – $ 179
Supreme	$ 142 – $ 193
Tahoe	$ 231 – $ 313
Tahoe SX	$ 301 – $ 408
Team	$ 620 – $ 838
Thrill	$ 187 – $ 253
Thrill SX	$ 236 – $ 319
Touring Series I	$ 329 – $ 445
Touring Series II	$ 432 – $ 585

Gary Fisher

Model	Price Range
Alfresco	$ 315 – $ 426
Aquila	$ 290 – $ 392
Avant Garde	$ 192 – $ 260
Big Sur	$ 403 – $ 545
Hoo Koo E Koo	$ 368 – $ 499
Joshua X	$ 549 – $ 743
Joshua Y	$ 743 – $ 1,005
Joshua Z	$ 969 – $ 1,311
Kaitai	$ 335 – $ 454
Klunker	$ 432 – $ 585
Mamba	$ 301 – $ 408
Maniac	$ 177 – $ 240
Marlin	$ 212 – $ 287
Minnosaurus	$ 101 – $ 137
Montare	$ 484 – $ 655
Mt. Tam	$ 549 – $ 743

C: – Components   F: – Fork

MODEL	PRICE RANGE

Gary Fisher *(continued)*

Model	Price Range
Nirvana	$ 347 – $ 469
Paragon	$ 549 – $ 743
Procaliber	$ 842 – $ 1,139
Procaliber Ltd.	$ 999 – $ 1,352
Shortcut	$ 122 – $ 165
Supercaliber	$ 770 – $ 1,042
Tassajara	$ 241 – $ 326
Tyro	$ 137 – $ 186
Utopia	$ 452 – $ 612
Wahoo	$ 182 – $ 247
X-Caliber	$ 473 – $ 639
X-Caliber RX	$ 585 – $ 792
Zebrano	$ 246 – $ 332

Giant

Model	Price Range
Animator	$ 56 – $ 76
ATX 750	$ 329 – $ 445
ATX 760	$ 407 – $ 551
ATX 780	$ 503 – $ 680
ATX 830	$ 248 – $ 335
ATX 840	$ 283 – $ 383
ATX 860	$ 341 – $ 462
ATX 870	$ 395 – $ 534
ATX 875	$ 395 – $ 534
ATX 880	$ 503 – $ 680
ATX 890	$ 615 – $ 832
ATX 970	$ 375 – $ 508
ATX 980	$ 560 – $ 758
ATX 990	$ 744 – $ 1,006
Awesome	$ 120 – $ 162
Boulder	$ 108 – $ 146

C: – Components   F: – Fork

MODEL	PRICE RANGE
Giant *(continued)*	🚲
Boulder 500	$ 113 – $ 152
Boulder 520	$ 134 – $ 182
Boulder 550	$ 149 – $ 201
CFR-1	$ 689 – $ 932
CFR-2	$ 624 – $ 844
CFR-3	$ 440 – $ 596
Commotion	$ 100 – $ 136
Farrago	$ 149 – $ 201
Frantic	$ 81 – $ 109
HCM-1	$ 440 – $ 596
Iguana 630	$ 172 – $ 233
Iguana 640	$ 191 – $ 258
Iguana 640 SE	$ 223 – $ 302
Iguana 650	$ 228 – $ 308
Iguana 650 SE	$ 272 – $ 369
Innova	$ 223 – $ 302
Kronos	$ 307 – $ 416
Kronos GS	$ 207 – $ 280
MCM-1	$ 884 – $ 1,196
MCM-2	$ 732 – $ 990
Mosh	$ 100 – $ 136
Mosh AL	$ 196 – $ 265
Nutra	$ 177 – $ 239
Prodigy	$ 354 – $ 479
Pudd'n	$ 56 – $ 76
Taffy	$ 76 – $ 102
Totally Awesome	$ 160 – $ 217
Giordana	🚲
Replica	$ 648 – $ 877
Stelvio Veloce	$ 743 – $ 1,005

C: – Components   F: – Fork

1996

MODEL   PRICE RANGE

Giordana *(continued)*   🚲

Titanium AL	$ 770 – $ 1,042
XL-Eco	$ 863 – $ 1,168
XL-Strada	$ 645 – $ 872
XL-Super Leggero	$ 946 – $ 1,280

Gonzo   🚲

KGB #1	$ 729 – $ 986

GT   🚲

Avalanche F: GT Bologna Lite	$ 432 – $ 585
Avalanche F: Rock Shox Quadra 21R	$ 499 – $ 675
Avalanche LE	$ 582 – $ 787
Backwoods	$ 285 – $ 385
Force	$ 361 – $ 488
Fueler	$ 207 – $ 280
Fury	$ 655 – $ 886
Interceptor	$ 140 – $ 190
Karakoram F: GT Bologna Lite	$ 331 – $ 448
Karakoram F: Rock Shox Quadra 21R	$ 376 – $ 508
LTS-1	$ 826 – $ 1,118
LTS-2	$ 667 – $ 903
LTS-3	$ 450 – $ 608
Mach One	$ 158 – $ 214
Mach Two	$ 209 – $ 306
Mini Mach One	$ 156 – $ 211
Outpost	$ 147 – $ 198
Outpost Trail	$ 125 – $ 169
Pantera F: GT Bologna Lite	$ 339 – $ 458
Pantera F: Rock Shox Quadra 21R	$ 412 – $ 557
Performer	$ 158 – $ 214
Pro Freestyle Tour	$ 236 – $ 320

C: – Components   F: – Fork

1996 (side tab)

MODEL	PRICE RANGE

GT *(continued)*

Model		Price Range	
Pro Freestyle Tour Team	$	320 – $	433
Pro Series	$	218 – $	294
Pro Series 24	$	224 – $	303
Pro Series Team	$	304 – $	412
Rage	$	589 – $	797
Rebound	$	223 – $	302
Ricochet	$	316 – $	427
RTS-1	$	812 – $	1,099
RTS-2	$	629 – $	851
RTS-3	$	415 – $	562
Speed Series	$	265 – $	358
Speed Series Team	$	350 – $	474
Strike	$	483 – $	653
Talera	$	179 – $	243
Tempest	$	223 – $	302
Tequesta	$	260 – $	352
Timberline F: GT	$	211 – $	285
Timberline F: Rock Shox Quadra 5	$	284 – $	385
Vertigo	$	134 – $	181
Zaskar	$	737 – $	997

Guerciotti

Model		Price Range	
Cromor Avanti	$	542 – $	733
Cromor Mirage	$	576 – $	780
Cromor Mirage Triple	$	590 – $	799
Cromor Veloce	$	611 – $	827
EL-OS Athena	$	878 – $	1,188
EL-OS Chorus	$	927 – $	1,254
EL-OS Record	$	990 – $	1,340
Genius Athena	$	901 – $	1,219
Genius Chorus	$	945 – $	1,278

C: – Components   F: – Fork

1996

MODEL PRICE RANGE

Guerciotti(*continued*)

Model	Price Range
Genius Record	$ 996 – $ 1,348
PRX Veloce	$ 713 – $ 964
PRX Athena	$ 946 – $ 1,280
PRX Chorus	$ 876 – $ 1,185
PRX Record	$ 967 – $ 1,308
SL Athena	$ 780 – $ 1,056
SL Chorus	$ 848 – $ 1,147
SL Veloce	$ 669 – $ 905

Guru

Model	Price Range
Kuku DH II	$ 989 – $ 1,338
R66	$ 808 – $ 1,093
Sestrieres	$ 964 – $ 1,328
Sherpa-FTE	$ 982 – $ 1,328

Hampton

Model	Price Range
Hampton Cruiser-3CB	$ 137 – $ 186
Hampton Cruiser-6	$ 127 – $ 172
Hampton Cruiser Alloy	$ 101 – $ 137
Hampton Cruiser Steel	$ 91 – $ 123

Hanebrink

Model	Price Range
Extreme Terrain 2000	$ 968 – $ 1,310

Haro

Model	Price Range
Basher	$ 190 – $ 257
Blaster	$ 86 – $ 116
Elite Cruiser	$ 368 – $ 499
Elite Junior	$ 355 – $ 481
Elite Pro	$ 368 – $ 499
Escape A0	$ 278 – $ 377

C: – Components F: – Fork

1996

154

MODEL

PRICE RANGE

Haro *(continued)*

Model	Price Range
Escape A1	$ 390 – $ 528
Escape A2	$ 558 – $ 755
Escape A3	$ 740 – $ 1,001
Escape A4	$ 985 – $ 1,333
Extreme EX-1	$ 473 – $ 639
Extreme EX-2	$ 714 – $ 966
Group 1 Ci	$ 137 – $ 186
Group 1 Si	$ 170 – $ 230
Group 1 Si 24	$ 200 – $ 270
Group 1 Si Al	$ 255 – $ 344
Group 1 Ti	$ 106 – $ 144
Group 1 Zi	$ 99 – $ 134
Shredder	$ 142 – $ 193
Shredder Deluxe	$ 142 – $ 193
Shredder Mag	$ 157 – $ 212
Super Blammo	$ 386 – $ 522
Ultra	$ 347 – $ 469
Vector V0I	$ 132 – $ 179
Vector V1E	$ 150 – $ 203
Vector V20S	$ 185 – $ 250
Vector V24	$ 137 – $ 186
Vector V24S	$ 187 – $ 253
Vector V2C	$ 170 – $ 230
Vector V3A	$ 195 – $ 263
Vector V3S	$ 217 – $ 293
Vector V4R	$ 231 – $ 313
Vector V4S	$ 278 – $ 377

High Zoot

Model	Price Range
Stealth Elite	$ 988 – $ 1,337
Stealth Premium	$ 936 – $ 1,267

C: – Components   F: – Fork

1996

MODEL	PRICE RANGE

High Zoot (continued)

Model	Price Range
Talon AMP Elite	$ 969 – $ 1,311
Talon AMP Premium	$ 897 – $ 1,214
Talon Strut Elite	$ 982 – $ 1,329

Hoffman

Model	Price Range
Big Daddy	$ 292 – $ 395
Condor	$ 326 – $ 442
Sugar Baby	$ 238 – $ 322
Taj	$ 253 – $ 342

Ibis

Model	Price Range
EZ Street	$ 945 – $ 1,279
Mojo	$ 898 – $ 1,215
Szazbo	$ 983 – $ 1,330

Iron Horse

Model	Price Range
ARS 600	$ 255 – $ 345
ARS 680	$ 377 – $ 528
ARS 700	$ 492 – $ 692
ARS 800	$ 769 – $ 1,040
ARS 900	$ 900 – $ 1,218
ARS Comp	$ 311 – $ 420
AT 20	$ 117 – $ 158
AT 50	$ 142 – $ 193
AT 70	$ 177 – $ 240
Flite	$ 96 – $ 130
FS Works2 Manitou	$ 512 – $ 692
FS Works2 RST	$ 473 – $ 639
IFR	$ 117 – $ 158
MT 100	$ 202 – $ 273
MT 200	$ 250 – $ 339

C: – Components   F: – Fork

MODEL

PRICE RANGE

Iron Horse *(continued)*

Model	Price Range
MT 400	$ 264 – $ 358
MT 400 Suspension	$ 315 – $ 426
MT 500	$ 346 – $ 469
MT 500 Suspension	$ 432 – $ 585
Quest	$ 106 – $ 144
Typhoon	$ 157 – $ 213

Jamis

Model	Price Range
Aragon	$ 182 – $ 247
Aurora	$ 420 – $ 568
Boss Cruiser-6	$ 147 – $ 199
Boss Cruiser-CB	$ 122 – $ 165
Bossy	$ 80 – $ 123
Citizen	$ 142 – $ 193
Coda	$ 390 – $ 528
Cross Country	$ 162 – $ 220
Dakar	$ 743 – $ 1,005
Dakar Sport	$ 574 – $ 777
Dakar Team	$ 965 – $ 1,305
Dakota	$ 500 – $ 677
Dakota Al	$ 609 – $ 825
Diablo	$ 346 – $ 469
Diablo LE	$ 420 – $ 568
Dragon	$ 696 – $ 942
Durango	$ 226 – $ 306
Durango Al	$ 260 – $ 351
Earth Cruiser-1	$ 127 – $ 172
Earth Cruiser-2	$ 106 – $ 144
Earth Cruiser-6	$ 152 – $ 206
Eclipse	$ 574 – $ 777
Eureka	$ 373 – $ 504

C: – Components   F: – Fork

MODEL	PRICE RANGE

Jamis *(continued)*

Model	Price Range
Exile	$ 288 – $ 389
Explorer C: Shimano MJ-II	$ 152 – $ 206
Explorer C: Shimano Tourney TY-22	$ 132 – $ 179
Quest	$ 407 – $ 551
Tangier	$ 231 – $ 313
Taxi	$ 145 – $ 196
Ukiah	$ 187 – $ 253

Joyride

Model	Price Range
Bannana Split Swinger	$ 157 – $ 212
Daddy O' Stretch Cruiser	$ 231 – $ 312
Shockwave Stretch Cruiser	$ 255 – $ 344
Swinger	$ 182 – $ 246
Two Long Tandem Stretch Cruiser	$ 432 – $ 584

Just Two Bikes

Model	Price Range
Montage	$ 999 – $ 1,352

KHS

Model	Price Range
Aero Comp	$ 729 – $ 986
Aero Sport	$ 221 – $ 299
Aero Track	$ 324 – $ 438
Aero Turbo	$ 549 – $ 742
Alite 500	$ 255 – $ 344
Alite 1000	$ 346 – $ 468
Alite 3000	$ 472 – $ 639
Alite 4000	$ 619 – $ 838
Fleet Wood	$ 390 – $ 527
FXT Comp	$ 684 – $ 925
FXT Descent	$ 472 – $ 639
FXT Pro	$ 795 – $ 1,076

C: – Components   F: – Fork

Sidebar: 1996

MODEL	PRICE RANGE

KHS *(continued)*

Model	Price Range
FXT Team	$ 932 – $ 1,261
Montana	$ 119 – $ 161
Montana Comp	$ 381 – $ 515
Montana Crest	$ 197 – $ 266
Montana Descent	$ 319 – $ 432
Montana Pro	$ 472 – $ 639
Montana Raptor	$ 111 – $ 150
Montana Sport	$ 167 – $ 226
Montana Summit	$ 255 – $ 344
Montana T-Rex	$ 121 – $ 164
Montana Team	$ 714 – $ 966
Montana Trail	$ 137 – $ 185
Tandemania Al	$ 652 – $ 883
Tandemania Comp	$ 602 – $ 815
Tandemania Sport	$ 346 – $ 468

Klein

Model	Price Range
Adroit F: Klein Strata	$ 842 – $ 1,139
Adroit F: Rock Shox Judy SL	$ 985 – $ 1,333
Aeolus	$ 969 – $ 1,310
Attitude	$ 932 – $ 1,261
Pulse Comp F: Rock Shox Judy XC	$ 743 – $ 1,005
Pulse Comp F: Rock Shox Quadra 21R	$ 511 – $ 692
Pulse Comp F: Spinner	$ 432 – $ 584
Pulse II C: Deore XT	$ 795 – $ 1,076
Pulse II C: Deore XT/LX	$ 743 – $ 1,005
Quantum F: Klein Proprietary C: Mirage	$ 629 – $ 852
Quantum F: Klein Proprietary C: 105SC	$ 714 – $ 966
Quantum F: Klein Proprietary C: 600 Ultegra	$ 795 – $ 1,076

C: – Components   F: – Fork

MODEL	PRICE RANGE

Klein *(continued)* 🚲

Quantum II C: Campagnolo Chorus	$ 992 – $ 1,341
Quantum II C: Campagnolo Mirage	$ 751 – $ 1,016
Quantum II C: 105SC	$ 819 – $ 1,109
Quantum II C: 600 Ultegra	$ 883 – $ 1,194
Quantum Pro	$ 992 – $ 1,341

Kona 🚲

A' Ha	$ 301 – $ 407
AA	$ 567 – $ 767
Cinder Cone	$ 411 – $ 556
Explosif	$ 714 – $ 966
Fire Mountain	$ 269 – $ 363
Hahanna	$ 240 – $ 325
Hot	$ 842 – $ 1,139
Humuhumu	$ 207 – $ 279
Kapu	$ 668 – $ 904
Kilauea	$ 492 – $ 665
Koa	$ 337 – $ 456
Ku	$ 842 – $ 1,139
Kula	$ 783 – $ 1,059
Lava Dome	$ 337 – $ 456
Muni Mula	$ 452 – $ 612
Sex One	$ 668 – $ 904
Sex Two	$ 783 – $ 1,059
Sex Three	$ 917 – $ 1,241

Land Rover 🚲

| APB | $ 793 – $ 1,073 |

C: – Components   F: – Fork

MODEL	PRICE RANGE

Land Shark
Roadshark	$ 984 – $ 1,331

LeMond
Alpe d'Huez	$ 492 – $ 666
Chambrey	$ 901 – $ 1,219
Maillot Jaune	$ 969 – $ 1,311
Tourmalet	$ 473 – $ 639
Zurich	$ 714 – $ 966

Lightning
M-5	$ 901 – $ 1,219
P-38	$ 794 – $ 1,075
P-38X	$ 957 – $ 1,295
Stealth	$ 547 – $ 740
Stealth LX	$ 669 – $ 905

Linear
LWB recumbent	$ 549 – $ 743
SWB Sonic	$ 549 – $ 743
Tandem Recumbent	$ 946 – $ 1,280

Litespeed
Catalyst	$ 992 – $ 1,343
Classic	$ 958 – $ 1,296
Hiawassee	$ 683 – $ 924
Natchez	$ 683 – $ 924
Obed F: Rock Shox Judy XC	$ 897 – $ 1,214
Obed F: Rock Shox Quadra 21R	$ 823 – $ 1,114
Obed F/S F: Rock Shox Judy XC	$ 932 – $ 1,261
Obed F/S F: Rock Shox Quadra 21R	$ 862 – $ 1,166
Ocoee	$ 993 – $ 1,343

C: – Components   F: – Fork

1996

MODEL   PRICE RANGE

Litespeed *(continued)*   🚲

| Tachyon | $ 900 – $ 1,218 |
| Ultimate | $ 998 – $ 1,350 |

Living Extreme   🚲

Ozzi Roo Expert	$ 585 – $ 791
Ozzi Roo Pro	$ 743 – $ 1,005
Ozzi Roo Sport I	$ 390 – $ 527
Ozzi Roo Sport II	$ 472 – $ 639
Team 1	$ 549 – $ 742
Team II	$ 714 – $ 966
Team III	$ 795 – $ 1,076

LOCOMotion   🚲

3Al/2.5V Titanium	$ 985 – $ 1,333
7005 Aluminum	$ 901 – $ 1,219
IFS	$ 993 – $ 1,343

Lovely Lowrider   🚲

Type C 16 Mini-Stingrey	$ 253 – $ 342
Type C 20 Stingrey	$ 253 – $ 342
Type C 24 Large Stingrey	$ 253 – $ 342
Type C 26 Cruiser	$ 253 – $ 342

Mandaric   🚲

853	$ 965 – $ 1,305
Genius	$ 953 – $ 1,290
Thron	$ 666 – $ 900

Marin   🚲

| Bear Valley F: Answer Manitou Mach 5 Comp XC | $ 395 – $ 534 |
| Bear Valley F: Marin Lite | $ 324 – $ 438 |

C: – Components   F: – Fork

MODEL	PRICE RANGE

Marin (continued)

Bear Valley SE F: Answer Manitou Mach 5 Comp XC	$ 416 – $ 563
Bear Valley SE F: Answer Manitou Mach 5 Pro XC	$ 476 – $ 644
Bear Valley SE F: Answer Manitou Mach 5 SX	$ 429 – $ 580
Bear Valley SE F: Marin Lite	$ 346 – $ 468
Bear Valley SE F: Rock Shox Judy SL	$ 555 – $ 751
Bear Valley SE F: Rock Shox Judy XC	$ 485 – $ 656
Bobcat Trail	$ 211 – $ 286
Bolinas Ridge	$ 172 – $ 233
Eldrige Grade F: Answer Manitou Mach 5 Comp XC	$ 493 – $ 667
Eldrige Grade F: Answer Manitou Mach 5 Pro XC	$ 548 – $ 742
Eldrige Grade F: Answer Manitou Mach 5 SX	$ 505 – $ 683
Eldrige Grade F: Marin Lite	$ 428 – $ 578
Eldrige Grade F: Rock Shox Judy SL	$ 622 – $ 842
Eldrige Grade F: Rock Shox Judy XC	$ 557 – $ 753
Hawk Hill	$ 211 – $ 286
Hidden Canyon	$ 162 – $ 219
Indian Fire Trail F: Answer Manitou Mach 5 Comp XC	$ 620 – $ 839
Indian Fire Trail F: Answer Manitou Mach 5 Pro XC	$ 668 – $ 904
Indian Fire Trail F: Answer Manitou Mach 5 SX	$ 630 – $ 853
Indian Fire Trail F: Marin Lite	$ 563 – $ 762
Indian Fire Trail F: Rock Shox Judy SL	$ 731 – $ 989
Indian Fire Trail F: Rock Shox Judy XC	$ 675 – $ 914
Larkspur	$ 162 – $ 219
Monocoque F: Answer Manitou Mach 5 Comp XC	$ 632 – $ 856
Monocoque F: Not included	$ 530 – $ 717
Muir Woods F: Answer Manitou Mach 5 Comp XC	$ 320 – $ 433
Muir Woods F: Marin Lite	$ 245 – $ 332
Nail FRS	$ 833 – $ 1,127
Nail Trail F: Answer Manitou Mach 5 Comp XC	$ 428 – $ 580
Nail Trail F: Answer Manitou Mach 5 Pro XC	$ 488 – $ 660
Nail Trail F: Answer Manitou Mach 5 SX	$ 441 – $ 597

C: – Components   F: – Fork

MODEL		PRICE RANGE
Marin (continued)		🚲
Nail Trail F: Marin Lite	$ 359	– $ 486
Nail Trail F: Rock Shox Judy SL	$ 566	– $ 766
Palisades Trail F: Answer Manitou Mach 5 Comp XC	$ 373	– $ 505
Palisades Trail F: Marin Lite	$ 301	– $ 407
Pine Mountain F: Answer Manitou Mach 5 Comp XC	$ 535	– $ 723
Pine Mountain F: Answer Manitou Mach 5 Pro XC	$ 588	– $ 796
Pine Mountain F: Marin Lite	$ 472	– $ 639
Pine Mountain F: Rock Shox Judy SL	$ 658	– $ 891
Pine Mountain F: Rock Shox Judy XC	$ 596	– $ 806
Pine Mountain F: Rock Shox Quadra 21R	$ 546	– $ 739
Point Reyes	$ 448	– $ 606
Redwood	$ 359	– $ 486
Rocky Ridge F: Answer Manitou Mach 5 Comp XC	$ 512	– $ 693
Rocky Ridge F: Answer Manitou Mach 5 Pro XC	$ 567	– $ 767
Rocky Ridge F: Marin Lite	$ 448	– $ 606
Rocky Ridge F: Rock Shox Judy SL	$ 639	– $ 864
Rocky Ridge F: Rock Shox Judy XC	$ 575	– $ 778
Rocky Ridge F: Rock Shox Quadra 21R	$ 524	– $ 709
San Rafael	$ 211	– $ 286
Sausalito	$ 264	– $ 357
Stinson	$ 187	– $ 253
Team FRS	$ 833	– $ 1,127
Team Issue F: Answer Manitou Mach 5 Comp XC	$ 620	– $ 839
Team Issue F: Answer Manitou Mach 5 Pro XC	$ 668	– $ 904
Team Issue F: Answer Manitou Mach 5 SX	$ 630	– $ 853
Team Issue F: Not included	$ 563	– $ 762
Team Issue F: Rock Shox Judy SL	$ 731	– $ 989
Team Issue F: Rock Shox Judy XC	$ 675	– $ 914
Team Marin F: Answer Manitou Mach 5 Comp XC	$ 589	– $ 797
Team Marin F: Answer Manitou Mach 5 SX	$ 600	– $ 812
Team Marin F: Marin Lite	$ 530	– $ 717

C: – Components   F: – Fork

MODEL	PRICE RANGE

Marin *(continued)*

Model	Price Range
Team Marin F: Rock Shox Judy XC	$ 639 – $ 865
Team Titanium F: Answer Manitou Mach 5 Comp XC	$ 875 – $ 1,184
Team Titanium F: Answer Manitou Mach 5 Pro XC	$ 902 – $ 1,221
Team Titanium F: Answer Manitou Mach 5 SX	$ 881 – $ 1,192
Team Titanium F: Not included	$ 842 – $ 1,139
Team Titanium F: Rock Shox Judy SL	$ 935 – $ 1,265
Team Titanium F: Rock Shox Judy XC	$ 906 – $ 1,226

Marinoni

Model	Price Range
Corsa C: Athena	$ 681 – $ 922
Corsa C: Chorus	$ 796 – $ 1,076
Corsa C: Veloce	$ 571 – $ 772
Estasi C: Chorus	$ 859 – $ 1,162
Estasi C: Record	$ 952 – $ 1,288
Giro C: Chorus	$ 838 – $ 1,133
Giro C: Record	$ 939 – $ 1,271
Leggero C: Chorus	$ 869 – $ 1,176
Leggero F: Record	$ 957 – $ 1,295
Panache F: Chorus	$ 888 – $ 1,202
Panache F: Record	$ 968 – $ 1,309
Squadra F: Athena	$ 704 – $ 952
Squadra F: Chorus	$ 820 – $ 1,109
Squadra F: Record	$ 929 – $ 1,257
Tourismo F: Athena	$ 696 – $ 942
Ultimo F: Chorus	$ 888 – $ 1,202

Masi

Model	Price Range
Gran Corsa Components Sachs 5000 Other Features	$ 542 – $ 734
Gran Corsa Components Sachs 5000 Other Features	$ 628 – $ 849
Gran Corsa C: Sachs New Success Other Features	$ 696 – $ 942
Gran Corsa C: Sachs New Success Other Features	$ 785 – $ 1,062

C: – Components   F: – Fork

MODEL		PRICE RANGE
Masi (continued)		🚲
Gran Corsa C: 600 Ultegra	$ 802 –	$ 1,085
Gran Corsa C: Dura-Ace	$ 958 –	$ 1,296
Gran Corsa F: Masi C: Campagnolo Athena	$ 749 –	$ 1,013
Gran Corsa F: Masi C: Campagnolo Chorus	$ 809 –	$ 1,095
Gran Corsa F: Masi C: Campagnolo Record	$ 922 –	$ 1,247
Gran Corsa F: Masi C: Campagnolo Veloce	$ 673 –	$ 911
Gran Criterium C: Campagnolo Athena	$ 903 –	$ 1,222
Gran Criterium C: Campagnolo Chorus	$ 939 –	$ 1,271
Gran Criterium C: Campagnolo Record	$ 993 –	$ 1,343
Gran Criterium C: Campagnolo Veloce	$ 854 –	$ 1,155
Gran Criterium C: Sachs 5000 Other Features	$ 763 –	$ 1,032
Gran Criterium C: Sachs 5000 Other Features	$ 823 –	$ 1,114
Gran Criterium C: Sachs New Success Other Features	$ 869 –	$ 1,176
Gran Criterium C: Sachs New Success Other Features	$ 925 –	$ 1,252
Gran Criterium C: 600 Ultegra	$ 935 –	$ 1,265
Nuova Strada C: Campagnolo Athena	$ 769 –	$ 1,040
Nuova Strada C: Campagnolo Chorus	$ 826 –	$ 1,118
Nuova Strada C: Campagnolo Record	$ 933 –	$ 1,262
Nuova Strada C: Campagnolo Veloce	$ 696 –	$ 941
Nuova Strada C: Sachs 5000 Other Features	$ 569 –	$ 770
Nuova Strada C: Sachs 5000 Other Features	$ 652 –	$ 882
Nuova Strada C: Sachs New Success Other Features	$ 718 –	$ 972
Nuova Strada C: Sachs New Success Other Features	$ 803 –	$ 1,087
Nuova Strada C: 600 Ultegra	$ 820 –	$ 1,109
Nuova Strada C: Dura-Ace	$ 966 –	$ 1,306
Team 3V C: Campagnolo Athena	$ 846 –	$ 1,145
Team 3V C: Campagnolo Chorus	$ 893 –	$ 1,208
Team 3V C: Campagnolo Record	$ 971 –	$ 1,314
Team 3V C: Campagnolo Veloce	$ 785 –	$ 1,063
Team 3V C: Sachs 5000 Other Features	$ 678 –	$ 917
Team 3V C: Sachs 5000 Other Features	$ 749 –	$ 1,013

C: – Components   F: – Fork

MODEL	PRICE RANGE

Masi *(continued)*

Team 3V	C: Sachs New Success Other Features	$ 805 – $ 1,089
Team 3V	C: Sachs New Success Other Features	$ 874 – $ 1,183
Team 3V	C: 600 Ultegra	$ 887 – $ 1,200
Team 3V	C: Dura-Ace	$ 991 – $ 1,341
Tre Volumetrica	C: Campagnolo Athena	$ 876 – $ 1,186
Tre Volumetrica	C: Campagnolo Chorus	$ 917 – $ 1,241
Tre Volumetrica	C: Campagnolo Record	$ 984 – $ 1,331
Tre Volumetrica	C: Campagnolo Veloce	$ 821 – $ 1,111
Tre Volumetrica	C: Sachs 5000 Other Features	$ 722 – $ 977
Tre Volumetrica	C: Sachs 5000 Other Features	$ 787 – $ 1,065
Tre Volumetrica	C: Sachs New Success Other Features	$ 839 – $ 1,135
Tre Volumetrica	C: Sachs New Success Other Features	$ 901 – $ 1,219
Tre Volumetrica	C: 600 Ultegra	$ 913 – $ 1,235
Tre Volumetrica	C: Dura-Ace	$ 998 – $ 1,350

MCS

Hurricane Jr.	$ 187 – $ 253
Magnum Pro	$ 182 – $ 246
Magnum XLX Team	$ 278 – $ 377

Merlin

Mountain	$ 992 – $ 1,342
RSR	$ 896 – $ 1,212
Taiga	$ 878 – $ 1,188

Mikado

Azimut	$ 296 – $ 401
Cartier	$ 202 – $ 273
de Champlain	$ 259 – $ 351
Marco Polo	$ 452 – $ 612
Radisson	$ 364 – $ 492
Zenith	$ 328 – $ 444

C: – Components   F: – Fork

MODEL		PRICE RANGE

Mohawk 🚲

200 Industrial Trike	$ 255 – $ 344
240 Industrial Trike	$ 283 – $ 382

Mondonico 🚲

Diamond Extra	C: Campagnolo Athena	$ 845 – $ 1,143
Diamond Extra	C: Campagnolo Chorus	$ 891 – $ 1,206
Diamond Extra	C: Campagnolo Record	$ 971 – $ 1,313
Diamond Extra	C: Campagnolo Veloce	$ 784 – $ 1,061
Diamond Extra	C: Sachs 5000 Other Features	$ 676 – $ 915
Diamond Extra	C: Sachs 5000 Other Features	$ 757 – $ 1,024
Diamond Extra	C: Sachs New Success Other Features	$ 803 – $ 1,087
Diamond Extra	C: Sachs New Success Other Features	$ 873 – $ 1,181
Diamond Extra	C: 600 Ultegra	$ 886 – $ 1,199
Diamond Extra	C: Dura-Ace	$ 991 – $ 1,341
Diamond SLX	C: Campagnolo Athena	$ 830 – $ 1,123
Diamond SLX	C: Campagnolo Chorus	$ 879 – $ 1,189
Diamond SLX	C: Campagnolo Record	$ 964 – $ 1,304
Diamond SLX	C: Campagnolo Veloce	$ 767 – $ 1,037
Diamond SLX	C: Sachs 5000 Other Features	$ 654 – $ 885
Diamond SLX	C: Sachs 5000 Other Features	$ 728 – $ 985
Diamond SLX	C: Sachs New Success Other Features	$ 786 – $ 1,064
Diamond SLX	C: Sachs New Success Other Features	$ 860 – $ 1,163
Diamond SLX	C: 600 Ultegra	$ 873 – $ 1,181
Diamond SLX	C: Dura-Ace	$ 987 – $ 1,335
Elos	C: Campagnolo Athena	$ 901 – $ 1,219
Elos	C: Campagnolo Chorus	$ 937 – $ 1,268
Elos	C: Campagnolo Record	$ 992 – $ 1,342
Elos	C: Campagnolo Veloce	$ 851 – $ 1,151
Elos	C: Sachs 5000 Other Features	$ 759 – $ 1,027
Elos	C: Sachs 5000 Other Features	$ 820 – $ 1,109
Elos	C: Sachs New Success Other Features	$ 866 – $ 1,172

C: – Components   F: – Fork

MODEL	PRICE RANGE

Mondonico (continued)

Model			Price Range
Elos	C:	Sachs New Success Other Features	$ 923 – $ 1,249
Elos	C:	600 Ultegra	$ 933 – $ 1,262
Futura	C:	Campagnolo Athena	$ 737 – $ 997
Futura	C:	Campagnolo Chorus	$ 798 – $ 1,080
Futura	C:	Campagnolo Record	$ 915 – $ 1,238
Futura	C:	Campagnolo Veloce	$ 659 – $ 891
Futura	C:	Sachs 5000 Other Features	$ 526 – $ 712
Futura	C:	Sachs 5000 Other Features	$ 613 – $ 829
Futura	C:	Sachs New Success Other Features	$ 683 – $ 924
Futura	C:	Sachs New Success Other Features	$ 774 – $ 1,047
Futura	C:	600 Ultegra	$ 791 – $ 1,070
Futura	C:	Dura-Ace	$ 953 – $ 1,289
Futura Leggro	C:	Campagnolo Athena	$ 777 – $ 1,051
Futura Leggro	C:	Campagnolo Chorus	$ 833 – $ 1,127
Futura Leggro	C:	Campagnolo Record	$ 939 – $ 1,270
Futura Leggro	C:	Campagnolo Veloce	$ 705 – $ 954
Futura Leggro	C:	Sachs 5000 Other Features	$ 581 – $ 785
Futura Leggro	C:	Sachs 5000 Other Features	$ 662 – $ 895
Futura Leggro	C:	Sachs New Success Other Features	$ 727 – $ 984
Futura Leggro	C:	Sachs New Success Other Features	$ 811 – $ 1,097
Futura Leggro	C:	600 Ultegra	$ 827 – $ 1,119
Futura Leggro	C:	Dura-Ace	$ 969 – $ 1,311

Mongoose

Model	Price Range
Alta	$ 336 – $ 454
Alta SX	$ 440 – $ 596
Amplifier 2 Comp	$ 699 – $ 946
Amplifier 2 Team	$ 1,188 – $ 1,607
Crossway 250	$ 166 – $ 225
Crossway 450	$ 214 – $ 290
Crossway 650	$ 261 – $ 353

C: – Components   F: – Fork

MODEL		PRICE RANGE	

Mongoose *(continued)*

Crossway 850	$	341 – $	462
Hill Topper	$	255 – $	345
Hill Topper SX	$	352 – $	477
IBOC Comp SX	$	800 – $	1,083
IBOC Pro SX	$	1,088 – $	1,472
IBOC Road	$	670 – $	907
IBOC Team SX	$	1,248 – $	1,689
IBOC Zero-G	$	446 – $	603
IBOC Zero-G SX	$	616 – $	834
Maneuver	$	161 – $	218
Omega	$	435 – $	589
Rockadile	$	402 – $	544
Rockadile SX	$	494 – $	668
Stormer	$	154 – $	209
Switchback	$	208 – $	282
Sycamore	$	226 – $	306
Sycamore SX	$	313 – $	423
Threshold	$	184 – $	250
Threshold Sport	$	184 – $	250

Montague

Backcountry	$	236 – $	319
Crosstown	$	255 – $	345
The Urban	$	390 – $	528
TriFrame Tandem	$	900 – $	1,218

Motiv

Al T Tube	$	157 – $	212
Back Country	$	127 – $	171
Cross Creek	$	172 – $	233
Ground Pounder	$	197 – $	266

C: – Components   F: – Fork

MODEL   PRICE RANGE

Moulton

Model	Price Range
AM 5	$ 985 – $ 1,333
AM 14	$ 999 – $ 1,352
APB 3	$ 599 – $ 811
APB 14 Sachs	$ 692 – $ 936
APB 14 Plus	$ 757 – $ 1,024

Mountain Cycle

Model	Price Range
Moho 7.0	$ 863 – $ 1,168
Moho CXS	$ 894 – $ 1,209
San Andreas 8.0	$ 901 – $ 1,219
San Andreas 8.6	$ 965 – $ 1,305

Mountain Sport

Model	Price Range
Adventure	$ 106 – $ 144

Mrazek Cycles

Model	Price Range
Unity HT MOC	$ 909 – $ 1,230
Unity HT Neos	$ 603 – $ 815
Unity HT Quarz	$ 757 – $ 1,024
Unity HT XT	$ 793 – $ 1,073

MountianTEK

Model	Price Range
6006 FS	$ 302 – $ 408
7008 FS	$ 347 – $ 469
Boulder	$ 147 – $ 199
Comp Al	$ 283 – $ 383
Comp St	$ 283 – $ 383
Comp XT	$ 432 – $ 585
Extreme	$ 187 – $ 253
Peak	$ 264 – $ 358
Team Issue	$ 969 – $ 1,311

C: – Components   F: – Fork

MODEL	PRICE RANGE

MTN TEK *(continued)*

Model	Price Range
Teton	$ 157 – $ 213
Traverse	$ 217 – $ 293
Vertical	$ 231 – $ 313

Nashbar

Model	Price Range
Dualie F: Rock Shox Judy XC	$ 538 – $ 727
Dualie F: Rock Shox Mag 21	$ 525 – $ 710
Dualie F: Rock Shox Quadra 5	$ 491 – $ 665
Flashback	$ 250 – $ 338

New Sense

Model	Price Range
Grant Hardtail World Cup	$ 743 – $ 1,005
Grant Pro	$ 699 – $ 946

Nishiki

Model	Price Range
Backroads	$ 217 – $ 293
Blazer	$ 142 – $ 193
Blazer FS	$ 217 – $ 293
Bravo	$ 112 – $ 151
Cascade	$ 315 – $ 426
Century	$ 145 – $ 196
Colorado	$ 269 – $ 364
Hill Razer	$ 117 – $ 158
Manitoba	$ 182 – $ 247
Pinnacle	$ 411 – $ 556
Pueblo	$ 162 – $ 220
Sport	$ 165 – $ 223

Norco

Model	Price Range
Arctic	$ 182 – $ 246
Avanti	$ 292 – $ 395

C: – Components   F: – Fork

MODEL	PRICE RANGE

Norco *(continued)*

Model	Price Range
Axia	$ 346 – $ 468
Bigfoot	$ 264 – $ 357
Bush Pilot	$ 177 – $ 239
Cherokee	$ 127 – $ 171
FTS	$ 917 – $ 1,241
Java	$ 585 – $ 791
Katmandu	$ 157 – $ 212
Kokanee	$ 207 – $ 279
Magnum	$ 324 – $ 438
Mocha	$ 492 – $ 665
Monterey Cross	$ 226 – $ 306
Mountaineer	$ 144 – $ 195
Nitro	$ 511 – $ 692
Rampage	$ 831 – $ 1,124
Sasquatch	$ 432 – $ 584
Tango	$ 368 – $ 498
Team Issue LE	$ 952 – $ 1,288
Team Issue WCS	$ 932 – $ 1,261
Torrent	$ 831 – $ 1,124

Novara

Model	Price Range
A7000	$ 278 – $ 377
A7000S	$ 278 – $ 377
Alight	$ 243 – $ 329
Alu-Pro	$ 618 – $ 836
Arriba	$ 313 – $ 423
Arroyo	$ 163 – $ 220
Aspen	$ 205 – $ 277
Corsa	$ 170 – $ 230
Dirt Rider	$ 112 – $ 158
Ponderosa	$ 388 – $ 525

C: – Components   F: – Fork

MODEL	PRICE RANGE

Novara *(continued)*

Randonne	$ 299 – $ 405
X-R	$ 231 – $ 313

Oryx

1000	$ 278 – $ 376
1000-S	$ 342 – $ 462
2000	$ 342 – $ 462
2000-S	$ 415 – $ 561
3000	$ 377 – $ 510
3000-S	$ 472 – $ 639
4000-S	$ 639 – $ 865
6000	$ 613 – $ 829
8000	$ 842 – $ 1,139

Otis Guy

Smoothie 105 Steel	$ 860 – $ 1,164
Smoothie Chorus Steel	$ 963 – $ 1,303
Smoothie Dura-Ace Steel	$ 976 – $ 1,320
Smoothie Ultegra Steel	$ 898 – $ 1,215
Soft Tail LX Steel	$ 822 – $ 1,113
Soft Tail XT Steel	$ 904 – $ 1,224
Soft Tail XTR Steel	$ 994 – $ 1,344

Outback

Hasbeltsi	$ 920 – $ 1,245
Stormin' Norman C: Uncle Sam All-American	$ 981 – $ 1,328
Stormin' Norman C: Unspecified	$ 844 – $ 1,142
The Thing	$ 934 – $ 1,264
Tricky Dic C: Uncle Sam All-American	$ 966 – $ 1,307
Tricky Dic C: Unspecified	$ 806 – $ 1,090

C: – Components   F: – Fork

MODEL

PRICE RANGE

Parkpre		
Ace	$ 137 –	$ 186
Alucomp F: RST 171B	$ 340 –	$ 460
Alucomp F: Spinner	$ 302 –	$ 408
Alumax F: Answer Manitou Mach 5 Comp XC	$ 450 –	$ 608
Alumax F: Answer Manitou Mach 5 Pro XC	$ 463 –	$ 626
Alumax F: Answer Manitou Mach 5 SX-CR	$ 511 –	$ 692
Alumax F: Rock Shox Judy SL	$ 520 –	$ 703
Alumax F: Rock Shox Quadra 21R	$ 463 –	$ 626
Alumax F: Spinner	$ 396 –	$ 536
Aluteam F: Answer Manitou Mach 5 Comp XC	$ 566 –	$ 766
Aluteam F: Answer Manitou Mach 5 Pro XC	$ 578 –	$ 782
Aluteam F: Answer Manitou Mach 5 SX-AL	$ 628 –	$ 850
Aluteam F: Answer Manitou Mach 5 SX-CR	$ 619 –	$ 838
Aluteam F: Rock Shox Judy SL	$ 693 –	$ 938
Aluteam F: Rock Shox Judy XC	$ 628 –	$ 849
Aluteam F: Rock Shox Quadra 21R	$ 577 –	$ 780
Aluteam F: Spinner	$ 517 –	$ 700
Comp Limited F: RST 381	$ 333 –	$ 451
Comp Limited F: Spinner	$ 281 –	$ 380
Deuce	$ 165 –	$ 223
Deuce Four	$ 170 –	$ 230
Deuce Four Yo Yo	$ 306 –	$ 414
Duece Pro-XL	$ 278 –	$ 377
Grand Sport	$ 157 –	$ 213
Leisure Sport	$ 137 –	$ 186
Mountain Comp F: RST 171B	$ 283 –	$ 383
Mountain Comp F: Spinner	$ 243 –	$ 329
Pro 825 F: Answer Manitou Mach 5 Pro XC	$ 706 –	$ 956
Pro 825 F: Answer Manitou Mach 5 SX-AL	$ 748 –	$ 1,012
Pro 825 F: Answer Manitou Mach 5 SX-CR	$ 742 –	$ 1,004
Pro 825 F: Rock Shox Judy SL	$ 801 –	$ 1,084

C: – Components   F: – Fork

MODEL   PRICE RANGE

Parkpre (continued)

Model	Price Range
Pro 825 F: Rock Shox Judy XC	$ 747 – $ 1,011
Pro 825 F: Rock Shox Quadra 21R	$ 705 – $ 954
Pro 825 F: Spinner	$ 656 – $ 887
Pro Elite F: Answer Manitou Mach 5 Pro XC	$ 925 – $ 1,252
Pro Elite F: Answer Manitou Mach 5 SX-AL	$ 946 – $ 1,279
Pro Elite F: Answer Manitou Mach 5 SX-CR	$ 943 – $ 1,276
Pro Elite F: Rock Shox Judy SL	$ 969 – $ 1,311
Pro Elite F: Rock Shox Judy XC	$ 945 – $ 1,279
Pro Elite F: Rock Shox Quadra 21R	$ 925 – $ 1,251
Pro Elite F: Spinner	$ 898 – $ 1,215
Pro Image F: Answer Manitou Mach 5 Comp XC	$ 698 – $ 945
Pro Image F: Answer Manitou Mach 5 SX-AL	$ 781 – $ 1,057
Pro Image F: Answer Manitou Mach 5 SX-CR	$ 776 – $ 1,050
Pro Image F: Rock Shox Judy DH	$ 801 – $ 1,084
Pro Image F: Rock Shox Judy SL	$ 831 – $ 1,124
Pro Image F: Rock Shox Judy XC	$ 781 – $ 1,057
Pro Image F: Rock Shox Quadra 21R	$ 741 – $ 1,003
Pro Image F: Spinner	$ 695 – $ 940
Scepter Comp F: Answer Manitou Mach 5 Comp XC	$ 417 – $ 564
Scepter Comp F: Answer Manitou Mach 5 Pro XC	$ 431 – $ 583
Scepter Comp F: Answer Manitou Mach 5 SX-CR	$ 481 – $ 651
Scepter Comp F: Rock Shox Judy XC	$ 490 – $ 662
Scepter Comp F: Rock Shox Quadra 21R	$ 429 – $ 581
Scepter Comp F: Spinner	$ 358 – $ 484
Solitude F: RST 171B	$ 243 – $ 329
Solitude F: Spinner	$ 202 – $ 273
Sport Limited F: RST 156	$ 219 – $ 296
Sport Limited F: Spinner	$ 185 – $ 250
Team 925 F: Answer Manitou Mach 5 Comp XC	$ 519 – $ 702
Team 925 F: Answer Manitou Mach 5 Pro XC	$ 532 – $ 720
Team 925 F: Answer Manitou Mach 5 SX-AL	$ 585 – $ 791

C: – Components   F: – Fork

MODEL	PRICE RANGE

Parkpre *(continued)*

Model	Price Range
Team 925 F: Answer Manitou Mach 5 SX-CR	$ 578 – $ 782
Team 925 F: Rock Shox Judy SL	$ 652 – $ 883
Team 925 F: Rock Shox Judy XC	$ 584 – $ 791
Team 925 F: Rock Shox Quadra 21R	$ 530 – $ 717
Team 925 F: Spinner	$ 469 – $ 634
Team Image	$ 222 – $ 313
X-Comp	$ 290 – $ 392

Pashley

Model	Price Range
DP23 Frontload Trike	$ 578 – $ 782
MW3 Worktrike	$ 684 – $ 926
No. 33 food vending trike	$ 653 – $ 883
Picabac Sprint	$ 618 – $ 836
Picador Sprint	$ 585 – $ 791
Premiere	$ 762 – $ 1,031
Prestige	$ 729 – $ 986
Prospero Original 3 Plus	$ 385 – $ 521
Prospero Princess Original 3 Plus	$ 390 – $ 527
Prospero Princess Sovereign 5	$ 469 – $ 634
Prospero Sovereign 5	$ 444 – $ 601
RH3 Carrier Bicycle w/carrier	$ 471 – $ 637
Roadster	$ 324 – $ 439
SW6	$ 440 – $ 596
SW8 Delibike w/carrier	$ 508 – $ 687
TB2 Police Cruiser	$ 525 – $ 710

Performance

Model	Price Range
Gryphon LX	$ 619 – $ 838
Gryphon XT	$ 714 – $ 966
M-006	$ 699 – $ 946
M-206	$ 411 – $ 556

C: – Components   F: – Fork

MODEL	PRICE RANGE

Performance *(continued)* 🚲

Model	Price Range
M-306	$ 381 – $ 515
M-406	$ 255 – $ 344
M-406 S	$ 296 – $ 401
M-506	$ 211 – $ 286
M-506 S	$ 255 – $ 344
M-606	$ 192 – $ 259
M-706	$ 157 – $ 212
R-006	$ 770 – $ 1,041
R-206	$ 324 – $ 438
Salmagundi	$ 882 – $ 1,193

Peugeot 🚲

Model	Price Range
Attitude	$ 127 – $ 171
Biarritz	$ 530 – $ 717
Chrono	$ 197 – $ 266
Dune Racing	$ 182 – $ 246
Dune Racing Suspension	$ 207 – $ 279
Evasion	$ 137 – $ 185
Grey Stone	$ 231 – $ 312
Horizon	$ 235 – $ 319
Hurricane Creek	$ 255 – $ 344
Liberty	$ 211 – $ 286
Nature	$ 216 – $ 293
Panorama	$ 147 – $ 199
Quantum	$ 142 – $ 192
Sprint	$ 197 – $ 266
Success	$ 368 – $ 498
Urbano	$ 157 – $ 212
X-generation	$ 157 – $ 212

C: – Components   F: – Fork

MODEL	PRICE RANGE

Pinarello

Model	Price Range
Arriba	$ 583 – $ 789
Monviso	$ 863 – $ 1,168
Ole	$ 549 – $ 742
Vuelta	$ 917 – $ 1,241

Powerlite

Model	Price Range
P-19	$ 109 – $ 148
P-28	$ 152 – $ 206
P-38	$ 172 – $ 233
P-47	$ 264 – $ 377
P-51	$ 322 – $ 436
P-61	$ 371 – $ 519
Pro Freestyle	$ 246 – $ 332
Pro Freestyle Expert	$ 160 – $ 216

ProFlex

Model	Price Range
656	$ 585 – $ 791
756	$ 652 – $ 883
856	$ 770 – $ 1,041
Animal	$ 795 – $ 1,076
Attack	$ 472 – $ 639
Attack LE	$ 549 – $ 742
Beast	$ 743 – $ 1,005

Python

Model	Price Range
Anaconda	$ 117 – $ 158
Boa	$ 346 – $ 469
Bonecrusher	$ 200 – $ 270
Mamba	$ 137 – $ 186
Medusa	$ 245 – $ 332
Opello	$ 96 – $ 130

C: – Components   F: – Fork

MODEL	PRICE RANGE

Python *(continued)*

Serpent	$ 106 – $	44
Strangler	$ 147 – $	199
Vermin	$ 96 – $	130

Quadracycle

Qudrasport Other Features	$ 652 – $	883
Qudrasport Other Features	$ 794 – $	1,075
Qudraspree Juvenile	$ 301 – $	407
Qudraspree Type A	$ 301 – $	407

Quintana Roo

Kilo	$ 762 – $	1,031
Kilo Private Reserve	$ 943 – $	1,276
QMTN	$ 653 – $	883
QMTN Pro	$ 999 – $	1,352

Race Team Ross

150 Race Tri-moly	$ 132 – $	179
152 Race Mini	$ 145 – $	196
154 Race Chromoly	$ 157 – $	213
156 Comp Chromoly	$ 207 – $	280
158 Pro Aluminum	$ 335 – $	454
Freestyle Aluminum	$ 267 – $	361
Freestyle Chromoly	$ 172 – $	233
Stock Trials	$ 585 – $	792
Trials Aluminum	$ 473 – $	639
Trials Chromoly	$ 276 – $	374

Raleigh

C30	$ 130 – $	175
C40	$ 148 – $	200

C: – Components   F: – Fork

MODEL	PRICE RANGE

Raleigh (continued)

Model	Price Range
M20	$ 100 – $ 135
M30	$ 127 – $ 172
M30FS	$ 194 – $ 263
M40	$ 146 – $ 197
M50	$ 168 – $ 227
M55	$ 190 – $ 257
M60	$ 194 – $ 263
M80	$ 241 – $ 326
M200	$ 229 – $ 309
M400	$ 307 – $ 415
M800	$ 407 – $ 550
M7000	$ 369 – $ 500
M8000	$ 478 – $ 646
M9000	$ 604 – $ 817
MCC8	$ 574 – $ 777
MCC9	$ 632 – $ 855
Mountain Scout	$ 105 – $ 141
R500	$ 343 – $ 463
R600	$ 443 – $ 599

Rans

Model	Price Range
Nimbus	$ 683 – $ 924
Response	$ 583 – $ 789
Rocket	$ 510 – $ 690
Stratus	$ 683 – $ 924
Tailwind	$ 467 – $ 631
V-Rex	$ 645 – $ 872
V-Rex 24	$ 645 – $ 872
Zero-G	$ 471 – $ 637

C: – Components   F: – Fork

MODEL   PRICE RANGE

ReBike   🚲

ReBike 2600 LE	$	315 – $	426
ReBike 2600 SE	$	301 – $	408
ReBike 707	$	255 – $	345
ReBike 818	$	278 – $	377
ReTrike 707	$	346 – $	469
ReTrike 707 VP	$	346 – $	469

Redline   🚲

MR 140	$	157 – $	213
PL-24	$	207 – $	280
Proline	$	212 – $	287
RL 240	$	157 – $	213
RL 340	$	119 – $	162
RL 340 Junior	$	106 – $	144
RL 440	$	157 – $	213
RL 640	$	219 – $	296

Research Dynamics   🚲

Coyote 975	$	132 – $	178
Coyote AFS Six	$	770 – $	1,041
Coyote Alu Five	$	492 – $	665
Coyote Cruiser	$	135 – $	182
Coyote Mow Tan	$	346 – $	468
Coyote One	$	135 – $	182
Coyote Pro Four	$	364 – $	492
Coyote STX FS	$	390 – $	527
Coyote STX Singletrack	$	283 – $	382
Coyote Team	$	207 – $	279
Coyote Team Extreme F: RD 24	$	135 – $	182
Coyote Team Extreme F: Unspecified	$	101 – $	136
Coyote Team Rider	$	175 – $	237

C: – Components   F: – Fork

MODEL	PRICE RANGE

Research Dynamics *(continued)*

Coyote Team Six	$ 606 – $ 820
Coyote Titan	$ 883 – $ 1,194
Coyote Two	$ 155 – $ 210

Rhygin

Aluminum C: Campagnolo Athena	$ 889 – $ 1,203
Aluminum C: Campagnolo Chorus	$ 923 – $ 1,249
Aluminum C: Campagnolo Record	$ 981 – $ 1,328
Aluminum C: 105SC	$ 831 – $ 1,124
Aluminum C: 600 Ultegra	$ 853 – $ 1,154
Aluminum C: Dura-Ace	$ 926 – $ 1,253
Juke C: Deore LX	$ 883 – $ 1,194
Juke C: Deore XT	$ 917 – $ 1,241
Juke C: XTR	$ 994 – $ 1,345
Metax C: Campagnolo Athena	$ 915 – $ 1,238
Metax C: Campagnolo Chorus	$ 944 – $ 1,277
Metax C: Campagnolo Record	$ 991 – $ 1,341
Metax C: 105SC	$ 863 – $ 1,168
Metax C: 600 Ultegra	$ 883 – $ 1,194
Metax C: Dura-Ace	$ 947 – $ 1,281

Ritchey

Comp	$ 743 – $ 1,005
Everest	$ 933 – $ 1,262
P-21	$ 901 – $ 1,219
Soft Tail	$ 958 – $ 1,296
Team Replica	$ 978 – $ 1,323

Robinson

| Cruiser | $ 255 – $ 345 |
| JR | $ 231 – $ 313 |

C: – Components   F: – Fork

1996

MODEL	PRICE RANGE

Robinson *(continued)*

Model	Price Range
MX	$ 172 – $ 233
Pro	$ 243 – $ 329
Rebel	$ 117 – $ 158
SST	$ 155 – $ 210
Team	$ 347 – $ 469

Rocky Mountain

Model	Price Range
Altitude	$ 850 – $ 1,150
Altitude T.O.	$ 978 – $ 1,323
Blizzard	$ 741 – $ 1,003
Cardiac	$ 255 – $ 344
Element	$ 651 – $ 881
Equipe F: Rock Shox Quadra 21R	$ 618 – $ 836
Equipe F: Tange	$ 545 – $ 738
Fusion	$ 313 – $ 423
Fusion Suspension	$ 368 – $ 499
Hammer	$ 388 – $ 525
Hammer Race	$ 471 – $ 637
Speed	$ 909 – $ 1,230
Thin Air	$ 635 – $ 859
Vertex	$ 850 – $ 1,150
Vertex T.O.	$ 978 – $ 1,323
Whistler	$ 255 – $ 344

Romic

Model	Price Range
Athena Sport	$ 783 – $ 1,059
Athena Tourer	$ 782 – $ 1,057
Chorus Eagle	$ 853 – $ 1,154
Chorus Sport	$ 838 – $ 1,133
Chorus Tourer	$ 820 – $ 1,109
Dura Ace Racer	$ 983 – $ 1,330

C: – Components   F: – Fork

MODEL	PRICE RANGE

Romic *(continued)*

Eco Sport	$ 732 – $ 990
Eco Tourer	$ 733 – $ 992
Record Racer	$ 966 – $ 1,307
RX-100 Sport Tour	$ 684 – $ 925
Texas Track Sprint	$ 684 – $ 925
Ultegra Sport	$ 798 – $ 1,080
Romic Ultegra STI Racer	$ 799 – $ 1,081
XTR Super Tourer	$ 897 – $ 1,214

Ross

Adventurer	$ 112 – $ 151
Amazon	$ 83 – $ 112
Aristocrat	$ 207 – $ 280
Beach Commander	$ 106 – $ 144
Bitsy Lady	$ 54 – $ 73
Boomerang	$ 78 – $ 105
Cherokee Country	$ 301 – $ 408
Cherokee SE	$ 207 – $ 280
Cherokee Sport SE	$ 255 – $ 345
Chimera	$ 132 – $ 179
Compact 3 CB	$ 112 – $ 151
Compact Clic	$ 101 – $ 137
Diamond Cruiser	$ 112 – $ 151
Diamond Trimatic	$ 137 – $ 186
Dune Commander	$ 106 – $ 144
Endo	$ 106 – $ 144
Eurotour	$ 112 – $ 151
Frenzy	$ 83 – $ 112
Gran Tour	$ 132 – $ 179
Grand Cherokee Laredo	$ 531 – $ 718
Grand Cherokee Limited	$ 743 – $ 1,005

C: – Components   F: – Fork

MODEL		PRICE RANGE		
Ross (continued)				🚲
Grand Cherokee SE	$	432	– $	585
Griffon	$	157	– $	213
Little Lady	$	75	– $	102
Mini Radical	$	75	– $	102
Mt. Crusier	$	132	– $	179
Mt. Jefferson	$	101	– $	137
Mt. Katahdin	$	207	– $	280
Mt. Pocono	$	112	– $	151
Mt. Rushmore	$	127	– $	172
Mt. Washington	$	152	– $	206
Peryton	$	106	– $	144
Petite Lady	$	70	– $	95
Piranha Pro	$	99	– $	134
Piranha Pro 6sp	$	122	– $	165
Piranha Pro CB	$	99	– $	134
Piranha Pro FW	$	112	– $	151
Pronto	$	54	– $	73
Renegade	$	324	– $	439
Shark	$	132	– $	179
Slinger	$	70	– $	95
Tailspin	$	67	– $	91
Teeny Lady	$	67	– $	91
Unicorn	$	101	– $	137
Wrangler Rio Grande	$	157	– $	213
Wrangler S	$	132	– $	179
Wrangler Sahara	$	182	– $	247
Wrangler SE	$	106	– $	151
Wrangler SE Sport	$	132	– $	179
Young Lady	$	78	– $	105
Zwoom	$	122	– $	165
Zwoom XII	$	157	– $	213

C: – Components   F: – Fork

MODEL	PRICE RANGE

Rotator

Model	Price Range
Coaster	$ 219 – $ 296
Coaster 7	$ 267 – $ 361
Interceptor	$ 917 – $ 1,241
Pursuit	$ 475 – $ 642

Ryan Recumbent Cycles

Model	Price Range
Duplex	$ 996 – $ 1,348
Vanguard	$ 699 – $ 946

S & B Recumbent

Model	Price Range
Single	$ 278 – $ 377
Single Alum	$ 585 – $ 792
Tandem	$ 917 – $ 1,240
Tri-Cycle	$ 401 – $ 542

Saint Marks

Model	Price Range
LR-16/B	$ 121 – $ 164
LR-20	$ 116 – $ 157
LR-20/B	$ 127 – $ 171
LR-20/BT	$ 137 – $ 185

SainTropez

Model	Price Range
Commander	$ 58 – $ 79
Contender	$ 58 – $ 79
HillWinder	$ 112 – $ 151
Lil Stuff	$ 41 – $ 55
Lookin Good	$ 58 – $ 79
Miss Sassy	$ 58 – $ 79
PathWinder	$ 91 – $ 123
Ruff Stuff	$ 54 – $ 73
SandWinder	$ 86 – $ 116

C: – Components   F: – Fork

MODEL	PRICE RANGE

Sain Tropez (continued) 🚲

TrailWinder	$ 101 – $ 137
Tuff Stuff	$ 41 – $ 55
Unicorn	$ 54 – $ 73

Santa Cruz 🚲

Heckler F: Rock Shox Judy SL	$ 818 – $ 1,107
Heckler F: Rock Shox Judy XC	$ 769 – $ 1,040
Heckler F: Rock Shox Quadra 21R	$ 741 – $ 1,003
Tazmon F: Rock Shox Judy SL	$ 925 – $ 1,252
Tazmon F: Rock Shox Judy XC	$ 892 – $ 1,207
Tazmon F: Rock Shox Quadra 21R	$ 873 – $ 1,181

Santana 🚲

Arriva	$ 996 – $ 1,348
Cilantro	$ 996 – $ 1,348
Fusion	$ 996 – $ 1,348
Rio	$ 917 – $ 1,240
Visa	$ 917 – $ 1,240
Vision	$ 917 – $ 1,240

Schwinn 🚲

Clear Creek	$ 208 – $ 282
Cruiser	$ 149 – $ 201
Cruiser Classic	$ 185 – $ 250
Cruiser Deluxe	$ 267 – $ 361
Cruiser Six	$ 191 – $ 258
Cruiser SS	$ 167 – $ 225
Cruiser Supreme	$ 185 – $ 250
Express	$ 196 – $ 266
Frontier	$ 143 – $ 193
Frontier GS	$ 155 – $ 209

C: – Components   F: – Fork

MODEL

PRICE RANGE

Schwinn *(continued)*

Model	Price Range
High Plains	$ 244 – $ 329
High Sierra	$ 313 – $ 423

Homegrown
  F: Rock Shox Judy XC
  C: Grip Shift/Deore XT
	$ 1,084 – $ 1,467

Homegrown F: Rock Shox Judy XC C: Deore XT	$ 973 – $ 1,317
Homegrown F: Rock Shox Judy XC C: Deore XT/LX	$ 893 – $ 1,208
Homegrown Factory	$ 1,184 – $ 1,602
Homegrown Factory Suspension	$ 1,323 – $ 1,790
Homegrown Factory USA	$ 1,432 – $ 1,938
Le Tour	$ 272 – $ 369
Moab.1	$ 391 – $ 529
Moab.2	$ 313 – $ 423
Moab.3	$ 267 – $ 361
Passage	$ 445 – $ 602
Range	$ 226 – $ 306
Ridge	$ 261 – $ 353
S[96].1	$ 669 – $ 905
S[96].10	$ 1,045 – $ 1,414
S[96].2	$ 570 – $ 771
S[96].20	$ 776 – $ 1,050
S[96].3	$ 519 – $ 702
S[96].30	$ 669 – $ 905
S[96].40	$ 570 – $ 771
Sidewinder	$ 185 – $ 250
Super Sport	$ 645 – $ 872
Transit	$ 161 – $ 217

Scorpio

Model	Price Range
AL-100	$ 157 – $ 213

C: – Components   F: – Fork

MODEL		PRICE RANGE

Scorpio (continued) 🚲

Model	Price Range
AL-200	$ 207 – $ 280
AL-400	$ 324 – $ 438
AL-400X	$ 432 – $ 584
AT-45	$ 85 – $ 115
AT-50	$ 96 – $ 129
AT-100	$ 119 – $ 162
AT-190	$ 132 – $ 178
AT-200	$ 142 – $ 193
AT-200X	$ 170 – $ 230
AT-400	$ 278 – $ 376
AT-400X	$ 390 – $ 527
AT-J20	$ 75 – $ 102
AZ Pro	$ 91 – $ 123
EX-200	$ 145 – $ 196
Primrose	$ 106 – $ 144
RA-200	$ 302 – $ 408
RS-100	$ 157 – $ 213

Scott 🚲

Model	Price Range
AFD-306	$ 419 – $ 567
AFD-606	$ 547 – $ 739
AFD-906	$ 934 – $ 1,263
Arapahoe	$ 197 – $ 267
Boulder	$ 348 – $ 471
Comp CST	$ 526 – $ 712
Comp Jr	$ 138 – $ 186
Dual Pro	$ 754 – $ 1,021
Elite Racing	$ 754 – $ 1,021
Expression	$ 505 – $ 684
Instinct	$ 197 – $ 266
Mahaka	$ 223 – $ 302

C: – Components   F: – Fork

1
9
9
6

MODEL	PRICE RANGE

Scott *(continued)*

Model	Price Range
Peak	$ 181 – $ 245
Pro Racing	$ 797 – $ 1,078
Santa Cruz	$ 271 – $ 367
Seattle	$ 165 – $ 223
Summit	$ 314 – $ 425
Tampico	$ 260 – $ 351
Team Jr	$ 153 – $ 208
Vantage M15	$ 339 – $ 459
Vantage M16	$ 382 – $ 517
Vertigo LSD	$ 783 – $ 1,060
Vertigo LSD Pro	$ 967 – $ 1,308
Waimea	$ 505 – $ 683
Waimea Pro	$ 946 – $ 1,280
Yecora	$ 260 – $ 351

Serotta

Model	Price Range
Atlanta Road	$ 920 – $ 1,244
ATX	$ 945 – $ 1,279
CSI-Road	$ 997 – $ 1,349

Signature

Model	Price Range
Centaur	$ 301 – $ 408
Minotaur 5	$ 255 – $ 345
Mt Hood CF 21	$ 390 – $ 528
Mt McKinley CK 24	$ 757 – $ 1,024
Mt Whitney CK 24	$ 531 – $ 718
Mt. Olympus CA 21	$ 255 – $ 345
Mt. Rainier	$ 452 – $ 612
Mt. St. Helens CA 21	$ 301 – $ 408
Pegasus 4	$ 207 – $ 280
Super Gran Tour	$ 157 – $ 213

C: – Components   F: – Fork

MODEL	PRICE RANGE

Signature (continued) 🚲

Model	Price Range
Triad	$ 347 – $ 469
Zemopi 484	$ 324 – $ 439
Zemopi 584	$ 432 – $ 585
Zemopi 684	$ 653 – $ 883
Zemopi 784	$ 883 – $ 1,194

Sling Shot 🚲

Model	Price Range
MT-1	$ 713 – $ 964
MT-2	$ 651 – $ 881
MT-3	$ 583 – $ 789
MTQ-1	$ 741 – $ 1,003
MTQ-2	$ 683 – $ 924
MTQ-3	$ 618 – $ 836
RD-1 700c	$ 794 – $ 1,075
RD-2 650c	$ 683 – $ 924
RD-2 700c	$ 683 – $ 924
RD 650c	$ 794 – $ 1,075
RDQ-1 650c	$ 818 – $ 1,107
RDQ-1 700c	$ 818 – $ 1,107
RDQ-2 650c	$ 713 – $ 964
RDQ-2 700c	$ 713 – $ 964
TR-1 650c	$ 769 – $ 1,040
TR-2	$ 651 – $ 881
TRQ-1	$ 794 – $ 1,075
TRQ-2	$ 683 – $ 924

Softride 🚲

Model	Price Range
360	$ 407 – $ 551
Century	$ 606 – $ 820
Contour	$ 677 – $ 915
Husky	$ 362 – $ 490

C: – Components   F: – Fork

MODEL   PRICE RANGE

Softride (continued)

Model	Price Range
Powerwing 650	$ 982 – $ 1,328
Powerwing 700	$ 995 – $ 1,346
Qualifier	$ 820 – $ 1,109
Sherpa	$ 492 – $ 666
Solo	$ 863 – $ 1,168
Sully	$ 820 – $ 1,109
Traveler	$ 606 – $ 820

Specialized

Model	Price Range
A1 Road	$ 552 – $ 747
A1 Sport Road	$ 646 – $ 874
Allez Sport	$ 456 – $ 617
Crossroads	$ 152 – $ 206
Crossroads Elite	$ 300 – $ 406
Crossroads Sport	$ 169 – $ 228
Crossroads Ultra	$ 211 – $ 286
Globe 3	$ 185 – $ 250
Globe 7	$ 274 – $ 371
Ground Control	$ 424 – $ 573
Ground Control A1	$ 561 – $ 759
Ground Control A1 Comp	$ 727 – $ 983
Hardrock	$ 173 – $ 235
Hardrock 20	$ 114 – $ 154
Hardrock FS	$ 248 – $ 335
Hardrock GX	$ 173 – $ 235
Hardrock Sport	$ 195 – $ 264
Hardrock Sport GX	$ 195 – $ 264
Hardrock Ultra	$ 243 – $ 329
Hotrock 20	$ 91 – $ 124
M2 Road Comp	$ 776 – $ 1,049
M2 Road Pro	$ 957 – $ 1,295

C: – Components   F: – Fork

MODEL	PRICE RANGE

Specialized *(continued)*

Model	Price Range
Rockhopper	$ 237 – $ 321
Rockhopper 24	$ 141 – $ 190
Rockhopper 26	$ 130 – $ 176
Rockhopper A1	$ 300 – $ 405
Rockhopper A1 FS	$ 350 – $ 473
Rockhopper Comp A1	$ 375 – $ 507
Rockhopper Comp A1 FS	$ 447 – $ 605
Rockhopper FS	$ 300 – $ 405
Sharkcruiser	$ 141 – $ 191
Shockrock	$ 179 – $ 242
Stumpjumper	$ 470 – $ 636
Stumpjumper A1 FS	$ 561 – $ 759
Stumpjumper FS	$ 646 – $ 874
Stumpjumper M2	$ 516 – $ 698
Stumpjumper M2 FS	$ 726 – $ 983
Stumpjumper M2 FS Comp	$ 871 – $ 1,179

Spectrum

Model	Price Range
Custom Steel F: Record	$ 999 – $ 1,352
Custom Steel F: Track	$ 901 – $ 1,219

Star Cruiser

Model	Price Range
Tradition	$ 91 – $ 123
Tradition-6	$ 104 – $ 141
Tradition LT	$ 101 – $ 137
Tradition LT-6	$ 112 – $ 151

Steelman

Model	Price Range
CC Chorus	$ 901 – $ 1,219
CC Ultegra	$ 831 – $ 1,124
Eurocross Chorus	$ 901 – $ 1,219

C: – Components   F: – Fork

MODEL	PRICE RANGE

Steelman *(continued)*

Model	Price Range
Eurocross Ultegra	$ 831 – $ 1,124
SR 105	$ 785 – $ 1,062
SR Athena	$ 863 – $ 1,168
SR Chorus	$ 901 – $ 1,219
SR Dura Ace	$ 917 – $ 1,241
SR Record	$ 972 – $ 1,314
SR Ultegra	$ 831 – $ 1,124
ST LX	$ 723 – $ 978
ST XT	$ 873 – $ 1,181
ST XTR	$ 967 – $ 1,308

Supercross

Model	Price Range
Racer-X	$ 207 – $ 279
Speed	$ 255 – $ 344
Stealth	$ 157 – $ 212
Team Speed	$ 328 – $ 444

Supergo

Model	Price Range
Access Max	$ 683 – $ 925

Terry

Model	Price Range
Athene	$ 344 – $ 466
Classic	$ 705 – $ 954
Jacaranda S	$ 633 – $ 857
Symmetry	$ 473 – $ 639

Ti Cycles

Model	Price Range
AMP style full suspension, Chro-mo	$ 853 – $ 1,154
AMP style full suspension, Titaniu	$ 939 – $ 1,271
Fillet Brazed Cyclocross	$ 771 – $ 1,043
Fillet brazed Mountain	$ 840 – $ 1,136

C: – Components   F: – Fork

MODEL	PRICE RANGE

Ti Cycles *(continued)* 🚲

Model	Price Range
Rigid Mountain, Titanium	$ 994 – $ 1,345
Road, Fillet Brazed F: Kestrel EMS C: Campagnolo Record	$ 985 – $ 1,332
Road, Fillet Brazed F: Kestrel EMS C: Dura-Ace	$ 981 – $ 1,328
Road, Lugged F: Kestrel EMS C: Campagnolo Record	$ 991 – $ 1,341
Road, Lugged F: Kestrel EMS C: Dura-Ace	$ 988 – $ 1,337
Road, Tig welded F: Kestrel EMS C: Campagnolo Record	$ 978 – $ 1,323
Road, Tig welded F: Kestrel EMS C: Dura-Ace	$ 974 – $ 1,318
Semi-unified Full suspension, Tita	$ 996 – $ 1,348
Tandem Mountain, TIG welded	$ 998 – $ 1,350
Tandem road, TIG welded	$ 999 – $ 1,352
TIG welded Cyclocross	$ 746 – $ 1,009
TIG welded Mountain	$ 818 – $ 1,107

Titan 🚲

Model	Price Range
Alpha	$ 432 – $ 584
Blaze	$ 142 – $ 192
Omega	$ 324 – $ 438
Prime	$ 255 – $ 344
Punisher	$ 226 – $ 306
Razorback	$ 207 – $ 279
Screamin' Eagle	$ 106 – $ 157
Titanium Compe	$ 985 – $ 1,333
Warphog	$ 177 – $ 239
Cyborg AL	$ 933 – $ 1,262
HCR Comp Ti	$ 841 – $ 1,138
Titus SFS Comp AL	$ 794 – $ 1,075

C: – Components   F: – Fork

MODEL		PRICE RANGE

TNT 🚲

Model		Price Range
Hwa Fong Daddy		$ 288 – $ 389
M-80		$ 167 – $ 227
Quarterstick		$ 197 – $ 267
TRX		$ 245 – $ 332
TRX Team		$ 342 – $ 463

Torelli 🚲

Model	Components	Price Range
Corsa Strada	C: Campagnolo Athena	$ 702 – $ 950
Corsa Strada	C: Campagnolo Chorus	$ 768 – $ 1,040
Corsa Strada	C: Campagnolo Record	$ 895 – $ 1,211
Corsa Strada	C: Campagnolo Veloce	$ 620 – $ 839
Corsa Strada	C: Sachs 5000 Other Features	$ 424 – $ 574
Corsa Strada	C: Sachs 5000 Other Features	$ 513 – $ 694
Corsa Strada	C: Sachs New Success Other Features	$ 646 – $ 873
Corsa Strada	C: Sachs New Success Other Features	$ 742 – $ 1,004
Corsa Strada	C: 600 Ultegra	$ 761 – $ 1,029
Corsa Strada	C: Dura-Ace	$ 937 – $ 1,268
Countach OS	C: Campagnolo Athena	$ 761 – $ 1,029
Countach OS	C: Campagnolo Chorus	$ 820 – $ 1,109
Countach OS	C: Campagnolo Record	$ 929 – $ 1,257
Countach OS	C: Veloce	$ 686 – $ 929
Countach OS	C: Sachs 5000 Other Features	$ 559 – $ 756
Countach OS	C: Sachs 5000 Other Features	$ 642 – $ 869
Countach OS	C: Sachs New Success Other Features	$ 710 – $ 960
Countach OS	C: Sachs New Success Other Features	$ 796 – $ 1,077
Countach OS	C: 600 Ultegra	$ 813 – $ 1,100
Countach OS	C: Dura-Ace	$ 963 – $ 1,302
Express	C: Athena	$ 830 – $ 1,123
Express	C: Chorus	$ 879 – $ 1,189
Express	C: Record	$ 964 – $ 1,304
Express	C: Veloce	$ 767 – $ 1,037

C: – Components   F: – Fork

MODEL   PRICE RANGE

Torelli (continued)

Model	Components		Price Range	
Express	C:	Sachs 5000 Other Features	$ 655	– $ 886
Express	C:	Sachs 5000 Other Features	$ 728	– $ 985
Express	C:	Sachs New Success Other Features	$ 786	– $ 1,064
Express	C:	Sachs New Success Other Features	$ 860	– $ 1,163
Express	C:	600 Ultegra	$ 873	– $ 1,181
Express	C:	Dura-Ace	$ 987	– $ 1,335
Express OS	C:	Athena	$ 845	– $ 1,143
Express OS	C:	Chorus	$ 891	– $ 1,206
Express OS	C:	Record	$ 971	– $ 1,313
Express OS	C:	Veloce	$ 784	– $ 1,061
Express OS	C:	Sachs 5000 Other Features	$ 676	– $ 914
Express OS	C:	Sachs 5000 Other Features	$ 747	– $ 1,011
Express OS	C:	Sachs New Success Other Features	$ 803	– $ 1,087
Express OS	C:	Sachs New Success Other Features	$ 873	– $ 1,181
Express OS	C:	600 Ultegra	$ 886	– $ 1,199
Express OS	C:	Dura-Ace	$ 991	– $ 1,341
Nitro Express	C:	Athena	$ 885	– $ 1,197
Nitro Express	C:	Chorus	$ 924	– $ 1,250
Nitro Express	C:	Record	$ 987	– $ 1,335
Nitro Express	C:	Veloce	$ 831	– $ 1,125
Nitro Express	C:	Sachs 5000 Other Features	$ 735	– $ 994
Nitro Express	C:	Sachs 5000 Other Features	$ 798	– $ 1,080
Nitro Express	C:	Sachs New Success Other Features	$ 848	– $ 1,148
Nitro Express	C:	Sachs New Success Other Features	$ 909	– $ 1,230
Nitro Express	C:	600 Ultegra	$ 920	– $ 1,244
Nitro Express	C:	Dura-Ace	$ 999	– $ 1,351
Super Strada	C:	Athena	$ 737	– $ 997
Super Strada	C:	Chorus	$ 798	– $ 1,080
Super Strada	C:	Record	$ 915	– $ 1,238
Super Strada	C:	Veloce	$ 659	– $ 891
Super Strada	C:	Sachs 5000 Other Features	$ 526	– $ 712

C: – Components   F: – Fork

MODEL		PRICE RANGE

Torelli (continued)

Super Strada	C: Sachs 5000 Other Features	$ 613 – $ 829
Super Strada	C: Sachs New Success Other Features	$ 683 – $ 924
Super Strada	C: Sachs New Success Other Features	$ 774 – $ 1,047
Super Strada	C: 600 Ultegra	$ 791 – $ 1,070
Super Strada	C: Dura-Ace	$ 952 – $ 1,289

Trailmate

Banana Peel	$ 176 – $ 239
Class Act Cruiser	$ 150 – $ 203
Class Act Tandem	$ 269 – $ 364
De Soto Classic	$ 243 – $ 329
Easy Ride	$ 150 – $ 203
EZ Roll Regal	$ 221 – $ 300
Funcycle	$ 199 – $ 269
Joyrider Other Features	$ 237 – $ 321
Joyrider Other Features	$ 274 – $ 370
Lowrider	$ 231 – $ 313

Trek

420	$ 244 – $ 330
470	$ 368 – $ 497
520	$ 523 – $ 708
700	$ 179 – $ 242
700 Sport	$ 149 – $ 202
720	$ 202 – $ 274
730	$ 244 – $ 330
750	$ 309 – $ 418
800	$ 163 – $ 220
800 Sport	$ 133 – $ 180
820	$ 192 – $ 259
830	$ 218 – $ 295

C: – Components   F: – Fork

MODEL	PRICE RANGE

Trek *(continued)*

Model	Price Range
830 SHX	$ 259 – $ 350
850	$ 259 – $ 350
850 SHX	$ 329 – $ 445
930	$ 259 – $ 350
930 SHX	$ 368 – $ 497
950	$ 406 – $ 549
970	$ 506 – $ 684
970 SHX	$ 579 – $ 784
990	$ 653 – $ 883
990 SHX	$ 801 – $ 1,083
1220	$ 461 – $ 624
1400	$ 506 – $ 684
2100	$ 633 – $ 856
2120	$ 672 – $ 909
2300	$ 783 – $ 1,060
5000	$ 851 – $ 1,152
5020	$ 943 – $ 1,276
5200	$ 971 – $ 1,314
5500	$ 1,181 – $ 1,598
7000	$ 343 – $ 465
7000 SHX	$ 424 – $ 574
7600	$ 475 – $ 642
7900	$ 549 – $ 743
8000	$ 447 – $ 605
8000 SHX	$ 549 – $ 743
8500	$ 672 – $ 909
8500 SHX	$ 818 – $ 1,107
9700 SHX	$ 748 – $ 1,012
9800 SHX	$ 883 – $ 1,195
9900 SHX	$ 1,131 – $ 1,531
Calypso	$ 173 – $ 234

C: – Components   F: – Fork

MODEL	PRICE RANGE

Trek (continued)

Model	Price Range
Cruiser Classic	$ 139 – $ 187
Mountain Cub	$ 81 – $ 110
Mountain Lion 220	$ 144 – $ 195
Mountain Lion 220SHX	$ 189 – $ 256
Mountain Lion 30	$ 87 – $ 117
Mountain Lion 40	$ 101 – $ 136
Mountain Lion 60	$ 125 – $ 169
Mountain Lion 60SHX	$ 165 – $ 224
Mountain Lion 80	$ 179 – $ 242
Mountain Track 240	$ 179 – $ 242
OCLV Team Kit	$ 1,131 – $ 1,530
ST 120	$ 549 – $ 743
T100	$ 592 – $ 800
T200	$ 1,023 – $ 1,384
Y Team Kit	$ 1,165 – $ 1,577
Y11	$ 747 – $ 1,011
Y22	$ 971 – $ 1,314
Y33	$ 1,165 – $ 1,577

Trophy Products

Model	Price Range
Lawwill Legend	$ 999 – $ 1,352
Lawwill Legend-Team	$ 999 – $ 1,352
XC	$ 794 – $ 1,075
XCR	$ 900 – $ 1,218
XCR-Team	$ 945 – $ 1,279

Univega

Model	Price Range
Activa Action	$ 142 – $ 193
Activa Country	$ 171 – $ 232
Activa Trail	$ 194 – $ 263
Alpina 500	$ 316 – $ 428

C: – Components   F: – Fork

MODEL   PRICE RANGE

Univega (continued)

Model	Price Range	
Alpina 502	$ 316 – $	428
Alpina 504	$ 390 – $	528
Alpina 506	$ 472 – $	639
Alpina 600	$ 327 – $	442
Alpina 602	$ 390 – $	528
Aluminum 700	$ 316 – $	428
Aluminum 700 SE	$ 250 – $	339
Aluminum 702	$ 369 – $	500
Aluminum 704	$ 442 – $	598
Aluminum 800	$ 390 – $	528
Aluminum 802	$ 442 – $	598
Aluminum 804	$ 522 – $	706
Aluminum 806	$ 685 – $	927
Aluminum 808	$ 812 – $	1,099
Carousel	$ 69 – $	94
Caveman	$ 69 – $	94
Cobra	$ 148 – $	200
Dual Action Comp	$ 570 – $	771
Dual Action Pro	$ 685 – $	927
Dual Action Team	$ 910 – $	1,231
Gran Rally	$ 663 – $	897
Hornet BMX	$ 96 – $	129
Hornet CX	$ 93 – $	126
Islander One	$ 125 – $	169
Islander Six	$ 148 – $	200
Islander Springer	$ 148 – $	200
Jamboree	$ 96 – $	145
Mad Dog	$ 75 – $	102
Merry Go Round	$ 75 – $	102
Mountain Force 102	$ 119 – $	161
Mountain Force 104	$ 125 – $	170

C: – Components   F: – Fork

MODEL	PRICE RANGE

Univega *(continued)* 🚲

Mountain Force 106	$ 142 – $ 193
Pro Comp	$ 812 – $ 1,099
Rover 300	$ 131 – $ 177
Rover 302	$ 142 – $ 193
Rover 304	$ 171 – $ 232
Rover 306	$ 194 – $ 263
Sportour	$ 272 – $ 369
Super G Comp	$ 188 – $ 255
Super G Cruiser	$ 194 – $ 263
Super G Pro	$ 261 – $ 354
Superstrada	$ 396 – $ 535
Tandem Sport	$ 380 – $ 514
Tandem Tour	$ 589 – $ 797
Via Carisma	$ 250 – $ 339
Via De Oro	$ 354 – $ 478
Via Montega	$ 305 – $ 413
Willow	$ 87 – $ 118

Valley Cycles 🚲

RS50	$ 917 – $ 1,241
RS100	$ 985 – $ 1,333

Ventana 🚲

El Chiquillo	$ 865 – $ 1,171
El Habanero	$ 865 – $ 1,171

Vision 🚲

R-40A	$ 471 – $ 637
R-40B	$ 531 – $ 718
R-40E	$ 492 – $ 666
R-40F	$ 540 – $ 730

C: – Components   F: – Fork

1996

MODEL	PRICE RANGE

Vision (continued)

R-42A	$ 653 – $ 883
R-42B	$ 684 – $ 926
R-42E	$ 653 – $ 883
R-42F	$ 684 – $ 926
R-45A	$ 883 – $ 1,194
R-45E	$ 901 – $ 1,219
R-82U	$ 996 – $ 1,348

VooDoo

Bizango F: Rock Shox Judy SL	$ 987 – $ 1,335
Bizango F: Rock Shox Judy XC	$ 807 – $ 1,092
Bizango F: Rock Shox Quadra 21R	$ 714 – $ 966
Bokor F: Rock Shox Judy XC	$ 961 – $ 1,300
Bokor F: Rock Shox Mag 21	$ 628 – $ 849
Bokor F: Rock Shox Quadra 21R	$ 684 – $ 925
Canzo AL F: Rock Shox Judy DH	$ 952 – $ 1,288
Canzo AL F: Rock Shox Judy XC	$ 901 – $ 1,219
Canzo ST F: Rock Shox Judy XC	$ 905 – $ 1,224
Canzo ST F: Rock Shox Mag 21	$ 842 – $ 1,139
Canzo ST F: Rock Shox Quadra 21R	$ 736 – $ 995
Canzo ST/AL	$ 813 – $ 1,101
Canzo Ti/AL	$ 969 – $ 1,311
D-Jab F: Rock Shox Judy XC	$ 909 – $ 1,230
D-Jab F: Rock Shox Mag 21	$ 795 – $ 1,076
Hoodoo F: Rock Shox Judy XC	$ 644 – $ 872
Hoodoo F: Rock Shox Quadra 21R	$ 530 – $ 717
Hoodoo F: Tange	$ 379 – $ 513
Wanga F: Rock Shox Judy XC	$ 756 – $ 1,023
Wanga F: Rock Shox Mag 21	$ 660 – $ 894
Wanga F: Rock Shox Quadra 21R	$ 511 – $ 692

C: – Components   F: – Fork

204

MODEL	PRICE RANGE

Windy City

Cruiser	$ 101 – $ 137
Explorer	$ 70 – $ 95
Trailblazer	$ 75 – $ 102

Wolf Creek

Renegade	$ 883 – $ 1,194

Worksman Cycle

Adult Lite Trike	$ 235 – $ 319
FMB3CB	$ 147 – $ 199
Industrial INB	$ 147 – $ 199
Mover M2626-CB	$ 301 – $ 407

Yellow Mushroom

Funky Expert	$ 743 – $ 1,005
Funky Mushroom World Cup	$ 795 – $ 1,076
Funky Pro	$ 770 – $ 1,041

Zerobike

Cannibal	$ 873 – $ 1,181
Mojo	$ 219 – $ 296
Red Zone CC	$ 999 – $ 1,352

C: – Components   F: – Fork

1997

MODEL	PRICE RANGE

Aegis

Model	Price Range
650 CHI/1	$ 1,238 – $ 1,675
650 CHI/2	$ 1,175 – $ 1,589
650 CHI/3	$ 1,048 – $ 1,418
650 CHI/4	$ 1,008 – $ 1,363
650 CHI/Special	$ 975 – $ 1,319
700 ARO/1	$ 1,238 – $ 1,675
700 ARO/2	$ 1,175 – $ 1,589
700 ARO/3	$ 1,048 – $ 1,418
700 ARO/4	$ 1,008 – $ 1,363
700 ARO/5	$ 1,313 – $ 1,777
700 ARO/6	$ 1,208 – $ 1,634
700 ARO/7	$ 1,138 – $ 1,539

Aero-Fast

Model	Price Range
#2448 Super Deluxe	$ 184 – $ 249
#2449 Heavy Duty	$ 162 – $ 220
#2454 Workhorse	$ 228 – $ 309
#2500 Deluxe Springer	$ 388 – $ 525
#2501 Deluxe Truss Rod	$ 333 – $ 451
#2502 Economy	$ 388 – $ 525
#2503 Beach Bomber	$ 243 – $ 329
#2504 Beach Bomber Economy	$ 184 – $ 249
#2505 St. Moritz	$ 228 – $ 309
#2506 Claybrook	$ 214 – $ 289
#2507 Gliderider	$ 254 – $ 344

Alex Moulton

Model	Price Range
AM 5	$ 1,273 – $ 1,722
APB 14 Shimano Plus	$ 975 – $ 1,319
APB 14 Shimano Plus-T	$ 1,008 – $ 1,364
APB 3	$ 787 – $ 1,065

C: – Components   F: – Fork

MODEL	PRICE RANGE
Alex Moulton (*continued*)	🚲
APB 5	$ 828 – $ 1,120
APB 7	$ 867 – $ 1,173
Jubilee APB 21-T	$ 1,040 – $ 1,406
Alpine Designs	🚲
Adventure 24 Shock	$ 184 – $ 249
Adventure 20	$ 124 – $ 168
Adventure 24	$ 161 – $ 217
Explore	$ 184 – $ 249
Fly Ti	$ 1,197 – $ 1,620
Phat Cat Deluxe LX	$ 975 – $ 1,319
Phat Cat Deluxe RC	$ 867 – $ 1,173
Phat Cat Deluxe XT	$ 1,125 – $ 1,522
Phat Cat Deluxe XTR	$ 1,238 – $ 1,675
Steely Man	$ 1,098 – $ 1,486
XC-1	$ 848 – $ 1,147
XC-2	$ 724 – $ 979
XC-3	$ 562 – $ 761
XC-3.5	$ 462 – $ 625
XC-4	$ 377 – $ 510
XC-Shock	$ 300 – $ 406
XC-Sport	$ 243 – $ 329
American Flyer	🚲
Bobcat	$ 1,133 – $ 1,532
Terminator	$ 1,084 – $ 1,467
Z-1	$ 1,084 – $ 1,467
AMP Research	🚲
B3	$ 741 – $ 1,003
B4 F: AMP Research F3 XC	$ 1,234 – $ 1,670
B4 F: AMP Research F4 BLT	$ 1,268 – $ 1,715

C: – Components   F: – Fork

MODEL	PRICE RANGE

Angletech 🚲

Tri Speeder	$ 1,273 – $ 1,722

Angletech/Rans 🚲

Rocket BLT 63	$ 745 – $ 1,008
Rocket GL63-T	$ 1,024 – $ 1,385
Stratus GL 63-T	$ 1,098 – $ 1,486
V-Rex GL63-T	$ 1,098 – $ 1,485

Angletech/Vision 🚲

Metro GL21	$ 901 – $ 1,219
VR30 Elan	$ 998 – $ 1,351
VR44 GL63	$ 1,117 – $ 1,511

Balance 🚲

Al-150 F: Balance	$ 319 – $ 431
Al-150 F: RST 161B	$ 380 – $ 515
Al-250 F: Balance	$ 380 – $ 515
Al-250 F: RST 171B	$ 444 – $ 600
Al-350 F: Balance	$ 440 – $ 595
Al-350 F: RST 381L	$ 540 – $ 731
Al-450 F: Balance	$ 528 – $ 714
Al-450 F: Rock Shox Indy C	$ 582 – $ 787
Al-550 F: Balance	$ 660 – $ 893
Al-550 F: Rock Shox Indy SL	$ 771 – $ 1,043
Al-750 F: Balance	$ 865 – $ 1,170
Al-750 F: Rock Shox Judy XC	$ 1,036 – $ 1,402
FS-350	$ 857 – $ 1,160
FS-550	$ 973 – $ 1,317
Killer B	$ 287 – $ 397
Stinger B	$ 170 – $ 229
Super B	$ 225 – $ 305

C: – Components   F: – Fork

MODEL	PRICE RANGE
Balance *(continued)*	🚲
Super FRS	$ 353 – $ 477
XR-150 F: Balance	$ 240 – $ 325
XR-150 F: RST 161B	$ 297 – $ 402
XR-250 F: Balance	$ 297 – $ 402
XR-250 F: RST 171B	$ 353 – $ 477
Barracuda	🚲
Cuda Comp	$ 975 – $ 1,319
A2B	$ 328 – $ 443
A2BS	$ 423 – $ 572
A2E	$ 724 – $ 979
A2F	$ 184 – $ 249
A2FS	$ 243 – $ 329
A2M	$ 562 – $ 761
A2R	$ 382 – $ 517
A2RS	$ 500 – $ 677
A2T	$ 1,125 – $ 1,522
A2V	$ 828 – $ 1,120
A2Z	$ 272 – $ 367
A2ZS	$ 355 – $ 481
C2A	$ 513 – $ 694
C2F	$ 657 – $ 889
C2K	$ 787 – $ 1,065
XX Team	$ 634 – $ 857
XXC	$ 586 – $ 793
XXFX	$ 1,125 – $ 1,522
XXXC	$ 1,125 – $ 1,522
Beyond Fabrications	🚲
BE-401 MMC	$ 1,294 – $ 1,751
G3	$ 1,227 – $ 1,661

C: – Components   F: – Fork

MODEL	PRICE RANGE

Beyond Fabrications (continued)

Hey Chubby	$ 722 – $ 976
Metro Police	$ 700 – $ 947

Bianchi

Advantage	$ 253 – $ 343
Alloro	$ 1,102 – $ 1,491
Avenue	$ 210 – $ 284
Boardwalk	$ 313 – $ 424
Bobcat	$ 154 – $ 209
Campione D'Italia	$ 648 – $ 877
Denali	$ 622 – $ 841
Eros	$ 663 – $ 898
Grizzly RC	$ 1,102 – $ 1,491
Ibex	$ 464 – $ 628
Lynx	$ 259 – $ 351
Lynx SX	$ 325 – $ 440
Milano	$ 401 – $ 543
Ocelot	$ 210 – $ 284
Osprey	$ 401 – $ 543
Peregrine	$ 525 – $ 711
Premio	$ 337 – $ 456
San Remo	$ 719 – $ 973
Strada	$ 173 – $ 234
Super GL	$ 1,511 – $ 2,045
Super GX	$ 769 – $ 1,041
Super GY	$ 1,103 – $ 1,492
Timber Wolf	$ 192 – $ 260
Trofeo	$ 509 – $ 689
Veloce	$ 846 – $ 1,144
Volpe	$ 448 – $ 606

C: – Components   F: – Fork

MODEL   PRICE RANGE

Bike Friday

Model	Price Range
Air Friday Tri Day	$ 1,124 – $ 1,520
AirFriday	$ 1,196 – $ 1,618
AirFriday Paris-Brest-Paris	$ 940 – $ 1,271
New World Tourist	$ 560 – $ 757
Pocket Llama Expedition	$ 865 – $ 1,170
Pocket Llama OR2 (Oregon Off Road)	$ 636 – $ 861
Pocket Rocket C: 105SC	$ 826 – $ 1,117
Pocket Rocket C: 600 Ultegra	$ 939 – $ 1,270
Pocket Rocket C: RSX	$ 700 – $ 947
Two'sDay C: RSX/Sachs Neos	$ 1,138 – $ 1,540
Two'sDay C: Sachs Centera	$ 1,024 – $ 1,385

BikeE

Model	Price Range
All Around F: Custom Other Features	$ 459 – $ 621
All Around F: Custom Other Features	$ 525 – $ 711
RoadE Other Features	$ 518 – $ 701
RoadE Other Features	$ 582 – $ 787

Bilenky

Model	Price Range
Clubsman	$ 1,172 – $ 1,586
Clubsman Sport	$ 1,068 – $ 1,445
Deluxe Sport	$ 1,313 – $ 1,776
Deluxe Trans Am	$ 1,124 – $ 1,520
Eco Trail Mix	$ 1,313 – $ 1,776
EcoSport	$ 1,237 – $ 1,674
EcoSport Tinker Tandem BTC	$ 1,313 – $ 1,776
Hedgehog Twinn	$ 1,287 – $ 1,741
Katahn	$ 1,068 – $ 1,445
Midlands	$ 1,068 – $ 1,445
Midlands 853	$ 1,124 – $ 1,520
Midlands Inox	$ 1,217 – $ 1,647

C: – Components   F: – Fork

MODEL   PRICE RANGE

Bilenky (continued)

Mud Puppy	$ 1,068 – $ 1,445
Nor'Easter	$ 973 – $ 1,317
Signature Clubsman	$ 1,174 – $ 1,588
Signature Pro Am	$ 1,280 – $ 1,732
Tinker Tandem BTC	$ 1,313 – $ 1,776
Trans Am Inox	$ 1,264 – $ 1,711
Travel Clubsman	$ 1,174 – $ 1,588
Travel Midlands	$ 1,055 – $ 1,427

BLT

Basic Loaded Touring	$ 641 – $ 867

Bontrager

B1	$ 242 – $ 328
B29	$ 242 – $ 328
B52	$ 382 – $ 517
Privateer	$ 562 – $ 760
Privateer Comp	$ 866 – $ 1,172
Privateer S	$ 656 – $ 888
Race Lite	$ 1,069 – $ 1,447
Ti Lite	$ 1,238 – $ 1,675

Boulder Bikes

Defiant	$ 975 – $ 1,319
Starship AL F: Rock Shox Indy XC	$ 1,175 – $ 1,589
Starship AL F: Rock Shox Judy SL	$ 1,272 – $ 1,722
Starship DH	$ 1,238 – $ 1,675
Starship LT	$ 1,197 – $ 1,620

Bouncer

Bouncing Scooter Bike	$ 124 – $ 168

C: – Components   F: – Fork

MODEL	PRICE RANGE

Breezer

Ignaz X	$ 396 – $ 536
Jet Stream	$ 1,068 – $ 1,445
Lightning	$ 1,218 – $ 1,648
Storm	$ 538 – $ 728
Thunder	$ 745 – $ 1,008
Twister	$ 1,097 – $ 1,484

Brompton

Brompton L3	$ 372 – $ 504
Brompton L5	$ 436 – $ 590
Brompton T5	$ 509 – $ 688

Bruce Gordon

Rock'n Road Tour	$ 1,098 – $ 1,486
Rock'n Road Tour EX	$ 1,098 – $ 1,486

Burley

Duet	$ 966 – $ 1,308
Rock'n Roll	$ 966 – $ 1,308
Rumba	$ 828 – $ 1,120
Samba	$ 787 – $ 1,065
Samba Softride	$ 904 – $ 1,224
Zydeco	$ 610 – $ 826
Zydeco Mixte-X	$ 645 – $ 873

Calfee

Luna Pro C: Athena	$ 1,151 – $ 1,557
Luna Pro C: Chorus	$ 1,201 – $ 1,634
Luna Pro C: Record	$ 1,292 – $ 1,758
Luna Pro C: 105SC	$ 1,012 – $ 1,369
Luna Pro C: 600 Ultegra	$ 1,072 – $ 1,450

C: – Components   F: – Fork

MODEL	PRICE RANGE

Calfee (continued)

Model	Price Range
Luna Pro C: Dura-Ace Other Features	$ 1,171 – $ 1,584
Luna Pro C: Dura-Ace Other Features	$ 1,217 – $ 1,647
Luna Tri F: Luna Tri C: 600 Ultegra	$ 1,072 – $ 1,450
Luna Tri F: Luna Tri C: Dura-Ace	$ 1,181 – $ 1,598
Tetra Custom C: 105SC	$ 1,284 – $ 1,737
Tetra Custom C: 600 Ultegra	$ 1,310 – $ 1,772
Tetra Custom F: Tetra Pro Ti	$ 1,293 – $ 1,750
Tetra Custom F: Tetra Pro Total Carbon	$ 1,301 – $ 1,760
Tetra Pro C: 105SC F: Tetra Pro	$ 1,231 – $ 1,666
Tetra Pro C: 600 Ultegra F: Tetra Pro	$ 1,266 – $ 1,713
Tetra Pro C: Athena F: Tetra Pro	$ 1,308 – $ 1,769
Tetra Pro C: 105SC F: Tetra Pro Ti	$ 1,243 – $ 1,682
Tetra Pro C: 105SC F: Tetra Pro Total Carbon	$ 1,254 – $ 1,696
Tetra Pro C: 600 Ultegra F: Tetra Pro Ti	$ 1,276 – $ 1,727
Tetra Pro C: 600 Ultegra F: Tetra Pro Total Carbon	$ 1,285 – $ 1,738
Tetra Tri F: Tetra Tri	$ 1,298 – $ 1,756
Tetra Tri F: Tetra Tri Ti	$ 1,306 – $ 1,767
Tetra Tri F: Tetra Tri Total Carbon	$ 1,313 – $ 1,776

Caloi

Model	Price Range
Comp	$ 495 – $ 670
Comp FS	$ 951 – $ 1,286
Comp XC	$ 641 – $ 867
Elite	$ 371 – $ 502
Elite FS	$ 773 – $ 1,046
Elite XC	$ 461 – $ 624
Expert	$ 299 – $ 405
Expert XC	$ 382 – $ 517
Pro	$ 336 – $ 455
Pro FS	$ 736 – $ 996
Pro XC	$ 417 – $ 565

C: – Components   F: – Fork

1
9
9
7

MODEL   PRICE RANGE

Caloi (continued)

Model	Price Range
Sigma	$ 425 – $ 575
Sigma FS	$ 818 – $ 1,107
Sigma XC	$ 512 – $ 693
Sport	$ 260 – $ 351
Supra	$ 228 – $ 309
Team FS	$ 1,175 – $ 1,589
Team XC	$ 923 – $ 1,248

Cannondale

Model	Price Range
B900 Beast of the East	$ 539 – $ 730
F300	$ 344 – $ 466
F500	$ 458 – $ 620
F500i	$ 419 – $ 567
F700	$ 539 – $ 730
F900	$ 643 – $ 869
F1000	$ 763 – $ 1,032
F2000	$ 915 – $ 1,239
Killer V 900 F: Cannondale Headshock DD60	$ 643 – $ 869
Killer V 900 F: Cannondale P-Bone	$ 539 – $ 730
M300 LE	$ 267 – $ 361
M300 SE	$ 267 – $ 361
M500	$ 344 – $ 466
M700	$ 402 – $ 544
M900	$ 539 – $ 730
M1000	$ 667 – $ 903
MT900	$ 830 – $ 1,123
MT1000	$ 994 – $ 1,345
MT3000	$ 1,320 – $ 1,786
Multisport 500	$ 539 – $ 730
Multisport 500 Polished	$ 591 – $ 800
Multisport 4000	$ 1,195 – $ 1,616

C: – Components   F: – Fork

1
9
9
7

MODEL	PRICE RANGE
Cannondale *(continued)*	🚲
R200	$ 344 – $ 465
R300	$ 429 – $ 581
R500	$ 512 – $ 693
R500T	$ 539 – $ 730
R600	$ 666 – $ 902
R800	$ 830 – $ 1,123
R900	$ 899 – $ 1,216
R4000	$ 1,195 – $ 1,616
RC600	$ 666 – $ 902
RMS800	$ 808 – $ 1,093
RT2000	$ 1,032 – $ 1,396
Silk Path 500	$ 501 – $ 678
Silk Path 700	$ 566 – $ 765
Silk Path 900	$ 642 – $ 869
Silk Road 500	$ 691 – $ 935
Silk Road 900	$ 1,031 – $ 1,395
Super V 500	$ 946 – $ 1,280
Super V 700	$ 799 – $ 1,081
Super V 900	$ 915 – $ 1,239
Super V 1000	$ 994 – $ 1,345
Super V 1000 Polished	$ 1,032 – $ 1,396
Super V 2000E	$ 1,165 – $ 1,576
Super V 2000R	$ 1,180 – $ 1,597
T 500	$ 401 – $ 543
T 900	$ 539 – $ 729
T 2000	$ 691 – $ 935
Catamount	🚲
MFS C: Deore LX	$ 1,070 – $ 1,447
MFS C: Deore XT	$ 1,151 – $ 1,557
MFS C: XTR 950	$ 1,288 – $ 1,742

C: – Components   F: – Fork

MODEL	PRICE RANGE

Cignal 🚲

Model	Price Range
Bimini	$ 196 – $ 265
Hot Rodasaurus	$ 63 – $ 85
Kokomo	$ 167 – $ 225
Lady Bug	$ 63 – $ 85
Lil Fox	$ 75 – $ 102
Melbourne Express	$ 339 – $ 458
Miss Daisy	$ 69 – $ 94
Montauk	$ 124 – $ 168
Montero	$ 155 – $ 209
Ozark	$ 184 – $ 249
Ozark 20	$ 100 – $ 135
Ozark 24	$ 118 – $ 160
Ozark SX 24	$ 149 – $ 201
Ranger	$ 106 – $ 144
Ranger SX	$ 137 – $ 185
Rialto	$ 137 – $ 185
Top Gun	$ 69 – $ 102
Village Velo Other Features	$ 161 – $ 217
Village Velo Other Features	$ 178 – $ 241
Village Velo Other Features	$ 231 – $ 313

Co-Motion 🚲

Model	Price Range
Breve	$ 1,124 – $ 1,520
Cappuccino	$ 1,260 – $ 1,705
Co-Pilot OR BTC C: Deore LX	$ 904 – $ 1,224
Co-Pilot OR BTC C: Deore XT	$ 1,013 – $ 1,370
Co-Pilot OR BTC C: XTR 950	$ 1,219 – $ 1,650
Co-Pilot Road BTC C: 105SC	$ 931 – $ 1,260
Co-Pilot Road BTC C: 600 Ultegra	$ 983 – $ 1,329
Co-Pilot Road BTC C: Chorus	$ 1,147 – $ 1,551
Custom Cyclocross	$ 1,119 – $ 1,513

C: – Components   F: – Fork

MODEL	PRICE RANGE
Co-Motion *(continued)*	
Custom Mountain	$ 1,290 – $ 1,746
Custom Mountain BTC	$ 1,088 – $ 1,472
Custom Road C: Record	$ 1,283 – $ 1,736
Custom Road C: Dura-Ace	$ 1,293 – $ 1,750
Custom Track	$ 1,024 – $ 1,385
Espresso C: 600 Ultegra	$ 971 – $ 1,314
Espresso C: Chorus	$ 1,183 – $ 1,600
Espresso C: Dura-Ace	$ 1,225 – $ 1,658
Espresso C: Record	$ 1,254 – $ 1,697
Speedster	$ 1,217 – $ 1,647
Conejo	
AP/5 F: Rock Shox Judy C Other Features	$ 1,065 – $ 1,441
AP/5 F: Rock Shox Judy C Other Features	$ 1,146 – $ 1,550
AP/5 F: Rock Shox Judy DH Other Features	$ 1,094 – $ 1,480
AP/5 F: Rock Shox Judy DH Other Features	$ 1,227 – $ 1,659
AP/5 F: Rock Shox Judy SL	$ 1,238 – $ 1,675
AP/5 F: Rock Shox Judy XC Other Features	$ 1,095 – $ 1,481
AP/5 F: Rock Shox Judy XC Other Features	$ 1,206 – $ 1,632
Corima	
T 2000	$ 1,307 – $ 1,768
Dahon	
Classic III PT631	$ 196 – $ 265
Explorer PT073	$ 243 – $ 329
Express PT074	$ 355 – $ 481
Getaway PT01	$ 137 – $ 185
Mariner PT053M	$ 254 – $ 344
Mariner ST683M	$ 311 – $ 421
Mountain Classic ST680D	$ 243 – $ 329

C: – Components   F: – Fork

MODEL

PRICE RANGE

Dahon (*continued*)

Stowaway PT03	$ 202 – $ 273
Stowaway PT05	$ 202 – $ 273
Venture ST674	$ 355 – $ 481

De Rosa

Giro	$ 1,255 – $ 1,698
Primato	$ 1,313 – $ 1,777
San Remo	$ 1,112 – $ 1,504

Dean

Bam Bam C: XT F: Answer Manitou SX	$ 1,276 – $ 1,727
Bam Bam C: XT/LX F: Answer Manitou SX	$ 1,204 – $ 1,629
Bam Bam C: XT/LX F: Rock Shox Judy SL	$ 1,244 – $ 1,682
Bam Bam C: XT F: Rock Shox Judy SL	$ 1,304 – $ 1,765
Bam Bam C: XT F: Rock Shox Judy DH	$ 1,291 – $ 1,747
Bam Bam C: XT F: Rock Shox Judy XC	$ 1,269 – $ 1,716
Bam Bam C: XT/LX F: Rock Shox Judy DH	$ 1,224 – $ 1,657
Bam Bam C: XT/LX F: Rock Shox Judy XC	$ 1,193 – $ 1,614
Carbanza C: 105SC	$ 1,080 – $ 1,461
Carbanza C: 600 Ultegra	$ 1,134 – $ 1,535
Carbanza C: Dura-Ace	$ 1,246 – $ 1,686
Carducci C: 105SC	$ 968 – $ 1,310
Carducci C: 600 Ultegra	$ 1,033 – $ 1,398
Carducci C: Dura-Ace	$ 1,172 – $ 1,586
Castanza F: Kestrel EMS	$ 1,207 – $ 1,633
Castanza C: 105SC	$ 1,019 – $ 1,379
Castanza C: 600 Ultegra	$ 1,080 – $ 1,461
Colonel C: XT F: Rock Shox Judy XC	$ 1,169 – $ 1,581
Colonel C: XT/LX F: Rock Shox Judy XC	$ 1,064 – $ 1,439
Colonel C: XTR F: Rock Shox Judy XC	$ 1,256 – $ 1,699
Colonel C: XT F: Answer Manitou SX	$ 1,181 – $ 1,597

C: – Components   F: – Fork

MODEL	PRICE RANGE

Dean (continued)

Model	Price Range
Colonel C: XT F: Rock Shox Indy SL	$ 1,159 – $ 1,568
Colonel C: XT F: Rock Shox Judy SL	$ 1,223 – $ 1,655
Colonel C: XT/LX F: Answer Manitou SX	$ 1,078 – $ 1,459
Colonel C: XT/LX F: Rock Shox Indy SL	$ 1,052 – $ 1,423
Colonel C: XT/LX F: Rock Shox Judy SL	$ 1,133 – $ 1,533
Colonel C: XTR F: Answer Manitou SX	$ 1,264 – $ 1,711
Colonel C: XTR F: Rock Shox Indy SL	$ 1,249 – $ 1,690
Colonel C: XTR F: Rock Shox Judy SL	$ 1,295 – $ 1,752
Duke XC F: Answer Manitou SX	$ 1,285 – $ 1,738
Duke XC F: Rock Shox Indy SL	$ 1,271 – $ 1,720
Duke XC F: Rock Shox Judy SL	$ 1,311 – $ 1,774
Duke XC F: Rock Shox Judy XC	$ 1,277 – $ 1,728
Felix C: Deore LX	$ 688 – $ 931
Felix C: Deore XT	$ 897 – $ 1,214
Jester C: XT F: Answer Manitou SX	$ 1,126 – $ 1,524
Jester C: XT/LX F: Answer Manitou SX	$ 1,011 – $ 1,368
Jester C: XTR F: Rock Shox Judy XC	$ 1,214 – $ 1,643
Jester C: XTR F: Answer Manitou SX	$ 1,224 – $ 1,657
Jester C: XT F: Rock Shox Judy SL	$ 1,176 – $ 1,591
Jester C: XT F: Rock Shox Judy XC	$ 1,113 – $ 1,506
Jester C: XT F: Rock Shox Indy SL	$ 1,102 – $ 1,491
Jester C: XT/LX F: Rock Shox Indy SL	$ 982 – $ 1,328
Jester C: XT/LX F: Rock Shox Judy SL	$ 1,072 – $ 1,451
Jester C: XT/LX F: Rock Shox Judy XC	$ 995 – $ 1,346
Jester C: XTR F: Rock Shox Indy SL	$ 1,259 – $ 1,706
Jester C: XTR F: Rock Shox Judy SL	$ 1,261 – $ 1,706
Oscar C: XT F: Rock Shox Judy SL	$ 1,169 – $ 1,581
Oscar C: XT F: Rock Shox Judy XC	$ 1,105 – $ 1,495
Oscar C: XT/LX F: Rock Shox Judy SL	$ 1,064 – $ 1,439
Oscar C: XT/LX F: Rock Shox Judy XC	$ 985 – $ 1,333
Oscar C: XTR F: Rock Shox Judy SL	$ 1,256 – $ 1,699

C: – Components   F: – Fork

MODEL	PRICE RANGE

Dean *(continued)*

Model	Price Range
Oscar C: XTR F: Rock Shox Judy XC	$ 1,208 – $ 1,634
Oscar C: XT F: Answer Manitou SX	$ 1,119 – $ 1,513
Oscar C: XT F: Rock Shox Indy SL	$ 1,094 – $ 1,480
Oscar C: XT/LX F: Answer Manitou SX	$ 1,001 – $ 1,355
Oscar C: XT/LX F: Rock Shox Indy SL	$ 972 – $ 1,314
Oscar C: XTR F: Answer Manitou SX	$ 1,218 – $ 1,648
Oscar C: XTR F: Rock Shox Indy SL	$ 1,199 – $ 1,623
Sputnik C: XT F: Rock Shox Indy SL	$ 1,121 – $ 1,517
Sputnik C: XT F: Rock Shox Judy SL	$ 1,192 – $ 1,612
Sputnik C: XT F: Rock Shox Judy XC	$ 1,132 – $ 1,531
Sputnik C: XT/LX F: Rock Shox Indy SL	$ 1,005 – $ 1,359
Sputnik C: XT/LX F: Rock Shox Judy SL	$ 1,093 – $ 1,478
Sputnik C: XT/LX F: Rock Shox Judy XC	$ 1,018 – $ 1,377
Sputnik C: XT/LX F: Answer Manitou SX	$ 1,033 – $ 1,398
Sputnik C: XTR F: Answer Manitou SX	$ 1,238 – $ 1,675
Sputnik C: XTR F: Rock Shox Indy SL	$ 1,220 – $ 1,651
Sputnik C: XTR F: Rock Shox Judy SL	$ 1,273 – $ 1,722
Sputnik C: XTR F: Rock Shox Judy XC	$ 1,228 – $ 1,662
Sputnik C: XT F: Answer Manitou SX	$ 1,144 – $ 1,548

Diamondback

Model	Price Range
Apex SE	$ 348 – $ 471
Approach	$ 192 – $ 260
Ascent 1.0	$ 393 – $ 531
Ascent 3.0	$ 478 – $ 647
Assault	$ 116 – $ 157
Assault EX	$ 162 – $ 219
Crestview	$ 146 – $ 198
Expert	$ 325 – $ 440
Ignitor CB	$ 80 – $ 108
Ignitor FW	$ 85 – $ 115

C: – Components   F: – Fork

MODEL	PRICE RANGE
Diamondback (continued)	
Impression	$ 75 – $ 101
Interval	$ 216 – $ 293
Lakeside	$ 302 – $ 409
Lil' One	$ 54 – $ 73
Micro Viper	$ 54 – $ 73
Mini Photon	$ 62 – $ 83
Mini Viper	$ 62 – $ 83
Outlook	$ 116 – $ 157
Outlook 24	$ 111 – $ 150
Parkway	$ 121 – $ 164
Photon	$ 75 – $ 101
Reactor	$ 207 – $ 280
Reactor 24	$ 207 – $ 280
Reactor Jr.	$ 207 – $ 280
Reactor Pro	$ 279 – $ 377
Reactor Team	$ 348 – $ 471
Recoil	$ 106 – $ 143
Response	$ 231 – $ 313
Sorrento	$ 167 – $ 226
Sorrento SE	$ 207 – $ 280
Topanga SE	$ 269 – $ 364
V-Link 1.1	$ 558 – $ 755
V-Link 3.1	$ 703 – $ 951
V-Link Pro	$ 1,109 – $ 1,501
Venom	$ 126 – $ 171
Venom Pro	$ 182 – $ 246
Viper	$ 93 – $ 126
WCF 2.1	$ 348 – $ 471
WCF 4.1	$ 436 – $ 590
WCF 6.1	$ 669 – $ 905
WCF Expert	$ 393 – $ 531

C: – Components   F: – Fork

MODEL	PRICE RANGE

Diamondback (continued)

Model	Price Range
WCF Master	$ 478 – $ 647
Wildwood	$ 157 – $ 212
Wildwood 24	$ 177 – $ 239
Zetec 2.1	$ 436 – $ 590
Zetec 4.1	$ 558 – $ 755
Zetec Pro	$ 855 – $ 1,157

Dirt Research

Model	Price Range
Bandelier F: Ballistic XL800A-Pro	$ 503 – $ 680
Bandelier F: Dirt Research	$ 401 – $ 543
Echo Canyon	$ 610 – $ 826
Hot Springs F: Ballistic XL460	$ 366 – $ 496
Hot Springs F: Dirt Research	$ 294 – $ 397
Kenai F: Dirt Research	$ 648 – $ 876
Kenai F: Rock Shox Judy SL	$ 800 – $ 1,082
Kings Canyon	$ 904 – $ 1,224
Kobuk F: Dirt Research	$ 336 – $ 455
Kobuk F: Rock Shox Indy XC	$ 415 – $ 561
Pecos F: Dirt Research	$ 454 – $ 614
Pecos F: Rock Shox Indy SL	$ 574 – $ 777
Voyageurs	$ 940 – $ 1,272
Wildcat Canyon	$ 1,313 – $ 1,777

DK East

Model	Price Range
Banshee	$ 158 – $ 213
Fury	$ 184 – $ 249
Legend	$ 383 – $ 518
Nemisis	$ 257 – $ 348
Onyx	$ 702 – $ 949
Promotion	$ 286 – $ 387

C: – Components   F: – Fork

MODEL | PRICE RANGE

DK West 🚲

Model	Price Range
Banshee	$ 158 – $ 213
Fury	$ 184 – $ 249
Legend	$ 383 – $ 518
Nemisis	$ 257 – $ 348
Onyx	$ 702 – $ 949
Promotion	$ 286 – $ 387

Dyno 🚲

Model	Price Range
Air	$ 184 – $ 249
Blaze	$ 103 – $ 139
Compe	$ 164 – $ 221
Nitro	$ 158 – $ 214
Nitro 24	$ 178 – $ 241
NSX CB	$ 103 – $ 139
NSX FW	$ 109 – $ 148
Slammer	$ 317 – $ 428
V-Max Sonic	$ 204 – $ 276
VFR	$ 129 – $ 174
VFR 12 w/training wheels	$ 79 – $ 107
VFR 16 w/training wheels	$ 93 – $ 126

Eddy Merckx 🚲

Model	Price Range
Corsa 0.1	$ 1,098 – $ 1,486
OV-Pro	$ 1,287 – $ 1,741
Strada	$ 939 – $ 1,270
Titanium AX	$ 1,197 – $ 1,620

Electra 🚲

Model	Price Range
Bomber 4	$ 300 – $ 406
Bomber 7	$ 355 – $ 481
Deluxe 1	$ 161 – $ 217

C: – Components   F: – Fork

MODEL	PRICE RANGE

Electra (continued)

Model	Price Range
Deluxe 4	$ 225 – $ 305
Deluxe 7	$ 289 – $ 390
Hawaii	$ 130 – $ 177
Rocket 7	$ 462 – $ 625
Rocket STX 21	$ 487 – $ 660
StreetRod 4	$ 300 – $ 406
StreetRod 7	$ 355 – $ 481
Sunny Garcia	$ 161 – $ 217

Elf

Model	Price Range
DX-II	$ 243 – $ 329
Factory Team Cruiser	$ 462 – $ 625
Factory Team Cruiser Double Cross	$ 475 – $ 642
Factory Team Series	$ 457 – $ 618
Junior	$ 269 – $ 363
Team Series Comp	$ 300 – $ 406
Team Series Double Cross	$ 309 – $ 418
ZR-1	$ 237 – $ 321

Feather Titanium

Model	Price Range
MF6	$ 1,237 – $ 1,674
RF5	$ 1,237 – $ 1,674

Free Agent

Model	Price Range
Air Raid	$ 213 – $ 289
Ambush	$ 166 – $ 233
Champ	$ 93 – $ 134
Cruiser Pro	$ 265 – $ 359
Eluder	$ 127 – $ 180
Enforcer	$ 294 – $ 397
Expert	$ 202 – $ 281

C: – Components   F: – Fork

1997

MODEL   PRICE RANGE

Free Agent (continued) 🚲

Model	Price Range
Ground Zero	$ 231 – $ 312
Maverick	$ 93 – $ 134
Team	$ 382 – $ 517

Fuji 🚲

Model	Price Range
Blaster-7	$ 137 – $ 185
Crosstown	$ 137 – $ 185
Del Rey	$ 260 – $ 352
Diamond	$ 702 – $ 949
Double Diamond	$ 828 – $ 1,120
Finest	$ 383 – $ 518
Folder	$ 199 – $ 269
Mt. Fuji-SX	$ 745 – $ 1,008
Nevada	$ 199 – $ 269
Odessa	$ 137 – $ 185
Pro-SX	$ 904 – $ 1,224
Professional	$ 1,125 – $ 1,522
Roubaix	$ 606 – $ 819
Sagres	$ 199 – $ 269
Sandblaster	$ 137 – $ 185
Suncrest SX	$ 606 – $ 819
Sunfire	$ 167 – $ 225
Supreme	$ 173 – $ 233
Tahoe	$ 322 – $ 436
Tahoe SX	$ 383 – $ 518
Team Fuji	$ 745 – $ 1,008
Thrill	$ 231 – $ 313
Thrill-SE	$ 260 – $ 352
Touring Series	$ 436 – $ 590
Triple Diamond	$ 1,024 – $ 1,385

C: – Components   F: – Fork

MODEL	PRICE RANGE
Gary Fisher	🚲
Alfresco	$ 300 – $ 406
Aquila	$ 355 – $ 481
Big Sur	$ 487 – $ 660
Cleo Moto	$ 143 – $ 193
Hard Warp	$ 161 – $ 217
Hoo Koo E Koo	$ 451 – $ 611
Joshua X0	$ 702 – $ 949
Joshua X1	$ 562 – $ 761
Joshua Z1	$ 1,151 – $ 1,557
Joshua Z2	$ 904 – $ 1,224
Kaitai	$ 383 – $ 518
Klunker	$ 513 – $ 694
Lush Rush Fuel	$ 249 – $ 336
Lush Rush Tool	$ 220 – $ 297
Mamba	$ 328 – $ 443
Marlin	$ 243 – $ 329
Minnosaurus	$ 106 – $ 144
Montare	$ 562 – $ 761
Mt. Jam	$ 155 – $ 209
Mud Puppy	$ 88 – $ 119
Nirvana	$ 300 – $ 406
Paragon	$ 657 – $ 889
Piranha	$ 167 – $ 225
Pure Bender Kick	$ 208 – $ 281
Pure Bender Spin	$ 167 – $ 225
Quick Pierce	$ 249 – $ 336
Shortcut	$ 143 – $ 193
Supercaliber	$ 975 – $ 1,319
Tassajara	$ 272 – $ 367
Trigger Fish Baked	$ 311 – $ 421
Trigger Fish Raw	$ 383 – $ 518

C: – Components   F: – Fork

MODEL	PRICE RANGE

Gary Fisher (continued)

Tyro	$ 155 – $ 209
Utopia	$ 399 – $ 539
Wahoo	$ 202 – $ 273
Xcaliber	$ 745 – $ 1,008
Zebrano	$ 214 – $ 289

Giant

Animator	$ 57 – $ 77
ATX 840	$ 361 – $ 488
ATX 860	$ 474 – $ 641
ATX 870	$ 523 – $ 707
ATX 875	$ 523 – $ 707
ATX 880	$ 617 – $ 835
ATX 890	$ 909 – $ 1,230
ATX 970	$ 498 – $ 674
ATX 980	$ 724 – $ 979
ATX 990	$ 973 – $ 1,316
Boulder	$ 134 – $ 181
Farrago	$ 196 – $ 265
Farrago 4	$ 209 – $ 282
Iguana	$ 237 – $ 335
Iguana SE	$ 245 – $ 346
Innova	$ 266 – $ 360
Kronos	$ 346 – $ 468
Kronos GS	$ 237 – $ 321
MCM 1	$ 1,080 – $ 1,462
MCM 980	$ 1,057 – $ 1,430
MCM 990	$ 1,185 – $ 1,604
MCR 1	$ 1,080 – $ 1,462
MCR 2	$ 951 – $ 1,287
Mosh 2	$ 85 – $ 122

C: – Components   F: – Fork

MODEL   PRICE RANGE

Giant (continued)   🚲

MOSH Pro	$ 193 – $	261
MOSH Pro S	$ 96 – $	137
MOSH Pro XL	$ 245 – $	332
MTX 125	$ 107 – $	144
MTX 200	$ 112 – $	152
MTX 225	$ 129 – $	174
MTX 250	$ 193 – $	261
Option	$ 126 – $	170
Perigee	$ 166 – $	225
Prodigy	$ 296 – $	401
Pudd'n	$ 57 – $	77
Rincon	$ 139 – $	189
Sedona	$ 271 – $	380
Sedona SE	$ 346 – $	481
Taffy	$ 85 – $	114
TCR 2	$ 637 – $	862
Upland	$ 101 – $	137
Yukon	$ 177 – $	254
Yukon SE	$ 219 – $	311

Giordana   🚲

XL-Eco	$ 1,124 – $	1,520
XL-Strada	$ 767 – $	1,037
XL-Super	$ 1,196 – $	1,618

Grandis   🚲

Over Max Chorus	$ 1,280 – $	1,731
Over Max Light Chorus	$ 1,290 – $	1,745
SLX Athena	$ 1,085 – $	1,469

C: – Components   F: – Fork

MODEL	PRICE RANGE

Green Gear Cycling

The Family Tandem	$ 715 – $ 967

Griffen

Full Suspension F: RST Mozo Pro-W C: Deore XT	$ 1,237 – $ 1,674
Full Suspension F: RST Mozo Pro-W C: XTR 950	$ 1,313 – $ 1,776
Hardtail F: RST Mozo Pro	$ 1,124 – $ 1,520
Hardtail F: RST Mozo Pro-W	$ 1,237 – $ 1,674
Road F: Aegis Fresh Ride C: 105SC	$ 1,068 – $ 1,445
Road F: Aegis Fresh Ride C: 600 Ultegra	$ 1,124 – $ 1,520
Road F: Corima Puma	$ 1,237 – $ 1,674
Tri F: Aegis Fresh Ride C: 105SC	$ 1,068 – $ 1,445
Tri F: Aegis Fresh Ride C: 600 Ultegra	$ 1,124 – $ 1,520
Tri F: Corima Puma	$ 1,237 – $ 1,674

GT

Aggressor	$ 220 – $ 298
Arette	$ 151 – $ 204
Avalanche F: GT	$ 467 – $ 631
Avalanche F: Rock Shox Indy SL	$ 572 – $ 773
Avalanche LE	$ 647 – $ 875
Backwoods	$ 323 – $ 437
Cirque	$ 218 – $ 294
Edge	$ 1,094 – $ 1,480
Force	$ 416 – $ 563
Fueler Pro XL	$ 243 – $ 329
Fury	$ 1,005 – $ 1,360
Interceptor	$ 160 – $ 217
Karakoram F: GT	$ 375 – $ 507
Karakoram F: Rock Shox Indy SL	$ 487 – $ 659

C: – Components   F: – Fork

MODEL	PRICE RANGE
GT (continued)	🚲
Legacy	$ 131 – $ 177
Lightning	$ 777 – $ 1,052
LTS-1	$ 1,005 – $ 1,360
LTS-1 Spin	$ 1,081 – $ 1,463
LTS-2	$ 762 – $ 1,031
LTS-3	$ 592 – $ 801
LTS-4	$ 515 – $ 697
LTS-5	$ 373 – $ 504
Mach One	$ 184 – $ 249
Mach One Cruiser	$ 183 – $ 248
Mach Two	$ 227 – $ 307
Mini Mach One	$ 183 – $ 248
Nomad	$ 277 – $ 375
Outpost	$ 166 – $ 225
Outpost Trail	$ 146 – $ 197
Palomar	$ 126 – $ 170
Pantera F: GT	$ 381 – $ 516
Pantera F: Rock Shox Indy XC	$ 458 – $ 620
Performer	$ 179 – $ 243
Pro Freestyle Tour	$ 271 – $ 367
Pro Freestyle Tour Team	$ 374 – $ 506
Rage	$ 657 – $ 889
Raider	$ 183 – $ 248
Rapid Transit w/fenders	$ 258 – $ 349
Rave	$ 272 – $ 369
Rebound	$ 277 – $ 375
Ricochet	$ 381 – $ 516
Saddleback	$ 191 – $ 258
Speed Series Cruiser	$ 246 – $ 333
Speed Series Jr.	$ 307 – $ 416
Speed Series Team XL	$ 420 – $ 569

C: – Components   F: – Fork

MODEL	PRICE RANGE

GT *(continued)*   🚲

Speed Series Team XL Spin	$ 600 – $ 811
Speed Series XL	$ 305 – $ 413
Strike	$ 515 – $ 697
STS-2	$ 988 – $ 1,337
Talera	$ 201 – $ 271
Tempest	$ 255 – $ 346
Tequesta	$ 300 – $ 406
Tequesta FS	$ 390 – $ 528
Timberline	$ 242 – $ 327
Timberline FS	$ 323 – $ 437
Vantara	$ 178 – $ 241
Vengeance Spin	$ 1,005 – $ 1,360
Vertigo	$ 153 – $ 207
Virage	$ 377 – $ 510
Zaskar	$ 821 – $ 1,111
Zaskar LE	$ 1,084 – $ 1,466

Guru   🚲

Cyberitic	$ 911 – $ 1,233
Hedonistic	$ 1,280 – $ 1,732
Java	$ 908 – $ 1,228
Millennium	$ 1,163 – $ 1,573
Nemo	$ 1,288 – $ 1,742
Sestrieres	$ 741 – $ 1,002

Hampton   🚲

Hampton-7	$ 137 – $ 185
Hampton-CB Other Features	$ 94 – $ 127
Hampton-CB Other Features	$ 112 – $ 152

C: – Components   F: – Fork

MODEL	PRICE RANGE

Haro

Model	Price Range
Basher	$ 176 – $ 237
Blammo	$ 482 – $ 657
Blaster	$ 106 – $ 144
Elite Junior	$ 399 – $ 539
Elite Pro	$ 498 – $ 673
Elite Pro 24	$ 498 – $ 673
Escape A0	$ 377 – $ 510
Escape A1	$ 475 – $ 642
Escape A1 Graphite	$ 485 – $ 656
Escape A2	$ 582 – $ 787
Escape A2 Polished	$ 591 – $ 800
Escape A3	$ 796 – $ 1,076
Escape A4	$ 1,310 – $ 1,772
Extreme EX-1	$ 603 – $ 816
Extreme EX-2	$ 940 – $ 1,272
FZR	$ 106 – $ 149
Group 1 AL	$ 214 – $ 289
Group 1 ALi	$ 322 – $ 458
Group 1 Ci	$ 158 – $ 218
Group 1 Ci 24	$ 176 – $ 237
Group 1 RSi	$ 263 – $ 356
Group 1 Si	$ 196 – $ 265
Group 1 Si 24	$ 217 – $ 293
Group 1 Si JR	$ 199 – $ 269
Group 1 Ti	$ 127 – $ 177
Group 1 Zi	$ 118 – $ 165
Mini Blaster	$ 88 – $ 119
Shredder	$ 176 – $ 242
Shredder Mag	$ 193 – $ 266
Shredder Super Deluxe	$ 237 – $ 325
Ultra	$ 459 – $ 621

C: – Components   F: – Fork

MODEL		PRICE RANGE		

Haro *(continued)*

Vector V0	$	155	– $	209
Vector V1	$	173	– $	233
Vector V2	$	220	– $	297
Vector V3	$	263	– $	356
Vector V20	$	149	– $	201
Vector V24	$	155	– $	209
YZF	$	106	– $	149
Zippo	$	155	– $	214

HH Racing Group

America	$	1,313	– $	1,776
Fudendo	$	724	– $	979
Furiosa	$	1,038	– $	1,404
Furiosa 2Ti	$	901	– $	1,219
Furiosa 7C	$	1,219	– $	1,650
Pista	$	923	– $	1,248
Professional	$	1,188	– $	1,608
Vitesse	$	1,228	– $	1,662

Hoffman

Big Daddy	$	347	– $	481
Condor	$	377	– $	520
Sugar Baby	$	265	– $	370
Taj	$	334	– $	464

Holiday

Cruiser	$	148	– $	200

Ibis

Alibi	$	933	– $	1,263
Hakkalugi	$	1,105	– $	1,495

C: – Components   F: – Fork

MODEL

PRICE RANGE

Ibis (continued)

Model	Price Range
Mojo	$ 1,146 – $ 1,550
Spanky	$ 973 – $ 1,317
Szazbo	$ 1,283 – $ 1,736

Independent Fabrication

Model	Price Range
Crown Jewel C: Athena	$ 1,242 – $ 1,680
Crown Jewel C: Chorus	$ 1,301 – $ 1,760
Crown Jewel C: 105SC	$ 1,085 – $ 1,469
Crown Jewel C: 600 Ultegra	$ 1,139 – $ 1,542
Crown Jewel C: Dura-Ace	$ 1,262 – $ 1,707
Deluxe C: Deore LX F: Rock Shox Indy SL	$ 1,033 – $ 1,427
Deluxe C: Deore LX F: Rock Shox Judy SL	$ 1,117 – $ 1,538
Deluxe C: Deore LX F: Rock Shox Judy XC	$ 1,055 – $ 1,457
Deluxe C: Deore XT F: Rock Shox Indy SL	$ 1,143 – $ 1,589
Deluxe C: Deore XT F: Rock Shox Judy SL	$ 1,211 – $ 1,674
Deluxe C: Deore XT F: Rock Shox Judy XC Other Features	$ 1,162 – $ 1,572
Deluxe C: Deore XT F: Rock Shox Judy XC Other Features	$ 1,192 – $ 1,612
Deluxe C: XTR F: Rock Shox Indy SL	$ 1,306 – $ 1,766
Special C: Deore LX F: Rock Shox Indy SL	$ 1,033 – $ 1,427
Special C: Deore LX F: Rock Shox Judy SL	$ 1,117 – $ 1,538
Special C: Deore LX F: Rock Shox Judy XC	$ 1,055 – $ 1,457
Special C: Deore XT F: Rock Shox Indy SL Other Features	$ 1,143 – $ 1,547
Special C: Deore XT F: Rock Shox Indy SL Other Features	$ 1,175 – $ 1,589
Special C: Deore XT F: Rock Shox Judy SL	$ 1,211 – $ 1,674
Special C: Deore XT F: Rock Shox Judy XC Other Features	$ 1,162 – $ 1,572
Special C: Deore XT F: Rock Shox Judy XC Other Features	$ 1,192 – $ 1,612
Special C: XTR F: Rock Shox Indy SL	$ 1,306 – $ 1,766

C: – Components   F: – Fork

MODEL	PRICE RANGE

Ionic 🚲

E3.XC-Bully	$ 828 – $ 1,120
E3.XC-Custom	$ 1,218 – $ 1,648
E3.XC-Team	$ 1,008 – $ 1,363
Ion-DH-Bully	$ 1,008 – $ 1,364
Ion-DH-Team	$ 1,157 – $ 1,565

Iron Horse 🚲

ARS Comp	$ 377 – $ 509
ARS680	$ 461 – $ 624
ARS700	$ 656 – $ 888
ARS900	$ 939 – $ 1,270
AT20	$ 136 – $ 184
AT50	$ 166 – $ 225
DS	$ 656 – $ 888
Flite	$ 118 – $ 159
IFR	$ 148 – $ 200
Maverick	$ 118 – $ 159
MT100	$ 207 – $ 281
MT200	$ 242 – $ 328
MT300	$ 327 – $ 443
MT400 F: Iron Horse	$ 349 – $ 473
MT400 F: Rock Shox Indy C	$ 419 – $ 567
MT500	$ 537 – $ 727
Quest	$ 124 – $ 168
Typhoon	$ 213 – $ 289
XT1500	$ 136 – $ 184
XT1800	$ 166 – $ 225
XT2100	$ 242 – $ 328

C: – Components   F: – Fork

MODEL	PRICE RANGE
Iron Horse/Custom Cycle Supply	
ARS Comp	$ 377 – $ 509
Flite	$ 118 – $ 168
IFR	$ 143 – $ 201
Typhoon	$ 196 – $ 273
Jamis	
Aragon	$ 214 – $ 289
Aurora	$ 388 – $ 525
Boss Cruiser 7	$ 167 – $ 225
Boss Cruiser CB	$ 137 – $ 185
Bossy 16	$ 94 – $ 127
Bossy 20	$ 100 – $ 135
Citizen	$ 161 – $ 217
Coda	$ 328 – $ 443
Cross Country	$ 190 – $ 257
Dakar	$ 975 – $ 1,319
Dakar Sport	$ 657 – $ 889
Dakar Team	$ 1,301 – $ 1,760
Dakota	$ 648 – $ 876
Dakota AL	$ 766 – $ 1,037
Diablo	$ 518 – $ 701
Dragon	$ 904 – $ 1,224
Durango	$ 272 – $ 367
Durango AL	$ 317 – $ 428
Durango Sport	$ 225 – $ 305
Durango Sport SX	$ 283 – $ 383
Durango SX	$ 366 – $ 495
Earth Cruiser 6	$ 167 – $ 225
Earth Cruiser I	$ 137 – $ 185
Earth Cruiser II	$ 112 – $ 152
Eclipse	$ 848 – $ 1,147

C: – Components   F: – Fork

MODEL	PRICE RANGE

Jamis (continued)

Model	Price Range
Eureka	$ 430 – $ 582
Exile	$ 372 – $ 503
Explorer	$ 149 – $ 201
Explorer 24	$ 149 – $ 201
Quest	$ 538 – $ 727
Tangier	$ 272 – $ 367
Taxi	$ 155 – $ 209

Jeep

Model	Price Range
Cherokee Country	$ 355 – $ 481
Cherokee SE	$ 243 – $ 329
Cherokee Sport	$ 300 – $ 406
Grand Cherokee Ltd.	$ 657 – $ 889
Grand Cherokee SE	$ 513 – $ 694
Grand Cherokee Sport	$ 657 – $ 889
Islander Cruiser	$ 91 – $ 124
Laredo SE	$ 243 – $ 329
Laredo Sport	$ 300 – $ 406
Laredo TSi	$ 355 – $ 481
Renegade Folding	$ 382 – $ 517
Renegade SE	$ 137 – $ 185
Renegade Sport Light blue fade	$ 155 – $ 209
Renegade Sport Opal satin fade	$ 184 – $ 249
Wrangler Rio Grande	$ 184 – $ 249
Wrangler S	$ 155 – $ 209
Wrangler Sahara	$ 214 – $ 289
Wrangler SE	$ 130 – $ 177
Wrangler Sport	$ 155 – $ 209

Just Two Bikes

Model	Price Range
Just 4 Fun F: Just Two Bikes C: Alivio/Nexus	$ 1,237 – $ 1,674

C: – Components   F: – Fork

MODEL	PRICE RANGE

Just Two Bikes *(continued)*

Just 4 Fun F: Just Two Bikes C: Nexus	$ 1,196 – $ 1,618
Just 4 Fun F: Just Two Bikes C: Unspecified	$ 1,149 – $ 1,555
Montage	$ 1,237 – $ 1,674

KHS

Aero Comp	$ 787 – $ 1,065
Aero Track	$ 382 – $ 517
Aero Turbo	$ 656 – $ 888
Alite 1000	$ 461 – $ 624
Alite 3000	$ 679 – $ 919
Alite 4000 F: Rock Shox Judy XC C: Deore XT	$ 975 – $ 1,319
Alite 4000 F: Rock Shox Judy XC C: XTR 950	$ 1,238 – $ 1,675
Alite 500	$ 242 – $ 328
Alite 500 X	$ 299 – $ 405
Brentwood	$ 202 – $ 273
Comp	$ 425 – $ 575
Descent X	$ 461 – $ 624
Fleetwood	$ 461 – $ 624
FXT Comp	$ 745 – $ 1,008
FXT Pro	$ 904 – $ 1,223
FXT Team	$ 1,175 – $ 1,589
Montana	$ 118 – $ 159
Pro	$ 610 – $ 825
Raptor	$ 124 – $ 168
Sport	$ 184 – $ 249
Sport X	$ 231 – $ 312
Summit	$ 299 – $ 405
Summit X	$ 409 – $ 553
T-Rex	$ 136 – $ 184

C: – Components   F: – Fork

MODEL	PRICE RANGE
KHS *(continued)*	🚲
Tandemania Alite	$ 827 – $ 1,119
Tandemania Comp	$ 652 – $ 882
Tandemania Pro FXT	$ 1,218 – $ 1,648
Tandemania Sport	$ 435 – $ 589
Team XT	$ 940 – $ 1,272
Team XTR	$ 1,218 – $ 1,648
Trail	$ 148 – $ 200
Trail X	$ 184 – $ 249
Wedgewood	$ 327 – $ 443
Westwood	$ 163 – $ 221
Klein	🚲
Attitude Comp	$ 866 – $ 1,172
Attitude Race	$ 1,008 – $ 1,363
Mantra Comp	$ 787 – $ 1,065
Mantra Race	$ 1,125 – $ 1,522
Pulse Comp	$ 409 – $ 553
Pulse Comp S	$ 461 – $ 624
Pulse Pro	$ 701 – $ 949
Pulse Race	$ 547 – $ 740
Quantum Race	$ 904 – $ 1,223
Stage	$ 537 – $ 727
Stage Comp	$ 787 – $ 1,065
Kona	🚲
AA	$ 701 – $ 949
A'ha	$ 327 – $ 443
Caldera	$ 745 – $ 1,008
Cinder Cone	$ 446 – $ 603
Explosif	$ 847 – $ 1,146
Fire Mountain	$ 338 – $ 458

C: – Components   F: – Fork

MODEL	PRICE RANGE

Kona *(continued)*

Hahanna	$ 260 – $ 351
Hot	$ 1,069 – $ 1,447
Kapu	$ 807 – $ 1,092
Kilauea	$ 586 – $ 793
Kilauea SE	$ 745 – $ 1,008
King Kikapu	$ 1,150 – $ 1,556
Koa	$ 371 – $ 502
Ku	$ 1,069 – $ 1,447
Kula	$ 922 – $ 1,248
Lava Dome	$ 338 – $ 458
Lava Dome SE	$ 299 – $ 405
Manomano	$ 766 – $ 1,036
Muni-Mula	$ 537 – $ 727
U'hu	$ 975 – $ 1,319
U'I	$ 586 – $ 793

Land Rover

APB	$ 1,040 – $ 1,406

Landshark

Roadshark	$ 1,286 – $ 1,740
Trackshark	$ 1,232 – $ 1,667
X-Shark	$ 1,149 – $ 1,555

LeMond

Alpe d'Huez	$ 610 – $ 826
Buenos Aries	$ 745 – $ 1,008
Chamberry	$ 1,098 – $ 1,486
Reno	$ 513 – $ 694
Tourmalet	$ 562 – $ 761
Zurich	$ 904 – $ 1,224

C: – Components   F: – Fork

MODEL	PRICE RANGE

Le Mond (continued)

P-38	$ 997 – $ 1,348
P-38C	$ 1,236 – $ 1,672
Stealth	$ 686 – $ 928

Linear

CLWB F: Akisu C: Recumbent Medley	$ 586 – $ 793
CLWB F: Akisu C: Nexus	$ 409 – $ 553
LWB	$ 657 – $ 889
Tandem	$ 1,197 – $ 1,620

Litespeed

Appalachian	$ 1,055 – $ 1,427
Catalyst F: Kinesis	$ 975 – $ 1,319
Catalyst F: Look C: Chorus	$ 1,238 – $ 1,675
Catalyst F: Look C: 600 Ultegra	$ 1,138 – $ 1,540
Classic F: Kinesis C: 105SC	$ 1,070 – $ 1,447
Classic F: Kinesis C: 105SC Polished	$ 1,112 – $ 1,504
Classic F: Look C: 600 Ultegra	$ 1,208 – $ 1,634
Classic F: Look C: 600 Ultegra Polished	$ 1,238 – $ 1,675
Classic F: Look C: Chorus	$ 1,288 – $ 1,742
Classic F: Look C: Chorus Polished	$ 1,307 – $ 1,769
Hiwassee F: Rock Shox Indy C	$ 865 – $ 1,170
Hiwassee F: Rock Shox Indy SL	$ 975 – $ 1,319
Hiwassee F: Rock Shox Judy XC	$ 1,163 – $ 1,573
Natchez F: Kinesis	$ 865 – $ 1,170
Natchez F: Look	$ 1,040 – $ 1,406
Obed F: Rock Shox Indy SL	$ 1,040 – $ 1,406
Obed F: Rock Shox Judy XC	$ 1,175 – $ 1,589
Ocoee F: Rock Shox Indy SL C: Deore XT/LX	$ 1,151 – $ 1,557
Ocoee F: Rock Shox Indy SL C: Deore XT/LX Polished	$ 1,186 – $ 1,605

C: – Components   F: – Fork

MODEL	PRICE RANGE

Litespeed *(continued)*

Model	Price Range
Ocoee F: Rock Shox Judy XC C: Deore XT	$ 1,256 – $ 1,699
Ocoee F: Rock Shox Judy XC C: Deore XT Polished	$ 1,280 – $ 1,732
Owl Hollow F: Rock Shox Indy SL	$ 1,233 – $ 1,668
Owl Hollow F: Rock Shox Judy XC	$ 1,310 – $ 1,773
Tachyon F: Kestrel EMS C: 600 Ultegra	$ 1,070 – $ 1,447
Tachyon F: Kestrel EMS C: Dura-Ace	$ 1,256 – $ 1,699

Living-X

Model	Price Range
Menage F: Answer Manitou Pro	$ 610 – $ 825
Menage F: Answer Manitou SX C: Deore XT	$ 827 – $ 1,119
Menage F: Answer Manitou SX C: XTR 950	$ 975 – $ 1,319
OzziRoo Expert	$ 701 – $ 949
OzziRoo Pro	$ 904 – $ 1,223
OzziRoo Sport I	$ 461 – $ 624
OzziRoo Sport II	$ 562 – $ 760
OzziRoo Team I	$ 656 – $ 888
OzziRoo Team II	$ 866 – $ 1,172
OzziRoo Team III	$ 975 – $ 1,319
Plant F: Answer Manitou Pro	$ 656 – $ 888
Plant F: Answer Manitou SX	$ 827 – $ 1,119
Plant F: Answer Manitou SX Ti	$ 1,008 – $ 1,363

Lovely Lowrider

Model	Price Range
Bondobike	$ 355 – $ 518

Mandaric

Model	Price Range
Genius CX	$ 975 – $ 1,319
Neuron	$ 973 – $ 1,317
Thron	$ 562 – $ 760
Thron CX	$ 562 – $ 760

C: – Components   F: – Fork

1997

MODEL	PRICE RANGE

Marin

Model	Price Range
Bear Valley F: Marin	$ 299 – $ 405
Bear Valley F: Rock Shox Quadra 5	$ 382 – $ 517
Bear Valley SE F: Answer Manitou Mach 5 Pro XC	$ 461 – $ 624
Bear Valley SE F: Marin	$ 355 – $ 480
Bobcat Trail	$ 237 – $ 320
Bolinas Ridge	$ 184 – $ 249
Eldridge Grade F: Answer Manitou Pro C	$ 562 – $ 760
Eldridge Grade F: Marin	$ 461 – $ 624
Hawk Hill	$ 242 – $ 328
Hidden Canyon F: Marin	$ 173 – $ 233
Hidden Canyon F: RST 161B	$ 196 – $ 265
Highway One	$ 656 – $ 888
Indian Fire Trail	$ 904 – $ 1,223
Larkspur	$ 184 – $ 249
Mount Vision	$ 904 – $ 1,223
Muir Woods F: Marin	$ 271 – $ 367
Muir Woods F: Rock Shox Quadra 5	$ 344 – $ 465
Nail Trail F: Answer Manitou Pro C	$ 508 – $ 687
Nail Trail F: Marin	$ 404 – $ 547
Nail Trail FRS	$ 745 – $ 1,008
Palisades Trail F: Marin	$ 333 – $ 451
Palisades Trail F: Rock Shox Indy C	$ 409 – $ 554
Pine Mountain	$ 656 – $ 888
Point Reyes	$ 512 – $ 693
Quake	$ 610 – $ 825
Quake 5.0	$ 787 – $ 1,065
Quake 9.0	$ 1,008 – $ 1,363
Redwood	$ 409 – $ 553
Rift Zone	$ 701 – $ 949
Rocky Ridge	$ 656 – $ 888
San Anselmo	$ 355 – $ 480

C: – Components   F: – Fork

MODEL	PRICE RANGE

Marin *(continued)* 🚲

San Rafael	$ 242 – $ 328
Sausalito	$ 349 – $ 473
Stinson	$ 225 – $ 304
Team Issue	$ 1,098 – $ 1,485
Team Marin	$ 787 – $ 1,065
Team Titanium	$ 1,069 – $ 1,447

Marinoni 🚲

Ciclo	$ 923 – $ 1,248
Estasi	$ 1,228 – $ 1,662
Leggero	$ 1,151 – $ 1,557
Piccola	$ 787 – $ 1,065
Pista	$ 1,055 – $ 1,427
Piuma	$ 1,280 – $ 1,732
Squadra	$ 904 – $ 1,224
Turismo	$ 848 – $ 1,147

Masi 🚲

Gran Corsa	C: Sachs 5000 Other Features	$ 690 – $ 934
Gran Corsa	C: Sachs 5000 Other Features	$ 813 – $ 1,099
Gran Corsa	C: Sachs New Success Other Features	$ 885 – $ 1,198
Gran Corsa	C: Sachs New Success Other Features	$ 1,004 – $ 1,359
Gran Corsa	F: Masi C: Athena	$ 976 – $ 1,320
Gran Corsa	F: Masi C: Chorus	$ 1,081 – $ 1,462
Gran Corsa	F: Masi C: Record	$ 1,239 – $ 1,676
Gran Corsa	F: Masi C: Veloce	$ 836 – $ 1,131
Gran Corsa	F: Masi C: Shimano 600 Ultegra	$ 889 – $ 1,203
Gran Corsa	F: Masi C: Shimano Dura-Ace	$ 1,176 – $ 1,591
Gran Criterium	C: Sachs 5000 Other Features	$ 1,028 – $ 1,390
Gran Criterium	C: Sachs 5000 Other Features	$ 1,112 – $ 1,504
Gran Criterium	C: Sachs New Success Other Features	$ 1,160 – $ 1,569

C: – Components   F: – Fork

MODEL	PRICE RANGE

Masi (*continued*)

Model	Price Range
Gran Criterium C: Sachs New Success Other Features	$ 1,234 – $ 1,669
Gran Criterium F: Masi C: Athena	$ 1,216 – $ 1,646
Gran Criterium F: Masi C: Chorus	$ 1,277 – $ 1,727
Gran Criterium F: Masi C: Veloce	$ 1,127 – $ 1,525
Gran Criterium F: Masi C: Shimano 600 Ultegra	$ 1,162 – $ 1,572
Nuova Strada C: Sachs 5000 Other Features	$ 750 – $ 1,015
Nuova Strada C: Sachs 5000 Other Features	$ 867 – $ 1,173
Nuova Strada C: Sachs New Success Other Features	$ 936 – $ 1,266
Nuova Strada C: Sachs New Success Other Features	$ 1,048 – $ 1,418
Nuova Strada F: Masi C: Athena	$ 1,021 – $ 1,381
Nuova Strada F: Masi C: Chorus	$ 1,119 – $ 1,514
Nuova Strada F: Masi C: Record	$ 1,263 – $ 1,709
Nuova Strada F: Masi C: Veloce	$ 889 – $ 1,203
Nuova Strada F: Masi C: Shimano 600 Ultegra	$ 939 – $ 1,271
Nuova Strada F: Masi C: Shimano Dura-Ace	$ 1,207 – $ 1,632
Team 3V C: Sachs 5000 Other Features	$ 868 – $ 1,174
Team 3V C: Sachs 5000 Other Features	$ 972 – $ 1,315
Team 3V F: Masi C: Athena	$ 1,107 – $ 1,497
Team 3V F: Masi C: Chorus	$ 1,190 – $ 1,610
Team 3V F: Masi C: Record	$ 1,306 – $ 1,766
Team 3V F: Masi C: Veloce	$ 991 – $ 1,341
Team 3V F: Masi C: Sachs New Success	$ 1,130 – $ 1,529
Team 3V F: Masi C: 600 Ultegra	$ 1,036 – $ 1,402
Team 3V F: Masi C: Dura-Ace	$ 1,262 – $ 1,707
Tre Volumetrica C: Sachs 5000 Other Features	$ 957 – $ 1,295
Tre Volumetrica C: Sachs 5000 Other Features	$ 1,050 – $ 1,421
MasiTre Volumetrica C: Sachs New Success Other Features	$ 1,104 – $ 1,494
Tre Volumetrica C: Sachs New Success Other Features	$ 1,189 – $ 1,609
Tre Volumetrica F: Masi C: Athena	$ 1,169 – $ 1,581

C: – Components   F: – Fork

MODEL	PRICE RANGE

Masi (continued)

Tre Volumetrica F: Masi C: Chorus	$ 1,240 – $ 1,678
Tre Volumetrica F: Masi C: Veloce	$ 1,067 – $ 1,444
Tre Volumetrica F: Masi C: 600 Ultegra	$ 1,107 – $ 1,498
Tre Volumetrica F: Masi C: Dura-Ace	$ 1,298 – $ 1,757

Maxam Inc.

Retreat	$ 219 – $ 296
Retreat 266	$ 286 – $ 387
Reveille	$ 299 – $ 405
Reveille LX	$ 398 – $ 539
Tre'vellion	$ 767 – $ 1,037

Merlin

Cyclocross	$ 1,301 – $ 1,760
R.S.R.	$ 1,218 – $ 1,648
Taiga	$ 1,125 – $ 1,522
Triathlon	$ 1,288 – $ 1,742

Mirage

Mirage	$ 657 – $ 889

Mondonico

Diamond Extra C: Sachs 5000 Other Features	$ 891 – $ 1,206
Diamond Extra C: Sachs 5000 Other Features	$ 992 – $ 1,343
Diamond Extra C: Sachs New Success Other Features	$ 1,051 – $ 1,422
Diamond Extra C: Sachs New Success Other Features	$ 1,145 – $ 1,549
Diamond Extra F: Mondonico C: Athena	$ 1,123 – $ 1,519
Diamond Extra F: Mondonico C: Chorus	$ 1,203 – $ 1,628
Diamond Extra F: Mondonico C: Record	$ 1,313 – $ 1,776
Diamond Extra F: Mondonico C: Veloce	$ 1,011 – $ 1,368
Diamond Extra F: Mondonico C: 600 Ultegra	$ 1,054 – $ 1,427

C: – Components   F: – Fork

MODEL	PRICE RANGE

Mondonico (continued)

Model	Price Range
Diamond Extra F: Mondonico C: Dura-Ace	$ 1,272 – $ 1,721
Elos C: Sachs 5000 Other Features	$ 1,012 – $ 1,369
Elos C: Sachs 5000 Other Features	$ 1,099 – $ 1,487
Elos C: Sachs New Success Other Features	$ 1,148 – $ 1,553
Elos C: Sachs New Success Other Features	$ 1,224 – $ 1,657
Elos F: Mondonico C: 600 Ultegra	$ 1,151 – $ 1,557
Elos F: Mondonico C: Athena	$ 1,206 – $ 1,632
Elos F: Mondonico C: Chorus	$ 1,269 – $ 1,717
Elos F: Mondonico C: Veloce	$ 1,115 – $ 1,508
Futura Leggero C: Sachs 5000 Other Features	$ 750 – $ 1,015
Futura Leggero C: Sachs 5000 Other Features	$ 867 – $ 1,173
Futura Leggero C: Sachs New Success Other Features	$ 936 – $ 1,266
Futura Leggero C: Sachs New Success Other Features	$ 1,048 – $ 1,418
Futura Leggero F: Mondonico C: 600 Ultegra	$ 939 – $ 1,271
Futura Leggero F: Mondonico C: Athena	$ 1,021 – $ 1,381
Futura Leggero F: Mondonico C: Chorus	$ 1,119 – $ 1,514
Futura Leggero F: Mondonico C: Dura-Ace	$ 1,207 – $ 1,632
Futura Leggero F: Mondonico C: Record	$ 1,263 – $ 1,709
Futura Leggero F: Mondonico C: Veloce	$ 889 – $ 1,203
Nemo C: Sachs 5000 Other Features	$ 1,037 – $ 1,403
Nemo C: Sachs 5000 Other Features	$ 1,120 – $ 1,515
Nemo C: Sachs New Success Other Features	$ 1,167 – $ 1,579
Nemo C: Sachs New Success Other Features	$ 1,239 – $ 1,676
Nemo F: Mondonico C: 600 Ultegra	$ 1,169 – $ 1,582
Nemo F: Mondonico C: Athena	$ 1,222 – $ 1,654
Nemo F: Mondonico C: Chorus	$ 1,281 – $ 1,733
Nemo F: Mondonico C: Veloce	$ 1,135 – $ 1,535

Mongoose

Model	Price Range
Alta	$ 287 – $ 388
Alta SX	$ 394 – $ 532

C: – Components   F: – Fork

MODEL	PRICE RANGE
Mongoose (continued)	🚲
Comp SX	$ 769 – $ 1,040
Crossway 250	$ 169 – $ 229
Crossway 450	$ 222 – $ 300
Crossway 650	$ 278 – $ 376
Crossway 850	$ 362 – $ 490
DMC	$ 446 – $ 604
Expert Comp	$ 149 – $ 202
Expert Pro	$ 189 – $ 256
Expert Pro Cruiser	$ 196 – $ 265
Hill Topper	$ 267 – $ 362
Hill Topper SX	$ 387 – $ 524
Menace	$ 129 – $ 175
Menace Cruiser	$ 136 – $ 184
Motivator	$ 109 – $ 147
Mt. Grizzly	$ 136 – $ 184
Pro SX	$ 1,020 – $ 1,380
Racer X	$ 95 – $ 129
RM 1.0	$ 1,133 – $ 1,533
Road F: Kinesis	$ 665 – $ 900
Road F: Mongoose	$ 470 – $ 637
Rockadile SX	$ 544 – $ 736
Solution Comp	$ 300 – $ 406
Solution Pro	$ 363 – $ 491
Solution Team	$ 515 – $ 696
Solution Team Cruiser	$ 515 – $ 696
Solution Team Jr.	$ 424 – $ 574
Stormer	$ 163 – $ 220
SuperGoose Comp	$ 189 – $ 256
SuperGoose Pro	$ 248 – $ 335
SuperGoose Pro Cruiser	$ 261 – $ 353
Switchback	$ 202 – $ 274

C: – Components   F: – Fork

MODEL	PRICE RANGE

Mongoose (continued)

Model	Price Range
Sycomore	$ 235 – $ 318
Sycomore SX	$ 325 – $ 439
Tetra SX	$ 455 – $ 615
The Fuzz	$ 440 – $ 596
Threshold	$ 182 – $ 247
Threshold Sport	$ 182 – $ 247
VRS 1.0	$ 631 – $ 854
VRS 3.0	$ 848 – $ 1,147
VRS 5.0	$ 1,337 – $ 1,808
Zero-G SX	$ 515 – $ 696

Montague

Model	Price Range
Backcountry	$ 300 – $ 406
Crosstown	$ 355 – $ 481
The Urban	$ 513 – $ 694
Triframe Tandem	$ 1,124 – $ 1,521

Monty

Model	Price Range
B-205 CG	$ 160 – $ 216
B-205 CN	$ 148 – $ 200
B-207 CE	$ 202 – $ 273
B-207 CJ	$ 268 – $ 363
B-219 X-Class	$ 240 – $ 325
B-219 X-Hydra	$ 430 – $ 582
B-219 X-Stam	$ 322 – $ 435
B-221 X-Lite	$ 701 – $ 949
B-221 X-Pro	$ 591 – $ 799
B-231 X-Lite	$ 901 – $ 1,219

Moving Violations

Model	Price Range
Banana Split Swinger	$ 184 – $ 249

C: – Components   F: – Fork

MODEL	PRICE RANGE

Moving Violations *(continued)*

Model	Price Range
Lowglide Stretch Cruiser	$ 271 – $ 367
Swinger	$ 184 – $ 249

Mrazek

Model	Price Range
BOH FS Quarz	$ 1,054 – $ 1,427
BOH FS XTR	$ 1,264 – $ 1,711
BOH FX LX/XT F: Rock Shox Indy SL C: Deore LX	$ 766 – $ 1,065
BOH FX Neos/Quarz	$ 766 – $ 1,036
BOH FX STX-RC	$ 679 – $ 919
BOH FX XT	$ 940 – $ 1,272
BOH FX Quarz	$ 866 – $ 1,172
BOH FX XTR	$ 1,150 – $ 1,556

Nishiki

Model	Price Range
Ambush	$ 243 – $ 329
Arroyo	$ 237 – $ 321
Backroads	$ 243 – $ 329
Blazer	$ 149 – $ 201
Bravo	$ 124 – $ 168
Cascade	$ 383 – $ 518
Century	$ 155 – $ 209
Colorado	$ 300 – $ 406
Hill Razer	$ 124 – $ 168
Manitoba	$ 196 – $ 265
Pinnacle	$ 462 – $ 625
Pueblo	$ 173 – $ 233
Sport	$ 178 – $ 241

Norco

Model	Price Range
Berretta	$ 254 – $ 344

C: – Components   F: – Fork

MODEL	PRICE RANGE

Norco *(continued)* 🚲

Model	Price Range
Bigfoot	$ 317 – $ 428
Bomber	$ 1,186 – $ 1,605
Bush Pilot	$ 190 – $ 257
Java	$ 724 – $ 979
Katmandu	$ 175 – $ 237
Kokanee	$ 220 – $ 297
Lobos Comp	$ 787 – $ 1,065
Lobos Pro	$ 787 – $ 1,065
Magnum	$ 420 – $ 568
Mocha	$ 601 – $ 813
Nitro	$ 657 – $ 889
Rampage	$ 848 – $ 1,147
Sasquatch	$ 538 – $ 728
Tango	$ 562 – $ 761
Team Issue	$ 1,112 – $ 1,504
Torrent	$ 1,040 – $ 1,406

North Star 🚲

Model	Price Range
Cielo	$ 562 – $ 760
El Sol	$ 787 – $ 1,065
Estrella	$ 355 – $ 480
Estrella Al	$ 409 – $ 553
La Luna Al	$ 512 – $ 693
Viento	$ 409 – $ 553

Novara 🚲

Model	Price Range
A7000	$ 342 – $ 462
A7000S	$ 342 – $ 462
Alight	$ 252 – $ 340
Arriba	$ 396 – $ 536
Aspen	$ 225 – $ 305

C: – Components   F: – Fork

MODEL	PRICE RANGE

Novara *(continued)* 🚲

Corsa	$ 193 – $ 261
Dirt Rider	$ 137 – $ 185
M-1000	$ 181 – $ 245
Ponderosa	$ 510 – $ 690
Pro-Ultimate	$ 459 – $ 621
Randonee	$ 369 – $ 499
Strada	$ 436 – $ 590
X-R	$ 240 – $ 325

Otis Guy 🚲

Purist F: Rock Shox Judy XC	$ 1,045 – $ 1,414
Purist F: Tange Silhouette	$ 1,192 – $ 1,612
Smoothie Other Features	$ 1,225 – $ 1,658
Smoothie Other Features	$ 1,262 – $ 1,708
Smoothie F: Tange Silhouette C: 600 Ultegra	$ 1,097 – $ 1,484
Softail	$ 1,155 – $ 1,563

Parkpre 🚲

Alu Comp F: Parkpre	$ 299 – $ 405
Alu Comp F: RST 171	$ 355 – $ 480
Alu Max F: Answer Manitou Pro	$ 492 – $ 666
Alu Max F: Answer Manitou Pro C	$ 522 – $ 707
Alu Max F: Answer Manitou SX	$ 555 – $ 751
Alu Max F: Parkpre	$ 409 – $ 553
Alu Max F: Rock Shox Indy C	$ 477 – $ 645
Alu Max F: Rock Shox Indy SL	$ 532 – $ 720
Alu Max F: Rock Shox Indy XC	$ 497 – $ 673
Alu Sport F: Parkpre	$ 282 – $ 382
Alu Sport F: RST 171B	$ 322 – $ 435
Alu Team F: Answer Manitou Pro	$ 610 – $ 825
Alu Team F: Answer Manitou Pro C	$ 596 – $ 806

C: – Components   F: – Fork

MODEL	PRICE RANGE
Parkpre (continued)	🚲
Alu Team F: Answer Manitou SX	$ 675 – $ 913
Alu Team F: Answer Manitou SX Ti	$ 736 – $ 996
Alu Team F: Parkpre	$ 547 – $ 740
Alu Team F: Rock Shox Indy SL	$ 656 – $ 888
Alu Team F: Rock Shox Indy XC	$ 619 – $ 838
Alu Team F: Rock Shox Judy XC	$ 684 – $ 925
Comp Limited F: Parkpre	$ 299 – $ 405
Comp Limited F: RST 381L	$ 344 – $ 465
Grand Sport	$ 166 – $ 225
Mountain Comp F: Parkpre	$ 260 – $ 351
Mountain Comp F: RST 171	$ 299 – $ 405
Pro 825 F: Answer Manitou Pro C	$ 736 – $ 996
Pro 825 F: Answer Manitou SX	$ 770 – $ 1,042
Pro 825 F: Answer Manitou SX Ti	$ 827 – $ 1,119
Pro 825 F: Rock Shox Indy SL	$ 753 – $ 1,019
Pro 825 F: Rock Shox Indy XC	$ 719 – $ 973
Pro 825 F: Rock Shox Judy SL	$ 866 – $ 1,172
Pro 825 F: Rock Shox Judy XC	$ 779 – $ 1,053
Pro 825 F: Tange	$ 656 – $ 888
Pro Elite F: Answer Manitou Pro C	$ 1,066 – $ 1,443
Pro Elite F: Answer Manitou SX	$ 1,087 – $ 1,470
Pro Elite F: Answer Manitou SX Ti	$ 1,120 – $ 1,515
Pro Elite F: Parkpre	$ 998 – $ 1,350
Pro Elite F: Rock Shox Indy SL	$ 1,075 – $ 1,455
Pro Elite F: Rock Shox Indy XC	$ 1,051 – $ 1,422
Pro Elite F: Rock Shox Judy SL	$ 1,145 – $ 1,550
Pro Elite F: Rock Shox Judy XC	$ 1,092 – $ 1,478
Pro Image F: Answer Manitou Pro C	$ 803 – $ 1,087
Pro Image F: Answer Manitou SX	$ 831 – $ 1,125
Pro Image F: Answer Manitou SX Ti	$ 885 – $ 1,198
Pro Image F: Rock Shox Indy SL	$ 811 – $ 1,098

C: – Components   F: – Fork

MODEL	PRICE RANGE

Parkpre (continued)

Model	Price Range
Pro Image F: Rock Shox Indy XC	$ 783 – $ 1,059
Pro Image F: Rock Shox Judy SL	$ 915 – $ 1,238
Pro Image F: Rock Shox Judy XC	$ 839 – $ 1,136
Pro Image F: Tange	$ 719 – $ 973
Scepter Comp F: Answer Manitou Pro	$ 451 – $ 610
Scepter Comp F: Answer Manitou Pro C	$ 482 – $ 652
Scepter Comp F: Answer Manitou SX	$ 517 – $ 700
Scepter Comp F: Parkpre	$ 371 – $ 502
Scepter Comp F: Rock Shox Indy C	$ 435 – $ 589
Scepter Comp F: Rock Shox Indy SL	$ 497 – $ 673
Scepter Comp F: Rock Shox Indy XC	$ 456 – $ 617
Solitude F: Parkpre	$ 219 – $ 296
Solitude F: RST 171B	$ 260 – $ 351
Sport Limited F: Parkpre	$ 202 – $ 273
Sport Limited F: RST 156	$ 231 – $ 312
Team 925 F: Answer Manitou Pro	$ 542 – $ 734
Team 925 F: Answer Manitou Pro C	$ 576 – $ 780
Team 925 F: Answer Manitou SX	$ 610 – $ 825
Team 925 F: Answer Manitou SX Ti	$ 675 – $ 913
Team 925 F: Parkpre	$ 461 – $ 624
Team 925 F: Rock Shox Indy SL	$ 591 – $ 799
Team 925 F: Rock Shox Indy XC	$ 552 – $ 747
Team 925 F: Rock Shox Judy XC	$ 638 – $ 863

Pashley

Model	Price Range
DP23 Frontload Trike	$ 767 – $ 1,037
MW1 Worktrike	$ 828 – $ 1,120
MW3 Worktrike	$ 886 – $ 1,198
No. 33 food vending trike	$ 867 – $ 1,173
Parabike 21	$ 652 – $ 882
Parabike 7	$ 562 – $ 761

C: – Components   F: – Fork

MODEL	PRICE RANGE
Pashley *(continued)*	🚲
Picabac Sprint 3	$ 756 – $ 1,022
Picabac Sprint 5	$ 787 – $ 1,065
Picador Sprint 3	$ 701 – $ 949
Picador Sprint 5	$ 741 – $ 1,003
Premier	$ 930 – $ 1,258
Princess Original 3 Plus	$ 508 – $ 687
Princess Sovereign	$ 610 – $ 825
Prospero Original 3 Plus	$ 487 – $ 660
Prospero Sovereign	$ 586 – $ 793
RH2 Equal Wheel Carrier	$ 513 – $ 694
RH3 Equal Wheel Carrier	$ 610 – $ 825
Roadster	$ 409 – $ 554
SW6 26/20 Carrier	$ 557 – $ 754
SW8 Delibike w/carrier	$ 652 – $ 882
TB2 Police Cruiser	$ 657 – $ 889
Tube Rider 1	$ 503 – $ 680
Tube Rider 5	$ 557 – $ 754
Performance	🚲
M-007	$ 939 – $ 1,270
M-107	$ 743 – $ 1,005
M-207	$ 537 – $ 727
M-307	$ 382 – $ 517
M-407	$ 282 – $ 382
M-507	$ 207 – $ 281
M-607	$ 178 – $ 241
M-707	$ 160 – $ 216
Picacho	$ 939 – $ 1,270
Picaro	$ 865 – $ 1,170
R-007 F: Advanced Composite C: Athena/Veloce	$ 1,038 – $ 1,404

C: – Components   F: – Fork

1
9
9
7

MODEL	PRICE RANGE

Performance (continued)

R-007 F: Advanced Composite C: Dura-Ace	$ 1,068 – $ 1,445
R-107	$ 560 – $ 757
R-207	$ 355 – $ 480
X-107	$ 196 – $ 265

Peugeot

Biarritz	$ 610 – $ 826
Chrono	$ 333 – $ 451
Dune 100	$ 137 – $ 185
Dune 200	$ 155 – $ 209
Dune 300	$ 178 – $ 241
Equipe 1000S	$ 328 – $ 443
Equipe 2000AS	$ 513 – $ 694
Equipe 4000AS	$ 702 – $ 949
Equipe 6000DS	$ 610 – $ 826
Hurricane Creek 100	$ 223 – $ 301
Hurricane Creek 200	$ 272 – $ 367
Legend	$ 257 – $ 348
Panorama	$ 155 – $ 209
Prestige	$ 342 – $ 462
Success	$ 436 – $ 590
Urbano	$ 202 – $ 273
X-Country	$ 409 – $ 554

Pinarello

Arriba	$ 848 – $ 1,147
Asolo	$ 1,124 – $ 1,520
Monviso	$ 1,174 – $ 1,588
Replica	$ 923 – $ 1,248
Stelvio	$ 1,006 – $ 1,362
Vuelta	$ 1,217 – $ 1,647

C: – Components   F: – Fork

MODEL	PRICE RANGE

Planet-X 🚲

X/1	$	143	– $	193
X/2	$	184	– $	249

Powerlite 🚲

Expert	$	336	– $	454
P-11	$	106	– $	144
P-17	$	113	– $	154
P-19	$	142	– $	192
P-28	$	197	– $	266
P-38	$	213	– $	288
P-47 Jr. AL	$	247	– $	335
P-51 Pro AL	$	354	– $	479
P-61 Pro XL AL Team	$	472	– $	638
P-61 Pro XL AL Team Spin	$	713	– $	964
P-Shooter	$	94	– $	127
Spitfire	$	206	– $	278

ProFlex 🚲

657	$	700	– $	947
757	$	891	– $	1,206
857	$	1,077	– $	1,457
957	$	1,235	– $	1,671
Animal	$	1,132	– $	1,531
Attack	$	485	– $	656
Beast	$	903	– $	1,221
Beast GDT	$	785	– $	1,062
Reptile	$	598	– $	810

Python 🚲

Anaconda	$	137	– $	185
Boa	$	409	– $	554

C: – Components   F: – Fork

MODEL

PRICE RANGE

Python *(continued)*

Bonecrusher	$ 234 – $	317
Mamba	$ 161 – $	217
Medusa	$ 289 – $	390
Opello	$ 112 – $	152
Serpent	$ 124 – $	168
Strangler	$ 172 – $	233
Vermin	$ 112 – $	152

Raleigh

C200	$ 199 – $	270
C30	$ 133 – $	180
C40	$ 154 – $	208
F500 (Police)	$ 353 – $	477
Jazzi	$ 70 – $	95
Lil' Honey	$ 62 – $	84
M20	$ 107 – $	145
M200	$ 224 – $	303
M30	$ 128 – $	173
M3000	$ 209 – $	283
M40	$ 149 – $	201
M400	$ 329 – $	446
M50	$ 174 – $	236
M55	$ 204 – $	276
M60	$ 204 – $	276
M600	$ 398 – $	538
M7000	$ 398 – $	538
M7500	$ 484 – $	655
M80	$ 258 – $	349
M800	$ 484 – $	655
M8000	$ 566 – $	765
Mountain Scout	$ 107 – $	145

C: – Components   F: – Fork

MODEL	PRICE RANGE

Raleigh *(continued)*

Model	Price Range
MXR	$ 70 – $ 95
MXR Mini	$ 62 – $ 91
MXR Pro	$ 81 – $ 109
R300	$ 306 – $ 414
R500	$ 329 – $ 446
R600	$ 442 – $ 598
R700	$ 566 – $ 765
Retroglide	$ 102 – $ 138
Retroglide 6	$ 123 – $ 166
Retroglide Ultra	$ 258 – $ 349
Rowdy	$ 97 – $ 131

Rans

Model	Price Range
Nimbus	$ 826 – $ 1,117
Rocket	$ 608 – $ 822
S-5	$ 904 – $ 1,224
Stratus	$ 826 – $ 1,117
Tailwind	$ 560 – $ 757
V-Rex	$ 785 – $ 1,062
V-Rex 24	$ 785 – $ 1,062
Zero G	$ 560 – $ 757
Zero G HT	$ 407 – $ 550

ReBike

Model	Price Range
ReBike 2600 LE	$ 277 – $ 375
ReBike 2600 SE	$ 277 – $ 375
ReBike 707	$ 202 – $ 273
ReBike 818	$ 231 – $ 313
ReTrike 707	$ 409 – $ 554
ReTrike 707 VP	$ 409 – $ 554

C: – Components   F: – Fork

MODEL	PRICE RANGE

Red Hot

Model	Price Range
Colors	$ 1,069 – $ 1,447
Colors Deluxe	$ 1,197 – $ 1,620
FS	$ 1,305 – $ 1,765

Redline

Model	Price Range
Proline AL	$ 277 – $ 390
Proline AL Team Issue	$ 374 – $ 518
RL 140	$ 193 – $ 261
RL 180 Junior	$ 193 – $ 261
RL 240 F: Redline	$ 164 – $ 229
RL 340 F: Redline	$ 118 – $ 164
RL 340 Junior F: Redline	$ 118 – $ 164
RL 440	$ 173 – $ 233
RL 480 F: Redline	$ 193 – $ 269
RL 540	$ 243 – $ 329
RL 544	$ 243 – $ 329
RL 640	$ 243 – $ 329

Research Dynamics

Model	Price Range
Coyote AFS Five	$ 701 – $ 949
Coyote AFS Six	$ 866 – $ 1,172
Coyote Alu Five	$ 586 – $ 793
Coyote BMX One	$ 118 – $ 159
Coyote BMX Three	$ 271 – $ 367
Coyote BMX Two	$ 142 – $ 192
Coyote Challenge	$ 225 – $ 304
Coyote Cruiser	$ 124 – $ 168
Coyote Mow Tan	$ 409 – $ 553
Coyote One	$ 148 – $ 200
Coyote Pro Four	$ 461 – $ 624
Coyote Single Track	$ 316 – $ 428

C: – Components   F: – Fork

1997

MODEL	PRICE RANGE
Research Dynamics (*continued*) 🚲	
Coyote STX FS	$ 461 – $ 624
Coyote Summit	$ 154 – $ 208
Coyote Team Extreme 20	$ 112 – $ 151
Coyote Team Extreme 24	$ 142 – $ 192
Coyote Team Rider	$ 178 – $ 241
Coyote Team Six	$ 827 – $ 1,119
Coyote Three	$ 202 – $ 273
Coyote Trail	$ 142 – $ 192
Coyote Two	$ 160 – $ 216
Rhygin 🚲	
853 C: Athena	$ 1,040 – $ 1,406
853 C: Chorus	$ 1,112 – $ 1,504
853 C: Record	$ 1,226 – $ 1,659
853 C: 105SC	$ 903 – $ 1,221
853 C: 600 Ultegra	$ 992 – $ 1,342
853 C: Dura-Ace	$ 1,213 – $ 1,641
Aluminum C: Chorus	$ 1,138 – $ 1,540
Aluminum C: Record	$ 1,245 – $ 1,685
Aluminum C: 105SC	$ 903 – $ 1,221
Aluminum C: 600 Ultegra	$ 965 – $ 1,305
Aluminum C: Dura-Ace	$ 1,233 – $ 1,668
Bangarang F: Marzocchi Bomber Z-2	$ 1,225 – $ 1,658
Bangarang F: Rock Shox Indy SL	$ 947 – $ 1,282
Bangarang F: Rock Shox Indy XC	$ 888 – $ 1,201
Bangarang F: Rock Shox Judy XC	$ 1,003 – $ 1,357
Custom Track	$ 1,138 – $ 1,540
Juke F: Marzocchi Bomber Z-2	$ 1,077 – $ 1,457
Juke F: Rock Shox Indy SL	$ 970 – $ 1,312
Juke F: Rock Shox Judy SL	$ 1,269 – $ 1,717
Juke F: Rock Shox Judy XC	$ 1,018 – $ 1,377

C: – Components   F: – Fork

MODEL	PRICE RANGE
Rhygin (*continued*)	🚲
Juke HS C: Deore LX	$ 1,003 – $ 1,357
Juke HS C: Deore XT	$ 1,062 – $ 1,437
Juke HS C: Deore XT/LX	$ 1,030 – $ 1,394
Juke HS C: XTR 950	$ 1,238 – $ 1,675
Juke SS F: Marzocchi Bomber Z-2	$ 1,164 – $ 1,575
Juke SS F: Rock Shox Judy SL	$ 1,311 – $ 1,774
Juke SS F: Rock Shox Judy XC	$ 1,106 – $ 1,497
Metax C: 105SC	$ 1,105 – $ 1,495
Metax C: 600 Ultegra	$ 1,151 – $ 1,557
Metax C: Athena	$ 1,186 – $ 1,605
Metax C: Chorus	$ 1,238 – $ 1,675
Metax C: Dura-Ace	$ 1,304 – $ 1,765
Metax C: Record	$ 1,312 – $ 1,775
Spike	$ 1,299 – $ 1,757
Time Trial	$ 1,040 – $ 1,406
Urbane	$ 1,084 – $ 1,467
X	$ 1,125 – $ 1,522
Ritchey	🚲
Comp	$ 940 – $ 1,272
P-20	$ 1,245 – $ 1,685
P-21	$ 1,091 – $ 1,476
Road Logic	$ 1,008 – $ 1,364
SoftTail	$ 1,273 – $ 1,722
SwissCross	$ 1,040 – $ 1,406
Robinson	🚲
Jr.	$ 358 – $ 484
MX	$ 209 – $ 282
Pro	$ 339 – $ 458
Pro Cruiser	$ 335 – $ 453

C: – Components   F: – Fork

MODEL	PRICE RANGE

Robinson *(continued)* 🚲

Rebel	$ 138 – $ 186
SST	$ 184 – $ 249
Team Pro XL	$ 488 – $ 660
Team Pro XL Spin	$ 694 – $ 939

Rocky Mountain 🚲

Altitude Team Only	$ 1,269 – $ 1,717
Blizzard	$ 1,001 – $ 1,355
Cardiac F: RMB	$ 327 – $ 443
Cardiac F: Rock Shox Quadra 5	$ 398 – $ 539
Element Race	$ 889 – $ 1,203
Equipe	$ 715 – $ 967
Fusion	$ 409 – $ 553
Hammer Race	$ 591 – $ 799
Oxygen Race	$ 688 – $ 931
Soul	$ 472 – $ 638
Speed	$ 1,175 – $ 1,589
Spice	$ 723 – $ 979
Thin Air	$ 1,001 – $ 1,355
Vertex Team Only	$ 1,313 – $ 1,777
Whistler	$ 327 – $ 443

Roland 🚲

Beach Cruiser With Fenders	$ 118 – $ 160
Big Bend	$ 299 – $ 405
Classic Cruiser	$ 118 – $ 160
Country	$ 124 – $ 168
Country Sport	$ 124 – $ 168
Foothills	$ 184 – $ 249
Packsaddle	$ 154 – $ 208
Packsaddle Comp	$ 213 – $ 289

C: – Components   F: – Fork

MODEL	PRICE RANGE

Romic

Model	Price Range
Club Tourer	$ 871 – $ 1,178
Eco Triple Tourer	$ 948 – $ 1,282
Racer F: Romic C: 600 Ultegra	$ 932 – $ 1,260
Racer F: Romic C: Dura-Ace	$ 1,197 – $ 1,620
Racer F: Romic C: Record	$ 1,284 – $ 1,737
Road Sport	$ 1,112 – $ 1,504
port F: Romic C: 105SC	$ 846 – $ 1,144
Sport F: Romic C: 600 Ultegra	$ 904 – $ 1,224
Sport F: Romic C: Dura-Ace	$ 1,150 – $ 1,556
Sport F: Romic C: Record	$ 1,203 – $ 1,627
SSuper Tourer	$ 1,167 – $ 1,578
Tourer F: Romic C: Chorus	$ 1,024 – $ 1,385
Tourer F: Romic C: Record	$ 1,213 – $ 1,641
Triple Tourer	$ 1,125 – $ 1,522
TX Track	$ 922 – $ 1,248

Ross

Model	Price Range
Adventurer	$ 130 – $ 177
Amazon	$ 91 – $ 123
Beach Commander	$ 124 – $ 168
Bitsy Lady w/training wheels	$ 57 – $ 77
Boomerang	$ 82 – $ 110
Bryce Canyon	$ 243 – $ 329
Centaur w/fenders	$ 355 – $ 481
Chimera	$ 124 – $ 168
Compact III w/fenders	$ 130 – $ 177
Diamond Cruiser	$ 130 – $ 177
Diamond Trimatic w/fenders	$ 161 – $ 217
Dune Commander	$ 124 – $ 168
Eurotour w/fenders	$ 130 – $ 177
Freestyle	$ 184 – $ 249

C: – Components   F: – Fork

MODEL		PRICE RANGE
Ross (continued)		🚲
Frenzy	$ 91 –	$ 123
Glen Canyon	$ 355 –	$ 481
Gran Tour	$ 155 –	$ 209
Little Lady	$ 77 –	$ 104
Minotaur w/fenders	$ 300 –	$ 406
Mt. Hood	$ 513 –	$ 694
Mt. Jefferson	$ 112 –	$ 152
Mt. Katahdin	$ 214 –	$ 289
Mt. Olympus	$ 328 –	$ 443
Mt. Pocono	$ 120 –	$ 163
Mt. Rushmore	$ 149 –	$ 201
Mt. St. Helens	$ 409 –	$ 554
Mt. Washington	$ 172 –	$ 233
Pegasus w/fenders	$ 243 –	$ 329
Petite w/training wheels	$ 75 –	$ 102
Piranha Pro 142	$ 106 –	$ 144
Piranha Pro 144	$ 112 –	$ 152
Piranha Pro 146	$ 124 –	$ 167
Piranha Pro 148	$ 137 –	$ 185
Pronto w/training wheels	$ 57 –	$ 77
Race Team 150	$ 149 –	$ 201
Race Team 152 Mini	$ 168 –	$ 227
Race Team 154	$ 170 –	$ 230
Race Team 156	$ 214 –	$ 289
Race Team 158	$ 355 –	$ 481
Race Team 176 Cruiser	$ 231 –	$ 313
Race Team 178 Cruiser	$ 382 –	$ 517
Radical	$ 77 –	$ 104
Shark	$ 155 –	$ 209
Slinger w/training wheels	$ 75 –	$ 102
Super Gran Tour	$ 214 –	$ 289

C: – Components   F: – Fork

MODEL	PRICE RANGE

Ross *(continued)*

Model	Price Range
Tailspin w/training wheels	$ 69 – $ 94
Teeny Lady w/training wheels	$ 69 – $ 94
Triad	$ 446 – $ 604
Trials 164	$ 342 – $ 462
Trials 166	$ 562 – $ 761
Trials 168	$ 702 – $ 949
Young Lady	$ 82 – $ 110
Zemopi 484	$ 382 – $ 517
Zemopi 584	$ 513 – $ 694
Zemopi 684	$ 786 – $ 1,063
Zemopi 784	$ 1,098 – $ 1,486
Zion Canyon	$ 300 – $ 406

Ruption

Model	Price Range
Chogger	$ 286 – $ 387
GLX	$ 231 – $ 313
Hacker	$ 260 – $ 352
LX	$ 176 – $ 237
Newboy	$ 184 – $ 249
SRI	$ 260 – $ 352
TX-5	$ 130 – $ 177

S & B

Model	Price Range
Beach Cruiser	$ 353 – $ 477
Single	$ 436 – $ 590
Single Trike	$ 518 – $ 701
Tandem	$ 1,197 – $ 1,620

Saint Marks

Model	Price Range
LR-20-68/Bent	$ 183 – $ 248

C: – Components   F: – Fork

MODEL   PRICE RANGE

Santa Cruz   🚲

Heckler C: Deore XT F: Rock Shox Indy SL	$ 1,032 – $ 1,396
Heckler C: Deore XT F: Rock Shox Indy XC	$ 1,000 – $ 1,353
Heckler C: Deore XT F: Rock Shox Judy DH	$ 1,090 – $ 1,474
Heckler C: Deore XT F: Rock Shox Judy DHO	$ 1,238 – $ 1,675
Heckler C: Deore XT F: Rock Shox Judy SL	$ 1,108 – $ 1,499
Heckler C: Deore XT F: Rock Shox Judy XC	$ 1,049 – $ 1,419
Heckler C: Deore XT/LX F: Rock Shox Indy SL	$ 953 – $ 1,289
Heckler C: Deore XT/LX F: Rock Shox Indy XC	$ 919 – $ 1,243
Heckler C: Deore XT/LX F: Rock Shox Judy DH	$ 1,018 – $ 1,377
Heckler C: Deore XT/LX F: Rock Shox Judy DHO	$ 1,188 – $ 1,608
Heckler C: Deore XT/LX F: Rock Shox Judy SL	$ 1,038 – $ 1,404
Heckler C: Deore XT/LX F: Rock Shox Judy XC	$ 973 – $ 1,317
Heckler C: XTR 950 F: Rock Shox Indy SL	$ 1,215 – $ 1,644
Heckler C: XTR 950 F: Rock Shox Indy XC	$ 1,194 – $ 1,615
Heckler C: XTR 950 F: Rock Shox Judy DH	$ 1,252 – $ 1,693
Heckler C: XTR 950 F: Rock Shox Judy SL	$ 1,264 – $ 1,710
Heckler C: XTR 950 F: Rock Shox Judy XC	$ 1,225 – $ 1,658
Tazmon C: Deore XT F: Rock Shox Indy SL	$ 1,105 – $ 1,495
Tazmon C: Deore XT F: Rock Shox Indy XC	$ 1,078 – $ 1,459
Tazmon C: Deore XT F: Rock Shox Judy DH	$ 1,156 – $ 1,563
Tazmon C: Deore XT F: Rock Shox Judy SL	$ 1,171 – $ 1,585
Tazmon C: Deore XT F: Rock Shox Judy XC	$ 1,120 – $ 1,515
Tazmon C: Deore XT/LX F: Rock Shox Indy SL	$ 1,035 – $ 1,400
Tazmon C: Deore XT/LX F: Rock Shox Indy XC	$ 1,003 – $ 1,357
Tazmon C: Deore XT/LX F: Rock Shox Judy DH	$ 1,093 – $ 1,478
Tazmon C: Deore XT/LX F: Rock Shox Judy SL	$ 1,110 – $ 1,502
Tazmon C: Deore XT/LX F: Rock Shox Judy XC	$ 1,052 – $ 1,423
Tazmon C: XTR 950 F: Rock Shox Indy SL	$ 1,261 – $ 1,706
Tazmon C: XTR 950 F: Rock Shox Indy XC	$ 1,244 – $ 1,684
Tazmon C: XTR 950 F: Rock Shox Judy DH	$ 1,291 – $ 1,747
Tazmon C: XTR 950 F: Rock Shox Judy SL	$ 1,300 – $ 1,759
Tazmon C: XTR 950 F: Rock Shox Judy XC	$ 1,270 – $ 1,718

C: – Components   F: – Fork

MODEL	PRICE RANGE

Santana

Arriva	$ 1,313 – $ 1,776
Cilantro	$ 1,313 – $ 1,776
Fusion	$ 1,313 – $ 1,776
Rio	$ 1,174 – $ 1,588
Visa	$ 1,174 – $ 1,588
Vision	$ 1,174 – $ 1,588
Frontier	$ 163 – $ 220

Schwinn

Frontier DLX	$ 267 – $ 362
Frontier GS	$ 189 – $ 256
Frontier GSX	$ 222 – $ 300
Homegrown F: Rock Shox Judy SL	$ 1,561 – $ 2,113
Homegrown F: Rock Shox Judy SL Polished	$ 1,615 – $ 2,185
Homegrown F: Rock Shox Judy XC C: Grip Shift/Deore XT	$ 1,215 – $ 1,644
Homegrown F: Rock Shox Judy XC C: Deore XT Other Features	$ 1,086 – $ 1,469
Homegrown F: Rock Shox Judy XC C: Deore XT Other Features	$ 1,404 – $ 1,900
Homegrown F: Rock Shox Judy XC C: Deore XT/LX	$ 946 – $ 1,279
Hydra Glide	$ 299 – $ 413
Le Tour	$ 299 – $ 404
Mesa	$ 248 – $ 335
Mesa GS	$ 299 – $ 405
Mesa GSX	$ 362 – $ 490
Moab 1 Finish: Black	$ 685 – $ 927
Moab 1 Finish: Red	$ 630 – $ 852
Moab 2 F: Rock Shox Indy C	$ 572 – $ 774
Moab 2 F: Rock Shox Indy XC	$ 543 – $ 735
Moab 3 F: Rock Shox Indy C	$ 424 – $ 573

C: – Components   F: – Fork

MODEL	PRICE RANGE

Schwinn (continued)

MODEL		PRICE RANGE	
Moab 3 F: Rock Shox Quadra 5	$	393 – $	532
Passage	$	454 – $	614
Power Glide F: Schwinn	$	196 – $	274
Predator CB F: Schwinn	$	123 – $	175
Predator FW F: Schwinn	$	130 – $	184
Predator Pro F: Schwinn	$	156 – $	220
S 10	$	896 – $	1,212
S 20	$	740 – $	1,001
S 30	$	630 – $	852
Searcher Express	$	222 – $	300
Searcher Horizon	$	312 – $	422
Searcher Range	$	267 – $	362
Searcher Ridge	$	312 – $	422
Searcher Transit	$	189 – $	256
Super Sport	$	572 – $	774
XS Pro Cruiser Modified 1	$	630 – $	852
XS Pro Cruiser Modified 2	$	484 – $	655
XS Pro Modified 1	$	630 – $	852
XS Pro Modified 2	$	484 – $	655
XS Pro Stock 1	$	331 – $	448
XS Pro Stock 1 Polished	$	343 – $	465
XS Pro Stock 2	$	254 – $	344
XS Pro Stock 2 Polished	$	274 – $	370
XS Super Stock 1	$	286 – $	388
XS Super Stock 1 Chrome Plated	$	299 – $	405
XS Super Stock 2	$	222 – $	300
XS Super Stock 2 Chrome Plated	$	228 – $	309
XS Super Stock 3	$	189 – $	256
XS Super Stock 3 Chrome Plated	$	196 – $	265
XS Super Stock Cruiser 3	$	202 – $	274

C: – Components   F: – Fork

MODEL	PRICE RANGE

Scorpio 🚲

Model	Price Range
A-Z Pro	$ 106 – $ 144
AL100	$ 196 – $ 265
AL400	$ 294 – $ 398
AT100	$ 137 – $ 185
AT200X	$ 196 – $ 265
AT400	$ 243 – $ 329
AT45	$ 118 – $ 160
AT50	$ 118 – $ 160
ATJ20	$ 94 – $ 127
Primrose	$ 124 – $ 168

Scott 🚲

Model	Price Range
AFD-307	$ 502 – $ 679
Boston	$ 202 – $ 273
Boulder	$ 497 – $ 673
Catalina	$ 288 – $ 390
Cheyenne	$ 610 – $ 825
Comp Jr	$ 166 – $ 225
Comp Racing	$ 610 – $ 825
Eldora	$ 265 – $ 359
Elite Racing	$ 839 – $ 1,136
Galena	$ 745 – $ 1,008
Navajo	$ 440 – $ 596
Neva	$ 885 – $ 1,198
Ouray	$ 190 – $ 257
Pro Racing	$ 1,039 – $ 1,406
Pro Racing World Cup	$ 1,313 – $ 1,777
Purgatory	$ 237 – $ 320
Team Jr	$ 178 – $ 241
Team Racing	$ 1,039 – $ 1,406
Tigua	$ 265 – $ 359

C: – Components   F: – Fork

MODEL	PRICE RANGE

Scott *(continued)*

Model	Price Range
Vail	$ 409 – $ 553
Vertigo Comp	$ 552 – $ 747
Vertigo Pro	$ 958 – $ 1,295
Waimea	$ 958 – $ 1,295
Yecora	$ 322 – $ 435

SE Racing

Model	Price Range
Assasin	$ 207 – $ 281
Assasin Killer XL	$ 446 – $ 603
Assasin Pro	$ 207 – $ 281
Assasin Pro XL	$ 271 – $ 367
Bronco	$ 136 – $ 184
Floval Flyer Killer	$ 497 – $ 673
Floval Flyer Killer Anodized	$ 537 – $ 727
Floval Flyer Killer Polished	$ 512 – $ 693
Floval Flyer Pro	$ 333 – $ 450
Floval Flyer Pro Anodized	$ 355 – $ 480
PK Ripper Killer XL	$ 461 – $ 624
PK Ripper Killer XL Anodized	$ 512 – $ 693
PK Ripper Killer XL Polished	$ 487 – $ 659
PK Ripper Pro	$ 299 – $ 405
PK Ripper Pro Anodized	$ 349 – $ 473
PK Ripper Pro Polished	$ 322 – $ 435
PK Ripper Pro XL	$ 299 – $ 405
PK Ripper Pro XL Anodized	$ 349 – $ 473
PK Ripper Pro XL Polished	$ 322 – $ 435
Quadangle Pro	$ 299 – $ 405

Softride

Model	Price Range
Firestorm	$ 867 – $ 1,173
Norwester	$ 610 – $ 826

C: – Components   F: – Fork

MODEL	PRICE RANGE
Softride *(continued)*	🚲
Powerwing	$ 1,175 – $ 1,589
RoadWing	$ 940 – $ 1,272
Windshear	$ 867 – $ 1,173
Specialized	🚲
Allez A1	$ 563 – $ 762
Allez A1 Sport	$ 724 – $ 979
Allez M2 Comp	$ 871 – $ 1,178
Crossroads	$ 168 – $ 228
Crossroads A1 Elite	$ 333 – $ 450
Crossroads A1 Expert	$ 263 – $ 356
Crossroads A1 Pro	$ 471 – $ 637
Crossroads Sport	$ 201 – $ 272
Crossroads Ultra	$ 234 – $ 317
Fatboy	$ 168 – $ 228
Fatboy Chrome-plated	$ 186 – $ 252
Fatboy A1	$ 246 – $ 333
Fatboy A1 Pro	$ 389 – $ 526
Fatboy A1 Team	$ 627 – $ 848
Globe 7	$ 304 – $ 411
Ground Control AIM A1	$ 563 – $ 762
Ground Control AIM A1 Comp	$ 676 – $ 914
Ground Control AIM A1 Pro	$ 871 – $ 1,178
Ground Control FSR	$ 1,088 – $ 1,472
Ground Control FSR Comp	$ 1,260 – $ 1,704
Hardrock	$ 168 – $ 228
Hardrock 20	$ 141 – $ 191
Hardrock AX	$ 275 – $ 372
Hardrock Classic	$ 186 – $ 252
Hardrock GX	$ 201 – $ 272
Hardrock GX FS	$ 275 – $ 372

C: – Components   F: – Fork

MODEL	PRICE RANGE
Specialized *(continued)*	🚲
Hardrock GX Sport	$ 234 – $ 317
Rockhopper	$ 281 – $ 380
Rockhopper 24	$ 156 – $ 211
Rockhopper A1	$ 333 – $ 450
Rockhopper A1 Comp FS	$ 524 – $ 709
Rockhopper A1 FS	$ 417 – $ 564
Rockhopper Comp FS	$ 471 – $ 637
Rockhopper FS	$ 372 – $ 504
S-Works C3 FSR	$ 1,401 – $ 1,896
S-Works M2	$ 1,023 – $ 1,384
Sirrus	$ 444 – $ 601
Stumpjumper M2	$ 627 – $ 848
Stumpjumper M2 Comp	$ 747 – $ 1,011
Stumpjumper M2 Pro	$ 871 – $ 1,178
Spectrum	🚲
Custom Steel – track	$ 1,098 – $ 1,486
Custom Steel F: Spectrum Custom C: Chorus	$ 1,247 – $ 1,687
Custom Steel F: Spectrum Custom C: Dura-Ace	$ 1,280 – $ 1,732
Stock Ti – Ultegra	$ 1,313 – $ 1,777
Spooky	🚲
Darkside XT	$ 1,070 – $ 1,447
Darkside XTR	$ 1,273 – $ 1,722
Junebug	$ 848 – $ 1,147
Mothership	$ 1,256 – $ 1,699
Supercross	🚲
Buzz Bomb 3.5	$ 1,196 – $ 1,618

C: – Components   F: – Fork

MODEL	PRICE RANGE

Supercross *(continued)*

Model	Price Range
Dirt	$ 300 – $ 406
Racer-X	$ 243 – $ 329
Racer-X 24	$ 266 – $ 360
Speed	$ 300 – $ 406
Speed 24	$ 322 – $ 436
Team Speed	$ 462 – $ 625
Team Speed 24	$ 487 – $ 660
Team Speed Jr.	$ 409 – $ 554

Terry

Model	Price Range
Classic	$ 855 – $ 1,157
Moo	$ 404 – $ 547
Symmetry	$ 513 – $ 694

Ti Cycles

Model	Price Range
Custom Mountain Chromoly	$ 1,055 – $ 1,427
Custom Road Chromoly	$ 1,235 – $ 1,671
Hyak	$ 1,214 – $ 1,643
Skookum	$ 1,136 – $ 1,536

Titus

Model	Price Range
HCR Mountain	$ 1,008 – $ 1,364
HCR Road	$ 1,197 – $ 1,620
Racer X AL	$ 1,273 – $ 1,722
SFS AL	$ 973 – $ 1,317

TNT

Model	Price Range
Hwa Fong Daddy	$ 339 – $ 458
M-80	$ 196 – $ 265
Quaterstick	$ 231 – $ 313
TRX	$ 289 – $ 390
TRX Team	$ 404 – $ 547

C: – Components   F: – Fork

MODEL

PRICE RANGE

Torelli

Model		Price Range
Corsa Strada	C: Sachs 5000 Other Features	$ 620 – $ 839
Corsa Strada	C: Sachs 5000 Other Features	$ 749 – $ 1,014
Corsa Strada	C: Sachs New Success Other Features	$ 826 – $ 1,118
Corsa Strada	C: Sachs New Success Other Features	$ 953 – $ 1,289
Corsa Strada	F: Torelli C: 600 Ultegra	$ 830 – $ 1,123
Corsa Strada	F: Torelli C: Athena	$ 922 – $ 1,248
Corsa Strada	F: Torelli C: Chorus	$ 1,035 – $ 1,401
Corsa Strada	F: Torelli C: Dura-Ace	$ 1,139 – $ 1,540
Corsa Strada	F: Torelli C: Record	$ 1,208 – $ 1,635
Corsa Strada	F: Torelli C: Veloce	$ 774 – $ 1,047
Countach OS	C: Sachs 5000 Other Features	$ 737 – $ 997
Countach OS	C: Sachs 5000 Other Features	$ 855 – $ 1,157
Countach OS	C: Sachs New Success Other Features	$ 925 – $ 1,251
Countach OS	C: Sachs New Success Other Features	$ 1,038 – $ 1,405
Countach OS	F: Torelli C: 600 Ultegra	$ 929 – $ 1,256
Countach OS	F: Torelli C: Athena	$ 1,011 – $ 1,368
Countach OS	F: Torelli C: Chorus	$ 1,111 – $ 1,503
Countach OS	F: Torelli C: Dura-Ace	$ 1,200 – $ 1,623
Countach OS	F: Torelli C: Record	$ 1,258 – $ 1,702
Countach OS	F: Torelli C: Veloce	$ 877 – $ 1,187
Express OS	C: Sachs 5000 Other Features	$ 891 – $ 1,206
Express OS	C: Sachs 5000 Other Features	$ 992 – $ 1,343
Express OS	C: Sachs New Success Other Features	$ 1,051 – $ 1,422
Express OS	C: Sachs New Success Other Features	$ 1,145 – $ 1,549
Express OS	F: Torelli C: 600 Ultegra	$ 1,054 – $ 1,427
Express OS	F: Torelli C: Athena	$ 1,123 – $ 1,519
Express OS	F: Torelli C: Chorus	$ 1,203 – $ 1,628
Express OS	F: Torelli C: Dura-Ace	$ 1,272 – $ 1,721
Express OS	F: Torelli C: Record	$ 1,313 – $ 1,776
Express OS	F: Torelli C: Veloce	$ 1,011 – $ 1,368
Nemo	C: Sachs 5000 Other Features	$ 1,011 – $ 1,368

C: – Components   F: – Fork

MODEL	PRICE RANGE

Torelli *(continued)*

Model	Price Range
Nemo C: Sachs 5000 Other Features	$ 1,098 – $ 1,485
Nemo C: Sachs New Success Other Features	$ 1,147 – $ 1,551
Nemo C: Sachs New Success Other Features	$ 1,223 – $ 1,655
Nemo F: Torelli C: 600 Ultegra	$ 1,149 – $ 1,555
Nemo F: Torelli C: Athena	$ 1,205 – $ 1,631
Nemo F: Torelli C: Chorus	$ 1,268 – $ 1,716
Nemo F: Torelli C: Veloce	$ 1,113 – $ 1,506
Nitro Express C: Sachs 5000 Other Features	$ 973 – $ 1,316
Nitro Express C: Sachs 5000 Other Features	$ 1,064 – $ 1,439
Nitro Express C: Sachs New Success Other Features	$ 1,117 – $ 1,511
Nitro Express C: Sachs New Success Other Features	$ 1,199 – $ 1,622
Nitro Express F: Torelli C: 600 Ultegra	$ 1,119 – $ 1,514
Nitro Express F: Torelli C: Athena	$ 1,180 – $ 1,596
Nitro Express F: Torelli C: Chorus	$ 1,249 – $ 1,689
Nitro Express F: Torelli C: Dura-Ace	$ 1,304 – $ 1,765
Nitro Express F: Torelli C: Veloce	$ 1,081 – $ 1,462
Super Strada C: Sachs 5000 Other Features	$ 677 – $ 916
Super Strada C: Sachs 5000 Other Features	$ 801 – $ 1,084
Super Strada C: Sachs New Success Other Features	$ 874 – $ 1,183
Super Strada C: Sachs New Success Other Features	$ 995 – $ 1,346
Super Strada F: Torelli C: 600 Ultegra	$ 878 – $ 1,188
Super Strada F: Torelli C: Athena	$ 966 – $ 1,307
Super Strada F: Torelli C: Chorus	$ 1,072 – $ 1,451
Super Strada F: Torelli C: Dura-Ace	$ 1,169 – $ 1,581
Super Strada F: Torelli C: Record	$ 1,233 – $ 1,668
Super Strada F: Torelli C: Veloce	$ 824 – $ 1,115

Torker

Model	Price Range
200 X	$ 115 – $ 160
280 X	$ 155 – $ 209
TFX	$ 149 – $ 201

C: – Components   F: – Fork

1997

MODEL	PRICE RANGE

Trailmate

Model				
Banana Peel	$	219	– $	296
Class Act Tandem	$	272	– $	368
DeSoto Classic	$	198	– $	268
Double Joyrider	$	508	– $	687
EZ Ride	$	121	– $	164
EZ Roll Regal	$	225	– $	305
Fun Cycle	$	243	– $	329
Joyrider	$	229	– $	310
Jr. Joyrider	$	226	– $	306
Low Rider	$	279	– $	377

Trek

Model				
420	$	256	– $	346
470	$	393	– $	532
520	$	565	– $	765
700	$	183	– $	248
700 Sport	$	159	– $	216
720	$	224	– $	303
730	$	270	– $	366
750	$	332	– $	450
800	$	171	– $	232
800 Sport	$	150	– $	203
820	$	204	– $	276
830	$	236	– $	319
830SHX	$	267	– $	362
850	$	270	– $	366
850SHX	$	332	– $	450
930	$	332	– $	450
930SHX	$	423	– $	572
1220	$	515	– $	696
1400	$	540	– $	731

C: – Components   F: – Fork

MODEL	PRICE RANGE
Trek (continued)	🚲
2100	$ 663 – $ 897
2120	$ 710 – $ 960
2300	$ 800 – $ 1,082
5000	$ 925 – $ 1,251
5020	$ 964 – $ 1,304
5200	$ 1,074 – $ 1,453
6000	$ 267 – $ 362
6000SHX	$ 332 – $ 450
6500	$ 332 – $ 450
6500SHX	$ 423 – $ 572
7000	$ 423 – $ 572
7000SHX	$ 494 – $ 668
7600	$ 484 – $ 654
8000SHX	$ 565 – $ 765
8500 SHX	$ 884 – $ 1,197
9700SHX	$ 843 – $ 1,140
970SHX	$ 663 – $ 897
9800SHX	$ 1,002 – $ 1,355
Calypso	$ 171 – $ 232
Cruiser Classic	$ 138 – $ 187
Mountain Cub	$ 84 – $ 113
Mountain Lion 30	$ 96 – $ 130
Mountain Lion 60	$ 138 – $ 187
Mountain Lion 60SHX	$ 195 – $ 264
Mountain Track 220	$ 150 – $ 203
Mountain Track 220SHX	$ 204 – $ 276
Mountain Track 240	$ 204 – $ 276
Pro Issue XL	$ 393 – $ 532
Sub-Atomic	$ 221 – $ 319
Sub-Atomic SS	$ 253 – $ 366
Sub-Culture	$ 318 – $ 431

C: – Components   F: – Fork

MODEL	PRICE RANGE

Trek *(continued)*	🚲
Sub-Culture SS	$ 393 – $ 532
Sub-Dude	$ 117 – $ 167
Sub-Head	$ 165 – $ 232
Sub-Mission	$ 138 – $ 195
Sub-Species	$ 256 – $ 346
Sub-Vert 1.0G	$ 165 – $ 232
Sub-Vert 2.0G	$ 204 – $ 276
Sub-Vert 3.0G	$ 270 – $ 366
T-100	$ 663 – $ 897
T-200	$ 1,002 – $ 1,355
UAV1	$ 565 – $ 765
UAV2	$ 710 – $ 960
Y 3	$ 515 – $ 696
Y 5	$ 710 – $ 960
Y 11	$ 884 – $ 1,197
Y 22	$ 1,074 – $ 1,453
Y 33	$ 1,310 – $ 1,772

Univega	🚲
Activa Action	$ 131 – $ 178
Activa Country	$ 170 – $ 230
Activa Trail	$ 195 – $ 264
Alpina 500	$ 233 – $ 315
Alpina 500S	$ 258 – $ 349
Alpina 502	$ 289 – $ 390
Alpina 502S	$ 361 – $ 489
Alpina 800S	$ 319 – $ 432
Alpina 802S	$ 409 – $ 553
Alpina 804S	$ 495 – $ 670
Alpina 806S	$ 606 – $ 820
Alpina 808S	$ 861 – $ 1,164

C: – Components   F: – Fork

MODEL	PRICE RANGE
Univega (continued)	🚲
Dual Action Comp	$ 551 – $ 746
Dual Action Pro	$ 712 – $ 963
Dual Action Team	$ 1,308 – $ 1,769
Rover 300	$ 131 – $ 178
Rover 302	$ 144 – $ 195
Rover 304	$ 170 – $ 230
Rover 306	$ 195 – $ 264
Sportour	$ 258 – $ 349
Superstrada	$ 409 – $ 553
Tandem Sport	$ 414 – $ 561
Tandem Tour	$ 633 – $ 856
Via Carisma	$ 227 – $ 307
Via De Oro	$ 367 – $ 497
Via Montega	$ 258 – $ 349
Valley Cycles	🚲
RS-100	$ 1,301 – $ 1,760
XS-100	$ 1,228 – $ 1,662
Ventana	🚲
El Chiquillo C: Deore LX F: Rock Shox Judy SL	$ 1,003 – $ 1,357
El Chiquillo C: Deore LX F: Rock Shox Judy XC	$ 938 – $ 1,269
El Chiquillo C: Deore LX F: Rock Shox Mag 21	$ 898 – $ 1,216
El Chiquillo C: Deore LX F: White Brothers SC70	$ 1,035 – $ 1,400
El Chiquillo C: Deore XT F: Rock Shox Judy SL	$ 1,118 – $ 1,513
El Chiquillo C: Deore XT F: Rock Shox Judy XC	$ 1,065 – $ 1,441
El Chiquillo C: Deore XT F: Rock Shox Mag 21	$ 1,031 – $ 1,396
El Chiquillo C: Deore XT F: White Brothers SC70	$ 1,144 – $ 1,548
El Chiquillo C: XTR 950 F: Rock Shox Judy SL	$ 1,279 – $ 1,731
El Chiquillo C: XTR 950 F: Rock Shox Judy XC	$ 1,248 – $ 1,688
El Chiquillo C: XTR 950 F: Rock Shox Mag 21	$ 1,227 – $ 1,660

C: – Components   F: – Fork

MODEL	PRICE RANGE

Ventana (continued)   🚲

Model	Price Range
El Chiquillo C: XTR 950 F: White Brothers SC70	$ 1,294 – $ 1,750
El Habanero C: Deore LX F: Rock Shox Judy SL	$ 1,181 – $ 1,598
El Habanero C: Deore LX F: Rock Shox Judy XC	$ 1,135 – $ 1,536
El Habanero C: Deore LX F: Rock Shox Mag 21	$ 1,106 – $ 1,496
El Habanero C: Deore LX F: White Brothers SC70	$ 1,204 – $ 1,628
El Habanero C: Deore XT F: Rock Shox Judy SL	$ 1,259 – $ 1,704
El Habanero C: Deore XT F: Rock Shox Judy XC	$ 1,224 – $ 1,656
El Habanero C: Deore XT F: Rock Shox Mag 21	$ 1,201 – $ 1,625
El Habanero C: Deore XT F: White Brothers SC70	$ 1,276 – $ 1,726
Marble Peak FS C: Deore LX F: Rock Shox Judy SL	$ 1,259 – $ 1,704
Marble Peak FS C: Deore LX F: Rock Shox Judy XC	$ 1,224 – $ 1,656
Marble Peak FS C: Deore LX F: Rock Shox Mag 21	$ 1,201 – $ 1,625
Marble Peak FS C: Deore LX F: White Brothers SC70	$ 1,276 – $ 1,726
Marble Peak FS C: Deore XT F: Rock Shox Judy XC	$ 1,290 – $ 1,746
Marble Peak FS C: Deore XT F: Rock Shox Mag 21	$ 1,274 – $ 1,724
Marble Peak FS F: Rock Shox Judy SL	$ 1,259 – $ 1,704
Marble Peak FS F: White Brothers SC70	$ 1,276 – $ 1,726

Vision   🚲

Model	Price Range
R30 NT	$ 475 – $ 642
R30 ST	$ 500 – $ 677
R40 A/E	$ 574 – $ 793
R40 B/F	$ 634 – $ 873
R42 A/E	$ 785 – $ 1,076
R42 B/F	$ 836 – $ 1,144
R44 A/E	$ 914 – $ 1,248
R45 A/E	$ 1,091 – $ 1,476

VooDoo   🚲

Model	Price Range
Bantu C: STX-RC F: Marzocchi Bomber Z-1	$ 647 – $ 876
Bantu C: STX-RC F: Rock Shox Indy C	$ 527 – $ 713

C: – Components   F: – Fork

MODEL	PRICE RANGE

VooDoo (continued)

Model	Price Range
Bantu C: STX-RC F: Rock Shox Indy SL	$ 588 – $ 796
Bantu C: STX-RC F: Rock Shox Indy XC	$ 552 – $ 747
Bantu C: STX-RC F: Rock Shox Judy C	$ 600 – $ 812
Bantu C: STX-RC F: Rock Shox Judy SL	$ 704 – $ 952
Bantu C: STX-RC F: Rock Shox Judy XC	$ 624 – $ 844
Bantu C: STX-RC F: Rock Shox Quadra 5	$ 502 – $ 679
Bantu C: STX-RC F: VooDoo	$ 451 – $ 610
Bantu C: STX F: Marzocchi Bomber Z-1	$ 576 – $ 780
Bantu C: STX F: Rock Shox Indy C	$ 451 – $ 610
Bantu C: STX F: Rock Shox Indy SL	$ 515 – $ 697
Bantu C: STX F: Rock Shox Indy XC	$ 477 – $ 645
Bantu C: STX F: Rock Shox Judy C	$ 527 – $ 713
Bantu C: STX F: Rock Shox Judy SL	$ 622 – $ 841
Bantu C: STX F: Rock Shox Judy XC	$ 552 – $ 747
Bantu C: STX F: Rock Shox Quadra 5	$ 425 – $ 575
Bantu C: STX F: VooDoo	$ 371 – $ 502
Bizango C: Deore LX F: Marzocchi Bomber Z-1	$ 885 – $ 1,198
Bizango C: Deore LX F: Rock Shox Indy C	$ 766 – $ 1,036
Bizango C: Deore LX F: Rock Shox Indy SL	$ 827 – $ 1,119
Bizango C: Deore LX F: Rock Shox Indy XC	$ 787 – $ 1,065
Bizango C: Deore LX F: Rock Shox Judy C	$ 837 – $ 1,133
Bizango C: Deore LX F: Rock Shox Judy SL	$ 949 – $ 1,284
Bizango C: Deore LX F: Rock Shox Judy XC	$ 866 – $ 1,172
Bizango C: Deore LX F: Rock Shox Quadra 5	$ 756 – $ 1,022
Bizango C: Deore LX F: VooDoo	$ 701 – $ 949
Bizango C: Deore XT F: Marzocchi Bomber Z-1	$ 1,024 – $ 1,385
Bizango C: Deore XT F: Rock Shox Indy C	$ 922 – $ 1,248
Bizango C: Deore XT F: Rock Shox Indy SL	$ 975 – $ 1,319
Bizango C: Deore XT F: Rock Shox Indy XC	$ 940 – $ 1,272
Bizango C: Deore XT F: Rock Shox Judy C	$ 983 – $ 1,330
Bizango C: Deore XT F: Rock Shox Judy SL	$ 1,077 – $ 1,456

C: – Components   F: – Fork

MODEL	PRICE RANGE
VooDoo *(continued)*	🚲
Bizango C: Deore XT F: Rock Shox Judy XC	$ 1,008 – $ 1,363
Bizango C: Deore XT F: Rock Shox Quadra 5	$ 913 – $ 1,235
Bizango C: Deore XT F: VooDoo	$ 866 – $ 1,172
Bizango C: Deore XT/LX F: Marzocchi Bomber Z-1	$ 949 – $ 1,284
Bizango C: Deore XT/LX F: Rock Shox Indy C	$ 837 – $ 1,133
Bizango C: Deore XT/LX F: Rock Shox Indy SL	$ 895 – $ 1,211
Bizango C: Deore XT/LX F: Rock Shox Indy XC	$ 857 – $ 1,159
Bizango C: Deore XT/LX F: Rock Shox Judy C	$ 904 – $ 1,223
Bizango C: Deore XT/LX F: Rock Shox Judy SL	$ 1,008 – $ 1,363
Bizango C: Deore XT/LX F: Rock Shox Judy XC	$ 931 – $ 1,260
Bizango C: Deore XT/LX F: Rock Shox Quadra 5	$ 827 – $ 1,119
Bizango C: Deore XT/LX F: VooDoo	$ 777 – $ 1,051
Bizango C: STX-RC F: Marzocchi Bomber Z-1	$ 837 – $ 1,133
Bizango C: STX-RC F: Rock Shox Indy C	$ 712 – $ 964
Bizango C: STX-RC F: Rock Shox Indy SL	$ 777 – $ 1,051
Bizango C: STX-RC F: Rock Shox Indy XC	$ 734 – $ 993
Bizango C: STX-RC F: Rock Shox Judy C	$ 787 – $ 1,065
Bizango C: STX-RC F: Rock Shox Judy SL	$ 904 – $ 1,223
Bizango C: STX-RC F: Rock Shox Judy XC	$ 817 – $ 1,106
Bizango C: STX-RC F: Rock Shox Quadra 5	$ 701 – $ 949
Bizango C: STX-RC F: VooDoo	$ 645 – $ 872
Bizango C: XTR 950 F: Marzocchi Bomber Z-1	$ 1,268 – $ 1,716
Bizango C: XTR 950 F: Rock Shox Indy C	$ 1,228 – $ 1,662
Bizango C: XTR 950 F: Rock Shox Indy SL	$ 1,242 – $ 1,681
Bizango C: XTR 950 F: Rock Shox Indy XC	$ 1,223 – $ 1,655
Bizango C: XTR 950 F: Rock Shox Judy C	$ 1,247 – $ 1,687
Bizango C: XTR 950 F: Rock Shox Judy SL	$ 1,280 – $ 1,732
Bizango C: XTR 950 F: Rock Shox Judy XC	$ 1,260 – $ 1,705
Bizango C: XTR 950 F: Rock Shox Quadra 5	$ 1,228 – $ 1,662
Bizango C: XTR 950 F: VooDoo	$ 1,18 – $ 1,597
Bokor C: Deore LX F: Marzocchi Bomber Z-1	$ 847 – $ 1,146

C: – Components   F: – Fork

MODEL

PRICE RANGE

Model		Price Range
Bokor C: Deore LX F: Rock Shox Indy C	$ 723 – $ 979
Bokor C: Deore LX F: Rock Shox Indy SL	$ 787 – $ 1,065
Bokor C: Deore LX F: Rock Shox Indy XC	$ 745 – $ 1,008
Bokor C: Deore LX F: Rock Shox Judy C	$ 797 – $ 1,079
Bokor C: Deore LX F: Rock Shox Judy SL	$ 913 – $ 1,235
Bokor C: Deore LX F: Rock Shox Judy XC	$ 827 – $ 1,119
Bokor C: Deore LX F: Rock Shox Quadra 5	$ 712 – $ 964
Bokor C: Deore LX F: VooDoo	$ 656 – $ 888
Bokor C: Deore XT F: Marzocchi Bomber Z-1	$ 989 – $ 1,339
Bokor C: Deore XT F: Rock Shox Indy C	$ 885 – $ 1,198
Bokor C: Deore XT F: Rock Shox Indy SL	$ 904 – $ 1,223
Bokor C: Deore XT F: Rock Shox Indy XC	$ 904 – $ 1,223
Bokor C: Deore XT F: Rock Shox Judy C	$ 949 – $ 1,284
Bokor C: Deore XT F: Rock Shox Judy SL	$ 1,047 – $ 1,416
Bokor C: Deore XT F: Rock Shox Judy XC	$ 975 – $ 1,319
Bokor C: Deore XT F: Rock Shox Quadra 5	$ 876 – $ 1,185
Bokor C: Deore XT F: VooDoo	$ 827 – $ 1,119
Bokor C: Deore XT/LX F: Marzocchi Bomber Z-1	$ 913 – $ 1,235
Bokor C: Deore XT/LX F: Rock Shox Indy C	$ 797 – $ 1,079
Bokor C: Deore XT/LX F: Rock Shox Indy SL	$ 857 – $ 1,159
Bokor C: Deore XT/LX F: Rock Shox Indy XC	$ 817 – $ 1,106
Bokor C: Deore XT/LX F: Rock Shox Judy C	$ 866 – $ 1,172
Bokor C: Deore XT/LX F: Rock Shox Judy SL	$ 975 – $ 1,319
Bokor C: Deore XT/LX F: Rock Shox Judy XC	$ 895 – $ 1,211
Bokor C: Deore XT/LX F: Rock Shox Quadra 5	$ 787 – $ 1,065
Bokor C: Deore XT/LX F: VooDoo	$ 734 – $ 993
Bokor C: STX-RC F: Marzocchi Bomber Z-1	$ 797 – $ 1,079
Bokor C: STX-RC F: Rock Shox Indy C	$ 668 – $ 903
Bokor C: STX-RC F: Rock Shox Indy SL	$ 734 – $ 993
Bokor C: STX-RC F: Rock Shox Indy XC	$ 690 – $ 934
Bokor C: STX-RC F: Rock Shox Judy C	$ 745 – $ 1,008

C: – Components   F: – Fork

MODEL	PRICE RANGE

VooDoo (continued)   🚲

Model	Price Range
Bokor C: STX-RC F: Rock Shox Judy SL	$ 866 – $ 1,172
Bokor C: STX-RC F: Rock Shox Judy XC	$ 777 – $ 1,051
Bokor C: STX-RC F: Rock Shox Quadra 5	$ 598 – $ 809
Bokor C: STX-RC F: VooDoo	$ 598 – $ 809
Bokor C: XTR 950 F: Marzocchi Bomber Z-1	$ 1,251 – $ 1,693
Bokor C: XTR 950 F: Rock Shox Indy C	$ 1,192 – $ 1,612
Bokor C: XTR 950 F: Rock Shox Indy SL	$ 1,223 – $ 1,655
Bokor C: XTR 950 F: Rock Shox Indy XC	$ 1,203 – $ 1,627
Bokor C: XTR 950 F: Rock Shox Judy C	$ 1,228 – $ 1,661
Bokor C: XTR 950 F: Rock Shox Judy SL	$ 1,294 – $ 1,751
Bokor C: XTR 950 F: Rock Shox Quadra 5	$ 1,185 – $ 1,603
Bokor C: XTR 950 F: VooDoo	$ 1,157 – $ 1,565
Canzo C: Deore LX F: Marzocchi Bomber Z-1	$ 1,091 – $ 1,476
Canzo C: Deore LX F: Marzocchi Bomber Z-1	$ 1,131 – $ 1,531
Canzo C: Deore LX F: Rock Shox Indy C	$ 1,000 – $ 1,352
Canzo C: Deore LX F: Rock Shox Indy C	$ 1,047 – $ 1,416
Canzo C: Deore LX F: Rock Shox Indy SL	$ 1,047 – $ 1,416
Canzo C: Deore LX F: Rock Shox Indy SL	$ 1,091 – $ 1,476
Canzo C: Deore LX F: Rock Shox Indy XC	$ 1,016 – $ 1,374
Canzo C: Deore LX F: Rock Shox Indy XC	$ 1,062 – $ 1,437
Canzo C: Deore LX F: Rock Shox Judy C	$ 1,054 – $ 1,427
Canzo C: Deore LX F: Rock Shox Judy C	$ 1,098 – $ 1,485
Canzo C: Deore LX F: Rock Shox Judy SL	$ 1,138 – $ 1,539
Canzo C: Deore LX F: Rock Shox Judy SL	$ 1,175 – $ 1,589
Canzo C: Deore LX F: Rock Shox Judy XC	$ 1,077 – $ 1,456
Canzo C: Deore LX F: Rock Shox Judy XC	$ 1,118 – $ 1,513
Canzo C: Deore LX F: Rock Shox Quadra 5	$ 991 – $ 1,341
Canzo C: Deore LX F: Rock Shox Quadra 5	$ 1,039 – $ 1,406
Canzo C: Deore XT F: Marzocchi Bomber Z-1	$ 1,192 – $ 1,612
Canzo C: Deore XT F: Marzocchi Bomber Z-1	$ 1,223 – $ 1,655
Canzo C: Deore XT F: Rock Shox Indy C	$ 1,118 – $ 1,513

C: – Components   F: – Fork

MODEL	PRICE RANGE

VooDoo (continued) 🚲

Model	Price Range
Canzo C: Deore XT F: Rock Shox Indy C	$ 1,157 – $ 1,565
Canzo C: Deore XT F: Rock Shox Indy SL	$ 1,157 – $ 1,565
Canzo C: Deore XT F: Rock Shox Indy SL	$ 1,192 – $ 1,612
Canzo C: Deore XT F: Rock Shox Indy XC	$ 1,131 – $ 1,531
Canzo C: Deore XT F: Rock Shox Indy XC	$ 1,169 – $ 1,581
Canzo C: Deore XT F: Rock Shox Judy C	$ 1,163 – $ 1,573
Canzo C: Deore XT F: Rock Shox Judy C	$ 1,197 – $ 1,620
Canzo C: Deore XT F: Rock Shox Judy SL	$ 1,228 – $ 1,662
Canzo C: Deore XT F: Rock Shox Judy SL	$ 1,256 – $ 1,699
Canzo C: Deore XT F: Rock Shox Judy XC	$ 1,180 – $ 1,597
Canzo C: Deore XT F: Rock Shox Judy XC	$ 1,213 – $ 1,641
Canzo C: Deore XT F: Rock Shox Quadra 5	$ 1,112 – $ 1,504
Canzo C: Deore XT F: Rock Shox Quadra 5	$ 1,150 – $ 1,556
Canzo C: Deore XT/LX F: Marzocchi Bomber Z-1	$ 1,163 – $ 1,573
Canzo C: Deore XT/LX F: Marzocchi Bomber Z-1	$ 1,175 – $ 1,589
Canzo C: Deore XT/LX F: Rock Shox Indy C	$ 1,054 – $ 1,427
Canzo C: Deore XT/LX F: Rock Shox Indy C	$ 1,098 – $ 1,485
Canzo C: Deore XT/LX F: Rock Shox Indy SL	$ 1,098 – $ 1,485
Canzo C: Deore XT/LX F: Rock Shox Indy SL	$ 1,138 – $ 1,539
Canzo C: Deore XT/LX F: Rock Shox Indy XC	$ 1,069 – $ 1,447
Canzo C: Deore XT/LX F: Rock Shox Indy XC	$ 1,112 – $ 1,504
Canzo C: Deore XT/LX F: Rock Shox Judy C	$ 1,105 – $ 1,495
Canzo C: Deore XT/LX F: Rock Shox Judy C	$ 1,144 – $ 1,548
Canzo C: Deore XT/LX F: Rock Shox Judy SL	$ 1,180 – $ 1,597
Canzo C: Deore XT/LX F: Rock Shox Judy SL	$ 1,213 – $ 1,641
Canzo C: Deore XT/LX F: Rock Shox Judy XC	$ 1,125 – $ 1,522
Canzo C: Deore XT/LX F: Rock Shox Judy XC	$ 1,163 – $ 1,573
Canzo C: Deore XT/LX F: Rock Shox Quadra 5	$ 1,047 – $ 1,416
Canzo C: Deore XT/LX F: Rock Shox Quadra 5	$ 1,091 – $ 1,476
Canzo C: STX-RC F: Marzocchi Bomber Z-1	$ 1,054 – $ 1,427
Canzo C: STX-RC F: Marzocchi Bomber Z-1	$ 1,098 – $ 1,485

C: – Components   F: – Fork

MODEL	PRICE RANGE

VooDoo (continued)

Model	Price Range
Canzo C: STX-RC F: Rock Shox Indy C	$ 958 – $ 1,295
Canzo C: STX-RC F: Rock Shox Indy C	$ 1,008 – $ 1,363
Canzo C: STX-RC F: Rock Shox Indy SL	$ 1,006 – $ 1,362
Canzo C: STX-RC F: Rock Shox Indy SL	$ 1,054 – $ 1,427
Canzo C: STX-RC F: Rock Shox Indy XC	$ 975 – $ 1,319
Canzo C: STX-RC F: Rock Shox Indy XC	$ 1,024 – $ 1,385
Canzo C: STX-RC F: Rock Shox Judy C	$ 1,016 – $ 1,374
Canzo C: STX-RC F: Rock Shox Judy C	$ 1,062 – $ 1,437
Canzo C: STX-RC F: Rock Shox Judy SL	$ 1,105 – $ 1,495
Canzo C: STX-RC F: Rock Shox Judy SL	$ 1,169 – $ 1,581
Canzo C: STX-RC F: Rock Shox Judy XC	$ 1,036 – $ 1,402
Canzo C: STX-RC F: Rock Shox Judy XC	$ 1,084 – $ 1,466
Canzo C: STX-RC F: Rock Shox Quadra 5	$ 949 – $ 1,284
Canzo C: STX-RC F: Rock Shox Quadra 5	$ 1,000 – $ 1,352
Canzo C: XTR 950 F: Rock Shox Indy C	$ 1,313 – $ 1,777
Canzo C: XTR 950 F: Rock Shox Quadra 5	$ 1,310 – $ 1,773
Canzo ESP C: Deore LX F: Marzocchi Bomber Z-1	$ 966 – $ 1,307
Canzo ESP C: Deore LX F: Rock Shox Indy C	$ 857 – $ 1,159
Canzo ESP C: Deore LX F: Rock Shox Indy SL	$ 913 – $ 1,235
Canzo ESP C: Deore LX F: Rock Shox Indy XC	$ 876 – $ 1,185
Canzo ESP C: Deore LX F: Rock Shox Judy C	$ 922 – $ 1,248
Canzo ESP C: Deore LX F: Rock Shox Judy SL	$ 1,024 – $ 1,385
Canzo ESP C: Deore LX F: Rock Shox Judy XC	$ 949 – $ 1,284
Canzo ESP C: Deore LX F: Rock Shox Quadra 5	$ 847 – $ 1,146
Canzo ESP C: Deore XT F: Marzocchi Bomber Z-1	$ 1,091 – $ 1,476
Canzo ESP C: Deore XT F: Rock Shox Indy C	$ 1,000 – $ 1,352
Canzo ESP C: Deore XT F: Rock Shox Indy SL	$ 1,047 – $ 1,416
Canzo ESP C: Deore XT F: Rock Shox Indy XC	$ 1,016 – $ 1,374
Canzo ESP C: Deore XT F: Rock Shox Judy C	$ 1,054 – $ 1,427
Canzo ESP C: Deore XT F: Rock Shox Judy SL	$ 1,138 – $ 1,539
Canzo ESP C: Deore XT F: Rock Shox Judy XC	$ 1,077 – $ 1,456

C: – Components   F: – Fork

MODEL	PRICE RANGE

VooDoo *(continued)*

Model	Price Range
Canzo ESP C: Deore XT F: Rock Shox Quadra 5	$ 991 – $ 1,341
Canzo ESP C: Deore XT/LX F: Marzocchi Bomber Z-1	$ 1,024 – $ 1,385
Canzo ESP C: Deore XT/LX F: Rock Shox Indy C	$ 922 – $ 1,248
Canzo ESP C: Deore XT/LX F: Rock Shox Indy SL	$ 975 – $ 1,319
Canzo ESP C: Deore XT/LX F: Rock Shox Indy XC	$ 940 – $ 1,272
Canzo ESP C: Deore XT/LX F: Rock Shox Judy C	$ 983 – $ 1,330
Canzo ESP C: Deore XT/LX F: Rock Shox Judy SL	$ 1,077 – $ 1,456
Canzo ESP C: Deore XT/LX F: Rock Shox Judy XC	$ 1,008 – $ 1,363
Canzo ESP C: Deore XT/LX F: Rock Shox Quadra 5	$ 913 – $ 1,235
Canzo ESP C: STX-RC F: Marzocchi Bomber Z-1	$ 922 – $ 1,248
Canzo ESP C: STX-RC F: Rock Shox Indy C	$ 807 – $ 1,092
Canzo ESP C: STX-RC F: Rock Shox Indy SL	$ 831 – $ 1,125
Canzo ESP C: STX-RC F: Rock Shox Indy XC	$ 827 – $ 1,119
Canzo ESP C: STX-RC F: Rock Shox Judy C	$ 876 – $ 1,185
Canzo ESP C: STX-RC F: Rock Shox Judy SL	$ 983 – $ 1,330
Canzo ESP C: STX-RC F: Rock Shox Judy XC	$ 904 – $ 1,223
Canzo ESP C: STX-RC F: Rock Shox Quadra 5	$ 797 – $ 1,079
Canzo ESP C: XTR 950 F: Marzocchi Bomber Z-1	$ 1,301 – $ 1,760
Canzo ESP C: XTR 950 F: Rock Shox Indy C	$ 1,256 – $ 1,699
Canzo ESP C: XTR 950 F: Rock Shox Indy SL	$ 1,280 – $ 1,732
Canzo ESP C: XTR 950 F: Rock Shox Indy XC	$ 1,264 – $ 1,711
Canzo ESP C: XTR 950 F: Rock Shox Judy C	$ 1,284 – $ 1,737
Canzo ESP C: XTR 950 F: Rock Shox Judy XC	$ 1,294 – $ 1,751
Canzo ESP C: XTR 950 F: Rock Shox Quadra 5	$ 1,251 – $ 1,693
D-Jab C: Deore LX F: Marzocchi Bomber Z-1	$ 1,039 – $ 1,406
D-Jab C: Deore LX F: Rock Shox Indy C	$ 940 – $ 1,272
D-Jab C: Deore LX F: Rock Shox Indy SL	$ 991 – $ 1,341
D-Jab C: Deore LX F: Rock Shox Indy XC	$ 958 – $ 1,295
D-Jab C: Deore LX F: Rock Shox Judy C	$ 1,000 – $ 1,352
D-Jab C: Deore LX F: Rock Shox Judy SL	$ 1,091 – $ 1,476

C: – Components   F: – Fork

MODEL   PRICE RANGE

VooDoo (continued)   🚲

Model				Price Range
D-Jab	C: Deore LX	F: Rock Shox Judy XC		$ 1,024 – $ 1,385
D-Jab	C: Deore LX	F: Rock Shox Quadra 5		$ 931 – $ 1,260
D-Jab	C: Deore LX	F: VooDoo		$ 885 – $ 1,198
D-Jab	C: Deore XT	F: Marzocchi Bomber Z-1		$ 1,150 – $ 1,556
D-Jab	C: Deore XT	F: Rock Shox Indy C		$ 1,069 – $ 1,447
D-Jab	C: Deore XT	F: Rock Shox Indy SL		$ 1,112 – $ 1,504
D-Jab	C: Deore XT	F: Rock Shox Indy XC		$ 1,083 – $ 1,465
D-Jab	C: Deore XT	F: Rock Shox Judy C		$ 1,118 – $ 1,513
D-Jab	C: Deore XT	F: Rock Shox Judy SL		$ 1,192 – $ 1,612
D-Jab	C: Deore XT	F: Rock Shox Judy XC		$ 1,137 – $ 1,538
D-Jab	C: Deore XT	F: Rock Shox Quadra 5		$ 1,062 – $ 1,437
D-Jab	C: Deore XT	F: VooDoo		$ 1,024 – $ 1,385
D-Jab	C: Deore XT/LX	F: Marzocchi Bomber Z-1		$ 1,091 – $ 1,476
D-Jab	C: Deore XT/LX	F: Rock Shox Indy C		$ 1,000 – $ 1,352
D-Jab	C: Deore XT/LX	F: Rock Shox Indy SL		$ 1,047 – $ 1,416
D-Jab	C: Deore XT/LX	F: Rock Shox Indy XC		$ 1,016 – $ 1,374
D-Jab	C: Deore XT/LX	F: Rock Shox Judy C		$ 1,054 – $ 1,427
D-Jab	C: Deore XT/LX	F: Rock Shox Judy SL		$ 1,138 – $ 1,539
D-Jab	C: Deore XT/LX	F: Rock Shox Judy XC		$ 1,077 – $ 1,456
D-Jab	C: Deore XT/LX	F: Rock Shox Quadra 5		$ 991 – $ 1,341
D-Jab	C: Deore XT/LX	F: VooDoo		$ 949 – $ 1,284
D-Jab	C: STX-RC	F: Marzocchi Bomber Z-1		$ 1,000 – $ 1,352
D-Jab	C: STX-RC	F: Rock Shox Indy C		$ 895 – $ 1,211
D-Jab	C: STX-RC	F: Rock Shox Indy SL		$ 949 – $ 1,284
D-Jab	C: STX-RC	F: Rock Shox Indy XC		$ 913 – $ 1,235
D-Jab	C: STX-RC	F: Rock Shox Judy C		$ 958 – $ 1,295
D-Jab	C: STX-RC	F: Rock Shox Judy SL		$ 1,054 – $ 1,427
D-Jab	C: STX-RC	F: Rock Shox Judy XC		$ 983 – $ 1,330
D-Jab	C: STX-RC	F: Rock Shox Quadra 5		$ 885 – $ 1,198
D-Jab	C: STX-RC	F: VooDoo		$ 837 – $ 1,133
D-Jab	C: XTR 950	F: Rock Shox Indy C		$ 1,291 – $ 1,747

C: – Components   F: – Fork

MODEL   PRICE RANGE

VooDoo (continued)   🚲

Model			Price Range
D-Jab C: XTR 950 F: Rock Shox Indy SL			$ 1,310 – $ 1,773
D-Jab C: XTR 950 F: Rock Shox Indy XC			$ 1,298 – $ 1,756
D-Jab C: XTR 950 F: Rock Shox Judy C			$ 1,313 – $ 1,777
D-Jab C: XTR 950 F: Rock Shox Quadra 5			$ 1,288 – $ 1,742
D-Jab C: XTR 950 F: VooDoo			$ 1,268 – $ 1,716
Erzulie C: STX-RC F: Marzocchi Bomber Z-1			$ 610 – $ 825
Erzulie C: STX-RC F: Rock Shox Indy C			$ 487 – $ 659
Erzulie C: STX-RC F: Rock Shox Indy SL			$ 550 – $ 744
Erzulie C: STX-RC F: Rock Shox Indy XC			$ 512 – $ 693
Erzulie C: STX-RC F: Rock Shox Judy C			$ 562 – $ 760
Erzulie C: STX-RC F: Rock Shox Judy SL			$ 668 – $ 903
Erzulie C: STX-RC F: Rock Shox Judy XC			$ 586 – $ 793
Erzulie C: STX-RC F: Rock Shox Quadra 5			$ 461 – $ 624
Erzulie C: STX-RC F: VooDoo			$ 409 – $ 553
Erzulie C: STX F: Marzocchi Bomber Z-1			$ 537 – $ 727
Erzulie C: STX F: Rock Shox Indy C			$ 409 – $ 553
Erzulie C: STX F: Rock Shox Indy SL			$ 474 – $ 642
Erzulie C: STX F: Rock Shox Indy XC			$ 435 – $ 589
Erzulie C: STX F: Rock Shox Judy C			$ 487 – $ 659
Erzulie C: STX F: Rock Shox Judy SL			$ 598 – $ 809
Erzulie C: STX F: Rock Shox Judy XC			$ 512 – $ 693
Erzulie C: STX F: Rock Shox Quadra 5			$ 382 – $ 517
Erzulie C: STX F: VooDoo			$ 327 – $ 443
HooDoo C: Deore LX F: Marzocchi Bomber Z-1			$ 745 – $ 1,008
HooDoo C: Deore LX F: Rock Shox Indy C			$ 610 – $ 825
HooDoo C: Deore LX F: Rock Shox Indy SL			$ 679 – $ 919
HooDoo C: Deore LX F: Rock Shox Indy XC			$ 633 – $ 857
HooDoo C: Deore LX F: Rock Shox Judy C			$ 690 – $ 934
HooDoo C: Deore LX F: Rock Shox Judy SL			$ 817 – $ 1,106
HooDoo C: Deore LX F: Rock Shox Judy XC			$ 723 – $ 979
HooDoo C: Deore LX F: Rock Shox Quadra 5			$ 598 – $ 809

C: – Components   F: – Fork

MODEL	PRICE RANGE

VooDoo (continued)

Model		Components	Fork	Price Range
HooDoo	C:	Deore LX	F: VooDoo	$ 537 – $ 727
HooDoo	C:	Deore XT	F: Marzocchi Bomber Z-1	$ 904 – $ 1,223
HooDoo	C:	Deore XT	F: Rock Shox Indy C	$ 787 – $ 1,065
HooDoo	C:	Deore XT	F: Rock Shox Indy SL	$ 847 – $ 1,146
HooDoo	C:	Deore XT	F: Rock Shox Indy XC	$ 807 – $ 1,092
HooDoo	C:	Deore XT	F: Rock Shox Judy C	$ 857 – $ 1,159
HooDoo	C:	Deore XT	F: Rock Shox Judy SL	$ 931 – $ 1,260
HooDoo	C:	Deore XT	F: Rock Shox Judy XC	$ 885 – $ 1,198
HooDoo	C:	Deore XT	F: Rock Shox Quadra 5	$ 777 – $ 1,051
HooDoo	C:	Deore XT	F: VooDoo	$ 723 – $ 979
HooDoo	C:	Deore XT/LX	F: Marzocchi Bomber Z-1	$ 817 – $ 1,106
HooDoo	C:	Deore XT/LX	F: Rock Shox Indy C	$ 690 – $ 934
HooDoo	C:	Deore XT/LX	F: Rock Shox Indy SL	$ 756 – $ 1,022
HooDoo	C:	Deore XT/LX	F: Rock Shox Indy XC	$ 712 – $ 964
HooDoo	C:	Deore XT/LX	F: Rock Shox Judy C	$ 766 – $ 1,036
HooDoo	C:	Deore XT/LX	F: Rock Shox Judy SL	$ 884 – $ 1,196
HooDoo	C:	Deore XT/LX	F: Rock Shox Judy XC	$ 797 – $ 1,079
HooDoo	C:	Deore XT/LX	F: Rock Shox Quadra 5	$ 679 – $ 919
HooDoo	C:	Deore XT/LX	F: VooDoo	$ 622 – $ 841
HooDoo	C:	STX-RC	F: Marzocchi Bomber Z-1	$ 690 – $ 934
HooDoo	C:	STX-RC	F: Rock Shox Indy C	$ 550 – $ 744
HooDoo	C:	STX-RC	F: Rock Shox Indy SL	$ 622 – $ 841
HooDoo	C:	STX-RC	F: Rock Shox Indy XC	$ 574 – $ 777
HooDoo	C:	STX-RC	F: Rock Shox Judy C	$ 633 – $ 857
HooDoo	C:	STX-RC	F: Rock Shox Judy SL	$ 766 – $ 1,036
HooDoo	C:	STX-RC	F: Rock Shox Judy XC	$ 668 – $ 903
HooDoo	C:	STX-RC	F: Rock Shox Quadra 5	$ 487 – $ 659
HooDoo	C:	STX-RC	F: VooDoo	$ 474 – $ 642
HooDoo	C:	XTR 950	F: Marzocchi Bomber Z-1	$ 1,192 – $ 1,612
HooDoo	C:	XTR 950	F: Rock Shox Indy C	$ 1,125 – $ 1,522
HooDoo	C:	XTR 950	F: Rock Shox Indy SL	$ 1,144 – $ 1,548

C: – Components   F: – Fork

MODEL	PRICE RANGE

VooDoo (continued)

Model	Price Range
HooDoo C: XTR 950 F: Rock Shox Indy XC	$ 1,131 – $ 1,531
HooDoo C: XTR 950 F: Rock Shox Judy C	$ 1,169 – $ 1,581
HooDoo C: XTR 950 F: Rock Shox Judy SL	$ 1,238 – $ 1,675
HooDoo C: XTR 950 F: Rock Shox Judy XC	$ 1,175 – $ 1,589
HooDoo C: XTR 950 F: Rock Shox Quadra 5	$ 1,125 – $ 1,522
HooDoo C: XTR 950 F: VooDoo	$ 1,091 – $ 1,476
Loa C: 105SC F: Marzocchi Pave'	$ 1,098 – $ 1,485
Loa C: 105SC F: VooDoo	$ 940 – $ 1,272
Wanga C: Deore LX F: Marzocchi Bomber Z-1	$ 807 – $ 1,092
Wanga C: Deore LX F: Rock Shox Indy C	$ 679 – $ 919
Wanga C: Deore LX F: Rock Shox Indy SL	$ 745 – $ 1,008
Wanga C: Deore LX F: Rock Shox Indy XC	$ 701 – $ 949
Wanga C: Deore LX F: Rock Shox Judy C	$ 756 – $ 1,022
Wanga C: Deore LX F: Rock Shox Judy SL	$ 876 – $ 1,185
Wanga C: Deore LX F: Rock Shox Judy XC	$ 787 – $ 1,065
Wanga C: Deore LX F: Rock Shox Quadra 5	$ 668 – $ 903
Wanga C: Deore LX F: VooDoo	$ 610 – $ 825
Wanga C: Deore XT F: Marzocchi Bomber Z-1	$ 958 – $ 1,295
Wanga C: Deore XT F: Rock Shox Indy C	$ 847 – $ 1,146
Wanga C: Deore XT F: Rock Shox Indy SL	$ 904 – $ 1,223
Wanga C: Deore XT F: Rock Shox Indy XC	$ 866 – $ 1,172
Wanga C: Deore XT F: Rock Shox Judy C	$ 913 – $ 1,235
Wanga C: Deore XT F: Rock Shox Judy SL	$ 1,016 – $ 1,374
Wanga C: Deore XT F: Rock Shox Judy XC	$ 940 – $ 1,272
Wanga C: Deore XT F: Rock Shox Quadra 5	$ 787 – $ 1,065
Wanga C: Deore XT F: VooDoo	$ 787 – $ 1,065
Wanga C: Deore XT/LX F: Rock Shox Indy C	$ 756 – $ 1,022
Wanga C: Deore XT/LX F: Rock Shox Indy SL	$ 817 – $ 1,106
Wanga C: Deore XT/LX F: Rock Shox Indy XC	$ 777 – $ 1,051
Wanga C: Deore XT/LX F: Rock Shox Judy C	$ 827 – $ 1,119
Wanga C: Deore XT/LX F: Rock Shox Judy SL	$ 895 – $ 1,211

C: – Components   F: – Fork

MODEL	PRICE RANGE

VooDoo (*continued*)

Wanga C: Deore XT/LX F: Rock Shox Judy SL	$ 940 – $ 1,272
Wanga C: Deore XT/LX F: Rock Shox Judy SL	$ 975 – $ 1,319
Wanga C: Deore XT/LX F: Rock Shox Quadra 5	$ 745 – $ 1,008
Wanga C: Deore XT/LX F: VooDoo	$ 690 – $ 934
Wanga C: STX-RC F: Marzocchi Bomber Z-1	$ 756 – $ 1,022
Wanga C: STX-RC F: Rock Shox Indy C	$ 622 – $ 841
Wanga C: STX-RC F: Rock Shox Indy SL	$ 668 – $ 903
Wanga C: STX-RC F: Rock Shox Indy XC	$ 645 – $ 872
Wanga C: STX-RC F: Rock Shox Judy C	$ 701 – $ 949
Wanga C: STX-RC F: Rock Shox Judy SL	$ 827 – $ 1,119
Wanga C: STX-RC F: Rock Shox Judy XC	$ 734 – $ 993
Wanga C: STX-RC F: Rock Shox Quadra 5	$ 610 – $ 825
Wanga C: STX-RC F: VooDoo	$ 550 – $ 744
Wanga C: XTR 950 F: Marzocchi Bomber Z-1	$ 1,233 – $ 1,668
Wanga C: XTR 950 F: Rock Shox Indy C	$ 1,169 – $ 1,581
Wanga C: XTR 950 F: Rock Shox Indy SL	$ 1,203 – $ 1,627
Wanga C: XTR 950 F: Rock Shox Indy XC	$ 1,180 – $ 1,597
Wanga C: XTR 950 F: Rock Shox Judy C	$ 1,208 – $ 1,634
Wanga C: XTR 950 F: Rock Shox Judy SL	$ 1,280 – $ 1,732
Wanga C: XTR 950 F: Rock Shox Judy XC	$ 1,223 – $ 1,655
Wanga C: XTR 950 F: Rock Shox Quadra 5	$ 1,163 – $ 1,573
Wanga C: XTR 950 F: VooDoo	$ 1,157 – $ 1,565
Wazoo C: 105SC F: Marzocchi Pave'	$ 975 – $ 1,319
Wazoo C: 105SC F: VooDoo	$ 787 – $ 1,065
Zobop C: STX-RC F: Marzocchi Bomber Z-1	$ 827 – $ 1,119
Zobop C: STX-RC F: Rock Shox Indy C	$ 723 – $ 979
Zobop C: STX-RC F: Rock Shox Indy SL	$ 777 – $ 1,051
Zobop C: STX-RC F: Rock Shox Indy XC	$ 745 – $ 1,008
Zobop C: STX-RC F: Rock Shox Judy C	$ 787 – $ 1,065
Zobop C: STX-RC F: Rock Shox Judy SL	$ 876 – $ 1,185
Zobop C: STX-RC F: Rock Shox Judy XC	$ 807 – $ 1,092

C: – Components   F: – Fork

MODEL	PRICE RANGE

VooDoo (continued)

Model	Price Range
Zobop C: STX-RC F: Rock Shox Quadra 5	$ 701 – $ 949
Zobop C: STX F: Marzocchi Bomber Z-1	$ 766 – $ 1,036
Zobop C: STX F: Rock Shox Indy SL	$ 712 – $ 964
Zobop C: STX F: Rock Shox Indy XC	$ 679 – $ 919
Zobop C: STX F: Rock Shox Judy C	$ 656 – $ 888
Zobop C: STX F: Rock Shox Judy C	$ 723 – $ 979
Zobop C: STX F: Rock Shox Judy SL	$ 817 – $ 1,106
Zobop C: STX F: Rock Shox Judy XC	$ 745 – $ 1,008
Zobop C: STX F: Rock Shox Quadra 5	$ 633 – $ 857

Wheeler

Model	Price Range
200	$ 124 – $ 168
600	$ 145 – $ 196
770	$ 132 – $ 179
800	$ 151 – $ 204
1600	$ 150 – $ 203
1800	$ 178 – $ 241
2600	$ 181 – $ 245
2800	$ 232 – $ 314
2800 ZX	$ 246 – $ 333
3900	$ 242 – $ 328
3900 ZX	$ 304 – $ 412
5000 ZX	$ 538 – $ 728
5200 ZX	$ 347 – $ 469
5500 ZX	$ 394 – $ 533
7000 ZX	$ 754 – $ 1,020
7900 ZX	$ 594 – $ 803
9000 ZX	$ 1,313 – $ 1,777
E-3ZX	$ 874 – $ 1,182
Expert	$ 109 – $ 148
FS	$ 155 – $ 209

C: – Components   F: – Fork

MODEL	PRICE RANGE

Windy City

Cruiser	$ 118 – $	160
Explorer	$ 82 – $	110
Trailblazer	$ 88 – $	119

WizWheelz

TerraTrike	$ 827 – $	1,119
TerraTrike Super 7	$ 827 – $	1,119

Worksman

ALT3CB	$ 299 – $	405
Industrial Newsboy	$ 178 – $	241

Yellow Mushroom

Cloud Nine Other Features	$ 1,255 – $	1,698
Cloud Nine Other Features	$ 1,287 – $	1,741
Groovy Tuesday Other Features	$ 1,068 – $	1,445
Groovy Tuesday Other Features	$ 1,124 – $	1,520
Hippie Shake Other Features	$ 865 – $	1,170
Hippie Shake Other Features	$ 939 – $	1,270
Peace Traveler Other Features	$ 700 – $	947
Peace Traveler Other Features	$ 785 – $	1,062

C: – Components   F: – Fork

MODEL	PRICE RANGE

Aegis

Model	Price Range
650 Bantam 1	$ 1,387 – $ 1,876
650 Bantam 2	$ 1,231 – $ 1,666
650 Bantam 3	$ 1,140 – $ 1,542
650 Bantam Special	$ 1,017 – $ 1,376
700 Aro Svelte 1	$ 1,426 – $ 1,929
700 Aro Svelte 2	$ 1,282 – $ 1,734
700 Aro Svelte 3	$ 1,214 – $ 1,642
700 Aro Svelte 4	$ 1,177 – $ 1,593
700 Aro Svelte 5	$ 1,524 – $ 2,062
700 Aro Svelte 6	$ 1,387 – $ 1,876
700 Aro Svelte 7	$ 1,159 – $ 1,568
Katahdin	$ 1,060 – $ 1,433
Katahdin CX	$ 1,100 – $ 1,489
Katahdin XC	$ 1,214 – $ 1,642
Katahdin XCR	$ 1,426 – $ 1,929
Shaman C	$ 1,017 – $ 1,376
Shaman CXR	$ 1,214 – $ 1,642

Alpine Designs

Model	Price Range
Adventure 20	$ 137 – $ 185
Adventure 24 Rigid	$ 203 – $ 275
Adventure 24 Shock	$ 242 – $ 327
Explore	$ 254 – $ 344
Fly-Ti LX	$ 1,282 – $ 1,734
Fly-Ti RC	$ 1,139 – $ 1,541
Fly-Ti Road	$ 1,533 – $ 2,074
Fly-Ti XT	$ 1,450 – $ 1,962
XC-1	$ 973 – $ 1,317
XC-2	$ 833 – $ 1,127
XC-3	$ 652 – $ 883
XC-3.5	$ 523 – $ 708

C: – Components   F: – Fork

MODEL	PRICE RANGE

Alpine Designs (continued)

XC-4	$ 453 – $ 612
XC-Shock	$ 349 – $ 473
XC-Sport	$ 299 – $ 405

AMP Research

B4 F3XC F: AMP Research F3 XC C: Deore LX	$ 1,036 – $ 1,402
B4 F3XC F: AMP Research F3 XC C: Deore XT	$ 1,237 – $ 1,673
B4 F3XC F: AMP Research F3 XC C: STX	$ 900 – $ 1,218
B4 F3XC Carbon F: AMP Research F3 XC C: Deore LX	$ 1,102 – $ 1,491
B4 F3XC Carbon F: AMP Research F3 XC C: Deore XT	$ 1,290 – $ 1,745
B4 F3XC Carbon F: AMP Research F3 XC C: STX	$ 924 – $ 1,249
B4 F4BLT	$ 1,290 – $ 1,745
B4 F4BLT Carbon	$ 1,340 – $ 1,812
B5 F4BLT F: AMP Research F4BLT C: Deore LX	$ 1,177 – $ 1,593
B5 F4BLT F: AMP Research F4BLT C: SDeore XT	$ 1,351 – $ 1,828
B5 F4BLT F: AMP Research F4BLT C: STX	$ 1,060 – $ 1,433
B5 F4BLT Carbon F: AMP Research F4BLT C: Deore LX	$ 1,235 – $ 1,671
B5 F4BLT Carbon F: AMP Research F4BLT C: Deore XT	$ 1,396 – $ 1,889
B5 F4BLT Carbon F: AMP Research F4BLT C: STX	$ 1,080 – $ 1,461

Angeltech/Lightning

P38-GL63	$ 1,438 – $ 1,946

C: – Components   F: – Fork

MODEL	PRICE RANGE
Angletech	🚲
TriSpeeder	$ 1,495 – $ 2,022
Angletech/Bike E	🚲
AT21GL	$ 1,017 – $ 1,376
Angletech/Rans	🚲
Gliss GL 63	$ 1,282 – $ 1,734
Stratus Miltegra 24	$ 1,177 – $ 1,593
V-Rex GL 63	$ 1,249 – $ 1,689
V Rex Sho	$ 1,450 – $ 1,962
Vivo GL63	$ 1,314 – $ 1,777
AutoBike	🚲
Classic	$ 203 – $ 275
Spirit	$ 203 – $ 275
Sport	$ 170 – $ 230
Balance	🚲
Al 150 F: Balance	$ 382 – $ 517
Al 150 F: RST 161B	$ 453 – $ 613
Al 250 F: Balance	$ 453 – $ 613
Al 250 F: RST 171B	$ 545 – $ 737
Al 350 F: Balance	$ 528 – $ 714
Al 350 F: RST 381L	$ 648 – $ 877
Al 450 F: Balance	$ 630 – $ 853
Al 450 F: Rock Shox Indy C	$ 760 – $ 1,029
Al 550 F: Balance	$ 791 – $ 1,070
Al 550 F: Rock Shox Indy SL	$ 924 – $ 1,251
Al 750	$ 1,244 – $ 1,684
FS 350	$ 771 – $ 1,043
FS 550	$ 1,312 – $ 1,774

C: – Components   F: – Fork

MODEL	PRICE RANGE

Balance (continued)

Model	Price Range
Killer B	$ 344 – $ 475
Stinger B	$ 235 – $ 318
Super B	$ 270 – $ 365
Super FRS	$ 267 – $ 362
Timber Wolf	$ 189 – $ 256
XR 150 F: Balance	$ 274 – $ 371
XR 150 F: RST 161B	$ 356 – $ 482
XR 250 F: RST 171B	$ 390 – $ 528
XR 250 F: Unspecified	$ 300 – $ 406

Barracuda

Model	Price Range
A2B	$ 423 – $ 573
A2BS	$ 453 – $ 613
A2E	$ 706 – $ 955
A2F	$ 236 – $ 319
A2FS	$ 268 – $ 362
A2M	$ 541 – $ 732
A2R	$ 453 – $ 613
A2RS	$ 483 – $ 653
A2T	$ 1,177 – $ 1,593
A2V	$ 833 – $ 1,127
A2Z	$ 331 – $ 532
A2ZS	$ 362 – $ 490
Cuda Cat X XC	$ 652 – $ 882
Cuda Cat XC	$ 453 – $ 613
Cuda Cat XX XC	$ 881 – $ 1,192
Cuda Comp	$ 1,100 – $ 1,489
Urban Assault	$ 331 – $ 448
X FR	$ 423 – $ 573
X FX	$ 928 – $ 1,256
XX FR	$ 625 – $ 846

C: – Components   F: – Fork

MODEL	PRICE RANGE

Barracuda *(continued)*

XX FX	$ 1,282 – $ 1,734
XX Team	$ 625 – $ 846

Bianchi

Advantage	$ 258 – $ 349
Alloro	$ 1,059 – $ 1,432
Avenue	$ 218 – $ 295
B.O.S.S. Single Speed	$ 522 – $ 706
Boardwalk	$ 342 – $ 62
Campione	$ 674 – $ 911
Denali	$ 752 – $ 1,017
Eros	$ 674 – $ 911
Grizzly	$ 962 – $ 1,301
Lynx	$ 290 – $ 393
Lynx SX	$ 393 – $ 531
Milano	$ 399 – $ 540
Ocelot	$ 218 – $ 295
Osprey	$ 616 – $ 834
Peregrine	$ 616 – $ 834
Premio	$ 355 – $ 480
San Remo	$ 735 – $ 995
Strada	$ 185 – $ 250
Trofeo	$ 534 – $ 722
Veloce	$ 911 – $ 1,233
Volpe	$ 411 – $ 556
Wildcat	$ 191 – $ 259
Wildcat 24	$ 144 – $ 195

BikeE

All Around AT21	$ 677 – $ 915
All Around AT7	$ 622 – $ 842

C: – Components   F: – Fork

MODEL	PRICE RANGE

BikeE *(continued)* 🚲

All Around CT21	$ 583 – $ 789
All Around CT7	$ 526 – $ 712
Road E AT21	$ 750 – $ 1,015
Road E AT7	$ 698 – $ 944
Road E CT21	$ 660 – $ 894
Road E CT7	$ 606 – $ 819

BLT 🚲

Basic Loaded Touring w/racks	$ 714 – $ 966

Bontrager 🚲

B1	$ 268 – $ 363
B29	$ 268 – $ 363
B52	$ 423 – $ 573
Privateer	$ 512 – $ 693
Privateer Comp	$ 783 – $ 1,060
Privateer S	$ 625 – $ 846
Race Lite	$ 973 – $ 1,317

Boulder Bikes 🚲

Defiant (LX)	$ 1,017 – $ 1,376
Finesse (XT)	$ 1,373 – $ 1,857
Paris-Roubaix (AC)	$ 1,450 – $ 1,962
Paris-Roubaix (CROMO)	$ 1,248 – $ 1,689
Starship (LX)	$ 1,282 – $ 1,734
Starship (XT)	$ 1,373 – $ 1,857
Starship (XTR)	$ 1,533 – $ 2,073
Starship DH (XT)	$ 1,533 – $ 2,073
Starship LT (XT)	$ 1,450 – $ 1,962
TSL 700 (AL)	$ 1,533 – $ 2,073

C: – Components   F: – Fork

MODEL	PRICE RANGE

Breezer

Ignaz X	$ 438 – $ 593
Jet Stream	$ 926 – $ 1,253
Lightning	$ 1,176 – $ 1,590
Storm	$ 509 – $ 689
Thunder	$ 729 – $ 987
Tornado	$ 1,312 – $ 1,775
Twister	$ 1,078 – $ 1,459

Brompton

L3	$ 412 – $ 557
L5	$ 483 – $ 654
T5	$ 565 – $ 764

Bruce Gordon

Rock N' Road Tour EX w/racks	$ 1,259 – $ 1,703
Rock N' Road Tour w/racks	$ 1,259 – $ 1,703

Burley

Birdy 3 x 7	$ 758 – $ 1,025
Birdy 7	$ 622 – $ 842
Duet	$ 1,177 – $ 1,593
Rock n' Roll	$ 1,090 – $ 1,475
Rumba	$ 951 – $ 1,287
Rumba S&S	$ 1,329 – $ 1,798
Rumba Softride	$ 1,080 – $ 1,461
Samba	$ 881 – $ 1,192
Samba Softride	$ 1,017 – $ 1,376
Zydeco	$ 679 – $ 919
Zydeco Mixte	$ 719 – $ 973

C: – Components   F: – Fork

MODEL	PRICE RANGE

Calfee Design 🚲

Model	Price Range
Luna Pro C: 600 Ultegra F: Kinesis	$ 1,279 – $ 1,739
Luna Pro C: 600 Ultegra F: Tetra Other Features	$ 1,308 – $ 1,777
Luna Pro C: 600 Ultegra F: Tetra Other Features	$ 1,328 – $ 1,827
Luna Pro C: Dura-Ace F: Kinesis	$ 1,440 – $ 1,948
Luna Pro C: Dura-Ace F: Tetra	$ 1,461 – $ 2,013
Luna Pro C: Chorus F: Kinesis	$ 1,395 – $ 1,887
Luna Pro C: Chorus F: Tetra Other Features	$ 1,418 – $ 1,941
Luna Pro C: Chorus F: Tetra Other Features	$ 1,448 – $ 1,959
Luna Pro C: Record F: Kinesis	$ 1,530 – $ 2,071
Luna Tri C: 600 Ultegra F: Kinesis Other Features	$ 1,339 – $ 1,811
Luna Tri C: 600 Ultegra F: Kinesis Other Features	$ 1,365 – $ 1,847
Luna Tri C: 600 Ultegra F: Kinesis Other Features	$ 1,383 – $ 1,892
Luna Tri C: Dura-Ace F: Kinesis	$ 1,427 – $ 1,930
Luna Tri C: Dura-Ace F: Tetra Other Features	$ 1,448 – $ 1,960
Luna Tri C: Dura-Ace F: Tetra Other Features	$ 1,464 – $ 1,997
Tetra Pro C: 600 Ultegra F: Kinesis	$ 1,471 – $ 1,996
Tetra Pro C: 600 Ultegra F: Tetra Other Features	$ 1,491 – $ 2,035
Tetra Pro C: 600 Ultegra F: Tetra Other Features	$ 1,508 – $ 2,055
Tetra Tri C: 600 Ultegra F: Kinesis	$ 1,511 – $ 2,044
Tetra Tri C: 600 Ultegra F: Tetra	$ 1,528 – $ 2,067

Caloi 🚲

Model	Price Range
BMX	$ 207 – $ 280
Busta Cruz	$ 253 – $ 343
Comp	$ 612 – $ 828
Comp FS	$ 869 – $ 1,176
Comp XC	$ 666 – $ 901
Elite	$ 354 – $ 479
Elite FS	$ 607 – $ 822

C: – Components   F: – Fork

MODEL	PRICE RANGE
Caloi (continued)	🚲
Elite XC	$ 438 – $ 593
Expert	$ 277 – $ 375
Expert XC	$ 354 – $ 479
Nexa Cruz	$ 322 – $ 435
Pan Am 1	$ 139 – $ 188
Pan Am 6	$ 160 – $ 216
Pro F: Caloi	$ 306 – $ 414
Pro F: Ritz RR-52023	$ 462 – $ 625
Pro FS	$ 546 – $ 739
Pro XC	$ 383 – $ 518
Rio Cruz	$ 139 – $ 188
Sigma FS	$ 666 – $ 901
Sigma XC	$ 493 – $ 667
Sport	$ 257 – $ 348
Super Cruz	$ 253 – $ 343
Supra	$ 227 – $ 308
Team	$ 802 – $ 1,085
Team FS	$ 1,130 – $ 1,529
Team XC	$ 969 – $ 1,312
Ultra 6	$ 223 – $ 302
Cannondale	🚲
Beast Of The East 900	$ 524 – $ 709
F400	$ 402 – $ 544
F500	$ 524 – $ 709
F700	$ 628 – $ 850
F900	$ 722 – $ 977
F1000	$ 802 – $ 1,085
F2000	$ 950 – $ 1,286
F3000	$ 1,127 – $ 1,525
FS4	$ 464 – $ 628

C: – Components   F: – Fork

MODEL	PRICE RANGE

Cannondale (continued) 🚲

Model	Price Range
H300	$ 294 – $ 398
H300 Mixte	$ 300 – $ 406
H500	$ 402 – $ 544
H700	$ 494 – $ 668
Killer V 700	$ 628 – $ 850
Killer V 900	$ 749 – $ 1,013
M300	$ 287 – $ 388
M300 Mixte	$ 294 – $ 398
M400	$ 306 – $ 415
M500	$ 402 – $ 544
M700	$ 463 – $ 627
M900	$ 524 – $ 709
MT1000	$ 997 – $ 1,348
MT3000	$ 1,463 – $ 1,980
Multisport 600	$ 749 – $ 1,013
Multisport 1000	$ 1,041 – $ 1,409
Multisport 4000	$ 1,408 – $ 1,905
R200	$ 402 – $ 544
R300	$ 463 – $ 627
R300 Compact	$ 464 – $ 628
R500	$ 611 – $ 827
R600	$ 722 – $ 977
R600 Compact	$ 695 – $ 940
R800	$ 853 – $ 1,154
R900	$ 902 – $ 1,220
R1000	$ 997 – $ 1,348
R4000 Other Features	$ 1,314 – $ 1,778
R4000 Other Features	$ 1,437 – $ 1,944
RT1000	$ 1,041 – $ 1,409
RT3000	$ 1,463 – $ 1,980
Silk Path 300	$ 463 – $ 627

C: – Components   F: – Fork

MODEL	PRICE RANGE

Cannondale (continued)

Model	Price Range
Silk Path 300 Mixte	$ 463 – $ 627
Silk Path 500	$ 553 – $ 749
Silk Path 500 Mixte	$ 553 – $ 749
Silk Path 700	$ 639 – $ 865
Silk Path 900	$ 722 – $ 977
Silk Road 500	$ 749 – $ 1,013
Silk Road 1000	$ 1,127 – $ 1,525
Super V 400	$ 668 – $ 903
Super V 500	$ 749 – $ 1,013
Super V 700	$ 878 – $ 1,187
Super V 700 Freeride	$ 1,061 – $ 1,435
Super V 900	$ 997 – $ 1,348
Super V 1000	$ 1,085 – $ 1,468
Super V 1000 Freeride	$ 1,244 – $ 1,683
Super V 2000	$ 1,244 – $ 1,683
Super V 2000 Freeride	$ 1,512 – $ 2,046
Super V Raven 2000	$ 1,463 – $ 1,980
T500	$ 433 – $ 586
T700	$ 524 – $ 709
T1000	$ 802 – $ 1,085
TS700	$ 695 – $ 940
XR800	$ 853 – $ 1,154
XS800	$ 950 – $ 1,286

Cignal

Model	Price Range
Hot Rodasaurus	$ 76 – $ 103
Kokomo	$ 177 – $ 239
Lady Bug	$ 76 – $ 103
Lil Fox	$ 90 – $ 121
Melbourne Express	$ 393 – $ 532
Miss Daisy	$ 83 – $ 112

C: – Components   F: – Fork

MODEL	PRICE RANGE

Cignal (continued)

Model	Price Range
Montauk	$ 137 – $ 185
Ozark	$ 203 – $ 275
Ozark 20	$ 124 – $ 167
Ozark 24	$ 144 – $ 194
Ozark SX 24	$ 183 – $ 248
Ranger	$ 130 – $ 176
Ranger SX	$ 164 – $ 221
Rialto	$ 150 – $ 203
Top Gun	$ 96 – $ 131
Top Gun CB	$ 83 – $ 121
Village Velo	$ 274 – $ 371
Village Velo CB	$ 216 – $ 293
Village Velo FW	$ 190 – $ 257

Co-Motion

Model	Price Range
Breve	$ 1,280 – $ 1,732
Cappuccino	$ 1,456 – $ 1,970
Co-Pilot OR BTC F: Cro-Motion Other Features	$ 1,098 – $ 1,486
Co-Pilot OR BTC F: Cro-Motion Other Features	$ 1,230 – $ 1,664
Co-Pilot OR BTC F: Rock Shox Judy XC	$ 1,151 – $ 1,557
Co-Pilot OR BTC F: Rock Shox Judy XC C: Deore XT	$ 1,275 – $ 1,725
Co-Pilot OR BTC F: Rock Shox Judy XC C: XTR	$ 1,440 – $ 1,948
Co-Pilot Road BTC F: Kinesis	$ 1,516 – $ 2,051
Co-Pilot Road BTC F: Kinesis C: Chorus	$ 1,383 – $ 1,871
Co-Pilot Road BTC F: Kinesis C: 105SC	$ 1,110 – $ 1,516
Co-Pilot Road BTC F: Kinesis C: 600 Ultegra	$ 1,240 – $ 1,685
Co-Pilot Road BTC F: Kinesis C: Dura-Ace	$ 1,416 – $ 1,916
Co-Pilot Road BTC F: Wound Up C: Chorus	$ 1,425 – $ 1,928

C: – Components   F: – Fork

MODEL	PRICE RANGE

Co-Motion (continued)

Co-Pilot Road BTC F: Wound Up C: 105SC	$ 1,171 – $ 1,598
Co-Pilot Road BTC F: Wound Up C: 600 Ultegra	$ 1,293 – $ 1,756
Co-Pilot Road BTC F: Wound Up C: Dura-Ace	$ 1,455 – $ 1,969
Expresso F: Kinesis	$ 1,486 – $ 2,011
Expresso F: Kinesis C: Chorus	$ 1,340 – $ 1,812
Expresso F: Kinesis C: 105SC	$ 1,049 – $ 1,419
Expresso F: Kinesis C: 105SC Triple	$ 1,060 – $ 1,433
Expresso F: Kinesis C: 600 Ultegra	$ 1,186 – $ 1,605
Expresso F: Kinesis C: 600 Ultegra Triple	$ 1,192 – $ 1,613
Expresso F: Kinesis C: Dura-Ace	$ 1,376 – $ 1,861
Expresso F: Wound Up	$ 1,518 – $ 2,054
Expresso F: Wound Up C: Chorus	$ 1,385 – $ 1,874
Expresso F: Wound Up C: 105SC	$ 1,112 – $ 1,505
Expresso F: Wound Up C: 105SC Triple	$ 1,124 – $ 1,521
Expresso F: Wound Up C: 600 Ultegra	$ 1,243 – $ 1,682
Expresso F: Wound Up C: 600 Ultegra Triple	$ 1,298 – $ 1,756
Expresso F: Wound Up C: Dura-Ace	$ 1,418 – $ 1,919
Speedster	$ 1,399 – $ 1,893

Columbia

Superb Limited Edition	$ 879 – $ 1,189

Conejo

AP/5 C: Deore LX F: Marzocchi Bomber Z-1 BAM	$ 1,399 – $ 1,893
AP/5 C: Deore LX F: Marzocchi Bomber Z-2 BAM	$ 1,373 – $ 1,858
AP/5 C: Deore LX F: Marzocchi Jr. T	$ 1,418 – $ 1,918
AP/5 C: Deore LX F: Marzocchi Mr. T	$ 1,520 – $ 2,057
AP/5 C: Deore LX F: Rock Shox Boxxer Pro	$ 1,526 – $ 2,064
AP/5 C: Deore LX F: Rock Shox Judy SL	$ 1,392 – $ 1,884

C: – Components   F: – Fork

MODEL	PRICE RANGE
Conejo (continued)	🚲
AP/5 C: Deore LX F: Rock Shox Judy XC	$ 1,362 – $ 1,842
AP/5 C: Deore LX F: Rock Shox Judy XL	$ 1,419 – $ 1,919
AP/5 C: Deore LX F: RST 381R	$ 1,294 – $ 1,750
AP/5 C: Deore LX F: RST Hi-5	$ 1,376 – $ 1,862
AP/5 C: Deore LX F: RST Mozo Pro	$ 1,328 – $ 1,797
AP/5 C: Deore LX F: White Brothers SC70	$ 1,411 – $ 1,909
AP/5 C: Deore LX F: White Brothers SC90	$ 1,419 – $ 1,919
AP/5 C: Deore XT F: Marzocchi Bomber Z-1 BAM	$ 1,493 – $ 2,019
AP/5 C: Deore XT F: Marzocchi Bomber Z-2 BAM	$ 1,472 – $ 1,992
AP/5 C: Deore XT F: Marzocchi Jr. T	$ 1,507 – $ 2,039
AP/5 C: Deore XT F: Rock Shox Judy SL	$ 1,487 – $ 2,012
AP/5 C: Deore XT F: Rock Shox Judy XC	$ 1,463 – $ 1,979
AP/5 C: Deore XT F: Rock Shox Judy XL	$ 1,508 – $ 2,040
AP/5 C: Deore XT F: RST 381R	$ 1,408 – $ 1,905
AP/5 C: Deore XT F: RST Hi-5	$ 1,475 – $ 1,995
AP/5 C: Deore XT F: RST Mozo Pro	$ 1,436 – $ 1,943
AP/5 C: Deore XT F: White Brothers SC70	$ 1,502 – $ 2,032
AP/5 C: Deore XT F: White Brothers SC90	$ 1,508 – $ 2,040
AP/5 F: Marzocchi Mr. T	$ 1,520 – $ 2,057
AP/5 F: Rock Shox Boxxer Pro	$ 1,526 – $ 2,064
AP/5 F: Rock Shox Judy XL	$ 1,508 – $ 2,040
AP/5 F: White Brothers SC90	$ 1,419 – $ 1,919
AP/5 Ti C: Deore LX F: RST 381R	$ 1,495 – $ 2,023
AP/5 Ti C: Deore LX F: RST Mozo Pro	$ 1,517 – $ 2,052
AP/5 Ti F: RST 381R	$ 1,495 – $ 2,023
AP/5 Ti F: RST Mozo Pro	$ 1,517 – $ 2,052
RBx5 C: Deore LX F: Marzocchi Bomber Z-1 BAM	$ 1,317 – $ 1,782
RBx5 C: Deore LX F: Marzocchi Bomber Z-2 BAM	$ 1,287 – $ 1,742
RBx5 C: Deore LX F: Marzocchi Jr. T	$ 1,339 – $ 1,811
RBx5 C: Deore LX F: Marzocchi Mr. T	$ 1,461 – $ 1,977
RBx5 C: Deore LX F: Rock Shox Judy SL	$ 1,420 – $ 1,921

C: – Components   F: – Fork

MODEL	PRICE RANGE

Conejo (continued)

RBx5 C: Deore LX F: Rock Shox Judy XC	$ 1,274 – $ 1,724
RBx5 C: Deore LX F: Rock Shox Judy XL	$ 1,340 – $ 1,813
RBx5 C: Deore LX F: RST 381R	$ 1,196 – $ 1,619
RBx5 C: Deore LX F: RST Hi-5	$ 1,291 – $ 1,746
RBx5 C: Deore LX F: RST Mozo Pro	$ 1,236 – $ 1,672
RBx5 C: Deore LX F: RST XXL	$ 1,518 – $ 2,053
RBx5 C: Deore LX F: White Brothers SC70	$ 1,331 – $ 1,801
RBx5 C: Deore LX F: White Brothers SC90	$ 1,340 – $ 1,813
RBx5 C: Deore XT F: Marzocchi Bomber Z-1 BAM	$ 1,428 – $ 1,931
RBx5 C: Deore XT F: Marzocchi Bomber Z-2 BAM	$ 1,403 – $ 1,898
RBx5 C: Deore XT F: Marzocchi Jr. T	$ 1,445 – $ 1,955
RBx5 C: Deore XT F: Rock Shox Judy SL	$ 1,421 – $ 1,922
RBx5 C: Deore XT F: Rock Shox Judy XC	$ 1,392 – $ 1,883
RBx5 C: Deore XT F: Rock Shox Judy XL	$ 1,446 – $ 1,956
RBx5 C: Deore XT F: RST 381R	$ 1,328 – $ 1,796
RBx5 C: Deore XT F: RST Hi-5	$ 1,406 – $ 1,902
RBx5 C: Deore XT F: RST Mozo Pro	$ 1,361 – $ 1,841
RBx5 C: Deore XT F: White Brothers SC70	$ 1,439 – $ 1,946
RBx5 C: Deore XT F: White Brothers SC90	$ 1,446 – $ 1,956
RBx5 C: XTR F: RST 381R	$ 1,521 – $ 2,057
RBx5 F: Marzocchi Mr. T	$ 1,461 – $ 1,977
RBx5 F: Rock Shox Judy SL C: Deore LX	$ 1,420 – $ 1,921
RBx5 F: Rock Shox Judy SL C: Deore XT	$ 1,421 – $ 1,922
RBx5 F: RST XXL	$ 1,518 – $ 2,053
RBx5 Ti C: Deore LX F: Marzocchi Bomber Z-1 BAM	$ 1,476 – $ 1,997
RBx5 Ti C: Deore LX F: Marzocchi Bomber Z-2 BAM	$ 1,454 – $ 1,968
RBx5 Ti C: Deore LX F: Marzocchi Jr. T	$ 1,491 – $ 2,017
RBx5 Ti C: Deore LX F: Rock Shox Judy SL	$ 1,470 – $ 1,989
RBx5 Ti C: Deore LX F: Rock Shox Judy XC	$ 1,445 – $ 1,955

C: – Components   F: – Fork

MODEL	PRICE RANGE

Conejo (continued) 🚲

Model	Price Range
RBx5 Ti C: Deore LX F: Rock Shox Judy XL	$ 1,492 – $ 2,018
RBx5 Ti C: Deore LX F: RST 381R	$ 1,387 – $ 1,877
RBx5 Ti C: Deore LX F: RST Hi-5	$ 1,457 – $ 1,971
RBx5 Ti C: Deore LX F: RST Mozo Pro	$ 1,417 – $ 1,917
RBx5 Ti C: Deore LX F: White Brothers SC70	$ 1,486 – $ 2,010
RBx5 Ti C: Deore LX F: White Brothers SC90	$ 1,492 – $ 2,018
RBx5 Ti C: Deore XT F: Rock Shox Judy XC	$ 1,527 – $ 2,066
RBx5 Ti C: Deore XT F: RST 381R	$ 1,483 – $ 2,007
RBx5 Ti C: Deore XT F: RST Mozo Pro	$ 1,506 – $ 2,038
RBx5 Ti F: Marzocchi Bomber Z-1 BAM	$ 1,476 – $ 1,997
RBx5 Ti F: Marzocchi Bomber Z-2 BAM	$ 1,454 – $ 1,968
RBx5 Ti F: Marzocchi Jr. T	$ 1,491 – $ 2,017
RBx5 Ti F: Rock Shox Judy SL	$ 1,470 – $ 1,989
RBx5 Ti F: Rock Shox Judy XL	$ 1,492 – $ 2,018
RBx5 Ti F: RST Hi-5	$ 1,457 – $ 1,971
RBx5 Ti F: White Brothers SC70	$ 1,486 – $ 2,010

Corima 🚲

Model	Price Range
Road	$ 1,425 – $ 1,928
TT Fox	$ 1,400 – $ 1,894
TT Puma	$ 1,425 – $ 1,928

da vinci Designs 🚲

Model	Price Range
In-2-ition	$ 1,533 – $ 2,074

Dahon 🚲

Model	Price Range
Classic III PT631	$ 203 – $ 275
Getaway PT010	$ 137 – $ 185
Himalaya SC614A	$ 331 – $ 448
Mariner PT053M	$ 287 – $ 388
Mariner SC614M	$ 368 – $ 498

C: – Components   F: – Fork

MODEL	PRICE RANGE

Dahon (continued)

Model	Price Range
Mountain Gold ST612	$ 268 – $ 362
Novel LC073	$ 268 – $ 362
Omega LC074N	$ 393 – $ 532
Stowaway PT051	$ 203 – $ 275
Venture SC674N	$ 393 – $ 532

Dean

Model	Price Range
Castanza F: Dean C: 105SC	$ 1,243 – $ 1,682
Castanza F: Dean C: 600 Ultegra	$ 1,328 – $ 1,796
Castanza F: Dean C: Dura-Ace	$ 1,456 – $ 1,970
Colonel Elite	$ 1,226 – $ 1,659
Colonel Expert	$ 1,328 – $ 1,796
Colonel Pro	$ 1,461 – $ 1,976
Duke XC Elite	$ 1,481 – $ 2,003
Felix Elite	$ 987 – $ 1,335
Felix Expert	$ 1,116 – $ 1,510
Felix Pro	$ 1,295 – $ 1,752
Jester XC Elite	$ 1,260 – $ 1,705
Jester XC Expert	$ 1,357 – $ 1,836
Lunar Elite	$ 1,435 – $ 1,941
Lunar Expert	$ 1,504 – $ 2,034
Newman	$ 1,100 – $ 1,489
Oscar Elite	$ 1,124 – $ 1,521
Oscar Expert	$ 1,238 – $ 1,675
Oscar Pro	$ 1,468 – $ 1,986
Sipowitz F: Dean C: 105SC	$ 1,143 – $ 1,547
Sipowitz F: Dean C: 600 Ultegra	$ 1,238 – $ 1,675
Sputnik CTi Elite	$ 1,530 – $ 2,070
Z-Link Elite	$ 1,417 – $ 1,917
Z-Link Expert	$ 1,469 – $ 1,987

C: – Components   F: – Fork

MODEL	PRICE RANGE

Dekerf 🚲

Generation	$ 1,026 – $ 1,388
Team SL	$ 1,385 – $ 1,874
Team ST	$ 1,422 – $ 1,924

Diamondback 🚲

Assault	$ 126 – $ 170
Assault Chrome-plated f	$ 143 – $ 193
Assault EX	$ 143 – $ 193
Coaster	$ 115 – $ 155
Crestview	$ 170 – $ 230
Drifter	$ 143 – $ 193
Expert	$ 329 – $ 445
Ignitor CB	$ 87 – $ 117
Ignitor FW	$ 92 – $ 125
Impression	$ 81 – $ 109
Interval	$ 224 – $ 303
Joker	$ 115 – $ 155
Lakeside	$ 251 – $ 339
Lil One	$ 58 – $ 78
Micro Photon	$ 67 – $ 90
Micro Viper	$ 58 – $ 78
Mini Viper	$ 67 – $ 90
Mr. Lucky	$ 170 – $ 230
Outlook	$ 115 – $ 155
Outlook 24	$ 109 – $ 148
Outlook DX	$ 143 – $ 193
Photon	$ 81 – $ 109
Reactor	$ 214 – $ 289
Reactor Chrome-plated f	$ 224 – $ 303
Reactor Jr.	$ 224 – $ 303
Reactor Team	$ 329 – $ 445

C: – Components   F: – Fork

MODEL	PRICE RANGE
Diamondback (*continued*)	🚲
Recoil	$ 115 – $ 155
Sherwood	$ 197 – $ 267
Sorrento	$ 159 – $ 215
Sorrento 24	$ 115 – $ 155
Sorrento SE	$ 224 – $ 303
Team Issue	$ 1,063 – $ 1,439
V-10	$ 1,180 – $ 1,596
V-6	$ 735 – $ 994
V-6 Team	$ 915 – $ 1,238
V-8	$ 978 – $ 1,324
V-Link 1.2	$ 476 – $ 643
V-Link 3.2	$ 567 – $ 767
Venom	$ 137 – $ 185
Venom X	$ 197 – $ 267
Venom XX	$ 251 – $ 339
Viper	$ 101 – $ 136
Voyager I	$ 224 – $ 303
Voyager II	$ 277 – $ 375
Voyager III	$ 379 – $ 513
Wildwood	$ 159 – $ 215
Wildwood DX	$ 186 – $ 252
DK	🚲
Banshee	$ 183 – $ 248
Fury	$ 203 – $ 275
Legend	$ 423 – $ 573
Promotion	$ 319 – $ 431
Air	$ 204 – $ 276
Air Chrome-plated	$ 211 – $ 286
Blaze	$ 114 – $ 154
Blaze Chrome-plated	$ 120 – $ 163

C: – Components   F: – Fork

MODEL	PRICE RANGE

DK *(continued)* 🚲

Model	Price Range
Compe	$ 184 – $ 249
Compe Chrome-plated	$ 191 – $ 259
Detour	$ 301 – $ 407
Detour Chrome-plated	$ 308 – $ 416
Nitro	$ 204 – $ 276
Nitro Chrome-plated	$ 211 – $ 286
Nitro 24	$ 211 – $ 286
NSX CB	$ 114 – $ 154
NSX CB Chrome-plated	$ 120 – $ 163
NSX FW	$ 121 – $ 164
NSX FW Chrome-plated	$ 128 – $ 173
Slammer	$ 530 – $ 717
VFR	$ 143 – $ 194
VFR Chrome-plated	$ 150 – $ 203
VFR 12	$ 81 – $ 110
VFR 12 Chrome-plated	$ 89 – $ 120
VFR 16	$ 98 – $ 133
VFR 16 Chrome-plated	$ 105 – $ 142
Zone	$ 143 – $ 194
Zone Chrome-plated	$ 158 – $ 214

Electra 🚲

Model	Price Range
Anniversary	$ 268 – $ 362
Bomber 21	$ 362 – $ 490
Bomber 7	$ 411 – $ 556
Deluxe 7 w/fenders	$ 300 – $ 406
Deluxe w/fenders	$ 183 – $ 248
Hawaii 4 w/fenders	$ 236 – $ 319
Hawaii w/fenders	$ 150 – $ 203
Rocket 7	$ 500 – $ 677
Rocket 24	$ 541 – $ 732

C: – Components   F: – Fork

MODEL	PRICE RANGE

Electra (continued)

StreetRod City w/lights & fenders	$ 411 – $ 556
StreetRod Race	$ 411 – $ 556
Sunny Garcia Surf Pro	$ 183 – $ 248

Ellsworth

Road	$ 1,425 – $ 1,928
Roots	$ 1,425 – $ 1,928
Specialist	$ 1,425 – $ 1,928
Sub 22	$ 1,425 – $ 1,928
Truth	$ 1,373 – $ 1,857

Fat Chance

Bro Eddy ! F: Rock Shox Judy SL C: Deore XT Other Features	$ 1,305 – $ 1,765
Bro Eddy ! F: Rock Shox Judy SL C: Deore XT Other Features	$ 1,339 – $ 1,811
Bro Eddy ! F: Rock Shox Judy SL C: XTR Other Features	$ 1,479 – $ 2,001
Bro Eddy ! F: Rock Shox Judy SL C: XTR Other Features	$ 1,506 – $ 2,037
Bro Eddy ! F: Rock Shox Judy XC C: Deore LX Other Features	$ 1,108 – $ 1,499
Bro Eddy ! F: Rock Shox Judy XC C: Deore LX Other Features	$ 1,135 – $ 1,536
Bro Eddy ! F: Rock Shox Judy XC C: Deore XT Other Features	$ 1,221 – $ 1,652
Bro Eddy ! F: Rock Shox Judy XC C: Deore XT Other Features	$ 1,259 – $ 1,704
Chris Chance F: Fat Chance C: 600 Ultegra	$ 1,214 – $ 1,643
Chris Chance F: Fat Chance C: Dura-Ace	$ 1,451 – $ 1,964
Chris Chance Ti	$ 1,528 – $ 2,067
Shock-A-Billy C: Deore LX Other Features	$ 1,431 – $ 1,936
Shock-A-Billy C: Deore LX Other Features	$ 1,448 – $ 1,958

C: – Components   F: – Fork

MODEL	PRICE RANGE

Fat Chance (continued) 🚲

Shock-A-Billy C: Deore XT Other Features	$ 1,499 – $ 2,028
Shock-A-Billy C: Deore XT Other Features	$ 1,520 – $ 2,057
Ti Fat Other Features	$ 1,498 – $ 2,027
Ti Fat Other Features	$ 1,512 – $ 2,046
Yo Betty ! F: Rock Shox Judy SL C: Deore XT Other Features	$ 1,305 – $ 1,765
Yo Betty ! F: Rock Shox Judy SL C: Deore XT Other Features	$ 1,339 – $ 1,811
Yo Betty ! F: Rock Shox Judy SL C: XTR Other Features	$ 1,479 – $ 2,001
Yo Betty ! F: Rock Shox Judy SL C: XTR Other Features	$ 1,506 – $ 2,037
Yo Betty ! F: Rock Shox Judy XC C: Deore LX Other Features	$ 1,108 – $ 1,499
Yo Betty ! F: Rock Shox Judy XC C: Deore LX Other Features	$ 1,135 – $ 1,536
Yo Betty ! F: Rock Shox Judy XC C: Deore XT Other Features	$ 1,221 – $ 1,652
Yo Betty ! F: Rock Shox Judy XC C: Deore XT Other Features	$ 1,259 – $ 1,704
Yo Eddy ! F: Rock Shox Judy SL C: Deore XT Other Features	$ 1,352 – $ 1,829
Yo Eddy ! F: Rock Shox Judy SL C: Deore XT Other Features	$ 1,383 – $ 1,871
Yo Eddy ! F: Rock Shox Judy SL C: XTR	$ 1,511 – $ 2,044
Yo Eddy ! F: Rock Shox Judy XC C: Deore LX Other Features	$ 1,168 – $ 1,580
Yo Eddy ! F: Rock Shox Judy XC C: Deore LX Other Features	$ 1,193 – $ 1,615
Yo Eddy ! F: Rock Shox Judy XC C: Deore XT Other Features	$ 1,274 – $ 1,724
Yo Eddy ! F: Rock Shox Judy XC C: Deore XT Other Features	$ 1,310 – $ 1,772

C: – Components   F: – Fork

MODEL	PRICE RANGE

Feather Titanium

MF6	$ 1,425 – $ 1,928
RF3	$ 1,425 – $ 1,928
RF5	$ 1,425 – $ 1,928

Fiore

BK2601F1	$ 170 – $ 230
BK2605F1	$ 197 – $ 266

Free Agent

Air Raid	$ 170 – $ 229
Ambush	$ 163 – $ 221
Ambush 24	$ 170 – $ 229
Bombardier	$ 392 – $ 531
Champ	$ 103 – $ 139
Eluder	$ 136 – $ 184
Ground Zero	$ 222 – $ 301
Limo	$ 267 – $ 362
Limo 24	$ 267 – $ 362
Limo Team Issue	$ 392 – $ 531
Speedway	$ 203 – $ 274
Speedy	$ 75 – $ 102

Fuji

Aloha	$ 732 – $ 990
Black Diamond	$ 569 – $ 770
Blaster	$ 124 – $ 185
Boulevard	$ 124 – $ 167
Cross	$ 881 – $ 1,192
Crosstown	$ 137 – $ 185
Del Rey	$ 268 – $ 363
Double Black Diamond	$ 783 – $ 1,060

C: – Components   F: – Fork

MODEL	PRICE RANGE

Fuji (continued)

Model	Price Range
Dynamic	$ 453 – $ 613
Finest	$ 393 – $ 532
Folder	$ 216 – $ 293
Gravity-One	$ 1,314 – $ 1,777
Mt. Fuji-SX	$ 1,533 – $ 2,074
Nevada	$ 203 – $ 275
Odessa	$ 137 – $ 185
Professional	$ 1,314 – $ 1,777
Quadruple Black Diamond	$ 1,214 – $ 1,642
Roubaix	$ 625 – $ 846
Sagres	$ 203 – $ 275
Sandblaster	$ 124 – $ 167
Suncrest-SX	$ 423 – $ 573
Sundance-SX	$ 625 – $ 846
Sunfire	$ 170 – $ 230
Supreme	$ 177 – $ 239
Tahoe	$ 268 – $ 363
Tahoe-SX	$ 331 – $ 448
Team	$ 900 – $ 1,218
Thrill	$ 242 – $ 328
Touring Series	$ 453 – $ 613
Triple Black Diamond	$ 973 – $ 1,317

Gary Fisher

Model	Price Range
Air Bob	$ 300 – $ 406
Aquila	$ 368 – $ 498
Big Sur	$ 569 – $ 770
Cleo Moto	$ 150 – $ 212
Dolph	$ 242 – $ 328
Gitche Gumee	$ 203 – $ 275
Hard Warp	$ 190 – $ 275

C: – Components   F: – Fork

MODEL	PRICE RANGE
Gary Fisher (continued)	
Hoo Koo E Koo	$ 512 – $ 693
Joshua X0	$ 783 – $ 1,060
Joshua X1	$ 625 – $ 846
Joshua Z0	$ 1,426 – $ 1,929
Joshua Z1	$ 1,017 – $ 1,376
Kaitai	$ 435 – $ 589
Level Betty FH0	$ 1,282 – $ 1,734
Level Betty FH1	$ 1,100 – $ 1,489
Level Betty FH2	$ 783 – $ 1,060
Lush Rush Cruiser	$ 242 – $ 328
Lush Rush Fuel	$ 242 – $ 328
Lush Rush Tool	$ 203 – $ 275
Marlin	$ 268 – $ 363
Minnosaurus	$ 117 – $ 158
Mr. Skinner	$ 137 – $ 194
Mt. Jam	$ 223 – $ 301
Mt. Tam	$ 1,017 – $ 1,376
Mud Puppy	$ 96 – $ 131
Nirvana	$ 287 – $ 388
Opie	$ 287 – $ 388
Paragon	$ 625 – $ 846
Pure Bender Kick	$ 229 – $ 310
Pure Bender Spin	$ 183 – $ 248
Quick Pierce	$ 203 – $ 275
Short Cut	$ 157 – $ 212
Supercaliber	$ 1,314 – $ 1,777
Tassajara	$ 306 – $ 414
Trigger Fish Baked	$ 268 – $ 363
Trigger Fish Raw	$ 344 – $ 465
Tyro	$ 170 – $ 230

C: – Components   F: – Fork

1998

MODEL	PRICE RANGE

Kaitai *(continued)* 🚲

Model	Price Range
Utopia	$ 423 – $ 573
Wahoo	$ 223 – $ 301
Zebrano	$ 229 – $ 310

Gazelle Bikes 🚲

Model	Price Range
Gazelle FS XT	$ 1,265 – $ 1,712
Gazelle FS XTR	$ 1,387 – $ 1,876
Rapture XT	$ 1,524 – $ 2,062

Giant 🚲

Model	Price Range
Acapulco	$ 115 – $ 156
Animator	$ 61 – $ 82
ATX 860	$ 401 – $ 543
ATX 865	$ 401 – $ 543
ATX 870	$ 529 – $ 716
ATX 890	$ 865 – $ 1,170
ATX 970	$ 529 – $ 716
ATX 1100	$ 884 – $ 1,196
ATX 1200	$ 1,081 – $ 1,462
Boulder	$ 136 – $ 184
Cypress	$ 162 – $ 235
Farrago	$ 191 – $ 274
Iguana	$ 237 – $ 336
Iguana SE	$ 271 – $ 381
Innova	$ 237 – $ 321
Kronos	$ 348 – $ 470
MCM 980	$ 1,274 – $ 1,724
MCR	$ 1,172 – $ 1,585
Morph	$ 168 – $ 227
Mosh 2	$ 85 – $ 115
Mosh Pro	$ 214 – $ 290

C: – Components   F: – Fork

1998

MODEL	PRICE RANGE

Giant *(continued)*

Model	Price Range
Mosh Pro XL	$ 320 – $ 434
Mosh Pro XL 4130	$ 191 – $ 259
MTX 125	$ 115 – $ 156
MTX 200	$ 115 – $ 156
MTX 225	$ 136 – $ 184
MTX 250	$ 208 – $ 282
Option	$ 133 – $ 180
Pudd'n	$ 61 – $ 82
Rincon	$ 156 – $ 211
Rincon SE	$ 203 – $ 274
Sedona SE	$ 293 – $ 396
Taffy	$ 85 – $ 115
TCR	$ 695 – $ 940
Upland	$ 109 – $ 148
Warp DS1	$ 320 – $ 434
Warp DS2	$ 427 – $ 578
Warp SE	$ 231 – $ 313
Yukon	$ 194 – $ 263
Yukon SE	$ 287 – $ 389

Grandis

Model	Price Range
Over Max Chorus	$ 1,473 – $ 1,993
Classic F: Aegis Fresh Ride	$ 1,176 – $ 1,590
Classic F: Aegis Hot Rod C: 600 Ultegra	$ 1,371 – $ 1,855
Classic F: Aegis Hot Rod C: Dura-Ace	$ 1,493 – $ 2,021
Classic Tri F: Aegis Hot Rod C: 600 Ultegra	$ 1,399 – $ 1,893
Classic Tri F: Aegis Hot Rod C: Dura-Ace	$ 1,513 – $ 2,048
Hard Tail F: Marzocchi Bomber Z-2	$ 1,312 – $ 1,775
Hard Tail F: Marzocchi Bomber Z-2 Atom Bomb	$ 1,425 – $ 1,928
Triton Tri F: Aegis Hot Rod C: 600 Ultegra	$ 1,425 – $ 1,928
Triton Tri F: Aegis Hot Rod C: Dura-Ace	$ 1,532 – $ 2,072

C: – Components   F: – Fork

1998

MODEL	PRICE RANGE

Grandis (continued) 🚲

Vulcan	$ 1,532 – $ 2,072
Vulcan Tri	$ 1,532 – $ 2,072

GT 🚲

Aggressor	$ 219 – $ 296
Attack	$ 672 – $ 909
Avalanche	$ 575 – $ 778
Avalanche LE	$ 757 – $ 1,024
Avalanche Spin	$ 755 – $ 1,022
Backwoods	$ 337 – $ 456
Course	$ 736 – $ 996
Edge Aero	$ 1,070 – $ 1,448
Force	$ 326 – $ 441
Forte Titanium	$ 1,100 – $ 1,488
Fueler	$ 281 – $ 380
Fury	$ 857 – $ 1,160
GTB-1	$ 379 – $ 513
Karakoram	$ 459 – $ 621
Lightning	$ 859 – $ 1,162
LTS-1000 DS	$ 1,214 – $ 1,642
LTS-2000	$ 824 – $ 1,114
LTS-2000 DS	$ 913 – $ 1,236
LTS-3000	$ 518 – $ 701
LTS-3000 DS	$ 649 – $ 878
LTS-4000	$ 425 – $ 575
Mach One	$ 158 – $ 221
Nomad	$ 324 – $ 439
Outpost	$ 174 – $ 236
Outpost Trail	$ 152 – $ 206
Palomar	$ 130 – $ 176
Performer	$ 202 – $ 273

C: – Components   F: – Fork

MODEL	PRICE RANGE

GT (continued)

Model	Price Range
Performer (Mag)	$ 220 – $ 297
Power Series	$ 180 – $ 244
Power Series 1.0	$ 222 – $ 301
Power Series 3.0	$ 291 – $ 394
Pro Performer	$ 257 – $ 348
Pro Series	$ 185 – $ 258
Pro Series 24	$ 190 – $ 258
Pro Series Mini	$ 185 – $ 250
Pulse	$ 945 – $ 1,278
Rebound	$ 254 – $ 344
Ricochet	$ 366 – $ 496
Show	$ 519 – $ 702
Slipstream	$ 177 – $ 240
Speed Series	$ 356 – $ 482
Speed Series Cruiser	$ 356 – $ 482
Speed Series Jr	$ 371 – $ 502
Speed Series Team	$ 519 – $ 702
Speed Series Team (Spin)	$ 632 – $ 855
Strike	$ 578 – $ 782
STS-1000 DS	$ 1,239 – $ 1,676
STS-1500 DS	$ 1,001 – $ 1,354
Team Trials	$ 649 – $ 879
Tequesta	$ 351 – $ 475
Timberline	$ 249 – $ 337
Tour	$ 501 – $ 677
Vertigo	$ 175 – $ 236
Virage	$ 460 – $ 623
Windstream	$ 154 – $ 208
Zaskar	$ 858 – $ 1,161
Zazkar LE	$ 1,239 – $ 1,676

C: – Components   F: – Fork

MODEL	PRICE RANGE

Habit 🚲

Bad Habit	$ 281 – $ 380

Hanebrink 🚲

Extreme Terrain Rigid	$ 1,400 – $ 1,894

Haro 🚲

Blammo	$ 453 – $ 613
Blaster	$ 107 – $ 144
Cozmo	$ 319 – $ 431
Del Sol	$ 157 – $ 212
Del Sol NX	$ 278 – $ 375
El Camino	$ 170 – $ 230
El Camino DX	$ 229 – $ 310
Escape A1	$ 408 – $ 552
Escape A2	$ 564 – $ 762
Escape A3	$ 821 – $ 1,110
Escape A4	$ 1,282 – $ 1,734
Escape AO	$ 278 – $ 375
Extreme DX2	$ 808 – $ 1,094
Extreme EX0	$ 462 – $ 625
Extreme EX1	$ 625 – $ 846
Extreme MX3	$ 1,130 – $ 1,529
Group 1 AL	$ 203 – $ 275
Group 1 ALi	$ 287 – $ 388
Group 1 Monocoque	$ 483 – $ 653
Group 1 Si	$ 170 – $ 230
Group 1 Si Mini	$ 200 – $ 270
Group 1 Zi	$ 124 – $ 167
Micro Blaster	$ 93 – $ 126
Mini Blaster	$ 100 – $ 135
Revo	$ 140 – $ 190

C: – Components   F: – Fork

MODEL	PRICE RANGE
Haro (continued)	🚲
Shredder	$ 213 – $ 288
Supra	$ 233 – $ 315
Supra DLX	$ 378 – $ 511
Ultra	$ 453 – $ 613
V2R	$ 200 – $ 270
Vector V0	$ 150 – $ 203
Vector V1	$ 170 – $ 230
Vector V2	$ 223 – $ 301
Vector V20	$ 137 – $ 185
Vector V24	$ 157 – $ 212
Vector V3	$ 274 – $ 371
Zippo	$ 177 – $ 239
Zippo Mag	$ 197 – $ 266
HH Racing Group	🚲
Fudendo	$ 808 – $ 1,094
Furiosa	$ 1,208 – $ 1,635
New Professional	$ 1,237 – $ 1,673
Pista	$ 1,017 – $ 1,376
Scarab	$ 1,489 – $ 2,015
STD	$ 1,519 – $ 2,055
Vitesse	$ 1,462 – $ 1,978
Vitesse ZTi	$ 1,275 – $ 1,725
Hoffman Bikes	🚲
Condor	$ 453 – $ 612
Ep	$ 435 – $ 588
Flash Pro	$ 280 – $ 379
Flash XL	$ 280 – $ 379
George	$ 229 – $ 309
Sugar Baby	$ 286 – $ 388
Taj	$ 411 – $ 555

C: – Components   F: – Fork

MODEL	PRICE RANGE

Hotta 🚲

| T 2000 | $ 1,504 – $ 2,034 |
| TT 2000 | $ 1,504 – $ 2,034 |

Huffy 🚲

B-52	$ 144 – $ 194
Delirium	$ 197 – $ 266
Enigma	$ 347 – $ 470
Half Ton	$ 164 – $ 221
MJ-12	$ 164 – $ 221
One Ton	$ 203 – $ 275
Quarter Ton	$ 144 – $ 194
Radius	$ 150 – $ 203
Radius 24	$ 157 – $ 212
SC-24	$ 137 – $ 185
Super Charger	$ 130 – $ 176
Super Deluxe	$ 255 – $ 345
Tremor	$ 110 – $ 149
Twister	$ 96 – $ 131

I.C.E. 🚲

Hammer C: Athena	$ 1,339 – $ 1,812
Hammer C: Chorus	$ 1,419 – $ 1,919
Hammer C: 105SC	$ 1,192 – $ 1,612
Hammer C: 600 Ultegra	$ 1,301 – $ 1,760
Hammer C: Dura-Ace	$ 1,464 – $ 1,981

Ibis 🚲

| Alibi | $ 985 – $ 1,332 |
| Mojo | $ 1,039 – $ 1,405 |

C: – Components   F: – Fork

MODEL

PRICE RANGE

Independent Fabrication

Model	Price Range
Crown Jewel C: 105SC F: Aegis	$ 1,242 – $ 1,680
Crown Jewel C: 105SC F: Steelman	$ 1,179 – $ 1,595
Crown Jewel C: 600 Ultegra F: Aegis	$ 1,353 – $ 1,830
Crown Jewel C: 600 Ultegra F: Steelman	$ 1,300 – $ 1,758
Crown Jewel C: Dura-Ace F: Aegis	$ 1,496 – $ 2,023
Crown Jewel C: Dura-Ace F: Steelman	$ 1,457 – $ 1,972
Crown Jewel C: Athena F: Aegis	$ 1,388 – $ 1,878
Crown Jewel C: Athena F: Steelman	$ 1,338 – $ 1,810
Crown Jewel C: Chorus F: Aegis	$ 1,469 – $ 1,987
Crown Jewel C: Chorus F: Steelman	$ 1,427 – $ 1,931
Deluxe C: Deore LX F: Marzocchi Bomber Z-2 Atom Bomb	$ 1,300 – $ 1,758
Deluxe C: Deore LX F: Marzocchi Bomber Z-2 BAM	$ 1,274 – $ 1,723
Deluxe C: Deore LX F: Rock Shox Judy SL	$ 1,290 – $ 1,745
Deluxe C: Deore LX F: Rock Shox Judy XC	$ 1,254 – $ 1,696
Deluxe C: Deore LX F: Rock Shox Sid	$ 1,351 – $ 1,828
Deluxe C: Deore XT F: Marzocchi Bomber Z-2 Atom Bomb	$ 1,384 – $ 1,872
Deluxe C: Deore XT F: Marzocchi Bomber Z-2 BAM	$ 1,361 – $ 1,842
Deluxe C: Deore XT F: Rock Shox Judy SL	$ 1,376 – $ 1,861
Deluxe C: Deore XT F: Rock Shox Judy XC	$ 1,344 – $ 1,818
Deluxe C: Deore XT F: Rock Shox Sid	$ 1,429 – $ 1,933
Deluxe C: XTR F: Marzocchi Bomber Z-2 Atom Bomb	$ 1,527 – $ 2,066
Deluxe C: XTR F: Marzocchi Bomber Z-2 BAM	$ 1,512 – $ 2,046
Deluxe C: XTR F: Rock Shox Judy SL	$ 1,522 – $ 2,059
Deluxe C: XTR F: Rock Shox Judy XC	$ 1,501 – $ 2,030
Planet X C: 105SC F: Steelman	$ 1,174 – $ 1,588
Planet X C: 600 Ultegra F: Steelman	$ 1,257 – $ 1,701
Special C: Deore LX F: Marzocchi Bomber Z-2 Atom Bomb	$ 1,300 – $ 1,758
Special C: Deore LX F: Marzocchi Bomber Z-2 BAM	$ 1,274 – $ 1,723

1998

C: – Components   F: – Fork

MODEL   PRICE RANGE

Independent Fabrication *(continued)*   🚲

Special C: Deore LX F: Rock Shox Judy SL	$ 1,290 – $ 1,745
Special C: Deore LX F: Rock Shox Judy XC	$ 1,254 – $ 1,696
Special C: Deore LX F: Rock Shox Sid	$ 1,351 – $ 1,828
Special C: Deore XT F: Marzocchi Bomber Z-2 Atom Bomb	$ 1,384 – $ 1,872
Special C: Deore XT F: Marzocchi Bomber Z-2 BAM	$ 1,361 – $ 1,842
Special C: Deore XT F: Rock Shox Judy SL	$ 1,376 – $ 1,861
Special C: Deore XT F: Rock Shox Judy XC	$ 1,344 – $ 1,818
Special C: Deore XT F: Rock Shox Sid	$ 1,429 – $ 1,933
Special C: XTR F: Marzocchi Bomber Z-2 Atom Bomb	$ 1,527 – $ 2,066
Special C: XTR F: Marzocchi Bomber Z-2 BAM	$ 1,512 – $ 2,046
Special C: XTR F: Rock Shox Judy SL	$ 1,522 – $ 2,059
Special C: XTR F: Rock Shox Judy XC	$ 1,501 – $ 2,030

Ionic   🚲

E3 Bully	$ 951 – $ 1,287
E3 CX F: Answer Manitou SX Ti	$ 1,519 – $ 2,055
E3 CX F: Rock Shox Judy SL	$ 1,502 – $ 2,032
E3 CX F: Rock Shox Sid	$ 1,533 – $ 2,074
E3 Expert F: Rock Shox Judy SL	$ 1,290 – $ 1,745
E3 Expert F: Rock Shox Judy XC	$ 1,240 – $ 1,678
Ion Bomber F: Answer Manitou X-Vert	$ 1,214 – $ 1,642
Ion Bomber F: Rock Shox Judy XC LT	$ 1,159 – $ 1,568
Ion Max	$ 1,426 – $ 1,929

Iron Horse   🚲

Adirondack	$ 137 – $ 185
Adventure	$ 170 – $ 230
ARS 2.0	$ 268 – $ 362
ARS 4.0	$ 387 – $ 523

C: – Components   F: – Fork

MODEL	PRICE RANGE

Iron Horse (continued)

Model	Price Range
ARS 6.8	$ 529 – $ 716
ARS 7.0	$ 706 – $ 955
ARS 9.0	$ 985 – $ 1,332
ARS Comp	$ 362 – $ 515
Expedition	$ 236 – $ 319
Flite	$ 124 – $ 176
G-Out	$ 453 – $ 613
G-Spot	$ 677 – $ 915
IFR	$ 144 – $ 203
Journey	$ 137 – $ 185
Maverick	$ 137 – $ 185
Outlaw	$ 117 – $ 158
Quest	$ 137 – $ 185
Sequoia	$ 203 – $ 275
Typhoon	$ 210 – $ 284

Jamis

Model	Price Range
Aragon	$ 216 – $ 293
Aurora	$ 393 – $ 532
Aurora Compact	$ 393 – $ 532
Boss 7	$ 183 – $ 248
Boss 7 Aluminum	$ 255 – $ 345
Boss Coaster	$ 150 – $ 203
Bossy	$ 110 – $ 149
Citizen	$ 170 – $ 230
Coda	$ 399 – $ 540
Comet	$ 928 – $ 1,256
Cross Country	$ 197 – $ 266
Dakar Expert	$ 803 – $ 1,087
Dakar Pro	$ 1,100 – $ 1,489
Dakar Sport	$ 483 – $ 653

C: – Components   F: – Fork

MODEL	PRICE RANGE
Jamis *(continued)*	🚲
Dakota	$ 668 – $ 904
Dakota AL	$ 808 – $ 1,094
Diablo	$ 1,494 – $ 2,022
Dragon	$ 1,039 – $ 1,405
Durango AL	$ 312 – $ 423
Durango Sport	$ 242 – $ 328
Durango Sport SX	$ 306 – $ 414
Durango SX	$ 405 – $ 548
EC 1	$ 144 – $ 194
EC 2	$ 124 – $ 167
EC 7	$ 177 – $ 239
EC 7 Aluminum	$ 325 – $ 440
Eclipse	$ 1,004 – $ 1,359
Eureka	$ 541 – $ 732
Explorer	$ 164 – $ 221
Explorer 24	$ 164 – $ 221
Komodo	$ 960 – $ 1,299
Quest	$ 641 – $ 868
Quest Compact	$ 641 – $ 868
Tangier	$ 312 – $ 423
Taxi	$ 170 – $ 230
Just Two Bikes	🚲
Montage I7	$ 1,472 – $ 1,992
Montage EX	$ 1,425 – $ 1,928
K2 Bike	🚲
ProFlex 1000	$ 652 – $ 882
ProFlex 2000	$ 783 – $ 1,060
ProFlex 3000	$ 928 – $ 1,256
ProFlex 4000	$ 1,140 – $ 1,542

C: – Components   F: – Fork

MODEL	PRICE RANGE

K2 Bike (continued)

ProFlex 4000 SE	$ 1,231 – $ 1,665
ProFlex 4500C	$ 1,265 – $ 1,712
ProFlex 5000	$ 1,413 – $ 1,912
ProFlex Animal	$ 1,265 – $ 1,712
ProFlex Beast	$ 1,017 – $ 1,376

Kestrel

200EMS	$ 1,484 – $ 2,008
200SCI F: Kestrel EMS C: 105SC	$ 1,177 – $ 1,592
200SCI F: Kestrel EMS C: 600 Ultegra	$ 1,265 – $ 1,712
200SCI F: Kestrel EMS C: Dura-Ace	$ 1,426 – $ 1,929
500SCI	$ 1,386 – $ 1,876
CS-X F: Rock Shox Indy C	$ 881 – $ 1,192
CS-X F: Rock Shox Judy XC	$ 1,017 – $ 1,376
CS-X F: Rock Shox Sid	$ 1,231 – $ 1,665
KM40	$ 1,450 – $ 1,962
Rubicon Comp F: Rock Shox Judy SL	$ 1,426 – $ 1,929
Rubicon Comp F: Rock Shox Judy XC	$ 1,313 – $ 1,777

KHS

Aero Comp	$ 881 – $ 1,192
Aero Track	$ 423 – $ 572
Aero Turbo	$ 732 – $ 990
Alite 500	$ 235 – $ 318
Alite 1000	$ 331 – $ 447
Alite 2000	$ 423 – $ 572
Alite 3000	$ 679 – $ 918
Alite 4000	$ 1,059 – $ 1,433
Brentwood	$ 229 – $ 309
Fleetwood	$ 453 – $ 612
FXT Desent	$ 453 – $ 612

C: – Components   F: – Fork

MODEL	PRICE RANGE
KHS (*continued*)	🚲
FXT Sport	$ 362 – $ 489
FXT Team	$ 1,426 – $ 1,929
Montana	$ 136 – $ 184
Montana Comp	$ 453 – $ 612
Montana Crest	$ 267 – $ 362
Montana Nomad	$ 299 – $ 405
Montana Pro	$ 540 – $ 731
Montana Raptor	$ 136 – $ 184
Montana Sport	$ 203 – $ 274
Montana T-Rex	$ 136 – $ 184
Montana Team	$ 1,017 – $ 1,376
Montana Town+Country	$ 222 – $ 301
Montana Trail	$ 156 – $ 212
Tandemania Alite	$ 973 – $ 1,316
Tandemania Comp	$ 624 – $ 845
Tandemania Roma	$ 1,100 – $ 1,488
Tandemania Sport	$ 482 – $ 652
Wedgewood	$ 331 – $ 447
Klein	🚲
Attitude Comp	$ 928 – $ 1,256
Attitude Pro	$ 1,533 – $ 2,074
Attitude Race	$ 1,282 – $ 1,734
Karma	$ 625 – $ 846
Karma Pave	$ 625 – $ 846
Mantra	$ 833 – $ 1,127
Mantra Comp	$ 973 – $ 1,317
Mantra Race	$ 1,249 – $ 1,689
Mantra Race LT	$ 1,313 – $ 1,777
Navigator	$ 833 – $ 1,127
Pulse	$ 453 – $ 613

C: – Components   F: – Fork

MODEL	PRICE RANGE

Klein (continued)

Pulse Comp	$ 569 – $ 770
Pulse Pro	$ 833 – $ 1,127
Pulse Race	$ 679 – $ 919
Quantum Pro	$ 1,533 – $ 2,074
Quantum Race	$ 1,100 – $ 1,489
Stage	$ 608 – $ 823
Stage Comp R	$ 833 – $ 1,127
Stage Comp T	$ 833 – $ 1,127

Kona

Caldera	$ 569 – $ 769
Cinder Cone	$ 511 – $ 692
Explosif	$ 951 – $ 1,286
Fire Mountain	$ 362 – $ 489
Hahanna	$ 254 – $ 344
Humu One	$ 254 – $ 344
Humu Seven	$ 362 – $ 489
Jake the Snake	$ 652 – $ 882
Kapu	$ 904 – $ 1,224
Kiluea	$ 732 – $ 990
King Kikapu	$ 1,248 – $ 1,689
Kula	$ 995 – $ 1,346
Lava Dome	$ 392 – $ 531
Manomano	$ 857 – $ 1,159
Mokomoko	$ 1,017 – $ 1,376
Muni-Mula	$ 624 – $ 845
Pahoehoe	$ 783 – $ 1,059
Stab	$ 1,313 – $ 1,777
U'Hu	$ 1,100 – $ 1,489

C: – Components   F: – Fork

MODEL	PRICE RANGE

LeMond 🚲

Model	Price Range
Alpe d'Huez	$ 679 – $ 919
Buenos Aires	$ 783 – $ 1,060
Maillot Jaune	$ 1,426 – $ 1,929
Reno	$ 541 – $ 732
Tourmalet	$ 597 – $ 808
Zurich	$ 1,017 – $ 1,376

Lenz Sport 🚲

Model	Price Range
Bouldervore XC	$ 1,473 – $ 1,993

Lightning 🚲

Model	Price Range
P-38	$ 1,138 – $ 1,539
P-38C	$ 1,425 – $ 1,928
Stealth	$ 758 – $ 1,025

Linear 🚲

Model	Price Range
LWB	$ 808 – $ 1,094
Mach III Club	$ 679 – $ 918
SWB	$ 808 – $ 1,094
SWB Sonic	$ 808 – $ 1,094
Tandem Folder	$ 1,473 – $ 1,993

Litespeed 🚲

Model	Price Range
Appalachian	$ 1,413 – $ 1,912
Blade	$ 1,484 – $ 2,008
Blue Ridge C: 105SC	$ 1,274 – $ 1,723
Blue Ridge C: 600 Ultegra	$ 1,373 – $ 1,857
Classic C: 105SC Other Features	$ 1,282 – $ 1,734
Classic C: 105SC Other Features	$ 1,298 – $ 1,756
Classic C: 600 Ultegra Other Features	$ 1,413 – $ 1,912
Classic C: 600 Ultegra Other Features	$ 1,426 – $ 1,929

C: – Components   F: – Fork

MODEL	PRICE RANGE
Litespeed *(continued)*	🚲
Classic F: Time Equipe	$ 1,484 – $ 2,008
Cohutta	$ 1,495 – $ 2,022
Hiwassee F: Rock Shox Judy SL	$ 1,321 – $ 1,788
Hiwassee F: Rock Shox Judy XC	$ 1,130 – $ 1,529
Natchez C: 105SC Other Features	$ 1,130 – $ 1,529
Natchez C: 105SC Other Features	$ 1,140 – $ 1,542
Natchez F: Look C: 600 Ultegra	$ 1,298 – $ 1,756
Obed F: Rock Shox Judy SL	$ 1,321 – $ 1,788
Obed F: Rock Shox Judy XC	$ 1,130 – $ 1,529
Ocoee F: Rock Shox Judy SL	$ 1,426 – $ 1,929
Ocoee F: Rock Shox Judy XC	$ 1,265 – $ 1,712
Owl Hollow F: Rock Shox Judy SL	$ 1,484 – $ 2,008
Owl Hollow F: Rock Shox Judy XC	$ 1,344 – $ 1,818
Owl Hollow MTS	$ 1,495 – $ 2,022
Tachyon F: Look C: 600 Ultegra	$ 1,314 – $ 1,777
Tachyon F: Look C: Dura-Ace	$ 1,473 – $ 1,993
Tuscany F: Look C: 105SC	$ 1,214 – $ 1,642
Tuscany F: Look C: 600 Ultegra	$ 1,373 – $ 1,857
Tuscany F: Time Equipe	$ 1,510 – $ 2,042
Unicoi F: Rock Shox Judy SL	$ 1,450 – $ 1,962
Unicoi F: Rock Shox Judy XC	$ 1,298 – $ 1,756
Lodestar	🚲
Destiny	$ 1,100 – $ 1,488
Obsession	$ 540 – $ 731
Renaissance	$ 732 – $ 990
Revenge	$ 569 – $ 769
Serenity	$ 758 – $ 1,025
Therapy	$ 652 – $ 882

C: – Components   F: – Fork

MODEL

PRICE RANGE

Lovely Lowrider 🚲

Model				
Bondobike	$	392	– $	531
Chromebike	$	170	– $	229
Goldbike	$	203	– $	274
Showbike	$	453	– $	612

Marin 🚲

Model				
Alpine Trail F.R.S.	$	569	– $	769
B-17 F.R.S	$	881	– $	1,192
Bear Valley	$	392	– $	531
Bobcat Trail	$	267	– $	362
Bolinas Ridge	$	203	– $	274
East Peak F.R.S.	$	679	– $	918
Eldridge Grade	$	488	– $	660
Hawk Hill	$	267	– $	362
Hidden Canyon	$	222	– $	301
Highway One	$	732	– $	990
Indian Fire Trail	$	732	– $	990
Larkspur	$	203	– $	274
Limited Edition	$	511	– $	692
Mount Vision F.R.S.	$	1,059	– $	1,433
Mount Vision Pro F.R.S.	$	1,400	– $	1,894
Muir Woods	$	305	– $	413
Nail Trail	$	423	– $	572
Palisades Trail	$	331	– $	447
Pine Mountain	$	624	– $	845
Point Reyes	$	546	– $	739
Rift Zone	$	833	– $	1,126
Rocky Ridge	$	511	– $	692
San Anselmo	$	368	– $	498
San Rafael	$	267	– $	362
Sausalito	$	386	– $	523

C: – Components   F: – Fork

MODEL	PRICE RANGE

Marin *(continued)*

Sausalito FS	$ 429 – $ 580
Stinson	$ 254 – $ 344
Team DH F.R.S	$ 1,426 – $ 1,929
Team Marin	$ 833 – $ 1,126
Wildcat Trail	$ 1,139 – $ 1,541

Marinoni

Bella Donna Chorus	$ 1,450 – $ 1,962
Ciclo Ultegra Triple	$ 996 – $ 1,347
Estasi Dura-Ace	$ 1,344 – $ 1,818
Fango RSX	$ 808 – $ 1,094
Leggero Chorus	$ 1,282 – $ 1,734
Piccola 105	$ 905 – $ 1,224
Pista Record	$ 1,100 – $ 1,489
Puima Record	$ 1,426 – $ 1,929
Sprint Veloce	$ 808 – $ 1,094
Squadra Athena	$ 1,100 – $ 1,489
Turismo Veloce	$ 940 – $ 1,271
Ultimo Ultegra	$ 1,177 – $ 1,593

Masi

Gran Corsa F: Masi C: 600 Ultegra	$ 1,043 – $ 1,411
Gran Corsa F: Masi C: Athena	$ 1,062 – $ 1,436
Gran Corsa F: Masi C: Chorus	$ 1,188 – $ 1,608
Gran Corsa F: Masi C: Dura-Ace	$ 1,306 – $ 1,767
Gran Corsa F: Masi C: Mirage	$ 836 – $ 1,130
Gran Corsa F: Masi C: Record	$ 1,395 – $ 1,887
Gran Corsa F: Masi C: Veloce	$ 910 – $ 1,231
Gran Criterium F: Masi C: Athena	$ 1,364 – $ 1,846
Gran Criterium F: Masi C: Chorus	$ 1,449 – $ 1,961
Gran Criterium F: Masi C: Mirage	$ 1,203 – $ 1,628

C: – Components   F: – Fork

MODEL	PRICE RANGE

Masi (continued)

Model	Price Range
Gran Criterium F: Masi C: Veloce	$ 1,257 – $ 1,701
Gran Criterium F: Masi C: 600 Ultegra	$ 1,353 – $ 1,830
Gran Criterium F: Masi C: Dura-Ace	$ 1,522 – $ 2,059
Nuova Strada F: Masi C: 600 Ultegra	$ 1,098 – $ 1,486
Nuova Strada F: Masi C: Athena	$ 1,114 – $ 1,508
Nuova Strada F: Masi C: Chorus	$ 1,235 – $ 1,671
Nuova Strada F: Masi C: Dura-Ace	$ 1,345 – $ 1,820
Nuova Strada F: Masi C: Mirage	$ 898 – $ 1,215
Nuova Strada F: Masi C: Record	$ 1,430 – $ 1,934
Nuova Strada F: Masi C: Veloce	$ 969 – $ 1,311
Record F: Masi C: 600 Ultegra	$ 1,176 – $ 1,590
Record F: Masi C: Athena	$ 1,196 – $ 1,618
Record F: Masi C: Chorus	$ 1,303 – $ 1,763
Record F: Masi C: Dura-Ace	$ 1,403 – $ 1,898
Record F: Masi C: Mirage	$ 993 – $ 1,344
Record F: Masi C: Record	$ 1,478 – $ 1,999
Record F: Masi C: Veloce	$ 1,057 – $ 1,431
Team 3V F: Masi C: 600 Ultegra	$ 1,210 – $ 1,637
Team 3V F: Masi C: Athena	$ 1,224 – $ 1,656
Team 3V F: Masi C: Chorus	$ 1,331 – $ 1,800
Team 3V F: Masi C: Dura-Ace	$ 1,426 – $ 1,929
Team 3V F: Masi C: Mirage	$ 1,030 – $ 1,394
Team 3V F: Masi C: Record	$ 1,495 – $ 2,022
Team 3V F: Masi C: Veloce	$ 1,094 – $ 1,481
Tre Volumetrica F: Masi C: 600 Ultegra	$ 1,288 – $ 1,743
Tre Volumetrica F: Masi C: Athena	$ 1,303 – $ 1,763
Tre Volumetrica F: Masi C: Chorus	$ 1,398 – $ 1,891
Tre Volumetrica F: Masi C: Dura-Ace	$ 1,481 – $ 2,003
Tre Volumetrica F: Masi C: Mirage	$ 1,126 – $ 1,523
Tre Volumetrica F: Masi C: Veloce	$ 1,185 – $ 1,603

C: – Components   F: – Fork

MODEL	PRICE RANGE

Mercedes-Benz

MB4	$ 1,495 – $ 2,022
Sport Cruiser	$ 1,015 – $ 1,373

Merlin

Cyclocross	$ 1,473 – $ 1,993
Mountain	$ 1,473 – $ 1,993
Road	$ 1,473 – $ 1,993
Road Long	$ 1,505 – $ 2,036
Road Short	$ 1,505 – $ 2,036
RSR	$ 1,231 – $ 1,666
Taiga	$ 1,214 – $ 1,642
TBA	$ 1,100 – $ 1,489
Triathlon	$ 1,473 – $ 1,993

Mirage

Mirage Folding	$ 732 – $ 990

Mondonico

Altec C: 600 Ultegra	$ 1,287 – $ 1,741
Altec C: Athena	$ 1,301 – $ 1,760
Altec C: Chorus	$ 1,396 – $ 1,889
Altec C: Dura-Ace	$ 1,480 – $ 2,002
Altec C: Mirage	$ 1,124 – $ 1,521
Altec C: Veloce	$ 1,183 – $ 1,600
Diamond Extra C: 600 Ultegra	$ 1,230 – $ 1,664
Diamond Extra C: Athena	$ 1,245 – $ 1,685
Diamond Extra C: Chorus	$ 1,348 – $ 1,824
Diamond Extra C: Dura-Ace	$ 1,441 – $ 1,949
Diamond Extra C: Mirage	$ 1,055 – $ 1,428
Diamond Extra C: Record	$ 1,508 – $ 2,040
Diamond Extra C: Veloce	$ 1,118 – $ 1,513

C: – Components   F: – Fork

MODEL	PRICE RANGE

Mondonico *(continued)*

Model	Price Range
EL OS C: 600 Ultegra	$ 1,335 – $ 1,806
EL OS C: Athena	$ 1,348 – $ 1,824
EL OS C: Chorus	$ 1,435 – $ 1,941
EL OS C: Dura-Ace	$ 1,511 – $ 2,044
EL OS C: Mirage	$ 1,183 – $ 1,600
EL OS C: Veloce	$ 1,238 – $ 1,675
Futura Leggero C: 600 Ultegra	$ 1,114 – $ 1,508
Futura Leggero C: Athena	$ 1,132 – $ 1,531
Futura Leggero C: Chorus	$ 1,250 – $ 1,692
Futura Leggero C: Dura-Ace	$ 1,359 – $ 1,838
Futura Leggero C: Mirage	$ 919 – $ 1,243
Futura Leggero C: Record	$ 1,441 – $ 1,949
Futura Leggero C: Veloce	$ 989 – $ 1,338
Nemo C: 600 Ultegra	$ 1,357 – $ 1,836
Nemo C: Athena	$ 1,369 – $ 1,852
Nemo C: Chorus	$ 1,453 – $ 1,965
Nemo C: Dura-Ace	$ 1,525 – $ 2,063
Nemo C: Mirage	$ 1,208 – $ 1,635
Nemo C: Veloce	$ 1,262 – $ 1,707
Wing C: 600 Ultegra	$ 1,312 – $ 1,775
Wing C: Athena	$ 1,326 – $ 1,794
Wing C: Chorus	$ 1,417 – $ 1,917
Wing C: Dura-Ace	$ 1,497 – $ 2,025
Wing C: Mirage	$ 1,155 – $ 1,563
Wing C: Veloce	$ 1,212 – $ 1,640

Mongoose

Model	Price Range
Crossway 250	$ 165 – $ 223
Crossway 350	$ 191 – $ 259
Crossway 450	$ 256 – $ 346
Crossway 850	$ 360 – $ 488

C: – Components   F: – Fork

MODEL	PRICE RANGE

Mongoose (continued)

Model	Price Range
DMC	$ 367 – $ 496
DMC Pro	$ 579 – $ 783
DX 5.3	$ 296 – $ 400
DX 6.5	$ 357 – $ 483
DX 6.7	$ 427 – $ 578
Expert	$ 167 – $ 226
Fuzz	$ 488 – $ 660
FX-1	$ 213 – $ 289
FX-2	$ 282 – $ 382
Hooligan	$ 254 – $ 344
MacFearsome	$ 853 – $ 1,154
Maneuver	$ 167 – $ 226
Maneuver CX	$ 188 – $ 254
Menace	$ 131 – $ 177
Menace 24	$ 160 – $ 216
Motivator F: Mongoose	$ 117 – $ 168
Motivator CB	$ 124 – $ 168
Motivator Mini F: Mongoose	$ 117 – $ 168
Mountain Grizzly F: Mongoose C: Juvenile Mix	$ 142 – $ 197
NX 7.1	$ 558 – $ 755
NX 7.3	$ 629 – $ 851
NX 7.5	$ 804 – $ 1,087
NX 7.7	$ 1,404 – $ 1,900
NX 8.1	$ 706 – $ 955
NX 8.3	$ 884 – $ 1,196
NX 8.5	$ 1,035 – $ 1,400
NX 9.5	$ 1,288 – $ 1,743
Phase 1	$ 287 – $ 388
Phase 2	$ 350 – $ 474
Rogue	$ 227 – $ 307
RX 5.3	$ 548 – $ 741

C: – Components   F: – Fork

MODEL	PRICE RANGE
Mongoose *(continued)*	
RX 5.5	$ 763 – $ 1,032
RX 7.7	$ 1,248 – $ 1,689
RX 9.7	$ 1,445 – $ 1,955
SGX	$ 248 – $ 335
SGX Polished	$ 268 – $ 363
Sniper	$ 145 – $ 206
Sniper Chrome-plated	$ 177 – $ 250
Stormer	$ 158 – $ 214
Stormer Chrome-plated	$ 170 – $ 229
Stormer Mini	$ 158 – $ 214
Supergoose	$ 191 – $ 259
Supergoose chrome-plated	$ 227 – $ 307
Supergoose Jr.	$ 227 – $ 307
Surge	$ 254 – $ 344
Switchback	$ 213 – $ 288
Switchback CX	$ 234 – $ 316
Threshold Sport	$ 191 – $ 259
Villain	$ 171 – $ 240
Montague	
Backcountry	$ 331 – $ 448
Crosstown	$ 393 – $ 532
Tandem	$ 1,281 – $ 1,733
Urban	$ 569 – $ 770
Monty	
B-205 CN	$ 185 – $ 251
B-219 X-Class	$ 279 – $ 378
B-219 X-Hydra	$ 498 – $ 674
B-219 X-Stam	$ 35 – $ 481
B-221 X-Pro	$ 826 – $ 1,117

C: – Components   F: – Fork

MODEL	PRICE RANGE

Monty (continued)

B-231 X-Lite	$ 1,039 – $ 1,406
B-231 X-Pro	$ 652 – $ 883

Moots

Rigor Mootis	$ 1,532 – $ 2,072

Mountain Cycle

Moho CXS	$ 1,367 – $ 1,849
Moho STS	$ 928 – $ 1,255
San Andreas	$ 1,367 – $ 1,849

Mountain Sport

Adventure	$ 130 $ 176
ALU-24	$ 242 $ 328

Mrazek

Boh FS LX/XT	$ 1,234 – $ 1,670
Boh FS XT	$ 1,332 – $ 1,802
Boh Fx Quarz	$ 1,332 – $ 1,802
Backroads	$ 312 – $ 423
Blazer	$ 177 – $ 239
Bravo	$ 150 – $ 203
Cascade	$ 423 – $ 573
Century	$ 183 – $ 248
Colorado	$ 362 – $ 490
Hill Razer	$ 150 – $ 203
Manitoba	$ 255 – $ 345
Meridian SC	$ 183 – $ 248
Optima SC	$ 255 – $ 345
Pinnacle	$ 524 – $ 708
Pueblo	$ 210 – $ 284
Pueblo Comp	$ 223 – $ 301
Sport	$ 216 – $ 293

C: – Components   F: – Fork

MODEL	PRICE RANGE

Norco

Model	Price Range
Alteres	$ 392 – $ 531
Arctic	$ 222 – $ 301
Avanti	$ 355 – $ 481
Axia	$ 417 – $ 564
Berretta	$ 318 – $ 430
Bushpilot	$ 209 – $ 283
Cherokee	$ 145 – $ 196
Firenza	$ 254 – $ 344
Katmandu	$ 189 – $ 256
Kokanee	$ 252 – $ 341
Magnum	$ 464 – $ 628
Monterey	$ 305 – $ 413
Mountaineer	$ 163 – $ 221
Nitro	$ 652 – $ 882
Rampage	$ 813 – $ 1,100
Reactor	$ 242 – $ 327
Sasquatch	$ 534 – $ 723
Stikine	$ 196 – $ 265
Team Issue	$ 1,282 – $ 1,734
Terrene	$ 464 – $ 628
Torrent	$ 1,131 – $ 1,531
Voltage Matte Blue, Red	$ 408 – $ 552
Voltage Orange/Black	$ 464 – $ 628
VPS-1	$ 1,473 – $ 1,993
VPS-2	$ 833 – $ 1,126
VPS-3	$ 679 – $ 918

Otis Guy

Model	Price Range
Purist Road	$ 1,183 – $ 1,615
Purist XT MB	$ 1,240 – $ 1,678
Purist XTR MB	$ 1,441 – $ 1,949

C: – Components   F: – Fork

MODEL	PRICE RANGE

Otis Guy (continued)

Model	Price Range
Smoothie Road F: Tange Silhouette C: Chorus	$ 1,334 – $ 1,840
Smoothie Road F: Tange Silhouette C: 600 Ultegra	$ 1,250 – $ 1,692
Softail XT MB	$ 1,284 – $ 1,738
Softail XTR MB	$ 1,473 – $ 1,993

ParkPre

Model	Price Range
Aria	$ 362 – $ 490
Crema	$ 362 – $ 490
Image One	$ 962 – $ 1,302
Latte	$ 450 – $ 609
Royale	$ 450 – $ 609
Sizzle	$ 541 – $ 732

Peugeot

Model	Price Range
Appalaches	$ 356 – $ 482
Biarritz Triple	$ 639 – $ 864
Canyon	$ 187 – $ 253
Chrono	$ 399 – $ 540
Cote D'azur	$ 274 – $ 371
Dune	$ 136 – $ 184
Equipe 1000S	$ 392 – $ 531
Equipe 6000DS	$ 660 – $ 894
Greystone	$ 235 – $ 318
Horizon	$ 271 – $ 367
Horizon Alum	$ 300 – $ 406
Hurricane Creek	$ 343 – $ 464
Monaco	$ 144 – $ 194
Nature	$ 305 – $ 413
Panorama	$ 170 – $ 229

C: – Components   F: – Fork

MODEL	PRICE RANGE

Peugeot *(continued)*

Model	Price Range
Paris	$ 216 – $ 293
Prestige	$ 300 – $ 406
Sprint	$ 267 – $ 362
Success Triple	$ 524 – $ 708
Urbano	$ 216 – $ 293
X-Country	$ 471 – $ 637

Porsche

Model	Price Range
Bike S	$ 1,196 – $ 1,618

Porter Frames

Model	Price Range
Blade F: Kinesis Road-D	$ 1,032 – $ 1,397
Blade F: Porter C: 105SC	$ 911 – $ 1,233
Blade F: Porter C: RX-100	$ 800 – $ 1,083
Loki F: Marzocchi Bomber Z-2 C: Deore XT	$ 1,216 – $ 1,645
Loki F: Marzocchi Bomber Z-2 C: XTR	$ 1,497 – $ 2,025
Loki F: Marzocchi Bomber Z-3 Light C: Deore LX	$ 913 – $ 1,235
Loki F: Marzocchi Bomber Z-3 Light C: STX-RC	$ 833 – $ 1,127
Loki F: Rock Shox Indy XC	$ 713 – $ 964
Odin F: Marzocchi Bomber Z-1 C: Deore LX	$ 1,403 – $ 1,898
Odin F: Marzocchi Bomber Z-1 C: Deore XT	$ 1,450 – $ 1,961
Odin F: Marzocchi Bomber Z-1 C: STX-RC	$ 1,087 – $ 1,471
Thor F: Aegis Hot Rod	$ 1,313 – $ 1,777
Thor F: Kinesis Road-D	$ 1,034 – $ 1,399
Thor F: Porter C: 105SC	$ 898 – $ 1,215
Thor F: Porter C: RX-100	$ 864 – $ 1,168

Powerlite

Model	Price Range
Chaos	$ 216 – $ 292
Chaos chrome-plated	$ 223 – $ 302

C: – Components   F: – Fork

MODEL	PRICE RANGE

Powerlite (continued)

Model	Price Range
Expert	$ 385 – $ 521
Expert ball-burnished	$ 402 – $ 543
Havoc	$ 169 – $ 228
Havoc chrome-plated	$ 176 – $ 238
P-11 Cobra	$ 114 – $ 154
P-11 Cobra chrome-plated	$ 120 – $ 163
P-17 Fireball	$ 121 – $ 164
P-17 Fireball chrome-plated	$ 128 – $ 173
P-19 Falcon	$ 143 – $ 194
P-19 Falcon chrome-plated, ghost flames	$ 150 – $ 203
P-28 Intruder	$ 190 – $ 256
P-28 Intruder chrome-plated	$ 196 – $ 265
P-40 Warhawk	$ 380 – $ 513
P-47 Thunderbolt	$ 368 – $ 498
P-47 Thunderbolt ball-burnished	$ 385 – $ 521
P-51 Mustang	$ 440 – $ 595
P-51 Mustang ball-burnished	$ 456 – $ 617
P-61	$ 572 – $ 774
P-61 ball-burnished	$ 587 – $ 795
P-Shooter	$ 98 – $ 133
P-Shooter chrome-plated	$ 106 – $ 143
Spitfire	$ 254 – $ 343
Spitfire clear brushed ano	$ 261 – $ 352
Toxic	$ 491 – $ 664

Quetzal

Model	Price Range
T105	$ 745 – $ 1,008

Quintana Roo

Model	Price Range
Kilo 650C	$ 879 – $ 1,189
Panamint	$ 971 – $ 1,314

C: – Components   F: – Fork

MODEL	PRICE RANGE

Raleigh	🚲
C-30	$ 155 – $ 210
C-40	$ 183 – $ 248
C-200	$ 216 – $ 292
F-500	$ 413 – $ 559
Jazzi	$ 82 – $ 111
Lil' Honey	$ 73 – $ 99
M-20	$ 127 – $ 172
M-30	$ 150 – $ 203
M-40	$ 178 – $ 240
M-45	$ 189 – $ 255
M-50	$ 216 – $ 292
M-60	$ 243 – $ 329
M-80	$ 307 – $ 415
M400	$ 383 – $ 519
M600	$ 481 – $ 651
M800	$ 528 – $ 715
M-7000 i	$ 481 – $ 651
M-7500 i	$ 574 – $ 777
M-8000i FM	$ 662 – $ 895
Mountain Scout	$ 127 – $ 172
MXR	$ 82 – $ 111
MXR Mini	$ 73 – $ 99
MXR Pro-CB	$ 99 – $ 134
MXR Pro-FW	$ 105 – $ 142
R-300 w/rear rack	$ 358 – $ 484
R-500	$ 383 – $ 519
R-600	$ 491 – $ 664
R-700	$ 683 – $ 924
Retroglide 1	$ 127 – $ 172
Retroglide 6	$ 150 – $ 203
Retroglide NX7	$ 189 – $ 255

C: – Components   F: – Fork

MODEL	PRICE RANGE

Raleigh (continued)

Model	Price Range
Rowdy	$ 82 – $ 111
SC-200	$ 216 – $ 292
SC-200 NX	$ 243 – $ 329
SC-30	$ 155 – $ 210
ReBike 606	$ 222 – $ 301
ReBike 818	$ 254 – $ 344
ReBike 2600	$ 305 – $ 413
ReTrike 606	$ 392 – $ 531

Redline

Model	Price Range
Proline	$ 331 – $ 448
Proline 24	$ 331 – $ 448
Proline EX	$ 258 – $ 350
RL 140	$ 216 – $ 293
RL 180	$ 216 – $ 293
RL 240	$ 190 – $ 257
RL 340	$ 134 – $ 181
RL 340 Jr. C/B	$ 132 – $ 178
RL 340 Jr. F/W	$ 137 – $ 185
RL 380	$ 150 – $ 203
RL 440	$ 216 – $ 293
RL 444	$ 210 – $ 284
RL 470	$ 191 – $ 259
RL 480	$ 249 – $ 336
RL 540	$ 268 – $ 363
RL 640	$ 293 – $ 397

Research Dynamics

Model	Price Range
Coyote AFS 400	$ 624 – $ 845
Coyote AFS 600	$ 757 – $ 1,025
Coyote AFS 800	$ 1,042 – $ 1,410

C: – Components   F: – Fork

MODEL	PRICE RANGE

Research Dynamics *(continued)*

Model	Price Range
Coyote AFS 900	$ 1,426 – $ 1,929
Coyote Alu 600	$ 624 – $ 845
Coyote Challenge S.E.	$ 222 – $ 301
Coyote Mow Tan	$ 470 – $ 636
Coyote Pro 400	$ 470 – $ 636
Coyote Single Track	$ 305 – $ 413
Coyote Team 800	$ 833 – $ 1,126
Coyote Team Extreme	$ 143 – $ 193
Coyote Team Rider	$ 183 – $ 247
Coyote Trail 21	$ 136 – $ 184
Coyote X 300	$ 392 – $ 531

Rhygin

Model	Price Range
Juke HS	$ 1,249 – $ 1,689
Metax Road	$ 1,231 – $ 1,666

Rideable Replicas

Model	Price Range
Classical Hi Wheeler	$ 781 – $ 1,056
Hi Wheeler Boneshaker	$ 540 – $ 731
Lowrider	$ 163 – $ 221

Ritchey

Model	Price Range
Chicane	$ 1,363 – $ 1,844
Montebello	$ 985 – $ 1,332
P-20 Pro F: Rock Shox Judy SL	$ 1,280 – $ 1,732
P-20 Pro F: Rock Shox Judy T2	$ 1,176 – $ 1,590
P-20 WCS F: Rock Shox Judy SL	$ 1,420 – $ 1,921
P-20 WCS F: Rock Shox Sid	$ 1,489 – $ 2,015
Plexus F: Rock Shox Judy SL	$ 1,472 – $ 1,992
Plexus F: Rock Shox Sid	$ 1,532 – $ 2,072
Road Logic	$ 1,161 – $ 1,570

C: – Components   F: – Fork

MODEL	PRICE RANGE

Ritchey (continued)

ST	$ 1,493 – $ 2,021
Swiss Cross	$ 1,296 – $ 1,754

Rivendell

All Rounder	$ 1,280 – $ 1,732
LongLow	$ 1,280 – $ 1,732
Mountain Expedition	$ 1,280 – $ 1,732
Road Standard	$ 1,280 – $ 1,732

Rocky Mountain

Blizzard	$ 1,055 – $ 1,427
Cardiac	$ 417 – $ 564
DH Race	$ 1,131 – $ 1,531
Element Race	$ 964 – $ 1,304
Fusion	$ 453 – $ 612
Hammer Race	$ 679 – $ 918
Oxygen Race	$ 762 – $ 1,032
Pipeline	$ 1,139 – $ 1,541
Route 66	$ 429 – $ 580
Soul	$ 529 – $ 715
Spice	$ 778 – $ 1,052
Thin Air	$ 1,076 – $ 1,455
Turbo	$ 1,192 – $ 1,612
Vertex T.O.	$ 1,484 – $ 2,008
Whistler	$ 411 – $ 555

Romic

Athena Ergo Tour	$ 1,132 – $ 1,531
Chorus Sport	$ 1,265 – $ 1,712
Chorus Tourer	$ 1,188 – $ 1,608
DA Track Sprint	$ 1,049 – $ 1,419

C: – Components   F: – Fork

MODEL	PRICE RANGE

Romic (continued)

Eco Triple Tour	$ 928 – $ 1,256
Mirage Tourer	$ 958 – $ 1,296
Record Eagle	$ 1,464 – $ 1,981
Road Sport	$ 927 – $ 1,254
Texas Eagle	$ 1,313 – $ 1,776
Track Eagle	$ 1,100 – $ 1,489
Ultegra Sport	$ 1,008 – $ 1,364
Velo Racer	$ 857 – $ 1,160

Ross

Amazon	$ 100 – $ 135
Beach Boss	$ 103 – $ 140
Beach Commander	$ 127 – $ 172
Beach Commander 24	$ 127 – $ 172
Bitsy Lady	$ 62 – $ 84
Boomerang	$ 90 – $ 121
Centaur	$ 393 – $ 532
Chimera	$ 137 – $ 185
Diamond Cruiser	$ 127 – $ 172
Frenzy	$ 90 – $ 121
Griffon	$ 203 – $ 275
Little Lady	$ 84 – $ 114
Minotaur	$ 331 – $ 448
Mt Hood	$ 307 – $ 416
Mt Jefferson	$ 117 – $ 158
Mt. Olympus	$ 197 – $ 266
Mt. Pocono	$ 127 – $ 172
Mt. St Helens	$ 210 – $ 284
Mt. Washington	$ 170 – $ 230
Pegasus	$ 268 – $ 362
Petite Lady	$ 83 – $ 112

C: – Components   F: – Fork

MODEL	PRICE RANGE

Ross *(continued)*

Model	Price Range
Pirahna Pro 6 Spd	$ 150 – $ 203
Pirahna Pro CB	$ 117 – $ 158
Pirahna Pro FW	$ 124 – $ 184
Pronto	$ 62 – $ 84
Radical	$ 84 – $ 114
Shark 7 Spd	$ 157 – $ 212
Slinger	$ 83 – $ 112
Super Gran Tour	$ 236 – $ 319
Tailspin	$ 76 – $ 103
Teeny Lady	$ 76 – $ 103
Urbanite	$ 236 – $ 319
Zemopi 474	$ 203 – $ 275
Zemopi 574	$ 268 – $ 362
Zemopi 674	$ 393 – $ 532

Rotator

Model	Price Range
Pursuit	$ 881 – $ 1,192
Tiger	$ 881 – $ 1,192

Rotec

Model	Price Range
Hardtail	$ 1,482 – $ 2,005

S & B

Model	Price Range
Single 2001	$ 509 – $ 689
Slingshot Trike	$ 1,026 – $ 1,388
Speedster Trike	$ 1,312 – $ 1,775
Tandem 2002	$ 1,399 – $ 1,893
Trike 4000	$ 768 – $ 1,039

S & M

Model	Price Range
Dirtbike Next Generation Other Features	$ 392 – $ 543

C: – Components   F: – Fork

MODEL		PRICE RANGE

S & M *(continued)* 🚲

Dirtbike Next Generation Other Features	$ 398 –	$ 551
Dirtbike O/S	$ 331 –	$ 447
Holmes Next Generation Other Features	$ 392 –	$ 543
Holmes Next Generation Other Features	$ 398 –	$ 551
Holmes O/S	$ 331 –	$ 447

Sampson 🚲

Classico CV	$ 973 –	$ 1,316
Classico SVCH	$ 1,177 –	$ 1,592
Classico SVDA	$ 1,195 –	$ 1,617
Classico SVRD	$ 1,329 –	$ 1,798
Classico SVRT	$ 1,120 –	$ 1,515
Classico SVX	$ 1,038 –	$ 1,405
Kalispell CV	$ 1,017 –	$ 1,376
Kalispell SVCH	$ 1,213 –	$ 1,642
Kalispell SVDA	$ 1,231 –	$ 1,665
Kalispell SVRD	$ 1,358 –	$ 1,838
Kalispell SVRT	$ 1,158 –	$ 1,567
Kalispell SVX	$ 1,080 –	$ 1,461
Supra CV	$ 881 –	$ 1,192
Supra SVCH	$ 1,100 –	$ 1,488
Supra SVDA	$ 1,265 –	$ 1,712
Supra SVRD	$ 1,265 –	$ 1,712
Supra SVRT	$ 1,038 –	$ 1,405
Supra SVX	$ 951 –	$ 1,286
Trihiti Tri	$ 1,213 –	$ 1,642
Vail XCS	$ 973 –	$ 1,316
Vail XTR	$ 1,177 –	$ 1,592
Zing CV	$ 833 –	$ 1,126
Zing SVCH	$ 1,059 –	$ 1,433
Zing SVDA	$ 1,080 –	$ 1,461

C: – Components   F: – Fork

MODEL	PRICE RANGE

Sampson (continued)

Zing SVRD	$ 1,248 – $ 1,689
Zing SVRT	$ 995 – $ 1,346
Zing SVX	$ 904 – $ 1,224

Santa Cruz

Chameleon	$ 758 – $ 1,025
Heckler F: Marzocchi Bomber Z-2 Atom Bomb	$ 1,429 – $ 1,933
Heckler F: Rock Shox Judy T2	$ 1,034 – $ 1,399
Heckler F: Rock Shox Judy XL	$ 1,292 – $ 1,747
Heckler SL F: Rock Shox Judy SL	$ 1,335 – $ 1,806
Heckler SL F: Rock Shox Sid	$ 1,531 – $ 2,071
Heckler X	$ 881 – $ 1,192
Tazmon	$ 1,347 – $ 1,822

Schwinn

Circuit	$ 793 – $ 1,073
Cruiser	$ 166 – $ 225
Cruiser Classic	$ 216 – $ 292
Cruiser Deluxe	$ 339 – $ 459
Cruiser Seven	$ 319 – $ 432
Cruiser Six	$ 230 – $ 311
Cruiser SS	$ 202 – $ 273
Cruiser Supreme	$ 216 – $ 292
Frontier	$ 173 – $ 235
Frontier GS	$ 202 – $ 273
Frontier GSX	$ 237 – $ 320
Heavy Duty	$ 216 – $ 292
Homegrown All Mountain LXT	$ 1,484 – $ 2,007
Homegrown All Mountain XT	$ 1,599 – $ 2,163
Homegrown Factory Suspension XT	$ 1,562 – $ 2,113
Homegrown Factory XT Other Features	$ 1,400 – $ 1,895

C: – Components   F: – Fork

MODEL	PRICE RANGE

Schwinn (continued)

Model	Price Range
Homegrown Factory XT Other Features	$ 1,562 – $ 2,113
Homegrown LXT	$ 1,016 – $ 1,375
Homegrown XT	$ 1,218 – $ 1,649
Hydramatic by Jay Miron	$ 353 – $ 477
Hydramatic Comp by Jay Miron	$ 485 – $ 656
Mesa	$ 271 – $ 367
Mesa GS	$ 333 – $ 450
Mesa GSX	$ 386 – $ 523
Moab 1 (aluminum)	$ 734 – $ 993
Moab 1 (cro-moly)	$ 674 – $ 911
Moab 2 (aluminum)	$ 612 – $ 828
Moab 2 (cro-moly)	$ 549 – $ 743
Moab 3	$ 517 – $ 700
Passage	$ 485 – $ 656
Peloton	$ 962 – $ 1,302
Powermatic	$ 216 – $ 301
Powermatic Mag	$ 230 – $ 311
Predator	$ 145 – $ 206
Predator CB	$ 131 – $ 187
Predator Pro	$ 180 – $ 254
Pro Stock 1	$ 386 – $ 523
Pro Stock 2	$ 285 – $ 385
Pro Stock 2 Cruiser	$ 292 – $ 395
Pro Stock 3	$ 216 – $ 292
Pro Stock 3 Cruiser	$ 243 – $ 329
Pro Stock 3 Mini	$ 230 – $ 311
S-10	$ 962 – $ 1,302
S-10 All Mountain	$ 1,120 – $ 1,515
S-20	$ 793 – $ 1,073
S-30	$ 674 – $ 911
Searcher	$ 216 – $ 292

C: – Components   F: – Fork

MODEL	PRICE RANGE

Schwinn (continued)

Model	Price Range
Searcher GS	$ 264 – $ 357
Searcher GSX	$ 319 – $ 432
Searcher SL	$ 549 – $ 743
Sierra	$ 237 – $ 320
Sierra GS	$ 285 – $ 385
Sierra GSX	$ 353 – $ 477
Sierra SL	$ 511 – $ 691
Super Sport	$ 612 – $ 828
Super Stock 1	$ 312 – $ 432
Super Stock 2	$ 250 – $ 348
Supermatic	$ 166 – $ 235

Scorpio

Model	Price Range
Balboa	$ 103 – $ 140
Cabrillo	$ 262 – $ 354
Capistrano	$ 154 – $ 208
Laguna	$ 110 – $ 149

Scott

Model	Price Range
Boulder	$ 512 – $ 693
Comp Racing	$ 625 – $ 846
Elite Racing	$ 928 – $ 1,256
Intoxica CFX	$ 1,373 – $ 1,857
Octane FX	$ 783 – $ 1,060
Octane FX Pro	$ 1,059 – $ 1,433
Pro Racing	$ 1,100 – $ 1,489
Pro Racing WCS	$ 1,533 – $ 2,074
Taos	$ 331 – $ 448
Waimea	$ 625 – $ 846
Waimea Pro	$ 1,314 – $ 1,777

C: – Components   F: – Fork

1998

MODEL   PRICE RANGE

SE Racing

Model	Price Range
Assassin	$ 216 – $ 292
Assassin X20	$ 261 – $ 353
Bronco	$ 150 – $ 202
Floval Flyer Killer	$ 511 – $ 692
Floval Flyer Pro	$ 368 – $ 498
Mini-Ripper	$ 423 – $ 572
PK Ripper STD Pro	$ 362 – $ 489
PK Ripper XL Killer	$ 506 – $ 684
PK Ripper XL Pro	$ 362 – $ 489
Quadangle AC Killer	$ 529 – $ 715
Quadangle AC Pro	$ 411 – $ 555
Ripper	$ 349 – $ 473

Seven Cycles

Model	Price Range
Axiom F: Wound Up C: 600 Ultegra	$ 1,416 – $ 1,916
Axiom F: Wound Up C: Chorus	$ 1,505 – $ 2,036
Sola	$ 1,396 – $ 1,889
Tsunami	$ 1,403 – $ 1,898

Simo Cycles

Model	Price Range
Simo Aero F: Simo C: 105SC	$ 1,177 – $ 1,593
Simo Aero F: Simo C: 600 Ultegra	$ 1,295 – $ 1,752
Simo Aero F: Simo C: Athena	$ 1,329 – $ 1,798
Simo Aero F: Simo C: Dura-Ace	$ 1,438 – $ 1,946
Simo Aero F: Simo C: Record	$ 1,407 – $ 1,903
Simo Elan F: Simo C: 105SC	$ 1,076 – $ 1,456
Simo Elan F: Simo C: 600 Ultegra	$ 1,207 – $ 1,632
Simo Elan F: Simo C: Athena	$ 1,120 – $ 1,516
Simo Elan F: Simo C: Chorus	$ 1,223 – $ 1,654
Simo Elan F: Simo C: Dura-Ace	$ 1,282 – $ 1,734
Simo Elan F: Simo C: Record	$ 1,395 – $ 1,887

C: – Components   F: – Fork

MODEL	PRICE RANGE

Simo Cycles *(continued)*

Model	Price Range
Simo Elite F: Simo C: 105SC	$ 1,140 – $ 1,542
Simo Elite F: Simo C: 600 Ultegra	$ 1,262 – $ 1,707
Simo Elite F: Simo C: Athena	$ 1,298 – $ 1,756
Simo Elite F: Simo C: Chorus	$ 1,380 – $ 1,867
Simo Elite F: Simo C: Dura-Ace	$ 1,413 – $ 1,912
Simo Elite F: Simo C: Record	$ 1,511 – $ 2,044
Simo Prestige Classic F: Simo C: 105SC	$ 1,039 – $ 1,405
Simo Prestige Classic F: Simo C: 600 Ultegra	$ 1,174 – $ 1,588
Simo Prestige Classic F: Simo C: Athena	$ 1,214 – $ 1,642
Simo Prestige Classic F: Simo C: Chorus	$ 1,306 – $ 1,767
Simo Prestige Classic F: Simo C: Record	$ 1,457 – $ 1,972
Simo Prestige OS F: Simo C: 105SC	$ 1,098 – $ 1,486
Simo Prestige OS F: Simo C: 600 Ultegra	$ 1,226 – $ 1,659
Simo Prestige OS F: Simo C: Athena	$ 1,264 – $ 1,710
Simo Prestige OS F: Simo C: Chorus	$ 1,350 – $ 1,826
Simo Prestige OS F: Simo C: Dura-Ace	$ 1,385 – $ 1,874
Simo Prestige OS F: Simo C: Record	$ 1,489 – $ 2,015

Slingshot

Model	Price Range
Cyclo-cross	$ 1,098 – $ 1,486
MTQ-1	$ 1,247 – $ 1,687
MTQ-2	$ 971 – $ 1,314
MTQ-3	$ 806 – $ 1,090
RDQ-1	$ 1,312 – $ 1,775
RDQ-2	$ 1,015 – $ 1,373
RDQ-3	$ 926 – $ 1,253
TRQ-1	$ 1,312 – $ 1,775

Softride

Model	Price Range
Century	$ 679 – $ 919
Firestorm	$ 995 – $ 1,347

C: – Components   F: – Fork

MODEL	PRICE RANGE

Softride *(continued)* 🚲

Model	Price Range
Norwester	$ 625 – $ 846
Powerwing MTB	$ 1,177 – $ 1,593
Roadwing	$ 1,140 – $ 1,542
Solo	$ 881 – $ 1,192

Specialized 🚲

Model	Price Range
Allez A1	$ 729 – $ 986
Allez A1 Comp	$ 977 – $ 1,322
Allez A1 Sport	$ 832 – $ 1,126
Crossroads	$ 180 – $ 244
Crossroads A1 Elite	$ 387 – $ 524
Crossroads A1 Expert	$ 282 – $ 382
Crossroads A1 Pro	$ 477 – $ 646
Crossroads Sport	$ 216 – $ 292
Fatboy	$ 161 – $ 217
Fatboy A1	$ 263 – $ 356
Fatboy A1 Cruiser	$ 282 – $ 382
Fatboy A1 Pro	$ 418 – $ 565
Fatboy Expert	$ 187 – $ 252
Globe Deluxe	$ 251 – $ 339
Gound Control FSR	$ 675 – $ 913
Gound Control FSR Comp	$ 807 – $ 1,091
Gound Control FSR Elite	$ 1,309 – $ 1,771
Gound Control FSR Extreme	$ 977 – $ 1,322
Gound Control FSR Pro	$ 1,503 – $ 2,033
Hardrock	$ 180 – $ 244
Hardrock A1	$ 282 – $ 382
Hardrock Classic	$ 200 – $ 270
Hardrock Sport	$ 216 – $ 292
Hardrock Sport FS	$ 282 – $ 382
Hotrock 20	$ 144 – $ 195

C: – Components   F: – Fork

MODEL	PRICE RANGE

Specialized *(continued)*

Model	Price Range
Hotrock 24	$ 167 – $ 226
Rockhopper	$ 307 – $ 416
Rockhopper A1 Comp FS	$ 592 – $ 801
Rockhopper A1 FS	$ 462 – $ 626
Rockhopper Comp FS	$ 547 – $ 740
Rockhopper FS	$ 387 – $ 524
S-Works M2	$ 1,153 – $ 1,560
Stumpjumper M2	$ 729 – $ 986
Stumpjumper M2 Comp	$ 832 – $ 1,126
Stumpjumper M2 Pro	$ 977 – $ 1,322

Spit

Model	Price Range
Underdog 4130	$ 319 – $ 431

Spooky

Model	Price Range
Darkside XT	$ 1,249 – $ 1,689
Darkside XTR	$ 1,426 – $ 1,929
Junebug LX	$ 973 – $ 1,317
Junebug XT	$ 1,128 – $ 1,526

Star Cruiser

Model	Price Range
Tradition LT	$ 130 – $ 176
Tradition LT-7	$ 144 – $ 194

Sunn

Model	Price Range
Exact	$ 1,261 – $ 1,706
Exact Flex	$ 1,279 – $ 1,730
Lecoupe	$ 426 – $ 576
Mini Sport	$ 221 – $ 299
Pro Sport	$ 239 – $ 323
Revolt GP Flex	$ 1,025 – $ 1,387

C: – Components   F: – Fork

MODEL	PRICE RANGE
Sunn *(continued)*	
Stirt	$ 327 – $ 442
Total	$ 563 – $ 762
Xchox	$ 826 – $ 1,117
Xircuit Max	$ 757 – $ 1,024
Terry	
Classic	$ 960 – $ 1,299
Symmetry	$ 569 – $ 770
Ti Cycles	
Custom Steel Road	$ 1,388 – $ 1,878
Hyak Ultegra	$ 1,433 – $ 1,939
Skookum	$ 1,309 – $ 1,771
Titan	
Alpha	$ 732 – $ 990
Chaos	$ 732 – $ 990
Omega	$ 569 – $ 769
Prime	$ 379 – $ 513
Punisher	$ 329 – $ 446
Razorback	$ 279 – $ 378
Warphog	$ 255 – $ 345
FCR Triathalon	$ 1,514 – $ 2,049
HCR MTN	$ 1,426 – $ 1,929
HCR Road	$ 1,344 – $ 1,818
Moto-Lite	$ 1,533 – $ 2,074
Racer X Al	$ 1,177 – $ 1,593
Titus	
SFS Al	$ 1,098 – $ 1,486

C: – Components   F: – Fork

MODEL		PRICE RANGE

Titus by Zenital 🚲

BK2004AP	$ 170 – $ 230

Torelli 🚲

ALU Wing C: 600 Ultegra	$ 1,155 – $ 1,563
ALU Wing C: Athena	$ 1,172 – $ 1,585
ALU Wing C: Chorus	$ 1,285 – $ 1,739
ALU Wing C: Dura-Ace	$ 1,388 – $ 1,878
ALU Wing C: Mirage	$ 967 – $ 1,308
ALU Wing C: Record	$ 1,465 – $ 1,983
ALU Wing C: Veloce	$ 1,034 – $ 1,399
Corsa Strada C: 600 Ultegra	$ 980 – $ 1,326
Corsa Strada C: Athena	$ 998 – $ 1,350
Corsa Strada C: Chorus	$ 1,132 – $ 1,531
Corsa Strada C: Dura-Ace	$ 1,257 – $ 1,701
Corsa Strada C: Mirage	$ 760 – $ 1,029
Corsa Strada C: Record	$ 1,354 – $ 1,832
Corsa Strada C: Veloce	$ 838 – $ 1,134
Countach OS C: 600 Ultegra	$ 1,092 – $ 1,478
Countach OS C: Athena	$ 1,108 – $ 1,499
Countach OS C: Chorus	$ 1,230 – $ 1,664
Countach OS C: Dura-Ace	$ 1,341 – $ 1,814
Countach OS C: Mirage	$ 891 – $ 1,205
Countach OS C: Record	$ 1,426 – $ 1,929
Countach OS C: Veloce	$ 962 – $ 1,302
Express OS C: 600 Ultegra	$ 1,230 – $ 1,664
Express OS C: Athena	$ 1,245 – $ 1,685
Express OS C: Chorus	$ 1,350 – $ 1,826
Express OS C: Dura-Ace	$ 1,441 – $ 1,949
Express OS C: Mirage	$ 1,055 – $ 1,428
Express OS C: Record	$ 1,509 – $ 2,041
Express OS C: Veloce	$ 1,118 – $ 1,513

C: – Components   F: – Fork

MODEL	PRICE RANGE
Torelli (continued)	🚲
Merak C: 600 Ultegra	$ 1,149 – $ 1,555
Merak C: Athena	$ 1,166 – $ 1,578
Merak C: Chorus	$ 1,280 – $ 1,732
Merak C: Dura-Ace	$ 1,384 – $ 1,872
Merak C: Mirage	$ 962 – $ 1,302
Merak C: Record	$ 1,461 – $ 1,976
Merak C: Veloce	$ 1,028 – $ 1,391
Nemo C: 600 Ultegra	$ 1,334 – $ 1,804
Nemo C: Athena	$ 1,345 – $ 1,820
Nemo C: Chorus	$ 1,433 – $ 1,939
Nemo C: Dura-Ace	$ 1,510 – $ 2,042
Nemo C: Mirage	$ 1,179 – $ 1,595
Nemo C: Veloce	$ 1,235 – $ 1,671
Nitro Express C: 600 Ultegra	$ 1,298 – $ 1,756
Nitro Express C: Athena	$ 1,312 – $ 1,775
Nitro Express C: Chorus	$ 1,405 – $ 1,901
Nitro Express C: Dura-Ace	$ 1,487 – $ 2,012
Nitro Express C: Mirage	$ 1,138 – $ 1,539
Nitro Express C: Veloce	$ 1,196 – $ 1,618
Record Carbonio C: 600 Ultegra	$ 1,060 – $ 1,433
Record Carbonio C: Athena	$ 1,078 – $ 1,459
Record Carbonio C: Chorus	$ 1,201 – $ 1,625
Record Carbonio C: Dura-Ace	$ 1,317 – $ 1,782
Record Carbonio C: Mirage	$ 855 – $ 1,157
Record Carbonio C: Record	$ 1,405 – $ 1,901
Record Carbonio C: Veloce	$ 926 – $ 1,253
Super Strada C: 600 Ultegra	$ 1,030 – $ 1,394
Super Strada C: Athena	$ 1,049 – $ 1,419
Super Strada C: Chorus	$ 1,177 – $ 1,593
Super Strada C: Dura-Ace	$ 1,296 – $ 1,754
Super Strada C: Mirage	$ 821 – $ 1,110

C: – Components   F: – Fork

MODEL	PRICE RANGE

Torelli (continued) 🚲

Super Strada C: Record	$ 1,388 – $ 1,878
Super Strada C: Veloce	$ 896 – $ 1,212

Torker 🚲

180X	$ 127 – $ 172
200X	$ 157 – $ 212
280X	$ 190 – $ 257
Dual	$ 203 – $ 275
Pro Cruiser	$ 268 – $ 363
Pro XL	$ 268 – $ 363
TFX	$ 164 – $ 221

Trailmate 🚲

Banana Peel	$ 267 – $ 361
Class Act	$ 268 – $ 362
Desoto Classic	$ 203 – $ 275
Double Joyrider Quadricycle	$ 675 – $ 914
EZ Ride	$ 139 – $ 188
EZ Roll Regal	$ 255 – $ 345
Fun Cycle	$ 293 – $ 397
Joyrider	$ 278 – $ 375
Jr. Joyrider	$ 274 – $ 371
Low Rider	$ 325 – $ 440

Trek 🚲

370	$ 288 – $ 390
420	$ 469 – $ 635
470	$ 455 – $ 615
520	$ 609 – $ 82
700	$ 176 – $ 238
720	$ 240 – $ 324

C: – Components   F: – Fork

MODEL	PRICE RANGE

Trek (continued)

Model	Price Range
730	$ 288 – $ 390
745	$ 321 – $ 434
800	$ 196 – $ 266
800 Sport	$ 161 – $ 218
820	$ 218 – $ 296
820 Comfort	$ 253 – $ 342
920	$ 287 – $ 388
930	$ 357 – $ 483
950	$ 469 – $ 635
1220	$ 498 – $ 673
2100	$ 609 – $ 824
2120	$ 817 – $ 1,105
2300	$ 913 – $ 1,235
5000	$ 1,004 – $ 1,359
5200	$ 1,171 – $ 1,584
5220	$ 1,171 – $ 1,584
5500	$ 1,522 – $ 2,059
6000	$ 357 – $ 483
6000 Comfort	$ 342 – $ 463
6500	$ 455 – $ 615
7000	$ 526 – $ 712
7500	$ 357 – $ 482
7600	$ 486 – $ 658
8000	$ 609 – $ 824
8500	$ 913 – $ 1,235
8900	$ 1,171 – $ 1,584
Cruiser Calypso	$ 184 – $ 248
Cruiser Classic	$ 148 – $ 200
Cruiser Cool Breeze	$ 205 – $ 277
ElecTrek	$ 767 – $ 1,038
Mountain Cub 12	$ 77 – $ 104

C: – Components   F: – Fork

MODEL	PRICE RANGE

Trek (continued)

Model	Price Range
Mountain Cub 16	$ 89 – $ 121
Mountain Lion 30	$ 104 – $ 141
Mountain Lion 60	$ 148 – $ 200
Mountain Track 220	$ 161 – $ 218
Mountain Track 240	$ 233 – $ 315
Sub-Atomic	$ 196 – $ 266
Sub-Atomic Special finish	$ 203 – $ 274
Sub-Atomic SS	$ 240 – $ 324
Sub-Atomic SS Special finish	$ 246 – $ 333
Sub-Culture	$ 270 – $ 365
Sub-Culture SS	$ 342 – $ 463
Sub-Dude	$ 132 – $ 179
Sub-Head	$ 184 – $ 248
Sub-Mission	$ 148 – $ 200
Sub-Species	$ 196 – $ 266
Sub-Vert 1.0	$ 184 – $ 248
Sub-Vert 1.0 Chrome-Plated	$ 187 – $ 253
Sub-Vert 2.0	$ 233 – $ 315
Sub-Vert 3.0	$ 302 – $ 408
T100	$ 817 – $ 1,105
T200	$ 1,090 – $ 1,475
Team Issue 1	$ 423 – $ 572
Team Issue 2	$ 288 – $ 390
Team Issue 3	$ 236 – $ 319
Team Issue Cruiser	$ 244 – $ 330
UAV	$ 663 – $ 897
Y 3	$ 554 – $ 750
Y 5	$ 767 – $ 1,038
Y 11	$ 1,004 – $ 1,359
Y 22	$ 1,246 – $ 1,686
Y 33	$ 1,522 – $ 2,059

C: – Components   F: – Fork

MODEL			PRICE RANGE

Trek (continued) 🚲

Y Foil 66	$ 1,350 – $ 1,826
Y Glide	$ 767 – $ 1,038
Y Glide Deluxe	$ 1,171 – $ 1,584

Univega 🚲

Alpina 500	$ 262 – $ 355
DS-900	$ 437 – $ 591
DS-950	$ 567 – $ 767
FS-700	$ 405 – $ 549
FS-750	$ 469 – $ 634
Islander	$ 154 – $ 208
Islander 6	$ 181 – $ 245
Jammer	$ 140 – $ 189
Mountain Force	$ 154 – $ 208
Rover 300	$ 154 – $ 208
Rover 303	$ 181 – $ 245
Rover 305	$ 229 – $ 309
Tandem Sport	$ 437 – $ 591
Via Carisma	$ 188 – $ 255
Via de Oro	$ 262 – $ 355
Via Montega	$ 222 – $ 300
Zig Zag	$ 188 – $ 255
Zig Zag NX	$ 295 – $ 400
Zig Zag Plus	$ 262 – $ 355

Valley Cycles 🚲

RS-100	$ 1,371 – $ 1,855
XS-100	$ 1,243 – $ 1,682

Ventana 🚲

El Chiquillo	$ 1,130 – $ 1,529

C: – Components   F: – Fork

MODEL	PRICE RANGE

Ventana *(continued)*

El Terremoto	$ 1,492 – $ 2,018
Marble Peak	$ 1,366 – $ 1,848

Vision

VR30NT	$ 597 – $ 808
VR30ST	$ 652 – $ 883
VR40 Standard	$ 652 – $ 883
VR40 Suspension	$ 781 – $ 1,056
VR42 Standard	$ 879 – $ 1,189
VR42 Suspension	$ 991 – $ 1,341
VR44 Standard	$ 1,028 – $ 1,391
VR44 Suspension	$ 1,110 – $ 1,502
VR45 Standard	$ 1,282 – $ 1,734
VR45 Suspension	$ 1,344 – $ 1,818

VooDoo

Bantu C: Deore LX F: Answer Manitou Spyder R	$ 725 – $ 981
Bantu C: Deore LX F: Answer Manitou SX-R	$ 819 – $ 1,108
Bantu C: Deore LX F: Marzocchi Bomber Z-1 BAM	$ 889 – $ 1,203
Bantu C: Deore LX F: Marzocchi Bomber Z-2 Atom Bomb	$ 877 – $ 1,187
Bantu C: Deore LX F: Marzocchi Bomber Z-3 Light	$ 781 – $ 1,056
Bantu C: Deore LX F: Rock Shox Indy	$ 670 – $ 907
Bantu C: Deore LX F: Rock Shox Indy C	$ 698 – $ 944
Bantu C: Deore LX F: Rock Shox Indy SL	$ 762 – $ 1,032
Bantu C: Deore LX F: Rock Shox Judy SL	$ 857 – $ 1,160
Bantu C: Deore LX F: Rock Shox Judy XC	$ 801 – $ 1,084
Bantu C: Deore LX F: Rock Shox Judy XL	$ 906 – $ 1,226
Bantu C: Deore LX F: Rock Shox Sid	$ 954 – $ 1,290
Bantu C: Deore LX F: Tange	$ 614 – $ 831
Bantu C: STX-RC F: Answer Manitou Spyder R	$ 597 – $ 807

C: – Components   F: – Fork

MODEL	PRICE RANGE

VooDoo (continued)

Bantu C: STX-RC F: Answer Manitou SX-R	$ 698 – $ 944
Bantu C: STX-RC F: Marzocchi Bomber Z-1 BAM	$ 773 – $ 1,045
Bantu C: STX-RC F: Marzocchi Bomber Z-2 Atom Bomb	$ 760 – $ 1,028
Bantu C: STX-RC F: Marzocchi Bomber Z-3 Light	$ 657 – $ 888
Bantu C: STX-RC F: Rock Shox Indy	$ 538 – $ 729
Bantu C: STX-RC F: Rock Shox Indy SL	$ 637 – $ 861
Bantu C: STX-RC F: Rock Shox Judy SL	$ 738 – $ 999
Bantu C: STX-RC F: Rock Shox Judy XL	$ 791 – $ 1,070
Bantu C: STX-RC F: Rock Shox Sid	$ 842 – $ 1,140
Bantu C: STX-RC F: Tange	$ 479 – $ 648
Bantu C: STX F: Answer Manitou Spyder R	$ 550 – $ 745
Bantu C: STX F: Answer Manitou SX-R	$ 653 – $ 884
Bantu C: STX F: Marzocchi Bomber Z-1 BAM	$ 730 – $ 988
Bantu C: STX F: Marzocchi Bomber Z-2 Atom Bomb	$ 717 – $ 970
Bantu C: STX F: Marzocchi Bomber Z-3 Light	$ 611 – $ 827
Bantu C: STX F: Rock Shox Indy	$ 490 – $ 663
Bantu C: STX F: Rock Shox Indy C	$ 521 – $ 704
Bantu C: STX F: Rock Shox Indy SL	$ 591 – $ 800
Bantu C: STX F: Rock Shox Judy SL	$ 695 – $ 941
Bantu C: STX F: Rock Shox Judy XC	$ 634 – $ 857
Bantu C: STX F: Rock Shox Judy XL	$ 749 – $ 1,013
Bantu C: STX F: Rock Shox Sid	$ 801 – $ 1,084
Bantu C: STX F: Tange	$ 429 – $ 581
Bizango C: Deore LX F: Answer Manitou Spyder R	$ 960 – $ 1,299
Bizango C: Deore LX F: Answer Manitou SX-R	$ 1,041 – $ 1,409
Bizango C: Deore LX F: Marzocchi Bomber Z-1 BAM	$ 1,101 – $ 1,489
Bizango C: Deore LX F: Marzocchi Bomber Z-2 Atom Bomb	$ 1,090 – $ 1,475
Bizango C: Deore LX F: Marzocchi Bomber Z-3 Light	$ 1,008 – $ 1,364
Bizango C: Deore LX F: Rock Shox Indy	$ 913 – $ 1,235

C: – Components   F: – Fork

MODEL	PRICE RANGE

VooDoo (continued)

Model	Price Range
Bizango C: Deore LX F: Rock Shox Indy C	$ 937 – $ 1,268
Bizango C: Deore LX F: Rock Shox Indy SL	$ 992 – $ 1,343
Bizango C: Deore LX F: Rock Shox Judy SL	$ 1,073 – $ 1,452
Bizango C: Deore LX F: Rock Shox Judy XC	$ 1,026 – $ 1,388
Bizango C: Deore LX F: Rock Shox Judy XL	$ 1,115 – $ 1,509
Bizango C: Deore LX F: Rock Shox Sid	$ 1,155 – $ 1,563
Bizango C: Deore LX F: Tange	$ 864 – $ 1,169
Bizango C: Deore XT F: Answer Manitou Spyder R	$ 1,235 – $ 1,672
Bizango C: Deore XT F: Answer Manitou SX-R	$ 1,297 – $ 1,755
Bizango C: Deore XT F: Marzocchi Bomber Z-1 BAM	$ 1,342 – $ 1,815
Bizango C: Deore XT F: Marzocchi Bomber Z-2 Atom Bomb	$ 1,334 – $ 1,805
Bizango C: Deore XT F: Rock Shox Indy	$ 1,199 – $ 1,622
Bizango C: Deore XT F: Rock Shox Indy C	$ 1,217 – $ 1,647
Bizango C: Deore XT F: Rock Shox Indy SL	$ 1,260 – $ 1,705
Bizango C: Deore XT F: Rock Shox Judy SL	$ 1,321 – $ 1,788
Bizango C: Deore XT F: Rock Shox Judy XC	$ 1,285 – $ 1,739
Bizango C: Deore XT F: Rock Shox Judy XL	$ 1,352 – $ 1,829
Bizango C: Deore XT F: Rock Shox Sid	$ 1,381 – $ 1,869
Bizango C: Deore XT F: Tange	$ 1,161 – $ 1,570
Bizango C: Deore XT/LX F: Answer Manitou Spyder R	$ 1,039 – $ 1,406
Bizango C: Deore XT/LX F: Answer Manitou SX-R	$ 1,115 – $ 1,509
Bizango C: Deore XT/LX F: Marzocchi Bomber Z-1 BAM	$ 1,170 – $ 1,583
Bizango C: Deore XT/LX F: Marzocchi Bomber Z-2 Atom Bomb	$ 1,161 – $ 1,570
Bizango C: Deore XT/LX F: Marzocchi Bomber Z-3 Light	$ 1,084 – $ 1,466
Bizango C: Deore XT/LX F: Rock Shox Indy	$ 995 – $ 1,346
Bizango C: Deore XT/LX F: Rock Shox Indy C	$ 1,017 – $ 1,376

C: – Components   F: – Fork

MODEL   PRICE RANGE

VooDoo (continued)

Bizango C: Deore XT/LX F: Rock Shox Indy SL	$ 1,069 – $ 1,446
Bizango C: Deore XT/LX F: Rock Shox Judy SL	$ 1,145 – $ 1,549
Bizango C: Deore XT/LX F: Rock Shox Judy XC	$ 1,101 – $ 1,489
Bizango C: Deore XT/LX F: Rock Shox Judy XL	$ 1,184 – $ 1,601
Bizango C: Deore XT/LX F: Rock Shox Sid	$ 1,221 – $ 1,652
Bizango C: Deore XT/LX F: Tange	$ 949 – $ 1,284
Bizango C: STX-RC F: Answer Manitou Spyder R	$ 891 – $ 1,206
Bizango C: STX-RC F: Answer Manitou SX-R	$ 977 – $ 1,321
Bizango C: STX-RC F: Marzocchi Bomber Z-1 BAM	$ 1,039 – $ 1,406
Bizango C: STX-RC F: Marzocchi Bomber Z-2 Atom Bomb	$ 1,028 – $ 1,391
Bizango C: STX-RC F: Marzocchi Bomber Z-3 Light	$ 941 – $ 1,274
Bizango C: STX-RC F: Rock Shox Indy	$ 842 – $ 1,139
Bizango C: STX-RC F: Rock Shox Indy C	$ 867 – $ 1,172
Bizango C: STX-RC F: Rock Shox Indy SL	$ 925 – $ 1,251
Bizango C: STX-RC F: Rock Shox Judy SL	$ 1,010 – $ 1,367
Bizango C: STX-RC F: Rock Shox Judy XC	$ 960 – $ 1,299
Bizango C: STX-RC F: Rock Shox Judy XL Other Features	$ 1,054 – $ 1,426
Bizango C: STX-RC F: Rock Shox Judy XL Other Features	$ 1,096 – $ 1,483
Bizango C: STX-RC F: Tange	$ 790 – $ 1,069
Bizango C: XTR F: Tange	$ 1,516 – $ 2,051
Bokor C: Deore LX F: Answer Manitou Spyder R	$ 913 – $ 1,235
Bokor C: Deore LX F: Answer Manitou SX-R	$ 997 – $ 1,349
Bokor C: Deore LX F: Marzocchi Bomber Z-1 BAM	$ 1,058 – $ 1,432
Bokor C: Deore LX F: Marzocchi Bomber Z-2 Atom Bomb	$ 1,048 – $ 1,418
Bokor C: Deore LX F: Marzocchi Bomber Z-3 Light	$ 963 – $ 1,302
Bokor C: Deore LX F: Rock Shox Indy	$ 864 – $ 1,169
Bokor C: Deore LX F: Rock Shox Indy C	$ 889 – $ 1,203
Bokor C: Deore LX F: Rock Shox Judy SL	$ 1,030 – $ 1,394

C: – Components   F: – Fork

MODEL

PRICE RANGE

VooDoo (*continued*)

Model	Price Range
Bokor C: Deore LX F: Rock Shox Judy XC	$ 981 – $ 1,327
Bokor C: Deore LX F: Rock Shox Judy XL	$ 1,073 – $ 1,452
Bokor C: Deore LX F: Rock Shox Sid	$ 1,115 – $ 1,509
Bokor C: Deore LX F: Tange	$ 814 – $ 1,101
Bokor C: Deore XT F: Answer Manitou Spyder R	$ 1,199 – $ 1,622
Bokor C: Deore XT F: Answer Manitou SX-R	$ 1,263 – $ 1,709
Bokor C: Deore XT F: Marzocchi Bomber Z-1 BAM	$ 1,310 – $ 1,773
Bokor C: Deore XT F: Marzocchi Bomber Z-2 Atom Bomb	$ 1,302 – $ 1,762
Bokor C: Deore XT F: Marzocchi Bomber Z-3 Light	$ 1,237 – $ 1,674
Bokor C: Deore XT F: Rock Shox Indy	$ 1,161 – $ 1,570
Bokor C: Deore XT F: Rock Shox Indy C	$ 1,180 – $ 1,596
Bokor C: Deore XT F: Rock Shox Indy SL	$ 1,225 – $ 1,657
Bokor C: Deore XT F: Rock Shox Judy SL	$ 1,289 – $ 1,744
Bokor C: Deore XT F: Rock Shox Judy XC	$ 1,251 – $ 1,693
Bokor C: Deore XT F: Rock Shox Judy XL	$ 1,321 – $ 1,788
Bokor C: Deore XT F: Rock Shox Sid	$ 1,352 – $ 1,829
Bokor C: Deore XT F: Tange	$ 1,121 – $ 1,517
Bokor C: Deore XT/LX F: Answer Manitou Spyder R	$ 995 – $ 1,346
Bokor C: Deore XT/LX F: Answer Manitou SX-R	$ 1,073 – $ 1,452
Bokor C: Deore XT/LX F: Marzocchi Bomber Z-1 BAM	$ 1,131 – $ 1,530
Bokor C: Deore XT/LX F: Marzocchi Bomber Z-2 Atom Bomb	$ 1,121 – $ 1,517
Bokor C: Deore XT/LX F: Marzocchi Bomber Z-3 Light	$ 1,041 – $ 1,409
Bokor C: Deore XT/LX F: Rock Shox Indy	$ 949 – $ 1,284
Bokor C: Deore XT/LX F: Rock Shox Indy C	$ 972 – $ 1,315
Bokor C: Deore XT/LX F: Rock Shox Indy SL	$ 1,026 – $ 1,388
Bokor C: Deore XT/LX F: Rock Shox Judy SL	$ 1,105 – $ 1,495
Bokor C: Deore XT/LX F: Rock Shox Judy XC	$ 1,058 – $ 1,432
Bokor C: Deore XT/LX F: Rock Shox Judy XL	$ 1,145 – $ 1,549

C: – Components   F: – Fork

MODEL   PRICE RANGE

VooDoo *(continued)*

Model	Price Range
Bokor C: Deore XT/LX F: Rock Shox Sid	$ 1,184 – $ 1,601
Bokor C: Deore XT/LX F: Tange	$ 901 – $ 1,219
Bokor C: STX-RC F: Answer Manitou Spyder R	$ 842 – $ 1,139
Bokor C: STX-RC F: Answer Manitou SX-R	$ 930 – $ 1,258
Bokor C: STX-RC F: Marzocchi Bomber Z-1 BAM	$ 995 – $ 1,346
Bokor C: STX-RC F: Marzocchi Bomber Z-2 Atom Bomb	$ 983 – $ 1,330
Bokor C: STX-RC F: Marzocchi Bomber Z-3 Light	$ 894 – $ 1,209
Bokor C: STX-RC F: Rock Shox Indy	$ 790 – $ 1,069
Bokor C: STX-RC F: Rock Shox Indy C	$ 816 – $ 1,104
Bokor C: STX-RC F: Rock Shox Indy SL	$ 877 – $ 1,186
Bokor C: STX-RC F: Rock Shox Judy SL	$ 965 – $ 1,306
Bokor C: STX-RC F: Rock Shox Judy XC	$ 913 – $ 1,235
Bokor C: STX-RC F: Rock Shox Judy XL	$ 1,010 – $ 1,367
Bokor C: STX-RC F: Rock Shox Sid	$ 1,054 – $ 1,426
Bokor C: STX-RC F: Tange	$ 738 – $ 998
Bokor C: XTR F: Rock Shox Indy	$ 1,516 – $ 2,051
Bokor C: XTR F: Rock Shox Indy C	$ 1,526 – $ 2,064
Bokor C: XTR F: Tange	$ 1,496 – $ 2,024
Canzo AL C: Deore LX F: Answer Manitou Spyder R	$ 1,228 – $ 1,662
Canzo AL C: Deore LX F: Answer Manitou SX-R	$ 1,291 – $ 1,746
Canzo AL C: Deore LX F: Marzocchi Bomber Z-1 BAM	$ 1,335 – $ 1,807
Canzo AL C: Deore LX F: Marzocchi Bomber Z-2 Atom Bomb	$ 1,328 – $ 1,796
Canzo AL C: Deore LX F: Rock Shox Indy	$ 1,191 – $ 1,612
Canzo AL C: Deore LX F: Rock Shox Indy C	$ 1,210 – $ 1,637
Canzo AL C: Deore LX F: Rock Shox Indy SL	$ 1,253 – $ 1,695
Canzo AL C: Deore LX F: Rock Shox Judy SL	$ 1,315 – $ 1,779
Canzo AL C: Deore LX F: Rock Shox Judy XC	$ 1,279 – $ 1,730
Canzo AL C: Deore LX F: Rock Shox Judy XL	$ 1,346 – $ 1,821
Canzo AL C: Deore LX F: Rock Shox Sid	$ 1,376 – $ 1,861

C: – Components   F: – Fork

MODEL   PRICE RANGE

VooDoo *(continued)*

Model	Price Range
Canzo AL C: Deore XT F: Answer Manitou Spyder R	$ 1,434 – $ 1,940
Canzo AL C: Deore XT F: Answer Manitou SX-R	$ 1,477 – $ 1,998
Canzo AL C: Deore XT F: Marzocchi Bomber Z-1 BAM	$ 1,507 – $ 2,039
Canzo AL C: Deore XT F: Marzocchi Bomber Z-2 Atom Bomb	$ 1,502 – $ 2,032
Canzo AL C: Deore XT F: Marzocchi Bomber Z-3 Light	$ 1,460 – $ 1,975
Canzo AL C: Deore XT F: Rock Shox Indy	$ 1,408 – $ 1,905
Canzo AL C: Deore XT F: Rock Shox Indy C	$ 1,421 – $ 1,923
Canzo AL C: Deore XT F: Rock Shox Indy SL	$ 1,452 – $ 1,964
Canzo AL C: Deore XT F: Rock Shox Judy SL	$ 1,493 – $ 2,021
Canzo AL C: Deore XT F: Rock Shox Judy XC	$ 1,469 – $ 1,988
Canzo AL C: Deore XT F: Rock Shox Judy XL	$ 1,514 – $ 2,049
Canzo AL C: Deore XT/LX F: Answer Manitou Spyder R	$ 1,289 – $ 1,744
Canzo AL C: Deore XT/LX F: Answer Manitou SX-R	$ 1,346 – $ 1,821
Canzo AL C: Deore XT/LX F: Marzocchi Bomber Z-1 BAM	$ 1,387 – $ 1,877
Canzo AL C: Deore XT/LX F: Marzocchi Bomber Z-2 Atom Bomb	$ 1,380 – $ 1,867
Canzo AL C: Deore XT/LX F: Marzocchi Bomber Z-3 Light	$ 1,323 – $ 1,790
Canzo AL C: Deore XT/LX F: Rock Shox Indy	$ 1,255 – $ 1,697
Canzo AL C: Deore XT/LX F: Rock Shox Indy C	$ 1,272 – $ 1,721
Canzo AL C: Deore XT/LX F: Rock Shox Indy SL	$ 1,312 – $ 1,775
Canzo AL C: Deore XT/LX F: Rock Shox Judy SL	$ 1,369 – $ 1,852
Canzo AL C: Deore XT/LX F: Rock Shox Judy XC	$ 1,335 – $ 1,807
Canzo AL C: Deore XT/LX F: Rock Shox Judy XL	$ 1,397 – $ 1,890
Canzo AL C: Deore XT/LX F: Rock Shox Sid	$ 1,424 – $ 1,926
Canzo AL C: STX-RC F: Answer Manitou Spyder R	$ 1,174 – $ 1,588
Canzo AL C: STX-RC F: Answer Manitou SX-R	$ 1,241 – $ 1,679

C: – Components   F: – Fork

MODEL	PRICE RANGE

VooDoo *(continued)*

Model	Price Range
Canzo AL C: STX-RC F: Marzocchi Bomber Z-1 BAM	$ 1,289 – $ 1,744
Canzo AL C: STX-RC F: Marzocchi Bomber Z-2 Atom Bomb	$ 1,281 – $ 1,733
Canzo AL C: STX-RC F: Marzocchi Bomber Z-3 Light	$ 1,214 – $ 1,642
Canzo AL C: STX-RC F: Rock Shox Indy	$ 1,135 – $ 1,536
Canzo AL C: STX-RC F: Rock Shox Indy C	$ 1,155 – $ 1,563
Canzo AL C: STX-RC F: Rock Shox Indy SL	$ 1,201 – $ 1,625
Canzo AL C: STX-RC F: Rock Shox Judy SL	$ 1,267 – $ 1,714
Canzo AL C: STX-RC F: Rock Shox Judy XC	$ 1,228 – $ 1,662
Canzo AL C: STX-RC F: Rock Shox Judy XL	$ 1,301 – $ 1,760
Canzo AL C: STX-RC F: Rock Shox Sid	$ 1,332 – $ 1,803
Canzo Ti C: Deore LX F: Answer Manitou Spyder R	$ 1,281 – $ 1,733
Canzo Ti C: Deore LX F: Answer Manitou SX-R	$ 1,339 – $ 1,811
Canzo Ti C: Deore LX F: Marzocchi Bomber Z-1 BAM	$ 1,380 – $ 1,867
Canzo Ti C: Deore LX F: Marzocchi Bomber Z-2 Atom Bomb	$ 1,373 – $ 1,857
Canzo Ti C: Deore LX F: Marzocchi Bomber Z-3 Light	$ 1,315 – $ 1,779
Canzo Ti C: Deore LX F: Rock Shox Indy	$ 1,246 – $ 1,686
Canzo Ti C: Deore LX F: Rock Shox Indy C	$ 1,263 – $ 1,709
Canzo Ti C: Deore LX F: Rock Shox Indy SL	$ 1,304 – $ 1,764
Canzo Ti C: Deore LX F: Rock Shox Judy SL	$ 1,361 – $ 1,842
Canzo Ti C: Deore LX F: Rock Shox Judy XC	$ 1,328 – $ 1,796
Canzo Ti C: Deore LX F: Rock Shox Judy XL	$ 1,390 – $ 1,881
Canzo Ti C: Deore LX F: Rock Shox Sid	$ 1,417 – $ 1,917
Canzo Ti C: Deore XT F: Answer Manitou Spyder R	$ 1,470 – $ 1,989
Canzo Ti C: Deore XT F: Answer Manitou SX-R	$ 1,509 – $ 2,042
Canzo Ti C: Deore XT F: Marzocchi Bomber Z-2 Atom Bomb	$ 1,531 – $ 2,072

C: – Components   F: – Fork

VooDoo (continued)

Model	Price Range
Canzo Ti C: Deore XT F: Marzocchi Bomber Z-3 Light	$ 1,493 – $ 2,021
Canzo Ti C: Deore XT F: Rock Shox Indy	$ 1,447 – $ 1,957
Canzo Ti C: Deore XT F: Rock Shox Indy C	$ 1,459 – $ 1,973
Canzo Ti C: Deore XT F: Rock Shox Indy SL	$ 1,486 – $ 2,010
Canzo Ti C: Deore XT F: Rock Shox Judy SL	$ 1,524 – $ 2,062
Canzo Ti C: Deore XT F: Rock Shox Judy XC	$ 1,502 – $ 2,032
Canzo Ti C: Deore XT/LX F: Answer Manitou Spyder R	$ 1,337 – $ 1,809
Canzo Ti C: Deore XT/LX F: Answer Manitou SX-R	$ 1,390 – $ 1,881
Canzo Ti C: Deore XT/LX F: Marzocchi Bomber Z-1 BAM	$ 1,428 – $ 1,932
Canzo Ti C: Deore XT/LX F: Marzocchi Bomber Z-2 Atom Bomb	$ 1,421 – $ 1,923
Canzo Ti C: Deore XT/LX F: Marzocchi Bomber Z-3 Light	$ 1,369 – $ 1,852
Canzo Ti C: Deore XT/LX F: Rock Shox Indy	$ 1,305 – $ 1,766
Canzo Ti C: Deore XT/LX F: Rock Shox Indy C	$ 1,321 – $ 1,788
Canzo Ti C: Deore XT/LX F: Rock Shox Indy SL	$ 1,358 – $ 1,838
Canzo Ti C: Deore XT/LX F: Rock Shox Judy SL	$ 1,410 – $ 1,908
Canzo Ti C: Deore XT/LX F: Rock Shox Judy XC	$ 1,380 – $ 1,867
Canzo Ti C: Deore XT/LX F: Rock Shox Judy XL	$ 1,437 – $ 1,944
Canzo Ti C: Deore XT/LX F: Rock Shox Sid	$ 1,461 – $ 1,977
Canzo Ti C: STX-RC F: Answer Manitou Spyder R	$ 1,230 – $ 1,664
Canzo Ti C: STX-RC F: Answer Manitou SX-R	$ 1,292 – $ 1,748
Canzo Ti C: STX-RC F: Marzocchi Bomber Z-1 BAM	$ 1,337 – $ 1,809
Canzo Ti C: STX-RC F: Marzocchi Bomber Z-2 Atom Bomb	$ 1,329 – $ 1,799
Canzo Ti C: STX-RC F: Marzocchi Bomber Z-3 Light	$ 1,267 – $ 1,714
Canzo Ti C: STX-RC F: Rock Shox Indy	$ 1,193 – $ 1,614
Canzo Ti C: STX-RC F: Rock Shox Indy C	$ 1,212 – $ 1,640
Canzo Ti C: STX-RC F: Rock Shox Indy SL	$ 1,255 – $ 1,697

C: – Components   F: – Fork

MODEL   PRICE RANGE

Model	Price Range
Canzo Ti C: STX-RC F: Rock Shox Judy SL	$ 1,316 – $ 1,781
Canzo Ti C: STX-RC F: Rock Shox Judy XC	$ 1,281 – $ 1,733
Canzo Ti C: STX-RC F: Rock Shox Judy XL	$ 1,348 – $ 1,823
Canzo Ti C: STX-RC F: Rock Shox Sid	$ 1,377 – $ 1,863
D-Jab C: Deore LX F: Answer Manitou Spyder R	$ 1,153 – $ 1,560
D-Jab C: Deore LX F: Answer Manitou SX-R	$ 1,221 – $ 1,652
D-Jab C: Deore LX F: Marzocchi Bomber Z-1 BAM	$ 1,270 – $ 1,719
D-Jab C: Deore LX F: Marzocchi Bomber Z-2 Atom Bomb	$ 1,262 – $ 1,707
D-Jab C: Deore LX F: Marzocchi Bomber Z-3 Light	$ 1,193 – $ 1,614
D-Jab C: Deore LX F: Rock Shox Indy	$ 1,113 – $ 1,506
D-Jab C: Deore LX F: Rock Shox Indy C	$ 1,133 – $ 1,533
D-Jab C: Deore LX F: Rock Shox Indy SL	$ 1,180 – $ 1,596
D-Jab C: Deore LX F: Rock Shox Judy SL	$ 1,248 – $ 1,688
D-Jab C: Deore LX F: Rock Shox Judy XC	$ 1,208 – $ 1,634
D-Jab C: Deore LX F: Rock Shox Judy XL	$ 1,282 – $ 1,735
D-Jab C: Deore LX F: Rock Shox Sid	$ 1,315 – $ 1,779
D-Jab C: Deore LX F: Tange	$ 1,071 – $ 1,449
D-Jab C: Deore XT F: Answer Manitou Spyder R	$ 1,380 – $ 1,867
D-Jab C: Deore XT F: Answer Manitou SX-R	$ 1,429 – $ 1,933
D-Jab C: Deore XT F: Marzocchi Bomber Z-1 BAM	$ 1,463 – $ 1,980
D-Jab C: Deore XT F: Marzocchi Bomber Z-2 Atom Bomb	$ 1,457 – $ 1,972
D-Jab C: Deore XT F: Marzocchi Bomber Z-3 Light	$ 1,409 – $ 1,906
D-Jab C: Deore XT F: Rock Shox Indy	$ 1,351 – $ 1,828
D-Jab C: Deore XT F: Rock Shox Indy C	$ 1,365 – $ 1,847
D-Jab C: Deore XT F: Rock Shox Indy SL	$ 1,400 – $ 1,894
D-Jab C: Deore XT F: Rock Shox Judy SL	$ 1,448 – $ 1,959
D-Jab C: Deore XT F: Rock Shox Judy XC	$ 1,420 – $ 1,921
D-Jab C: Deore XT F: Rock Shox Judy XL	$ 1,471 – $ 1,991
D-Jab C: Deore XT F: Rock Shox Sid	$ 1,493 – $ 2,021

C: – Components   F: – Fork

MODEL	PRICE RANGE

VooDoo (continued)

Model	Price Range
D-Jab C: Deore XT F: Tange	$ 1,320 – $ 1,786
D-Jab C: Deore XT/LX F: Answer Manitou Spyder R	$ 1,219 – $ 1,649
D-Jab C: Deore XT/LX F: Answer Manitou SX-R	$ 1,282 – $ 1,735
D-Jab C: Deore XT/LX F: Marzocchi Bomber Z-1 BAM	$ 1,328 – $ 1,796
D-Jab C: Deore XT/LX F: Marzocchi Bomber Z-2 Atom Bomb	$ 1,320 – $ 1,786
D-Jab C: Deore XT/LX F: Marzocchi Bomber Z-3 Light	$ 1,257 – $ 1,700
D-Jab C: Deore XT/LX F: Rock Shox Indy	$ 1,182 – $ 1,599
D-Jab C: Deore XT/LX F: Rock Shox Indy C	$ 1,201 – $ 1,625
D-Jab C: Deore XT/LX F: Rock Shox Indy SL	$ 1,244 – $ 1,683
D-Jab C: Deore XT/LX F: Rock Shox Judy SL	$ 1,307 – $ 1,768
D-Jab C: Deore XT/LX F: Rock Shox Judy XC	$ 1,270 – $ 1,719
D-Jab C: Deore XT/LX F: Rock Shox Judy XL	$ 1,339 – $ 1,811
D-Jab C: Deore XT/LX F: Rock Shox Sid	$ 1,369 – $ 1,852
D-Jab C: Deore XT/LX F: Tange	$ 1,143 – $ 1,547
D-Jab C: STX-RC F: Answer Manitou SX-R	$ 1,167 – $ 1,578
D-Jab C: STX-RC F: Marzocchi Bomber Z-1 BAM	$ 1,219 – $ 1,649
D-Jab C: STX-RC F: Marzocchi Bomber Z-2 Atom Bomb	$ 1,210 – $ 1,637
D-Jab C: STX-RC F: Marzocchi Bomber Z-3 Light	$ 1,137 – $ 1,538
D-Jab C: STX-RC F: Rock Shox Indy	$ 1,052 – $ 1,423
D-Jab C: STX-RC F: Rock Shox Indy C	$ 1,073 – $ 1,452
D-Jab C: STX-RC F: Rock Shox Indy SL	$ 1,123 – $ 1,519
D-Jab C: STX-RC F: Rock Shox Judy SL	$ 1,195 – $ 1,617
D-Jab C: STX-RC F: Rock Shox Judy XC	$ 1,153 – $ 1,560
D-Jab C: STX-RC F: Rock Shox Judy XL	$ 1,232 – $ 1,666
D-Jab C: STX-RC F: Rock Shox Sid	$ 1,267 – $ 1,714
D-Jab C: STX-RC F: Tange	$ 1,008 – $ 1,364
Erzulie C: Deore LX F: Answer Manitou Spyder R	$ 676 – $ 915
Erzulie C: Deore LX F: Answer Manitou SX-R	$ 773 – $ 1,045

C: – Components   F: – Fork

MODEL	PRICE RANGE

VooDoo *(continued)*   🚲

Model	Price Range
Erzulie C: Deore LX F: Marzocchi Bomber Z-1 BAM	$ 845 – $ 1,143
Erzulie C: Deore LX F: Marzocchi Bomber Z-2 Atom Bomb	$ 832 – $ 1,126
Erzulie C: Deore LX F: Marzocchi Bomber Z-3 Light	$ 733 – $ 992
Erzulie C: Deore LX F: Rock Shox Indy	$ 619 – $ 838
Erzulie C: Deore LX F: Rock Shox Indy C	$ 648 – $ 877
Erzulie C: Deore LX F: Rock Shox Indy SL	$ 714 – $ 966
Erzulie C: Deore LX F: Rock Shox Judy SL	$ 812 – $ 1,098
Erzulie C: Deore LX F: Rock Shox Judy XC	$ 754 – $ 1,020
Erzulie C: Deore LX F: Rock Shox Judy XL Other Features	$ 862 – $ 1,167
Erzulie C: Deore LX F: Rock Shox Judy XL Other Features	$ 911 – $ 1,233
Erzulie C: Deore LX F: Tange	$ 562 – $ 760
Erzulie C: STX-RC F: Answer Manitou Spyder R	$ 544 – $ 736
Erzulie C: STX-RC F: Answer Manitou SX-R	$ 648 – $ 877
Erzulie C: STX-RC F: Marzocchi Bomber Z-1 BAM	$ 725 – $ 981
Erzulie C: STX-RC F: Marzocchi Bomber Z-2 Atom Bomb	$ 712 – $ 963
Erzulie C: STX-RC F: Marzocchi Bomber Z-3 Light	$ 606 – $ 819
Erzulie C: STX-RC F: Rock Shox Indy	$ 485 – $ 656
Erzulie C: STX-RC F: Rock Shox Indy C	$ 515 – $ 697
Erzulie C: STX-RC F: Rock Shox Indy SL	$ 586 – $ 792
Erzulie C: STX-RC F: Rock Shox Judy SL	$ 689 – $ 933
Erzulie C: STX-RC F: Rock Shox Judy XC	$ 628 – $ 850
Erzulie C: STX-RC F: Rock Shox Judy XL	$ 744 – $ 1,007
Erzulie C: STX-RC F: Rock Shox Sid	$ 796 – $ 1,077
Erzulie C: STX-RC F: Tange	$ 423 – $ 573
Erzulie C: STX F: Answer Manitou Spyder R Other Features	$ 497 – $ 672
Erzulie C: STX F: Answer Manitou Spyder R Other Features	$ 538 – $ 729

C: – Components   F: – Fork

MODEL	PRICE RANGE

VooDoo *(continued)*

Model	Price Range
Erzulie C: STX F: Answer Manitou SX-R	$ 603 – $ 816
Erzulie C: STX F: Marzocchi Bomber Z-1 BAM	$ 681 – $ 922
Erzulie C: STX F: Marzocchi Bomber Z-2 Atom Bomb	$ 667 – $ 903
Erzulie C: STX F: Marzocchi Bomber Z-3 Light	$ 559 – $ 756
Erzulie C: STX F: Rock Shox Indy	$ 436 – $ 590
Erzulie C: STX F: Rock Shox Indy C	$ 466 – $ 631
Erzulie C: STX F: Rock Shox Judy SL	$ 645 – $ 873
Erzulie C: STX F: Rock Shox Judy XC	$ 582 – $ 788
Erzulie C: STX F: Rock Shox Judy XL	$ 701 – $ 948
Erzulie C: STX F: Rock Shox Sid	$ 754 – $ 1,020
Erzulie C: STX F: Tange	$ 373 – $ 504
HooDoo C: Deore LX F: Answer Manitou Spyder R	$ 788 – $ 1,066
HooDoo C: Deore LX F: Answer Manitou SX-R	$ 879 – $ 1,189
HooDoo C: Deore LX F: Marzocchi Bomber Z-1 BAM	$ 946 – $ 1,280
HooDoo C: Deore LX F: Marzocchi Bomber Z-2 Atom Bomb	$ 935 – $ 1,264
HooDoo C: Deore LX F: Marzocchi Bomber Z-3 Light	$ 842 – $ 1,139
HooDoo C: Deore LX F: Rock Shox Indy	$ 735 – $ 995
HooDoo C: Deore LX F: Rock Shox Indy C	$ 762 – $ 1,031
HooDoo C: Deore LX F: Rock Shox Indy SL	$ 824 – $ 1,115
HooDoo C: Deore LX F: Rock Shox Judy SL	$ 915 – $ 1,238
HooDoo C: Deore LX F: Rock Shox Judy XC	$ 862 – $ 1,166
HooDoo C: Deore LX F: Rock Shox Judy XL	$ 963 – $ 1,302
HooDoo C: Deore LX F: Rock Shox Sid	$ 1,008 – $ 1,364
HooDoo C: Deore LX F: Tange	$ 681 – $ 921
HooDoo C: Deore XT F: Answer Manitou Spyder R	$ 1,101 – $ 1,489
HooDoo C: Deore XT F: Answer Manitou SX-R	$ 1,172 – $ 1,586
HooDoo C: Deore XT F: Marzocchi Bomber Z-1 BAM	$ 1,225 – $ 1,657

C: – Components   F: – Fork

MODEL	PRICE RANGE

VooDoo (continued)

Model	Price Range
HooDoo C: Deore XT F: Marzocchi Bomber Z-2 Atom Bomb	$ 1,216 – $ 1,645
HooDoo C: Deore XT F: Marzocchi Bomber Z-3 Light	$ 1,143 – $ 1,547
HooDoo C: Deore XT F: Rock Shox Indy	$ 1,058 – $ 1,432
HooDoo C: Deore XT F: Rock Shox Indy C	$ 1,080 – $ 1,461
HooDoo C: Deore XT F: Rock Shox Indy SL	$ 1,129 – $ 1,528
HooDoo C: Deore XT F: Rock Shox Judy SL	$ 1,201 – $ 1,625
HooDoo C: Deore XT F: Rock Shox Judy XC	$ 1,159 – $ 1,568
HooDoo C: Deore XT F: Rock Shox Judy XL	$ 1,237 – $ 1,674
HooDoo C: Deore XT F: Rock Shox Sid	$ 1,272 – $ 1,721
HooDoo C: Deore XT F: Tange	$ 1,015 – $ 1,373
HooDoo C: Deore XT/LX F: Answer Manitou Spyder R	$ 877 – $ 1,186
HooDoo C: Deore XT/LX F: Answer Manitou SX-R	$ 963 – $ 1,302
HooDoo C: Deore XT/LX F: Marzocchi Bomber Z-1 BAM	$ 1,026 – $ 1,388
HooDoo C: Deore XT/LX F: Marzocchi Bomber Z-2 Atom Bomb	$ 1,015 – $ 1,373
HooDoo C: Deore XT/LX F: Marzocchi Bomber Z-3 Light	$ 927 – $ 1,254
HooDoo C: Deore XT/LX F: Rock Shox Indy	$ 827 – $ 1,118
HooDoo C: Deore XT/LX F: Rock Shox Indy C	$ 852 – $ 1,152
HooDoo C: Deore XT/LX F: Rock Shox Indy SL	$ 911 – $ 1,232
HooDoo C: Deore XT/LX F: Rock Shox Judy SL	$ 997 – $ 1,349
HooDoo C: Deore XT/LX F: Rock Shox Judy XC	$ 946 – $ 1,280
HooDoo C: Deore XT/LX F: Rock Shox Judy XL	$ 1,041 – $ 1,409
HooDoo C: Deore XT/LX F: Rock Shox Sid	$ 1,084 – $ 1,466
HooDoo C: Deore XT/LX F: Tange	$ 775 – $ 1,048
HooDoo C: STX-RC F: Answer Manitou Spyder R	$ 711 – $ 962
HooDoo C: STX-RC F: Answer Manitou SX-R	$ 806 – $ 1,090
HooDoo C: STX-RC F: Marzocchi Bomber Z-1 BAM	$ 877 – $ 1,186

C: – Components   F: – Fork

MODEL	PRICE RANGE

Model	Price Range
HooDoo C: STX-RC F: Marzocchi Bomber Z-2 Atom Bomb	$ 864 – $ 1,169
HooDoo C: STX-RC F: Marzocchi Bomber Z-3 Light	$ 767 – $ 1,038
HooDoo C: STX-RC F: Rock Shox Indy	$ 656 – $ 888
HooDoo C: STX-RC F: Rock Shox Indy C	$ 684 – $ 925
HooDoo C: STX-RC F: Rock Shox Indy SL	$ 749 – $ 1,013
HooDoo C: STX-RC F: Rock Shox Judy SL	$ 844 – $ 1,142
HooDoo C: STX-RC F: Rock Shox Judy XC	$ 788 – $ 1,066
HooDoo C: STX-RC F: Rock Shox Judy XL	$ 894 – $ 1,209
HooDoo C: STX-RC F: Rock Shox Sid	$ 941 – $ 1,274
HooDoo C: STX-RC F: Tange	$ 599 – $ 810
HooDoo C: XTR F: Answer Manitou Spyder R	$ 1,485 – $ 2,009
HooDoo C: XTR F: Answer Manitou SX-R	$ 1,522 – $ 2,059
HooDoo C: XTR F: Marzocchi Bomber Z-3 Light	$ 1,507 – $ 2,039
HooDoo C: XTR F: Rock Shox Indy	$ 1,462 – $ 1,978
HooDoo C: XTR F: Rock Shox Indy C	$ 1,474 – $ 1,994
HooDoo C: XTR F: Rock Shox Indy SL	$ 1,500 – $ 2,029
HooDoo C: XTR F: Rock Shox Judy XC	$ 1,515 – $ 2,050
HooDoo C: XTR F: Tange	$ 1,438 – $ 1,945
Loa C: 105SC F: Kinesis	$ 1,105 – $ 1,495
Loa C: 105SC F: Marzocchi Pave'	$ 1,291 – $ 1,746
Wanga C: Deore LX F: Answer Manitou Spyder R	$ 864 – $ 1,169
Wanga C: Deore LX F: Answer Manitou SX-R	$ 951 – $ 1,287
Wanga C: Deore LX F: Marzocchi Bomber Z-1 BAM	$ 1,015 – $ 1,373
Wanga C: Deore LX F: Marzocchi Bomber Z-2 Atom Bomb	$ 1,003 – $ 1,358
Wanga C: Deore LX F: Marzocchi Bomber Z-3 Light	$ 915 – $ 1,238
Wanga C: Deore LX F: Rock Shox Indy	$ 814 – $ 1,101
Wanga C: Deore LX F: Rock Shox Indy C	$ 839 – $ 1,135
Wanga C: Deore LX F: Rock Shox Indy SL	$ 898 – $ 1,215
Wanga C: Deore LX F: Rock Shox Judy SL	$ 985 – $ 1,333

C: – Components   F: – Fork

MODEL

PRICE RANGE

VooDoo (continued) 🚲

Model	Price Range
Wanga C: Deore LX F: Rock Shox Judy XC	$ 935 – $ 1,264
Wanga C: Deore LX F: Rock Shox Judy XL	$ 1,030 – $ 1,394
Wanga C: Deore LX F: Rock Shox Sid	$ 1,073 – $ 1,452
Wanga C: Deore LX F: Tange	$ 762 – $ 1,031
Wanga C: Deore XT F: Answer Manitou Spyder R	$ 1,161 – $ 1,570
Wanga C: Deore XT F: Answer Manitou SX-R	$ 1,228 – $ 1,662
Wanga C: Deore XT F: Marzocchi Bomber Z-1 BAM	$ 1,277 – $ 1,728
Wanga C: Deore XT F: Marzocchi Bomber Z-2 Atom Bomb	$ 1,269 – $ 1,717
Wanga C: Deore XT F: Marzocchi Bomber Z-3 Light	$ 1,201 – $ 1,625
Wanga C: Deore XT F: Rock Shox Indy	$ 1,121 – $ 1,517
Wanga C: Deore XT F: Rock Shox Indy C	$ 1,141 – $ 1,544
Wanga C: Deore XT F: Rock Shox Indy SL	$ 1,188 – $ 1,607
Wanga C: Deore XT F: Rock Shox Judy SL	$ 1,255 – $ 1,697
Wanga C: Deore XT F: Rock Shox Judy XC	$ 1,216 – $ 1,645
Wanga C: Deore XT F: Rock Shox Judy XL	$ 1,289 – $ 1,744
Wanga C: Deore XT F: Rock Shox Sid	$ 1,321 – $ 1,788
Wanga C: Deore XT F: Tange	$ 1,080 – $ 1,461
Wanga C: Deore XT/LX F: Answer Manitou Spyder R	$ 949 – $ 1,284
Wanga C: Deore XT/LX F: Answer Manitou SX-R	$ 1,030 – $ 1,394
Wanga C: Deore XT/LX F: Marzocchi Bomber Z-1 BAM	$ 1,090 – $ 1,475
Wanga C: Deore XT/LX F: Marzocchi Bomber Z-2 Atom Bomb	$ 1,080 – $ 1,461
Wanga C: Deore XT/LX F: Marzocchi Bomber Z-3 Light	$ 997 – $ 1,349
Wanga C: Deore XT/LX F: Rock Shox Indy	$ 901 – $ 1,219
Wanga C: Deore XT/LX F: Rock Shox Indy C	$ 925 – $ 1,251
Wanga C: Deore XT/LX F: Rock Shox Indy SL	$ 981 – $ 1,327
Wanga C: Deore XT/LX F: Rock Shox Judy SL	$ 1,063 – $ 1,438
Wanga C: Deore XT/LX F: Rock Shox Judy XC	$ 1,015 – $ 1,373
Wanga C: Deore XT/LX F: Rock Shox Judy XL	$ 1,105 – $ 1,495

C: – Components   F: – Fork

MODEL	PRICE RANGE

VooDoo (continued)

Model	Price Range
Wanga C: Deore XT/LX F: Rock Shox Sid	$ 1,145 – $ 1,549
Wanga C: Deore XT/LX F: Tange	$ 852 – $ 1,152
Wanga C: STX-RC F: Answer Manitou Spyder R	$ 790 – $ 1,069
Wanga C: STX-RC F: Answer Manitou SX-R	$ 881 – $ 1,192
Wanga C: STX-RC F: Marzocchi Bomber Z-1 BAM	$ 949 – $ 1,284
Wanga C: STX-RC F: Marzocchi Bomber Z-2 Atom Bomb	$ 937 – $ 1,268
Wanga C: STX-RC F: Marzocchi Bomber Z-3 Light	$ 844 – $ 1,142
Wanga C: STX-RC F: Rock Shox Indy	$ 738 – $ 998
Wanga C: STX-RC F: Rock Shox Indy C	$ 764 – $ 1,034
Wanga C: STX-RC F: Rock Shox Indy SL	$ 827 – $ 1,118
Wanga C: STX-RC F: Rock Shox Judy SL	$ 918 – $ 1,242
Wanga C: STX-RC F: Rock Shox Judy XC	$ 864 – $ 1,169
Wanga C: STX-RC F: Rock Shox Judy XL	$ 965 – $ 1,306
Wanga C: STX-RC F: Rock Shox Sid	$ 1,010 – $ 1,367
Wanga C: STX-RC F: Tange	$ 684 – $ 925
Wanga C: XTR F: Answer Manitou Spyder R	$ 1,516 – $ 2,051
Wanga C: XTR F: Rock Shox Indy	$ 1,496 – $ 2,024
Wanga C: XTR F: Rock Shox Indy C	$ 1,506 – $ 2,038
Wanga C: XTR F: Rock Shox Indy SL	$ 1,529 – $ 2,069
Wanga C: XTR F: Tange	$ 1,474 – $ 1,994
Wazoo C: 105SC F: Kinesis	$ 903 – $ 1,222
Wazoo C: 105SC F: Marzocchi Pave'	$ 1,125 – $ 1,522
Zobop C: Deore LX F: Answer Manitou Spyder R	$ 879 – $ 1,190
Zobop C: Deore LX F: Answer Manitou SX-R	$ 965 – $ 1,306
Zobop C: Deore LX F: Marzocchi Bomber Z-1 BAM	$ 1,028 – $ 1,391
Zobop C: Deore LX F: Marzocchi Bomber Z-2 Atom Bomb	$ 1,017 – $ 1,376
Zobop C: Deore LX F: Marzocchi Bomber Z-3 Light	$ 930 – $ 1,258
Zobop C: Deore LX F: Rock Shox Indy	$ 830 – $ 1,122
Zobop C: Deore LX F: Rock Shox Indy C	$ 855 – $ 1,156

C: – Components   F: – Fork

MODEL   PRICE RANGE

VooDoo (continued)   🚲

Model	Price Range
Zobop C: Deore LX F: Rock Shox Indy SL	$ 913 – $ 1,236
Zobop C: Deore LX F: Rock Shox Judy SL	$ 999 – $ 1,352
Zobop C: Deore LX F: Rock Shox Judy XC	$ 949 – $ 1,284
Zobop C: Deore LX F: Rock Shox Judy XL	$ 1,044 – $ 1,412
Zobop C: Deore LX F: Rock Shox Sid	$ 1,086 – $ 1,470
Zobop C: STX-RC F: Answer Manitou Spyder R	$ 762 – $ 1,032
Zobop C: STX-RC F: Answer Manitou SX-R	$ 855 – $ 1,156
Zobop C: STX-RC F: Marzocchi Bomber Z-1 BAM	$ 923 – $ 1,249
Zobop C: STX-RC F: Rock Shox Indy	$ 709 – $ 959
Zobop C: STX-RC F: Rock Shox Indy SL	$ 799 – $ 1,081
Zobop C: STX-RC F: Rock Shox Judy SL	$ 892 – $ 1,207
Zobop C: STX-RC F: Rock Shox Judy XC Other Features	$ 837 – $ 1,132
Zobop C: STX-RC F: Rock Shox Judy XL	$ 940 – $ 1,271
Zobop C: STX-RC F: Rock Shox Sid	$ 986 – $ 1,334
Zobop C: STX F: Answer Manitou Spyder R	$ 719 – $ 973
Zobop C: STX F: Answer Manitou SX-R	$ 814 – $ 1,102
Zobop C: STX F: Marzocchi Bomber Z-1 BAM	$ 884 – $ 1,196
Zobop C: STX F: Marzocchi Bomber Z-2 Atom Bomb	$ 872 – $ 1,180
Zobop C: STX F: Marzocchi Bomber Z-3 Light	$ 776 – $ 1,049
Zobop C: STX F: Rock Shox Indy	$ 665 – $ 899
Zobop C: STX F: Rock Shox Indy C	$ 693 – $ 937
Zobop C: STX F: Rock Shox Indy SL	$ 757 – $ 1,024
Zobop C: STX F: Rock Shox Judy SL	$ 852 – $ 1,153
Zobop C: STX F: Rock Shox Judy XC	$ 796 – $ 1,077
Zobop C: STX F: Rock Shox Judy XL	$ 901 – $ 1,219
Zobop C: STX F: Rock Shox Sid	$ 949 – $ 1,284

Waterford   🚲

Model	Price Range
1100 C: Ultegra	$ 1,080 – $ 1,461
2200 C: Dura Ace	$ 1,413 – $ 1,912

C: – Components   F: – Fork

MODEL   PRICE RANGE

Waterford (continued)   🚲

2400 C: Deore XT	$ 1,290 – $ 1,745
Adventure Cycle C: Ultegra	$ 1,214 – $ 1,642
RS-22	$ 1,249 – $ 1,689
X-11 Cyclocross	$ 1,090 – $ 1,475

Western Flyer   🚲

| Western Flyer | $ 423 – $ 573 |

Wheeler   🚲

800	$ 164 – $ 221
1800	$ 193 – $ 261
2800ZX	$ 258 – $ 349
3900ZX	$ 349 – $ 473
4900ZX	$ 423 – $ 572
5900ZX	$ 453 – $ 612
6770R Trekking	$ 374 – $ 506
7900ZX	$ 624 – $ 845
CZX3000	$ 453 – $ 612
CZX4000	$ 597 – $ 807
CZX5000	$ 795 – $ 1,076
DZX6000	$ 892 – $ 1,207
DZX7000	$ 1,213 – $ 1,641
DZX8000	$ 1,344 – $ 1,818
Pro	$ 170 – $ 229

WizWheelz   🚲

| TerraTrike | $ 1,100 – $ 1,488 |

Yeti   🚲

| A.R.C. XTR | $ 1,533 – $ 2,074 |
| A.S.-3 All Mountain XT | $ 1,514 – $ 2,049 |

C: – Components   F: – Fork

MODEL	PRICE RANGE

Yeti (continued)   🚲

Model	Price Range
A.S.-3 XC LXT	$ 1,177 – $ 1,593
F.R.O. Alloy LXT	$ 1,059 – $ 1,433
F.R.O. Alloy XT	$ 1,177 – $ 1,593
Road Project Dura Ace	$ 1,473 – $ 1,993
Road Project Ultegra	$ 1,177 – $ 1,593

Zap Electric Bikes   🚲

Model	Price Range
Electric Cruiser	$ 569 – $ 770
Power Bike	$ 569 – $ 770
World Bike	$ 331 – $ 448
Zap Trike	$ 597 – $ 808

Zephyr   🚲

Model	Price Range
Alpental	$ 164 – $ 221
Boardwalk	$ 126 – $ 170
Boardwalk 6	$ 162 – $ 220
Boardwalk AL	$ 132 – $ 179
Dare	$ 100 – $ 135
Express	$ 322 – $ 435
Rage	$ 87 – $ 118
Rocket	$ 73 – $ 99
Rockette	$ 73 – $ 99
Silvertip	$ 168 – $ 227
Sunflower	$ 87 – $ 118
Torque	$ 100 – $ 135
Wombat Jr.	$ 135 – $ 183

C: – Components   F: – Fork

MODEL	PRICE RANGE

Aegis

Model	Price
Aro Svelte 1	$ 2,950
Aro Svelte 2	$ 2,450
Aro Svelte 3	$ 2,250
Aro Svelte 4	$ 3,300
Aro Svelte 5	$ 2,750
Aro Svelte 6	$ 2,450
Aro Svelte 7	$ 2,150
Brutus Comp	$ 2,100
Brutus Pro	$ 3,000
Brutus Sport	$ 1,750
Pro Axe	$ 2,000
Pro Axe R5R	$ 3,200
Shaman Comp	$ 1,950
Shaman Pro	$ 2,250
Swift 1	$ 2,800
Swift 2	$ 2,500
Swift 3	$ 2,100
Swift 4	$ 3,150
Swift 5	$ 2,650
Swift 6	$ 2,300
Swift 7	$ 2,100
Trident Comp	$ 2,500
Trident Pro	$ 2,750

Airo-Series

Model	Price
Titan Flex 650c	$ 3,679
Titan Flex 700c	$ 2,599

AMP Research

Model	Price
B3	$ 1,250
B4	$ 2,365
B5	$ 3,410

C: – Components   F: – Fork

MODEL | PRICE RANGE

Bianchi

Model	Price
Advantage	$ 399
Alfana	$ 800
Avenue	$ 325
B.A.S.S.	$ 799
Boardwalk	$ 459
Brava	$ 669
Campione	$ 1,100
Eros	$ 1,100
Giro	$ 1,200
Lynx	$ 439
Lynx SX	$ 599
Milano	$ 499
Ocelot	$ 359
Osprey	$ 900
San Remo	$ 1,100
Super Bee	$ 1,279
Veloce	$ 1,499
Veloce X3	$ 1,499
Volpe	$ 689

Bike Friday

Model	Price
Air Glide GT	$ 2,195
Family Tandem	$ 1,195
New World Tourist	$ 1,075
Pocket Rocket	$ 1,395
Tandem Tuesday	$ 2,450

BikeE

Model	Price
AT 3.0	$ 995
CT 2.0	$ 650

C: – Components   F: – Fork

MODEL	PRICE RANGE

Bontrager

Model	Price
Privateer	$ 1,000
Privateer Comp	$ 1,700
Privateer S	$ 1,200

Bruce Gordon

Model	Price
BLT (Basic Loaded Touring)	$ 1,060
Rock 'n Road Tour	$ 2,235
Rock 'n Road Tour EX	$ 2,235

Bully

Model	Price
Burnout	$ 530
Hot Rod Pro	$ 450

Burley

Model	Price
Duet	$ 2,199
Duet S&S	$ 3,199
Duet Softride	$ 2,499
Rock n' Roll	$ 1,999
Rock n' Roll Softride	$ 2,299
Rumba	$ 1,699
BurleyRumba S&S	$ 2,699
Rumba Softride	$ 1,999
Samba	$ 1,549
Samba Softride	$ 1,849
Zydeco	$ 1,099
Zydeco Mixte-X	$ 1,175

Cannondale

Model	Price
F300	$ 650
F400	$ 759
F400 SRB	$ 813

C: – Components   F: – Fork

MODEL	PRICE RANGE
Cannondale (continued)	🚲
F500	$ 899
F600	$ 1,084
F700	$ 1,246
F900	$ 1,517
F1000	$ 1,679
F2000	$ 2,275
F3000	$ 2,709
F4000	$ 3,251
H300	$ 543
H500	$ 760
KV700	$ 1,246
M300 Mixte SRB	$ 542
M300 SRB	$ 542
M400	$ 542
M500 SRB	$ 650
MT2000	$ 2,168
MT3000	$ 3,251
Multisport 800	$ 1,299
Multisport 2000	$ 1,949
Multisport 4000	$ 3,034
R300 Compact Triple	$ 846
R300 Triple	$ 846
R500D	$ 1,084
R500 Triple	$ 1,084
R600	$ 1,354
R800	$ 1,625
R800 Compact	$ 1,625
R1000D	$ 1,842
R1000 Triple	$ 1,842
R2000	$ 2,384
R4000	$ 2,926

C: – Components   F: – Fork

MODEL	PRICE RANGE

Cannondale (continued)

Model	Price
RT1000	$ 1,950
RT3000	$ 3,251
Saeco/Cannondale Team Issue	$ 4,334
Silk Path 300	$ 813
Silk Path 500	$ 976
Silk Path 1000	$ 1,300
Silk Road 500 Triple	$ 1,299
Silk Road 1000	$ 2,167
Super V 400	$ 1,192
Super V 400 SRB	$ 1,192
Super V 500	$ 1,409
Super V 700	$ 1,896
Super V 900	$ 2,167
Super V 1000	$ 2,384
Super V 2000	$ 2,926
Super V Freeride 700	$ 2,167
Super V Freeride 900	$ 2,438
Super V Raven 700	$ 2,384
Super V Raven 900	$ 2,655
Super V Raven 1000	$ 3,142
Super V Raven 3000	$ 4,334
Super V Raven Freeride 2000	$ 3,901
T500	$ 705
T700	$ 868
T1000	$ 1,410
TS700	$ 1,192
XR800	$ 1,518
XS800	$ 1,735

Catamount

Model	Price
MFS Components: Deore LX	$ 1,850

C: – Components   F: – Fork

1999

MODEL   PRICE RANGE

Catamount (*continued*)   🚲

MFS C: Deore XT	$ 2,120
MFS C: Deore XTR	$ 2,750

Cherry   🚲

Cherry Bomb C: 105	$ 2,100
Cherry Bomb C: 105 Triple	$ 2,125
Cherry Bomb C: Athena	$ 2,500
Cherry Bomb C: Athena Triple	$ 2,500
Cherry Bomb C: Chorus	$ 2,775
Cherry Bomb C: Chorus Triple	$ 2,650
Cherry Bomb C: Dura Ace	$ 2,975
Cherry Bomb C: Dura Ace Aero	$ 2,600
Cherry Bomb C: LX GS Indy SL	$ 2,119
Cherry Bomb C: LX GS Jett XC	$ 1,999
Cherry Bomb C: LX RF Indy SL	$ 2,234
Cherry Bomb C: LX RF Jett XC	$ 3,453
Cherry Bomb C: Record	$ 3,425
Cherry Bomb C: Record Triple	$ 3,075
Cherry Bomb C: Ultegra	$ 2,440
Cherry Bomb C: Ultegra Aero	$ 2,400
Cherry Bomb C: Ultegra Triple	$ 2,460
Cherry Bomb C: Veloce	$ 2,175
Cherry Bomb C: Veloce Triple	$ 2,250
Cherry Bomb C: XT GS Indy SL	$ 2,459
Cherry Bomb C: XT GS Jett XC	$ 2,339
Cherry Bomb C: XT RF Indy SL	$ 2,589
Cherry Bomb C: XTR GS Indy SL	$ 3,199
Cherry Bomb C: XTR RF Indy SL	$ 3,309
Cherry Club C: 105	$ 1,850
Cherry Club C: 105 Triple	$ 1,875
Cherry Club C: Athena	$ 2,250

C: – Components   F: – Fork

MODEL	PRICE RANGE

Cherry *(continued)*

Model	Price
Cherry Club C: Athena Triple	$ 2,250
Cherry Club C: Chorus	$ 2,525
Cherry Club C: Chorus Triple	$ 2,400
Cherry Club C: Dura Ace	$ 2,725
Cherry Club C: Dura Ace Aero	$ 2,350
Cherry Club C: Record	$ 3,175
Cherry Club C: Record Triple	$ 2,825
Cherry Club C: Ultegra	$ 2,190
Cherry Club C: Ultegra Aero	$ 2,150
Cherry Club C: Ultegra Triple	$ 2,210
Cherry Club C: Veloce	$ 1,925
Cherry Club C: Veloce Triple	$ 2,000
Cherry Cordial C: 105	$ 2,300
Cherry Cordial C: 105 Triple	$ 2,325
Cherry Cordial C: Athena	$ 2,700
Cherry Cordial C: Athena Triple	$ 2,700
Cherry Cordial C: Chorus	$ 2,975
Cherry Cordial C: Chorus Triple	$ 2,850
Cherry Cordial C: Dura Ace	$ 3,175
Cherry Cordial C: Dura Ace Aero	$ 2,800
Cherry Cordial C: Record	$ 3,625
Cherry Cordial C: Record Triple	$ 3,275
Cherry Cordial C: Ultegra	$ 2,640
Cherry Cordial C: Ultegra Aero	$ 2,600
Cherry Cordial C: Ultegra Triple	$ 2,660
Cherry Cordial C: Veloce	$ 2,375
Cherry Cordial C: Veloce Triple	$ 2,450
Cherry Titanium DB C: LX GS Indy SL	$ 3,934
Cherry Titanium DB C: LX GS Jett XC	$ 3,699
Cherry Titanium DB C: LX GS Judy SL	$ 4,109
Cherry Titanium DB C: LX GS Judy XC	$ 3,859

C: – Components   F: – Fork

MODEL | PRICE RANGE

Cherry *(continued)*

Model	Price Range
Cherry Titanium DB C: LX GS Marzocchi	$ 3,909
Cherry Titanium DB C: LX RF Indy SL	$ 3,934
Cherry Titanium DB C: LX RF Jett XC	$ 3,814
Cherry Titanium DB C: LX RF Judy SL	$ 3,224
Cherry Titanium DB C: LX RF Marzocchi	$ 4,024
Cherry Titanium DB C: XT GS Indy SL	$ 4,159
Cherry Titanium DB C: XT GS Judy XC	$ 4,199
Cherry Titanium DB C: XT GS Marzocchi	$ 4,249
Cherry Titanium DB C: XT RF Indy SL	$ 4,289
Cherry Titanium DB C: XT RF Jett XC	$ 4,169
Cherry Titanium DB C: XT RF Judy SL	$ 4,579
Cherry Titanium DB C: XT RF Judy XC	$ 4,329
Cherry Titanium DB C: XT RF Marzocchi	$ 3,379
Cherry Titanium DB C: XTR GS Indy SL	$ 4,899
Cherry Titanium DB C: XTR GS Jett XC	$ 4,779
Cherry Titanium DB C: XTR GS Judy SL	$ 5,189
Cherry Titanium DB C: XTR GS Marzocchi	$ 4,989
Cherry Titanium DB C: XTR RF Indy SL	$ 5,009
Cherry Titanium DB C: XTR RF Jett XC	$ 4,889
Cherry Titanium DB C: XTR RF Judy SL	$ 4,299
Cherry Titanium DB C: XTR RF Judy XC	$ 5,049
Cherry Titanium DB C: XTR RF Marzocchi	$ 5,099
Cherry Titanium Straight Gauge C: LX GS Indy SL	$ 3,434
Cherry Titanium Straight Gauge C: LX GS Jett XC	$ 3,199
Cherry Titanium Straight Gauge C: LX GS Judy SL	$ 3,609
Cherry Titanium Straight Gauge C: LX GS Judy XC	$ 3,359
Cherry Titanium Straight Gauge C: LX GS Marzocchi	$ 3,409
Cherry Titanium Straight Gauge C: LX RF Indy SL	$ 3,434
Cherry Titanium Straight Gauge C: LX RF Jett XC	$ 3,314
Cherry Titanium Straight Gauge C: LX RF Judy SL	$ 3,724
Cherry Titanium Straight Gauge C: LX RF Judy XC	$ 3,474

C: – Components   F: – Fork

MODEL	PRICE RANGE

Cherry (*continued*)

Model	Price
Cherry Titanium Straight Gauge C: LX RF Marzocchi	$ 3,524
Cherry Titanium Straight Gauge C: XT GS Indy SL	$ 3,659
Cherry Titanium Straight Gauge C: XT GS Jett XC	$ 3,539
Cherry Titanium Straight Gauge C: XT GS Judy SL	$ 3,949
Cherry Titanium Straight Gauge C: XT GS Judy XC	$ 3,699
Cherry Titanium Straight Gauge C: XT GS Judy XC	$ 4,439
Cherry Titanium Straight Gauge C: XT GS Marzocchi	$ 3,749
Cherry Titanium Straight Gauge C: XT RF Indy SL	$ 3,789
Cherry Titanium Straight Gauge C: XT RF Jett XC	$ 3,669
Cherry Titanium Straight Gauge C: XT RF Judy SL	$ 4,079
Cherry Titanium Straight Gauge C: XT RF Judy XC	$ 3,829
Cherry Titanium Straight Gauge C: XT RF Marzocchi	$ 3,879
Cherry Titanium Straight Gauge C: XTR GS Indy SL	$ 4,399
Cherry Titanium Straight Gauge C: XTR GS Jett XC	$ 4,279
Cherry Titanium Straight Gauge C: XTR GS Judy SL	$ 4,689
Cherry Titanium Straight Gauge C: XTR GS Marzocchi	$ 4,489
Cherry Titanium Straight Gauge C: XTR RF Indy SL	$ 4,509
Cherry Titanium Straight Gauge C: XTR RF Jett XC	$ 4,389
Cherry Titanium Straight Gauge C: XTR RF Judy SL	$ 4,799
Cherry Titanium Straight Gauge C: XTR RF Judy XC	$ 4,549
Cherry Titanium Straight Gauge C: XTR RF Marzocchi	$ 4,599
Dear John C: LX GS Indy SL	$ 2,084
Dear John C: LX GS Jett XC	$ 1,849
Dear John C: LX GS Judy SL	$ 2,259
Dear John C: LX GS Judy XC	$ 2,009
Dear John C: LX GS Marzocchi	$ 2,059
Dear John C: LX RF Jett XC	$ 1,964
Dear John C: LX RF Judy SL	$ 2,374
Dear John C: LX RF Judy XC	$ 2,124
Dear John C: LX RF Marzocchi	$ 2,174
Dear John C: XT GS Indy SL	$ 2,184

C: – Components   F: – Fork

MODEL	PRICE RANGE

Cherry (continued)

Model	Price
Dear John C: XT GS Jett XC	$ 2,184
Dear John C: XT GS Judy SL	$ 2,729
Dear John C: XT GS Judy XC	$ 2,349
Dear John C: XT RF Indy SL	$ 2,319
Dear John C: XT RF Jett XC	$ 2,319
Dear John C: XT RF Judy SL	$ 2,599
Dear John C: XT RF Judy XC	$ 2,479
Dear John C: XT RF Marzocchi	$ 2,399
Dear John C: XTR GS Indy SL	$ 2,929
Dear John C: XTR GS Jett XC	$ 2,929
Dear John C: XTR GS Judy SL	$ 3,449
Dear John C: XTR GS Judy XC	$ 3,084
Dear John C: XTR GS Marzocchi	$ 3,249
Dear John C: XTR RF Indy SL	$ 3,039
Dear John C: XTR RF Jett XC	$ 3,039
Dear John C: XTR RF Judy SL	$ 3,339
Dear John C: XTR RF Judy XC	$ 3,199
Dear John C: XTR RF Marzocchi	$ 3,139
Fat Boy C: 105	$ 2,400
Fat Boy C: 105 Triple	$ 2,425
Fat Boy C: Athena Triple	$ 2,800
Fat Boy C: Chorus	$ 3,075
Fat Boy C: Chorus Triple	$ 2,950
Fat Boy C: Dura Ace	$ 3,275
Fat Boy C: Record	$ 3,725
Fat Boy C: Record Triple	$ 3,375
Fat Boy C: Ultegra	$ 2,740
Fat Boy C: Ultegra Triple	$ 2,760
Fat Boy C: Veloce	$ 2,475
Fat Boy C: Veloce Triple	$ 2,550
Wild Cherry C: LX GS Indy SL	Unspecified
Wild Cherry C: LX RF Indy SL	Unspecified

C: – Components   F: – Fork

MODEL	PRICE RANGE
Cignal	
Foxxy	$ 140
Hot Rod	$ 100
Kokomo	$ 220
Lady Bug	$ 100
Lil' Foxx	$ 130
Melbourne Express	$ 600
Miss Daisy	$ 110
Montauk	$ 220
Ozark Size: 9.5	$ 180
Ozark Size: 8.5	$ 210
Ozark Components: Mountain Mix	$ 280
Ozark SX	$ 270
Ranger	$ 180
Ranger SX	$ 260
Rialto	$ 220
Top Dog	$ 150
Top Gun Rear cog: 16 teeth	$ 110
Top Gun Rear cog: 18 teeth	$ 130
Top Gun full size	$ 140
Village Velo 3 speed	$ 410
Village Velo CB	$ 320
Village Velo FW	$ 280
Co-Motion	
Breve	$ 2,499
Cappuccino	$ 3,225
Co-Pilot	$ 4,115
Co-Pilot Road	$ 2,550
Custom Folding Tandem	$ 4,900
Custom Hybrid Tandem	$ 4,900
Custom Mountain Tandem	$ 4,900

C: – Components   F: – Fork

MODEL	PRICE RANGE
Co-Motion (*continued*)	🚲
Custom MTB	$ 3,200
Custom Road	$ 3,200
Custom Road Tandem	$ 4,900
Custom Touring	$ 2,900
Espresso Dura-Ace	$ 2,970
Espresso Ultegra	$ 2,240
Java	$ 3,679
Sky Cap	$ 4,340
Speedster	$ 2,995
Speedster AL	$ 4,140
Columbia	🚲
F9T Columbia Superb	$ 1,495
Dahon	🚲
Classic III PT631	$ 299
Getaway PT011C	$ 199
Mariner PT053M	$ 429
Mariner SC614M	$ 499
Mountain Gold ST612	$ 399
Novel 073	$ 399
Stowaway PT651	$ 299
Dean	🚲
Boogle Elite SID SL	$ 2,439
Castanza Ultegra	$ 2,528
Colonel Elite SID SL	$ 3,165
Discovery Expert Judy SL	$ 2,439
Discovery Expert SC 70 UL	$ 2,739
Discovery Expert SC 70 XC	$ 2,439
Discovery Expert SID SL	$ 2,739

C: – Components   F: – Fork

MODEL	PRICE RANGE

Dean *(continued)*

Model	Price
Discovery Expert Super Fly	$ 2,689
Duke Elite SID SL	$ 3,239
Jester Elite SID SL	$ 2,439
Oscar Elite SID SL	$ 2,039
Radium Ultegra	$ 2,078
Scout Elite SID SL	$ 2,589
Sputnik Elite SID SL	$ 2,689
Z-Link Elite SID SL	$ 2,539
Zircon Ultegra	$ 2,078

Diamondback

Model	Price
Assault	$ 245
Assault 24	$ 245
Assault EX	$ 300
Coaster	$ 220
Crestview	$ 310
DBR-X10	$ 2,900
DBR-X2	$ 1,000
DBR-X6	$ 1,600
DBR-XR4	$ 1,600
DBR-XR8	$ 2,500
Drifter	$ 270
Expert	$ 700
Ignitor CB	$ 165
Ignitor FW	$ 175
Impression	$ 150
Interval	$ 480
Joker	$ 220
Lil' One	$ 110
Micro Viper	$ 110
Mini Photon	$ 130

C: – Components   F: – Fork

MODEL	PRICE RANGE

Diamondback (continued)

Model	Price
Mini Viper	$ 130
Mr. Lucky	$ 350
Outlook	$ 200
Outlook 24	$ 200
Outlook DX	$ 230
Parkway	$ 240
Photon	$ 150
Reactor	$ 425
Reactor 24	$ 430
Reactor JR	$ 380
Reactor Team	$ 690
Recoil	$ 200
Response	$ 310
Response SE	$ 390
Sherwood	$ 390
Skin Dog	$ 270
Sorrento	$ 260
Sorrento 24	$ 250
Sorrento SE	$ 350
Team Issue	$ 2,300
Topanga SE	$ 500
Venom	$ 270
Venom X	$ 380
Venom XX	$ 480
Viper	$ 195
Viper XL	$ 195
Voyager I	$ 360
Voyager II	$ 430
Voyager III	$ 430
Wildwood	$ 250
Wildwood DX	$ 290

C: – Components   F: – Fork

MODEL	PRICE RANGE

Diamondback (continued)

Zetec	$	720
Zetec Comp	$	900

Dirtmaster

Big Bertha	$	570
Flatty	$	600
H.F.O.	$	570
Jump	$	340
Street	$	390

DK

Banshee	$	280
Fury	$	350
Legend	$	650

Dyno

Air	$	260
Air Chrome-Plated, Red Machine	$	270
Blaze	$	130
Blaze Chrome-Plated	$	140
Compe	$	230
Compe Chrome-Plated	$	240
Detour	$	390
Detour Chrome-Plated	$	400
Nitro	$	250
NSX CB	$	140
NSX CB Chrome-Plated	$	150
NSX FW	$	140
NSX FW Chrome-Plated	$	150
Slammer	$	700
VFR	$	180

C: – Components   F: – Fork

MODEL		PRICE RANGE
Dyno *(continued)*		
VFR Chrome-Plated	$	190
VFR 24	$	240
VFR JR 12	$	90
VFR JR 12 Chrome-Plated	$	100
VFR JR 16 Chrome-Plated	$	110
VFR JR 16	$	100
XR	$	250
XR Chrome-Plated	$	260
Zone	$	190
Zone Chrome-Plated	$	200
Easy Racers		
EZ-1	$	969
Gold Rush	$	2,995
Tour Easy Expedition	$	1,795
Tour Easy Speed & Sport	$	1,795
Fabweld		
E.R.	$	600
FW-02 Expert	$	585
FW-02 Jr. Cruiser	$	585
FW-02 Junior	$	440
FW-02 Mini	$	440
FW-02 Pro	$	600
FW-02 Pro Cruiser	$	600
FW-02 Pro XL	$	600
Free Agent		
Air Raid	$	294
Ambush	$	269
Ambush 24	$	269

C: – Components   F: – Fork

MODEL	PRICE RANGE

Free Agent *(continued)*

Model	Price
Champ	$ 154
Eluder	$ 194
Flying Fortress	$ 394
Ground Zero	$ 309
Limo	Unspecified
Limo 24	$ 489
Limo Team	$ 729
Maverick	$ 174
Raceway	Unspecified
Speedway	$ 329
Speedway Jr.	$ 329
Speedy	$ 109

Fuji

Model	Price
Aloha	$ 1,200
Boulevard	$ 180
Cambridge	$ 250
Captiva	$ 200
Cross	$ 1,200
Crosstown	$ 200
Del Rey	$ 400
Dynamic	$ 580
Finest	$ 600
Folder	$ 300
Monterey	$ 380
Nevada	$ 300
Odessa	$ 200
Palisade	$ 300
Roubaix	$ 1,100
Sagres	$ 320
Sandblaster	$ 170

C: – Components   F: – Fork

MODEL	PRICE RANGE

Fuji (continued)

Model	Price
Sanibel	$ 160
Silhouette	$ 400
Suncrest	$ 800
Sunfire	$ 250
Supreme	$ 270
Tahoe	$ 530
Team	$ 1,500
Thrill	$ 430
Touring Series	$ 700

Gary Fisher

Model	Price
Air Bob	$ 530
Alfresco	$ 540
Aquila	$ 650
Avant Garde	$ 330
Big Sur	$ 930
Cleo Moto	$ 280
Dolph	$ 330
Gitchie Gumee	$ 300
Hard Warp	$ 300
Hoo Koo E Koo	$ 850
Joshua F1	$ 2,900
Joshua F2	$ 1,800
Joshua F3	$ 1,400
Joshua F4	$ 1,100
Kaitai	$ 750
Level Betty	$ 1,800
Level Betty SE	$ 2,400
Lush Rush Cruiser	$ 390
Marlin	$ 440
Minnosaurus	$ 170

C: – Components   F: – Fork

MODEL	PRICE RANGE

Gary Fisher *(continued)*

Model	Price
Mr. Skinner	$ 230
Mt. Jam	$ 330
Mt. Tam	$ 1,600
Mud Puppy	$ 140
Opie	$ 450
Paragon	$ 1,200
Procaliber	$ 3,200
Pure Bender Flip	$ 250
Pure Bender Kick	$ 400
Pure Bender Spin	$ 300
Short Cut	$ 230
Supercaliber	$ 2,500
Tassajara	$ 500
Tyro	$ 250
Wahoo	$ 360
Xcaliber	$ 1,600
Zebrano	$ 430
Ziggurat	$ 1,400

Giant

Model	Price
ATX DS	$ 2,700
ATX TEAM	$ 4,000
Boulder	$ 270
EB COMP	$ 550
EB SPORT	$ 450
Farrago DS	$ 500
Farrago SE	$ 440
Iguana SE	$ 590
Innova	$ 490
MCM SE	$ 1,800
MCM TEAM	$ 3,500

C: – Components   F: – Fork

MODEL	PRICE RANGE

Giant *(continued)*

Model	Price
Option	$ 240
Sedona	$ 360
Sedona SE	$ 470
TCR 1R	$ 1,900
TCR 1T	$ 1,100
TCR 2R	$ 1,200
TCR 2T	$ 800
TCR TEAM	$ 4,000
Upland	$ 220
Warp DS1	$ 800
Warp DS2	$ 650
Warp SE	$ 440
XtC DS1	$ 1,500
XtC DS2	$ 1,200
XtC SE1	$ 1,225
XtC SE2	$ 925
Yukon SE	$ 490

GT

Model	Price
Aggressor	$ 370
Airstream	$ 370
Avalanche Color selection	$ 1,050
Avalanche Color selection	$ 1,000
Backwoods	$ 600
Bump	$ 300
Edge Aero	$ 1,600
Force	$ 600
Fueler	$ 470
GTB	$ 700
Interceptor	$ 210
Interceptor Chrome-Plated	$ 220

C: – Components   F: – Fork

MODEL	PRICE RANGE

GT (continued)

Model	Price
Jetstream	$ 470
Karakoram	$ 600
LOBO-1000 DH	$ 4,000
LTS-1000 DS	$ 3,500
LTS-2000 DS	$ 2,200
Mach One	$ 250
Mach One Chrome-Plated	$ 260
Nomad	$ 500
Outpost	$ 310
Outpost Trail	$ 270
Palomar	$ 230
Performer	$ 300
Performer Chrome-Plated	$ 310
Power Series	$ 260
Power Series 1.0	$ 380
Power Series 3.0	$ 500
Pro Performer	$ 310
Pro Performer Chrome-Plated	$ 320
Pro Series	$ 350
Pro Series 24	$ 300
Pro Series Micro	$ 270
Pro Series Mini	$ 270
Rebound	$ 500
Ricochet Color selection	$ 750
Ricochet Color selection	$ 800
Saddleback	$ 280
Show	$ 870
Slipstream	$ 300
Speed Series	Unspecified
Speed Series 24	$ 700
Speed Series Team	$ 1,050

C: – Components   F: – Fork

MODEL   PRICE RANGE

GT (continued)

Model	Price Range
Speed Series Team EX	$ 740
Speed Series Team JR.	$ 740
STS-XCR1000	$ 4,000
STS-XCR2000	$ 3,000
Timberline	$ 440
Tour	$ 830
Tour 2	$ 390
Tour 2 Chrome-Plated	$ 400
Transit Express	$ 340
Vertigo	$ 260
Vertigo Chrome-Plated	$ 270
Virage	$ 670
Windstream	$ 250
XCR-1000	$ 2,500
XCR-2000	$ 1,800
XCR-3000	$ 1,300
XCR-4000	$ 900
Xiang Team	$ 3,500
Zaskar Color selection	$ 1,550
Zaskar Color selection	$ 1,600
Zaskar LE	$ 2,200
Zaskar LE Team	$ 3,000
ZR-1000	$ 2,500
ZR-2000	$ 1,600
ZR-3000	$ 1,200
ZR-4000	$ 800

Gunnar

Model	Price Range
Cross Hairs C: 105	$ 1,540
Cross Hairs C: Ultegra	$ 1,775
Rock Hound C: LX/XT	$ 1,550

C: – Components   F: – Fork

MODEL	PRICE RANGE

GT (continued)

Rock Hound C: XT	$ 1,850
Rock Hound C: XTR	$ 2,795
Tire-Biter C: 105	$ 1,575
Tire-Biter C: Dura-Ace	$ 2,330
Tire-Biter C: Ultegra	$ 1,770

Hampton

7-speed	$ 240
Aluminum 7-speed	$ 300
Aluminum Coaster	$ 250
Classic	$ 160
Deluxe Coaster Brake	$ 190

Haro

Blammo	$ 570
Cozmo	$ 470
Del Sol SPF1	$ 190
Del Sol SPF21	$ 280
Del Sol SPF6	$ 250
Escape A7.0	$ 340
Escape A7.1	$ 440
Escape A7.2	$ 560
Escape A7.3	$ 710
Escape A7.4	$ 950
Escape A7.5	$ 1,950
Extreme EX0	$ 650
Extreme EX1	$ 890
Extreme EX2	$ 1,110
Extreme EX3	$ 3,150
Extreme MX2	$ 1,950
Extreme MX3	$ 3,150

C: – Components   F: – Fork

MODEL	PRICE RANGE

Haro (continued)

Model	Price
Group 1 1.0	$ 250
Group 1 2.0	$ 290
Group 1 2.0 24	$ 310
Group 1 3.0	$ 430
Group 1 Monocoque	$ 770
Group 1 Ri	$ 165
Group 1 Si Mini	$ 260
Group 1 Zi	$ 180
Master	$ 670
Micro Blaster	$ 135
Mini Blaster	$ 140
Mirra 540	$ 290
Mirra Pro	$ 720
Revo	$ 190
Revo Mag	$ 240
Shredder	$ 310
Supra	$ 240
Supra DLX	$ 570
Supra SX	$ 300
T-Bone Choice	$ 260
T-Bone Prime	$ 360
T-Bone Prime 24	$ 360
T-Bone Select	$ 210
Vector V0	$ 220
Vector V1	$ 270
Zippo	$ 260

Hoffman Bikes

Model	Price
Condor	$ 670
Deebo	$ 640
EP	$ 650

C: – Components   F: – Fork

MODEL	PRICE RANGE

Hoffman Bikes (continued)

Evel Knievel Signature Limited Edition	$ 800
Flash Pro	$ 420
Flash XL	$ 420
George	$ 340
George Jr.	$ 290
Lil' Deebo	$ 640
SD-4	$ 430

I.C.E

Hammer Road C: 105	$ 2,229
Hammer Road C: Ultegra	$ 2,409
Hammer Road C: Athena	$ 2,599
Hammer Road C: Chorus	$ 2,859
Hammer Road C: Dura-Ace	$ 2,929
Hammer Road C: Record	$ 3,459
Hammer Track	$ 1,299

Ibis

Alibi	$ 2,475
Bow Ti	$ 6,925
Hakkalugi	$ 2,625
Mai Tai	$ 3,800
Mojo	$ 2,625
Sonoma Road	$ 3,840
Spanky	$ 2,625
Szazbo	$ 3,225
Ti Mojo	$ 5,850
Ti Road	$ 5,175

Iron Horse

Adirondack	$ 240
Adventure	$ 259

C: – Components   F: – Fork

MODEL	PRICE RANGE

Iron Horse (continued)

Model	Price
ARS 2.0	$ 440
ARS 4.0 Mens	$ 599
ARS 4.0 Womens	$ 599
ARS 7.0	$ 849
ARS 8.0	$ 1,249
ARS 9.0	$ 1,499
ARS Team	$ 2,899
Catskill	$ 230
Expedition	$ 429
Flagstaff	$ 300
G-8	$ 549
G-Out	$ 699
G-Spot	$ 1,199
G-Spot DH	$ 2,699
Journey	$ 209
Maverick	$ 200
Outlaw	$ 180
Outlaw Jr.	$ 180
Victory	$ 1,499

Jamis

Model	Price
Aragon	$ 300
Boss Cruiser	Unspecified
Boss Cruiser 7	$ 270
Boss Cruiser Aluminum	$ 300
Bossy Crankset 4.5in, chainring 32 teeth	$ 130
Bossy Crankset 5.5 in., chainring 36 teeth	$ 140
Citizen	$ 230
Coda	$ 630
Comet	$ 1,500
Cross Country	$ 280

C: – Components   F: – Fork

MODEL	PRICE RANGE
Jamis (continued)	
Dakar Comp	$ 1,000
Dakar Expert	$ 1,400
Dakar Pro	$ 1,800
Dakar Sport	$ 1,000
Dakota	$ 1,100
Diablo Comp	$ 2,500
Diablo Pro	$ 3,300
Dragon	$ 2,400
Durango AL	$ 390
Durango Sport	$ 340
Durango Sport SX	$ 400
Durango SX	$ 500
Earth Cruiser 1	$ 210
Earth Cruiser 2	$ 180
Earth Cruiser 7	$ 270
Earth Cruiser Aluminum	$ 440
Eclipse	$ 2,000
El Diablo	Unspecified
Eureka	$ 800
Exile	$ 650
Explorer Color selection	$ 210
Explorer Color selection	$ 230
Komodo	$ 1,670
Quest	$ 1,050
Tangier	$ 430
Taxi	$ 240
Just Two Bikes	
Montage 17	$ 3,195
Montage EX	$ 2,995

C: – Components   F: – Fork

MODEL	PRICE RANGE

K2 Bike

Model	Price
900	$ 999
1000	$ 1,299
3000	$ 1,599
4000	$ 2,099
4000RS	$ 2,099
Arcadia	$ 475
Flying Monkey	$ 1,399
Maintime	Unspecified
McCoy Comp.	Unspecified
McCoy Pro	Unspecified
Newport	$ 475
Oz-M	$ 4,099
Oz-M Superlight	$ 3,850
Oz-X	$ 2,299
Parker Comp	Unspecified
Pick	Unspecified
Razorback	$ 1,599
Razorback RS	$ 2,299
Razorback RS Superlight	$ 3,550
Shovel	Unspecified
Zed M	$ 1,099
Zed V	$ 699
Zed X	$ 899

KHS

Model	Price
Aero Comp	$ 1,499
Aero Track	$ 649
Aero Turbo	$ 799
Alite 1000	$ 599
Alite 2000	$ 829
Brentwood	$ 299

C: – Components   F: – Fork

MODEL

PRICE RANGE

KHS (continued)

Comp	$	699
Crest	$	429
Eastwood	$	269
FXT Sport	$	649
FXT Trail	$	699
Hollywood	$	359
Montana	$	199
Nomad	$	509
Pro	$	1,099
Raptor	$	199
Sport	$	319
T-Rex	$	209
Tandemania Alite	$	1,599
Tandemania Rio	$	1,599
Tandemania Roma	$	2,099
Tandemania Sport	$	799
Town & Country	$	369
Trail	$	279

Klein

Androit Pro	$	4,100
Androit Race	$	2,700
Attitude	$	750
Attitude Comp	$	1,200
Attitude Race	$	1,900
Mantra Comp	$	2,200
Mantra Pro	$	4,300
Mantra Race	$	2,700
Quantum	$	1,800
Quantum Pro	$	3,800
Quantum Race	$	2,400
Quantum Race T	$	2,430

C: – Components   F: – Fork

MODEL	PRICE RANGE
Kona	🚲
Caldera	$ 929
Chute	$ 1,699
Cinder Cone	$ 799
Explosif	$ 1,499
Haole	$ 1,399
Hei Hei	$ 3,499
Hoo-Ha	$ 549
Humu Seven	$ 549
Humuhumu-Nukunuku-A-Pa'a	$ 399
Jake the Snake	$ 1,149
Kapu	$ 1,699
King Kahuna	$ 3,999
King Kikapu	$ 2,499
Kula	$ 1,799
Manomano	$ 1,599
Mokomoko	$ 1,899
Muni Mula	$ 1,049
NuNu	$ 699
Pahoehoe	$ 1,299
Stab	$ 2,599
Stab Dee-Lux	$ 4,999
Stinky	$ 1,899
Stinky Dee-Lux	$ 2,599
Yee-Ha	$ 349
LeMond	🚲
Alpe d'Huez	$ 1,800
Buenos Aires	$ 1,500
Buenos Aires T	$ 1,530
Chambrey	$ 2,400
Maillot Jaune	$ 3,200

C: – Components   F: – Fork

MODEL	PRICE RANGE

LeMond *(continued)*

Tourmalet	$ 1,000
Tourmalet Triple	$ 1,030
Zurich	$ 1,900
Zurich T	$ 1,950

Linear

CLWB (Mach III)	$ 1,099
LWB	$ 1,350
SWB Sonic	$ 1,350
Tandem	$ 3,200

Litespeed

Appalachian C: 105	Unspecified
Appalachian C: Ultegra	$ 3,050
Blade C: Dura-Ace	$ 4,070
Blade C: Ultegra	$ 3,520
Blue Ridge C: 105 Triple	Unspecified
Blue Ridge C: Ultegra Triple	$ 2,900
Classic C: 105	$ 2,820
Classic C: Chorus	$ 3,820
Classic C: Dura-Ace	$ 3,770
Classic C: Record	$ 5,395
Classic C: Ultegra	$ 3,170
Classic C: Ultegra Triple	$ 3,220
Natchez C: 105	$ 2,322
Natchez C: 105 Triple	$ 2,370
Natchez C: Ultegra	$ 2,720
Natchez C: Ultegra Triple	$ 2,770
Obed	$ 2,950
Ocoee C: Deore XT	$ 3,325
Ocoee C: XTR	$ 4,100

C: – Components   F: – Fork

MODEL	PRICE RANGE
Litespeed *(continued)*	🚲
Owl Hollow C: Deore XT	$ 3,625
Owl Hollow C: XTR	$ 4,400
Tachyon C: Dura-Ace	$ 3,545
Tachyon C: Ultegra	$ 2,770
Taliani	$ 7,350
Tellico C: eore XT	$ 4,500
Tellico C: XTR	$ 5,125
Tsali C: Deore XT	$ 4,275
Tsali C: XTR	$ 4,900
Tuscany C: 105	$ 2,545
Tuscany C: Dura-Ace	Unspecified
Tuscany C: Ultegra	$ 2,945
Ultimate C: Chorus	$ 4,795
Ultimate C: Dura-Ace	$ 4,745
Ultimate C: Record	$ 5,395
Ultimo Ultegra	$ 4,145
Unicoi C: Deore XT	$ 3,425
Unicoi C: XTR	$ 4,200
Vortex C: Dura-Ace	$ 4,845
Vortex C: Record	$ 5,395
Lodestar	🚲
CS-470	$ 899
Destiny	$ 2,899
Obesession	$ 999
Renaissance	$ 1,350
Serenity	$ 1,850
The truck	$ 495
The Vagabond	$ 269

C: – Components   F: – Fork

MODEL — PRICE RANGE

Lovely Lowrider

Model	Price
Showbike Basic	$ 249
Showbike Crown	$ 299
Showbike Deluxe	$ 349

Marin

Model	Price
B-17	$ 1,469
Bayview Trial 24	$ 279
Bear Valley	$ 579
Bolinas Ridge	$ 329
East Peak	$ 1,259
Eldridge Grade	$ 789
Hawk Hill	$ 429
Hidden Canyon	$ 299
Indian Fire Trail	$ 1,579
Juniper Trail	$ 1,150
Kentfield	$ 279
Larkspur	$ 329
Mount Vision	$ 2,099
Mount Vision Pro	$ 3,149
Muirwoods	$ 489
Nail Trail	$ 733
Palisades Trail	$ 529
Pine Mountain	$ 1,049
Point Reyes	$ 949
Rift Zone	$ 1,700
Rock Springs	$ 1,150
Rocky Ridge	$ 899
San Anselmo	$ 529
San Marino	$ 1,579
San Rafael	$ 428
Sausalito	$ 639

C: – Components   F: – Fork

MODEL	PRICE RANGE
Marin *(continued)*	🚲
Sausalito FS	$ 689
Shoreline Trail	$ 839
Team DH	$ 4,199
Team Marin	$ 1,489
Team Titanium	Unspecified
Treviso	$ 2,099
Verona	$ 1,150
Vicenza	$ 1,459
Wild cat Trail	$ 2,629
MCS	🚲
Gravedigger	$ 560
Hurricane	$ 390
Hurricane Cruiser	$ 420
Magnum Pro	$ 390
Mondonico	🚲
Altec C: 105	$ 2,320
Altec C: Athena	$ 2,530
Altec C: Chorus	$ 2,829
Altec C: Dura-Ace	$ 3,150
Altec C: Mirage	$ 2,115
Altec C: Record	$ 3,415
Altec C: Ultegra	$ 2,575
Altec C: Veloce	$ 2,229
Altec Megatube C: 105	$ 2,390
Altec Megatube C: Athena	$ 2,600
Altec Megatube C: Chorus	$ 2,899
Altec Megatube C: Mirage	$ 2,185
Altec Megatube C: Ultegra	$ 2,645
Altec Megatube C: Veloce	$ 2,299

C: – Components   F: – Fork

MODEL	PRICE RANGE

Mondonico (continued)

Model	Price
Altec Megatube C: Dura-Ace	$ 3,220
Altec Megatube C: Record	$ 3,485
Diamond Extra C: Mirage Color selection	$ 1,975
Diamond Extra C: Mirage Color selection	$ 2,035
Diamond Extra C: Veloce Color selection	$ 2,089
Diamond Extra C: Veloce Color selection	$ 2,150
Diamond Extra C: 105 Color selection	$ 2,180
Diamond Extra C: 105 Color selection	$ 2,245
Diamond Extra C: Athena Color selection	$ 2,390
Diamond Extra C: Athena Color selection	$ 2,450
Diamond Extra C: Chorus Color selection	$ 2,689
Diamond Extra C: Chorus Color selection	$ 2,750
Diamond Extra C: Dura-Ace	$ 3,075
Diamond Extra C: Record Color selection	$ 3,275
Diamond Extra C: Record Color selection	$ 3,335
Diamond Extra C: Ultegra Color selection	$ 2,498
Diamond Extra C: Ultegra Color selection	$ 2,435
EL OS C: 105	$ 2,550
EL OS C: Athena	$ 2,760
EL OS C: Chorus	$ 3,059
EL OS C: Dura-Ace	$ 3,380
EL OS C: Mirage	$ 2,345
EL OS C: Record	$ 3,649
EL OS C: Ultegra	$ 2,805
EL OS C: Veloce	$ 2,459
Futura Leggero C: 105 Color Selection	$ 1,889
Futura Leggero C: 105 Color Selection	$ 1,935
Futura Leggero C: Mirage Color Selection	$ 1,685
Futura Leggero C: Mirage Color Selection	$ 1,729
Futura Leggero C: Veloce Color Selection	$ 1,795
Futura Leggero C: Veloce Color Selection	$ 1,845

C: – Components   F: – Fork

MODEL	PRICE RANGE

Mondonico *(continued)*

Futura Leggero C: Athena Color Selection	$ 2,098
Futura Leggero C: Athena Color Selection	$ 2,145
Futura Leggero C: Chorus Color Selection	$ 2,395
Futura Leggero C: Chorus Color Selection	$ 2,445
Futura Leggero C: Dura-Ace Color Selection	$ 2,720
Futura Leggero C: Dura-Ace Color Selection	$ 2,765
Futura Leggero C: Record Color Selection	$ 2,979
Futura Leggero C: Record Color Selection	$ 3,029
Futura Leggero C: Ultegra	$ 2,190
Monza C: 105	$ 2,089
Monza C: Athena	$ 2,298
Monza C: Chorus	$ 2,595
Monza C: Dura-Ace	$ 2,920
Monza C: Mirage	$ 1,885
Monza C: Record	$ 3,180
Monza C: Ultegra	$ 2,345
Monza C: Veloce	$ 1,995
Nemo C: 105	$ 2,625
Nemo C: Athena	$ 2,835
Nemo C: Chorus	$ 3,135
Nemo C: Dura-Ace	$ 3,459
Nemo C: Mirage	$ 2,420
Nemo C: Record	$ 3,720
Nemo C: Ultegra	$ 2,885
Nemo C: Veloce	$ 2,535

Mongoose

AKA	$ 550
Californian	$ 550
Crossway 250	$ 250
Crossway 350	$ 300

C: – Components   F: – Fork

MODEL	PRICE RANGE

Mongoose (continued)

Model	Price
Crossway 450 Color selection	$ 390
Crossway 450 Color selection	$ 420
Crossway 850	$ 600
DX 3.3	$ 230
DX 3.5	$ 270
DX 5.3	$ 440
Expert	$ 240
Expert Chrome-Plated	$ 250
FX-1	$ 380
Hooligan	$ 380
Menace	$ 200
Menace Chrome-Plated, Chrome-Plated/Red	$ 210
Menace Cruiser	$ 200
Motivator	$ 160
Motivator Chrome-Plated	$ 170
Motivator Mini	$ 160
Mt. Grizzly	$ 220
NX 6.5 Color selection	$ 550
NX 6.5 Color selection	$ 580
NX 6.7 Color selection	$ 650
NX 6.7 Color selection	$ 680
NX 7.1	$ 750
NX 7.3	$ 1,050
NX 8.1 Color selection	$ 950
NX 8.1 Color selection	$ 980
NX 8.3	$ 1,400
NX 9.5	$ 3,500
NX 9.7	$ 5,000
Rogue	$ 320
Rogue Chrome-Plated	$ 330
SGX	$ 380

C: – Components   F: – Fork

MODEL		PRICE RANGE
Mongoose *(continued)*		
24	$	400
Sniper	$	220
Speed Limit	$	130
Stormer	$	250
Supergoose	$	330
Supergoose Jr.	$	330
SX 4.3 Color selection	$	330
SX 4.3 Color selection	$	360
SX 4.5 Color selection	$	380
SX 4.5 Color selection	$	410
The FUZZ	$	700
Villain	$	260
Villain Chrome-Plated	$	270
Montague		
Backcountry	$	500
Crosstown	$	600
Tri Frame	$	2,496
Urban	$	900
Moots		
Mootaineer	$	4,679
Psychlo X	$	4,242
Psychlo X YBB	$	4,396
Rigor Mootis	$	3,720
VaMoots	$	4,042
YBB	$	4,279
YBB SL	$	4,425
Nishiki		
Backroads	$	435
Blazer	$	260

C: − Components   F: − Fork

MODEL	PRICE RANGE

Nishiki (continued)

Model	Price
Bravo	$ 220
Cascade	$ 760
Century	$ 270
Colorado	$ 540
Hill Razer	$ 220
Manitoba	$ 320
Meridian SC	$ 250
Optima SC	$ 310
Sport	$ 330

Norco

Model	Price
Alteres	$ 629
Avanti	$ 469
Axia	$ 549
Bigfoot	$ 469
Bushpilot	$ 299
Charger	$ 599
Cherokee	$ 189
Cypress	$ 399
Kokanee	$ 349
Monterey	$ 399
Mountaineer	$ 219
Nitro	$ 899
Olympia	$ 219
Rampage	$ 1,299
Rideau	$ 279
Sasquatch	$ 699
Scrambler	$ 249
Team 853	$ 2,399
Team Titanium	$ 2,999
Terrene	$ 799

C: – Components   F: – Fork

_1999_

MODEL	PRICE RANGE

Norco *(continued)*

Model	Price
Torrent	$ 1,799
Vermont	$ 329
VPS-1	$ 3,699
VPS-2	$ 2,149
Wolverine	$ 319
XCS-1	$ 1,549
XCS-2	$ 1,099
Yorkville	$ 249

Oryx

Model	Price
1000S	$ 650
2000S	$ 740
3000S	$ 910
4000S	Unspecified
ACT 125	$ 1,120
ACT 250	$ 1,540
ACT 500	$ 1,699
Freak	$ 1,660
Gold 14K	$ 1,620
HTA 125	$ 810
HTA 250	$ 1,050
HTA 500	$ 1,350
Pure Gold	$ 2,699
Super Freak	$ 1,870

Otis Guy

Model	Price
Purist 105 Triple Road	$ 2,081
Purist Campy Chorus Road	$ 2,624
Purist Campy Chorus Triple Road	$ 2,538
Purist Campy Record Road	$ 3,175
Purist Campy Record Triple Road	$ 2,828

C: – Components   F: – Fork

MODEL	PRICE RANGE

Otis Guy (continued)

Model	Price
Purist Dura-Ace Road	$ 2,690
Purist LX MB	$ 2,073
Purist Ultegra Road	$ 2,220
Purist Ultegra Triple Road	$ 2,233
Purist XT MB	$ 2,325
Purist XTR MB	$ 3,098
Smoothie 105 Triple Road	$ 2,271
Smoothie Campy Chorus Road	$ 2,814
Smoothie Campy Chorus Triple Road	$ 2,728
Smoothie Campy Record Road	$ 3,365
Smoothie Campy Record Triple Road	$ 3,018
Smoothie Dura-Ace Road	$ 2,880
Smoothie Ultegra Road	$ 2,413
Smoothie Ultegra Triple Road	$ 2,423
Softail LX MB	$ 2,173
Softail XT MB	$ 2,425
Softail XTR MB	$ 3,152

Outland

Model	Price
VPP3 XC	$ 3,760
VPP5 Dual Crown	$ 4,420
VPP6 DH	$ 3,585
VPP6 RnD	$ 3,405
VPP6 XC	$ 3,600
VPP9 DH	Unspecified

Peugeot

Model	Price
Appalache	Unspecified
Attitude	$ 260
Biarritz Double	$ 1,565
Biarritz Triple	$ 1,250

C: – Components   F: – Fork

MODEL	PRICE RANGE

Peugeot *(continued)*

Model	Price
Chronot	$ 610
Cote D' Azur	$ 435
Dune GSX	$ 360
Dune Racing	$ 420
Elite	$ 2,050
Evasion	$ 260
Frasier	$ 380
Frontier Comfort	Unspecified
Frontier Plus	Unspecified
Greystone	$ 395
Hippo	$ 195
Horizon	$ 435
Horizon Alum	$ 615
Hudson	$ 240
Hurricane Creek	$ 585
Jasper	$ 220
Jasper Jr.	$ 220
Kazoom	$ 160
Kazoom BMX	$ 160
Liberty	$ 525
Magic	$ 150
Monaco	$ 235
Monaco Beach	$ 220
Nature	$ 499
ORCA	$ 335
Panorama	$ 335
Paris	$ 340
Prestige	$ 470
Rhino	$ 250
Riviera	$ 495
Sprint	$ 440

C: – Components F: – Fork

MODEL	PRICE RANGE

Peugeot (continued)

Success Triple	$ 920
Urbano	$ 335
Urbano suspension	$ 450

Powerlite

Blitz	$ 270
Blitz Chrome-Plated	$ 280
Expert Color selection	$ 450
Expert Color selection	$ 470
Havoc	$ 210
Havoc Chrome-Plated	$ 220
P-11 Cobra	$ 130
P-11 Cobra Chrome-Plated	$ 140
P-17 Fireball	$ 140
P-17 Fireball Chrome-Plated	$ 150
P-19 Falcon	$ 180
P-19 Falcon Chrome-Plated	$ 190
P-28 Intruder	$ 230
P-28 Intruder Chrome-Plated	$ 240
P-38 Lightening	$ 250
P-40 Warhawk Color selection	$ 480
P-40 Warhawk Color selection	$ 500
P-47 Thunderbolt Color selection	$ 410
P-47 Thunderbolt Color selection	$ 430
P-51 Mustang Color selection	$ 600
P-51 Mustang Color selection	$ 630
P-61 Color selection	$ 900
P-61 Color selection	$ 950
P-shooter Chrome-Plated	$ 110
P-shooter	$ 100
Riot	$ 280

C: – Components   F: – Fork

MODEL — PRICE RANGE

Powerlite *(continued)*

Model	Price Range
Riot Chrome-Plated	$ 290
Spitfire Color selection	$ 300
Spitfire Color selection	$ 320
Toxic	$ 660

Raleigh

Model	Price Range
C30	$ 270
C40	$ 325
C200	$ 420
F-500	$ 760
Jazzi	$ 130
Lil' Honey	$ 110
M20	$ 220
M30	$ 260
M40	$ 320
M50	$ 320
M55	$ 380
M60	$ 435
M80	$ 550
M600	$ 760
M800	$ 980
M7000	$ 870
M8000	$ 1,250
Mountain Scout	$ 220
MXR	$ 140
MXR Mini	$ 110
MXR Mini Chrome-Plated	$ 120
R300	$ 650
R500	$ 710
R600 Color selection	$ 1,030
R600 Color selection	$ 980

C: – Components   F: – Fork

MODEL	PRICE RANGE

Raleigh *(continued)*

Model	Price
R700	$ 1,300
Rave	$ 200
Retroglide 1	$ 250
Retroglide 6	$ 250
Retroglide NX7	$ 330
Rowdy	$ 190
Ruler	$ 220
SC-30	$ 250
SC-40	$ 310
SC200	$ 400
SC2000NX	$ 435
Speedway C: Juvenile Mix	$ 170
Speedway	$ 180
Superspeed	$ 250

Redline

Model	Price
Conquest Cyclo-X	$ 799

Research Dynamics

Model	Price
Coyote ALU 600	$ 1,039
Coyote Challenge S.E.	$ 249
Coyote Pro 400	$ 689
Coyote Team Extreme	$ 179
Coyote Trail 21	$ 199
Coyote X 200	$ 389
Coyote X 300	$ 499
Cruiser	$ 229
Lowrider 16	$ 229
Lowrider 20	$ 229

C: – Components   F: – Fork

MODEL	PRICE RANGE

Ritchey

Model	Price
Chicane	$ 3,295
NiTi	$ 2,795
P-20 WCS Judy SL	$ 3,425
P-20 WCS SID	$ 3,425
Plexus Judy SL	$ 3,325
Plexus SID	$ 3,525
Road Logic	$ 2,465
Swiss Cross	$ 2,595

Robinson

Model	Price
Defender	$ 400
Missle	$ 570
Patriot	$ 850
Patriot 24	$ 600
Patriot JR.	$ 500
Rebel Color selection	$ 190
Rebel Color selection	$ 200
Ruckus	$ 350
SST	$ 270
SST Chrome-Plated	$ 280

Rocky Mountain

Model	Price
Blizzard	$ 1,649
Cardiac	$ 589
Element Race	$ 1,619
Element T.O.	$ 3,426
Fusion	$ 669
Hammer Race	$ 1,369
Instinct	$ 2,259
Oxygen Race	$ 1,199
Pipeline	$ 2,159

C: – Components   F: – Fork

MODEL	PRICE RANGE

Rocky Mountain *(continued)*

Soul	$ 719
Spice	$ 1,199
Thin Air	$ 1,919
Turbo	$ 1,869
Turbo T.O.	$ 3,279
Vapor	$ 839
Vertex T.O.	$ 3,089

Rotator

Pursuit	$ 1,500
Tiger	$ 1,500

Rotec

Dual Sport	$ 3,995
Pro Downhill	$ 4,495
Pro XC	$ 4,495

S & B

Malibu/7-speed Price varies/ buyers choice	$ 795
Malibu/7-speed Price varies/ buyers choice	$ 895
Malibu/14-speed Price varies/ buyers choice	$ 1,095
Malibu/14-speed Price varies/ buyers choice	$ 995
Malibu/21-speed Price varies/ buyers choice	$ 1,050
Malibu/21-speed Price varies/ buyers choice	$ 1,150
Speedster	$ 2,800
Tandem	$ 2,800
Venice Beach/7-speed	$ 990
Venice Beach/14-speed	$ 1,195
Venice Beach/21-speed	$ 1,245

C: – Components   F: – Fork

MODEL		PRICE RANGE
Sampson		🚲
Ciaol C: 105	$	1,099
Ciaol C: Athena	$	1,749
Ciaol C: Dura-Ace	$	1,849
Ciaol C: Record	$	2,349
Ciaol C: Ultegra F: Ken carbon	$	1,399
Ciaol C: Ultegra F: Wound Up	$	1,699
Classico C: 105	$	1,599
Classico C: Athena	$	1,949
Classico C: Chorus	$	2,199
Classico C: Dura-Ace	$	2,249
Classico C: Record	$	2,699
Classico C: Ultegra	$	1,899
Kalispell Ti	$	2,749
Kalispell Ti C: 105	$	1,699
Kalispell Ti C: Athena	$	2,149
Kalispell Ti C: Chorus	$	2,299
Kalispell Ti C: Dura-Ace	$	2,349
Kalispell Ti C: Ultegra	$	1,899
Supra C: 105	$	1,399
Supra C: Chorus Road/Sport	$	1,899
Supra C: Chorus Road race & Triathalon	$	2,099
Supra C: Dura-Ace	$	2,199
Supra C: Record	$	2,499
Supra C: Ultegra F: Ken carbon	$	1,599
Supra C: Ultegra F: Wound Up	$	1,799
Trihiti C: 105	$	1,699
Trihiti C: Dura-Ace	$	2,299
Vail	$	1,699
Zing C: 105	$	1,199
Zing C: Athena	$	1,799
Zing C: Chorus	$	1,899

C: – Components   F: – Fork

MODEL   PRICE RANGE

Sampson *(continued)*

Model	Price
Zing C: Dura-Ace	$ 1,999
Zing C: Record	$ 2,399
Zing C: Ultegra F: Ken carbon	$ 1,499
Zing C: Ultegra F: Wound Up	$ 1,699

Santa Cruz

Model	Price
Bullit	$ 2,650
Chameleon C: LX/XT	$ 1,345
Chameleon C: XT	$ 1,910
Chameleon C: XTR	$ 2,525
Heckler C: LX/XT	$ 1,875
Heckler C: X	$ 1,499
Heckler C: XT F: Rock Shox Sid XC, 3.15 travel	$ 2,360
Heckler C: XT F: Marzocchi Bomber Z-1 BAM, 5.0 travel	$ 2,415
Heckler C: XTR	$ 3,135
Super 8	$ 3,995
Superlight C: LX/XT	$ 2,245
Superlight C: XT	$ 2,605
Superlight C: XTR	$ 3,330

Schwinn

Model	Price
4 Banger	$ 2,199
4 Banger All Mountain	$ 2,799
Aerostar	$ 180
AutoMatic Joey Garcia Signature Model	$ 520
AutoMatic C Joey Garcia Signature Model	$ 340
Gremlin	$ 140
Homegrown	$ 1,199
Homegrown 4 Banger	$ 3,299
Homegrown 4 Banger All Mountain	$ 3,899
Homegrown Elite	$ 1,599

C: – Components   F: – Fork

MODEL	PRICE RANGE
Schwinn (continued)	🚲
Homegrown Factory	$ 2,399
Homegrown Factory Suspension XT	$ 2,599
Homegrown Factory Team	$ 3,799
Homegrown Pro	$ 1,999
Homegrown Straight 8	$ 5,899
HydraMatic Jay Miron Signature Model	$ 550
HydraMatic C Jay Miron Signature Model	$ 760
Lil' Stardust	$ 140
Moab 1	$ 949
Moab 1 Disc	$ 1,399
Moab 2	$ 849
Moab 3	$ 649
PowerMatic	$ 320
PowerMatic Mag	$ 330
Predator C	$ 190
Predator FW	$ 200
Predator Pro	$ 270
Predator Pro Mini	$ 250
Pro Stock 1 Matt Pohlkamp Signature Model	$ 650
Pro Stock 2	$ 440
Pro Stock 3 20	$ 300
Pro Stock 3 24 Cruiser	$ 340
Pro Stock 3 Mini	$ 330
S-10	$ 1,899
S-20	$ 1,699
S-30	$ 1,399
S-40	$ 1,099
Stardust	$ 180
Super Stock 1 Brian Foster Signature Edition	$ 650
Super Stock 2 Brian Foster Signature Edition	$ 330
SuperMatic	$ 220

C: – Components   F: – Fork

MODEL	PRICE RANGE

Schwinn *(continued)*

Model	Price
Thrasher 2.0	$ 220
Thrasher 2.4	$ 220
Thrasher 2.4 F.S. A.L.	$ 360
Tiger	$ 120
Tigress	$ 120

Scorpio

Model	Price
A-Z Pro	$ 150
AL-200	$ 330
AT-30	$ 110
AT-50	$ 160
AT-100	$ 200
AT-200X	$ 270
AT-J20	$ 140
Balboa	$ 120
Cabrillo	$ 180
Capistrano	$ 300
FS-100	$ 250
FS-200	$ 370
Laguna	$ 150
Primrose	$ 200

SE Racing

Model	Price
Assassin	$ 325
Assassin X	$ 400
Bronco	$ 220
Floval Flyer Killer	$ 800
Floval Flyer Pro	$ 560
Mini-Ripper	$ 650
PK Ripper STD Killer	$ 790
PK Ripper STD Pro	$ 560

C: – Components   F: – Fork

MODEL	PRICE RANGE

SE Racing (continued)

PK Ripper XL Killer	$ 790
PK Ripper XL Pro	$ 560
Quadangle AL Killer	$ 830
Quadangle AL Pro	$ 630
Ripper Jr.	$ 530

Softride

PowerWing	$ 2,099
RoadWing	$ 2,099
RocketWing	$ 3,799
Solo	$ 1,599
Sully Adventure Tour	$ 1,399

Specialized

Allez	$ 1,000
Allez C	$ 1,500
Allez M4 Pro	$ 2,000
Allez Sport	$ 1,300
Crossroads	$ 290
Crossroads A1 Pro	$ 800
Crossroads Sport	$ 375
Crossroads Ultra	$ 480
Fatboy 415 Pro	$ 500
Fatboy C	$ 270
Fatboy Hemi C	$ 450
Fatboy Hemi C Cruiser	$ 500
Fatboy Hemi MX	$ 330
Fatboy Hemi Team	$ 700
Fatboy Hemi Team Cruiser	$ 750
Fatboy MX	$ 220
Fatboy Vegas	$ 300

C: – Components   F: – Fork

MODEL	PRICE RANGE
Specialized (continued)	🚲
Fatboy Vegas TJ	$ 500
Fatgirl C	$ 270
FSR	$ 1,100
FSR C	$ 1,400
FSR Elite	$ 2,500
FSR Expert	$ 1,700
FSR Pro	$ 2,500
Globe A1	$ 370
Globe A1 Deluxe	$ 450
Globe A1 Supreme	$ 600
Hardrock	$ 290
Hardrock A1 C FS	$ 500
Hardrock Classic	$ 300
Hardrock C	$ 350
Hardrock C FS	$ 450
Hardrock FS	$ 390
Hotrock Color selection	$ 210
Hotrock Color selection	$ 240
Rockhopper A1 FS	$ 700
Rockhopper A1 FS C	$ 900
Rockhopper FS	$ 600
S-Works FSR XC	$ 3,000
S-Works M4	$ 2,500
S-Works Road	$ 3,000
Stumpjumper C	$ 1,200
Stumpjumper FSR XC	$ 1,500
Stumpjumper FSR XC C	$ 1,800
Stumpjumper FSR XC Pro	$ 2,200
Stumpjumper Pro	$ 1,600

C: – Components   F: – Fork

MODEL	PRICE RANGE
Sun Cruiser 🚲	
Retro-Alloy	$ 180
Retro-Nexus	Unspecified
Swift 🚲	
Ace	$ 1,695
Deuce	$ 1,999
Flora	$ 575
Terry 🚲	
Symmetry	$ 900
Trixie	$ 1,200
Ti Cycles 🚲	
Cooley-ko	$ 3,735
Custom Steel Road	$ 3,085
Custom Ti Hardtail	$ 3,735
Custom Ti Road	$ 4,235
Custom Ti S & S	$ 4,780
Custom Ti Softride	$ 4,560
Custom Ti Tandem, Road	$ 8,335
Custom Ti Ultralight	$ 4,760
Hot Rod	$ 5,610
Hyak	$ 3,780
Skookum	$ 3,535
Tolo	$ 3,120
Titus 🚲	
Evolution AL	$ 2,900
Evolution Ti	$ 4,600
Full Custom Racer	$ 3,995
Full Custom Road Racer	$ 3,895

C: – Components   F: – Fork

MODEL	PRICE RANGE
Titus *(continued)*	🚲
Hard Core Racer	$ 2,395
Motolite	$ 3,500
Quasi Moto Al	$ 3,000
Quasi Moto Ti	$ 4,600
Racer X AL	$ 2,100
Racer X AL LTD.	$ 2,100
Racer X AL Ti	$ 3,750
Torelli	🚲
Alu Wing C: 105	$ 2,389
Alu Wing C: Athena	$ 2,598
Alu Wing C: Chorus	$ 2,895
Alu Wing C: Dura-Ace	$ 3,220
Alu Wing C: Mirage	$ 2,185
Alu Wing C: Record	$ 3,485
Alu Wing C: Ultegra	$ 2,645
Alu Wing C: Veloce	$ 2,295
Corsa Strada C: 105	$ 1,565
Corsa Strada C: Athena	$ 1,775
Corsa Strada C: Chorus	$ 2,075
Corsa Strada C: Dura-Ace	$ 2,395
Corsa Strada C: Mirage	$ 1,360
Corsa Strada C: Record	$ 2,659
Corsa Strada C: Ultegra	$ 1,820
Corsa Strada C: Veloce	$ 1,475
Countach OS C: 105	$ 1,829
Countach OS C: Athena	$ 2,035
Countach OS C: Chorus	$ 2,335
Countach OS C: Dura-Ace	$ 2,659
Countach OS C: Mirage	$ 1,620
Countach OS C: Record	$ 2,920

C: – Components   F: – Fork

MODEL	PRICE RANGE
Torelli (continued)	
Countach OS C: Ultegra	$ 2,085
Countach OS C: Veloce	$ 1,735
Express OS C: 105 Color Selection	$ 2,165
Express OS C: 105 Color Selection	$ 2,259
Express OS C: Athena Color Selection	$ 2,375
Express OS C: Athena Color Selection	$ 2,465
Express OS C: Chorus Color Selection	$ 2,675
Express OS C: Chorus Color Selection	$ 2,765
Express OS C: Dura-Ace Color Selection	$ 2,995
Express OS C: Dura-Ace Color Selection	$ 3,089
Express OS C: Mirage Color Selection	$ 1,960
Express OS C: Mirage Color Selection	$ 2,055
Express OS C: Record Color Selection	$ 3,259
Express OS C: Record Color Selection	$ 3,350
Express OS C: Ultegra Color Selection	$ 2,515
Express OS C: Ultegra Color Selection	$ 2,420
Express OS C: Veloce	$ 2,075
Nemo C: 105	$ 2,505
Nemo C: Athena	$ 2,715
Nemo C: Chorus	$ 3,015
Nemo C: Dura-Ace	$ 3,335
Nemo C: Mirage	$ 2,299
Nemo C: Record	$ 3,595
Nemo C: Ultegra	$ 2,760
Nemo C: Veloce	$ 2,410
Nito Express C: 105	$ 2,429
Nito Express C: Athena	$ 2,635
Nito Express C: Ultegra	$ 2,685
Nito Express C: Chorus	$ 2,935
Nito Express C: Dura-Ace	$ 3,259
Nito Express C: Mirage	$ 2,220

C: – Components   F: – Fork

MODEL	PRICE RANGE

Torelli (*continued*)

Model	Price
Nito Express C: Record	$ 3,520
Nito Express C: Veloce	$ 2,335
Record Carbonio C: 105	$ 2,055
Record Carbonio C: Athena	$ 2,265
Record Carbonio C: Chorus	$ 2,565
Record Carbonio C: Dura-Ace	$ 2,885
Record Carbonio C: Mirage	$ 1,850
Record Carbonio C: Record	$ 3,149
Record Carbonio C: Ultegra	$ 2,310
Record Carbonio C: Veloce	$ 1,965
Spada C: 105	$ 1,845
Spada C: Athena	$ 2,050
Spada C: Chorus	$ 2,350
Spada C: Dura-Ace	$ 2,675
Spada C: Mirage	$ 1,635
Spada C: Record	$ 2,935
Spada C: Ultegra	$ 2,098
Spada C: Veloce	$ 1,750
Super Countach C: 105	$ 2,075
Super Countach C: Athena	$ 2,285
Super Countach C: Chorus	$ 2,580
Super Countach C: Dura-Ace	$ 2,905
Super Countach C: Mirage	$ 1,865
Super Countach C: Record	$ 3,165
Super Countach C: Ultegra	$ 2,329
Super Countach C: Veloce	$ 1,985
Super Strada C: 105	$ 1,689
Super Strada C: Athena	$ 1,898
Super Strada C: Chorus	$ 2,195
Super Strada C: Dura-Ace	$ 2,520
Super Strada C: Mirage	$ 1,485

C: – Components   F: – Fork

MODEL   PRICE RANGE

Torelli (*continued*)

Super Strada C: Record	$ 2,779
Super Strada C: Ultegra	$ 1,945
Super Strada C: Veloce	$ 1,595

Torker

Epidemic	$ 525
Jester	$ 265
Plague	$ 300
TR .5	$ 250
TR 1.8	$ 175
TR 2.0	$ 189
TR 5.1	$ 350
TR 5.3	$ 350
TR 5.5	$ 500
TR 5.7	$ 500
Virus	$ 250
Wizard	$ 390

Trek

320	$ 620
520	$ 1,100
540	$ 1,500
700	$ 280
720	$ 390
800	$ 300
800 Sport	$ 250
820	$ 330
820 AL	$ 360
830 AL	$ 440
930	$ 650
1200T	$ 650

C: – Components   F: – Fork

PRICE RANGE		MODEL	PRICE RANGE	
	🚲	*Trek* (continued)		🚲
	Unspecified	1200T Titanium	$	750
	Unspecified	2000T	$	1,000
	Unspecified	2000T WSD	$	1,000
	Unspecified	2100T	$	1,200
	Unspecified	2200D	$	1,600
		2200T	$	1,630
	🚲	2200T WSD	$	1,550
$	1,775	2300D	$	1,850
$	1,526	2300T	$	1,880
$	2,220	2500	$	2,800
$	2,995	4000	$	460
$	3,489	5000D	$	2,050
$	696	5000T	$	2,100
$	1,949	5200D	$	2,500
$	753	5200T	$	2,530
$	1,570	5500	$	3,600
$	1,112	6000 women's	$	550
$	1,499	6000	$	900
		6500	$	750
	🚲	6500 Ladies	$	750
$	1,800	7000	$	900
$	2,250	7300	$	470
$	2,100	7500	$	570
$	2,300	7500 Shx	$	700
$	2,850	7700	$	1,000
$	2,350	8000	$	1,100
$	2,499	8000 WSD	$	1,100
	Unspecified	8500 LT	$	1,400
$	2,250	8900	$	2,000
	Unspecified	Cruiser Calypso	$	290
	Unspecified	Cruiser Classic	$	220

C: – Components   F: – Fork

C: – Components   F: – Fork

Trek (continued)

Model	Price
Elek Trek	$ 1,500
Elite XC 9.8	$ 2,700
Mt. Cub 12	$ 120
Mt. Cub 16	$ 140
Mt. Lion 30	$ 150
Mt. Lion 60	$ 250
Mt. Track 220	$ 250
Mt. Track 240	$ 320
Navigator 200	$ 300
Navigator 300	$ 440
Navigator 400	$ 600
Navigator 500	$ 750
Pro XC 9.9	$ 4,400
TI 1	$ 340
TI 2	$ 430
TI 24	$ 390
TI 3 Wade Bootes	$ 620
Town and Country	$ 330
TR-10	$ 220
TR-20	$ 270
TR-30 Jumping	$ 310
Vert 1	$ 240
Vert 2	$ 310
Vert 3	$ 410
Vert 4	$ 550
VRX 200	$ 1,100
VRX 300	$ 1,500
VRX 400	$ 1,750
VRX 500	$ 2,700
Y Foil 66D	$ 3,000
Y Foil 66T	$ 3,050

C: – Components   F: –

Ventana (continued)

El Fuego
El Matador
El Terremoto
El Toro
Marble Peak FS

VooDoo

Bizango
Bokor
Canzo AL
Canzo Ti
D-Jab
Hoodoo
Loa
Nzumbi
Rada
Wanga
Wazoo

Waterford

1100 C: 105
1200 C: Ultegra
1900 Adventure Cycle C: 105
1900 Adventure Cycle C: Ultegra
2200 C: Dura Ace
2200 C: Ultegra
2400 C: Deore XT
RS-11 C: 105
RS-12 C: Ultegra
RS-22 C: Record
X-11 Cyclocross C: 105

MODEL	PRICE RANGE
WizWheelz	
TerraTrike	$ 1,995
Yeti	
A.R.C. C L C: XT	$ 1,895
A.R.C. Pro XTR	$ 3,295
A.R.C. Race XT	$ 2,295
AS-3 C L C: XT	$ 2,295
AS-3 Race XT	$ 2,745
Lawwill DH-8	$ 5,895

C: – Components   F: – Fork